THE ENTROPY OF CAPITALISM

Studies in Critical Social Sciences Book Series

Haymarket Books is proud to be working with Brill Academic Publishers (www.brill.nl) to republish the *Studies in Critical Social Sciences* book series in paperback editions. This peer-reviewed book series offers insights into our current reality by exploring the content and consequences of power relationships under capitalism, and by considering the spaces of opposition and resistance to these changes that have been defining our new age. Our full catalog of *SCSS* volumes can be viewed at www.haymarketbooks.org/category/scss-series.

THE ENTROPY
OF CAPITALISM

ROBERT BIEL

Haymarket
Books
Chicago, IL

First published in 2012 by Brill Academic Publishers, The Netherlands.
© 2012 Koninklijke Brill NV, Leiden, The Netherlands

Published in paperback in 2013 by
Haymarket Books
P.O. Box 180165
Chicago, IL 60618
773-583-7884
www.haymarketbooks.org

ISBN: 978-1-60846-242-1

Trade distribution:
In the U.S. through Consortium Book Sales, www.cbsd.com
In the UK, Turnaround Publisher Services, www.turnaround-psl.com
In Australia, Palgrave Macmillan, www.palgravemacmillan.com.au
In all other countries by Publishers Group Worldwide, www.pgw.com

Cover design by Ragina Johnson.

This book was published with the generous support of Lannan Foundation
and the Wallace Global Fund.

10 9 8 7 6 5 4 3 2 1

Library of Congress Cataloging-in-Publication Data is available.

CONTENTS

LIST OF FIGURES

INTRODUCTION

The structure of this book reflects how the theory was actually developed: in a concrete way, derived from facts and referring back to them. In this introduction, I will briefly summarise the main lines of the argument in a more abstract way, but the reader must bear in mind that this general exposition could only have been written at the end of the process, not at the beginning.

The twenty-first century opens up what is possibly the most difficult and decisive period in human history. The ruling capitalist mode of production is hitting violently against its limits: it manufactures unmanageable amounts of poverty, and depletes the ecosystem more than the latter can bear. These violent shocks threaten immense deprivation ... but they also open up possibilities for renewal, if we can grasp them.

By employing the term *entropy*, in our title and as a central theme of the book, we aim to capture the flavour of a 'demise' of something. But is it the demise of humanity itself, or of the capitalist mode of production, whose decline might on the contrary herald a rebirth of humanity?

Radicals often speak of 'the system' to signify the socio-economic entity which currently oppresses us. The term implies that something (not just economic exploitation but ideological alienation, militarism etc.) has built up a momentum of its own and become a self-propagating force, severed from rational control and consuming the society which produced it. The premise of this book is that this intuition is exactly on the right lines, but will only reveal its true potential if we really push the systems notion to a point where we can be rigorous about its implications.

The task of a systems critique of capitalism could validly have been posed at any point of its history, but has special significance today, entering as we do a crisis of a new type where two systems – human and ecological – come into conflict and capitalism now consumes not just society itself, but its physical environment, to a point where neither can regenerate.

Systems are not fated to acquire a runaway 'bad' dynamic, it is possible for them to function sustainably. To understand this, systems theory suggests two complementary conceptual approaches:

thermodynamics and information. Information applies to internal structure, the extent to which an ensemble 'makes sense' and functions coherently. Thermodynamics addresses the energy flows. There must be an exchange of energy with a surrounding system (environment) if we are to maintain or improve society's internal coherence; otherwise (i.e., as a closed system) we would be condemned to degenerate in the direction of greater entropy. We can represent this entropy either as disorder, or, in a complementary formulation, as a descent into the wrong kind of 'orderedness', i.e. uniformity: a homogenised system which has lost the rich variety of signs is in no position to carry information.

Because we are lucky to have an environment, we can pursue a normative commitment to bettering the human condition. But we have to do this carefully. If we exhaust either the energy source or the environment's capacity to absorb disorder (heat, waste), the entropy will return to haunt us. Today, with peak oil and climate change, both kinds of revenge impinge together, and interact.

The Green movement recognises such external limits, but what we must emphasise is the drive from within pushing *against* them. This is where Marxism is essential. Our strategic goal of eventually stabilising humanity's relations with its environment must never be confused with stabilising the capitalist mode of production: were we side-tracked into attempting the latter (which is impossible anyway), we would disastrously amplify the causes of the problem. Only Marxism posits this distinction clearly.

As a basis for our subsequent argument, we therefore begin by re-stating the Marxist vision of capitalism's internal contradictions, re-interpreting it to emphasise the manipulation of, and ultimately surrender to, entropy. Thus, conflicts which would tear society apart are kept at bay only through massively unsustainable environmental demands: the symptoms of poverty are managed only through unnaturally cheap food, relying on artificial inputs which are ultimately unsustainable, each 'solution' being merely a temporary shuffling-off of the problem into a different region, or into the future. In particular, the core-periphery angle is emphasised: the system's worst features, the disorder from which the privileged seek to shield themselves, are shoved onto the colonies or the marginalised.

Systems of domination have always exploited fears of chaos to convince people that an iron hand is needed to maintain society's structure or predictability. Here, 'security' is equivalent to repression.

Capitalism is no different: while actually quite chaotic, it presents itself as a bastion of order. This is one aspect of the ruling discourse, the centralist one. We can refute it because systems theory shows that self-organisation is not only possible, but preferable to centralised order: society would not just fall into chaos if no longer ruled from the top, a superior self-organisation can be achieved, the condition being simply that we draw energy from our environment in a sustainable way. This is encouraging for the future.

But the discourse of top-down rule is only one option for maintaining dominance. The notion of self-organised order can also, in a strange way, be co-opted so as to disempower resistance. In some forms of structuralism, the emergent order may be recognised as alienating but nevertheless hard to shift, so this can lead to fatalism or an undervaluing of agency. More recent forms of capitalism perform this trick somewhat differently: neo-liberalism exploits the proposition (true in itself) that self-generated order is better than designed, as an excuse to outlaw social projects or any attempt to better the human condition. Our answer to this would have to focus on a particular aspect of information theory which emphasises 'information about the future': in human systems, structural emergent order inevitably has a strong dose of agency. The future is not predetermined; we can choose it, on the basis of existing possibilities.

Having established a systems reading of Marxism (or, a Marxist reading of systems theory), the book's main task is to address a question of burning contemporary relevance: if we view capitalism as an *adaptive* system, how, might it adapt to the symptoms of its own decay (entropy)?

Out of all the lessons of Marxism relevant to today's crisis, and its likely future development, surely the greatest is the emphasis on struggle. Although objective limits hover around somewhere (environmental carrying capacity, peak oil, exploiting society to a point where it cannot regenerate), the force which really bounces back the news of impending entropy is not, in some abstract way, the limits themselves, but rather the struggles (class struggle and social or national movements of various oppressed groups, which might be against exploitation or in favour of resource stewardship) which signal a refusal to tolerate the existing trajectory.

The issue is thus in an immediate sense political. In this context, it is significant that Marxism did begin to address a question of the declining phase of a mode of production, in the shape of its notion of imperialism. In affirming the centrality of imperialism, our book clearly identifies itself as Leninist, not just Marxist. But what is the relationship between imperialism and entropy? This is a vital question.

Again, we re-interpret certain formulations of imperialism theory from a systems angle: the notion of a 'highest stage' surely implies an era in which themes of decay are already manifested. But, we argue, this does not mean that capitalism ceases to function *adaptively*... simply, it adapts *to* its entropy, somehow embracing it symbiotically. It is from this peculiar relation of auto-parasitism that today's distorted features emerge.

Concretely, we argue that the capitalist adaptation is confused and ambiguous. What concerns us particularly is to define the range (or 'set') of responses available to capitalism in a structural crisis such as we now confront, and broadly we can identify the following four strands: 'greening' capitalism to make it survive a bit longer; burning up the remaining resources (institutional, as well as physical) in a final blaze, which is one aspect of the trend we call 'exterminism'; settling into a 'cold' or 'dark' form where energy demands are reduced and bad forms of chaos (e.g. diffuse militarism) squeeze out creative solutions; and co-opting parts of the human survival reflex as a basis of low-cost 'sustainable communities' solutions to local social order. Each of these four trends has certain antecedents within basic properties of imperialism, but the crisis brings them to the fore in a fundamentally new way. Crucially, we argue, twenty-first century adaptation takes the form not of *selecting* from these options, but of combining them. Sometimes they dovetail together, as when counter-'terrorism' style surveillance serves to keep sustainable communities in line, but in many respects they are strongly contradictory; it is exactly this which gives the dialectics its special flavour. Although these scenarios do not, separately or together, offer a viable solution (even for capitalism, let alone for humanity), it is precisely the different possible mixes between them which will determine the sub-phases of our immediate future... and its struggles.

The above ideas are explored in a general way in *Chapters 1 and 2,* in the first of which we propose a framework for the Marxism-systems dialogue, focusing on a number of illustrative cases. For example, the notion of a system escaping human control figures in the Marxian vocabulary as alienation. Here, systems theory offers clues about how alienating structures can become embedded, notably the role of feedback in entrenching certain lines of development. Since development is always lumpy, of key importance are phase transitions, and in capitalist political economy we represent these as the shifts between accumulation regimes which embody capitalist core values (exploitative efficiency) over certain periods. But as well as entrenching certain characteristics, feedback can also amplify distortions and hence prove highly disruptive, as we will see.

Our argument particularly critiques today's poverty discourse, as a cosmetic attempt to keep a lid on the destabilising effects of the auto-consumption of society. If we approach this from a relative perspective, the main issue is polarisation and its impact in destroying equilibrium. But there is also an absolute sense in which the regenerative capacity of society is under threat.

Driven by the force of such internal contradictions, capitalism is pushed not only into unceasing growth (with the devastating environmental impact we know), but also into the illusions of omnipotence which surface periodically, for example today with respect to genetic modification. The system thus artificially clings to its own small degree of surviving equilibrium, at the expense of subverting that of its environment.

We notably address the notion of complexity. Emergence is a self-created order coming about through the interplay of the system's different elements: since the whole is more than the sum of its parts, it cannot be *deduced* from them. The capacity for self-organisation only exists because, as an open system, we have an environment … but then we have to take on board that the latter is similarly complex! Complexity thus brings a paradoxical mix of fragility and robustness: messing up some part of the complex ecosystem could have unpredictable and devastating effects on the ensemble; on the other hand, the system may find unexpected pathways to a new equilibrium. This is encouraging with respect to society, but problematical with respect to the ecosystem: the new equilibrium may be one in which humanity could scarcely survive.

Within society itself, complexity seems to be on the increase. This can be embraced insofar as it implies more richness and variety, but only on the condition that our social and institutional arrangements are adequate: they should have diffuse capacity, be not too commandist, and possess 'reduncancy', in the sense of multiple pathways to creating solutions. This is precisely where capitalism tends to come unstuck. The system's 'limit' is in this sense not an absolute number but a degree of complexity, and when it loses hope in complexity, pathologies, long latent, rise to the surface.

This is not to say that capitalism is wholly unable to respond to the complexity challenge. It can do so, but only up to a point. In order to understand the parameters for this adaptation, and its limits, we must first explore what is meant by an adaptive system. This is the task of *Chapter 2*.

A key point in understanding adaptation is to recognise agency without sinking into conspiracy theory. Of course ruling forces consciously pursue their interests, whether at the 'macro' level of state policy, or as bosses of a particular firm. But agency necessarily dialogues with structural forces: complexity is such that accumulation regimes cannot wholly be thought of as planned, so they must to a significant extent self-engineer. On the other hand, in the more recent pathological phase, subjectivity may also unmoor itself from agency (at least in the sense of some rational pursuit of goals), and feed instead upon its own illusions.

Denial has thus become absolutely crucial to the system's mode of operation. Nevertheless, in this chapter we critically discuss what is seemingly the most rational and least denialist option, that of a low-energy form of capitalism. Something always seems to frustrate this option, at least at a whole-system level. We highlight for example the hidden entropy lurking beneath apparent virtualisation (this critique will be supplemented later by a discussion of the role of finance capital in profiting from depletion).

In order that accumulation regimes may stabilise capitalism over a period, a key goal is to concentrate and organise the system's internal forces. We argue that this particularly takes the form of consolidation within the historic core, the 'North'. In our systems reading of imperialism, the core is seen as a collective dominance regime. Since in the context of self-organising systems, reciprocity is a more natural mode of interaction than centralism or top-downism, the effect of the collective dominance regime is somehow to concentrate this benefit of the 'decentralisation dividend' within ... the centre! Nevertheless, the positive payoffs from collective imperialist exploitation are in fact fuelled by accentuated environmental degradation, and this again brings us back to the entropy problem: a constant intensification of resource exploitation is needed to maintain this regime.

In *Chapter 3*, as one of the book's major arguments, we propose a perspective on the past thirty years. In our analysis, the period breaks down into two main sections: the dynamic and triumphalist phase of the eighties, and a more recent, decadent sub-phase. In this chapter, we focus the first of these, a seemingly astonishing adaptation which would be hard to comprehend from conventional Left thinking. We draw particularly upon the dynamic contradiction between centralised and diffuse systems.

Self-organisation is genuinely more efficient than control, but this faculty can be co-opted in an abusive way, to create a kind of self-organising exploitation. Liberalism indeed always implied this possibility through its doctrine of laissez-faire, but the practice of 19th-century capitalist development had mostly gone the opposite way, towards top-down organisation; and this even got worse with imperialism: the forces of decay could seemingly only be repelled by centralising still further the system's remaining energies through statism and the giant corporations. But in escaping the seventies' structural crisis, capitalism learned to behave more like a 'proper system', permitting parts at least of the political economy to self-engineer.

Self-organisation as an objective property of *all* systems. But in dealing with *human* systems, we must always remember how big a role consciousness plays: the self-organising faculty thus takes the specific form of human capacity, which can be considered a free kind of energy. A totally centralised system cannot access this precious resource. Therefore, in order to survive, capitalism had no choice but to reverse its previous modernist line of development. Top-down control was partly relaxed, permitting the development of structures like industrial clusters and value chains. And these had a political equivalent: in the periphery, Cold War-style dictatorships were typically replaced by more complex structures, political forms of self-exploitation assembled from civil society actors, NGOs etc.

In Leninist theory, the imperialist era somehow 'prepares the groundwork' for a post-capitalist mode of production, and reading this in a modernist way it sounds as though imperialist centralism would be superceded in turn by a still more organised centrally-planned socialism. However, if we read it the opposite way, we could say that capitalism opens up the emergent properties of self-organising structures, but only in such a limited and truncated form that they are ultimately useless; it is up to socialism to realise their potential. Through a detailed analysis we show just how limited capitalist-inspired emergence really is, notably with respect to human capacity.

In a further step in our argument, we hypothesise a relationship between the energies unleashed through 'tame' emergence, and those required to constrict it within parameters acceptable to exploitation.

Though in some respects the centre-top is relaxed, in others it is *accentuated* precisely to police emergence, and it is this contradictory mix of centralism and decentralisation, of laissez-faire and surveillance, which marks out the neo-liberal phase. But our central question is: what happens when the energies of containment outstrip the exploitative benefit? We may expect the system to react ambiguously, on the one hand striving to re-centralise (an impossible goal, but with real and devastating impacts, for example in the destruction of civil liberties); on the other it may work with chaos, seeking to channel it away from creative chaotic forms (where the ruling attractor is loosened, and popular experimentation takes over), and towards a purely destructive form (often a parody of the constructively exploitative self organisation of the industrial system, as in military sub-contracting, for example).

At present, the approach of contained and limited self-organisation is not yet exhausted. It retains much exploitative potential at least in the productive sphere, where an insecure workforce desperately seeks 'niches' within the value chains.

But this equilibrium is fragile. In order to survive, capitalism must not just keep reproducing capital itself, but also also keep innovating institutionally (organising itself differently, at each level of the political economy). But the core has lost much of its freshness: in fact, it is the periphery of any system where its main area of vitality is often found, which is why for example global industry cultivates local 'embedding' and tacit knowledge. This undoubtedly creates some openings for Southern producers, and in a broader sense points in the direction of a (frustrated) non-Eurocentric displacement of capitalism, an issue to be addressed in Chapters 6–7. A key reason why we should keep thinking in terms of imperialism is to remind us that this is not just an economic system, but a politico-military one; it is at this latter level that the displacement to the periphery will ultimately be resisted.

The point where the shortcomings of capitalist emergent governance are really exposed is with the attempt to transplant self-organisation from the industrial to the political sphere. Ideally, Southern countries would be controlled at arm's length through an emergent subservient equilibrium using civil society, NGOs etc. But this is highly volatile in practice. What the ruling order particularly fears is a *contestatory* usage of systemic processes like networking, and it is this fear which determined the ideological form of the 'war on terror': by claiming to fight a networked enemy (itself a parody of capitalism's network-based rule over a complex and decentralised system), the system can experiment with the chaotic and 'dirty' means of repression which may subsequently be employed against society in general, once the crisis brings about a general weakening of order.

In *Chapter 4* we begin our detailed discussion of the system's responses to information of such an approaching disintegration. We emphasise the environmental parameters, notably peak oil and the food crisis. A key issue is the contradiction between increasing complexity (given that the ecological challenges are by definition complex) and the petulant, repressive reflex.

Most immediately, as we saw in Chapter 2, the very act of reproducing capital *is* a thermodynamic depletion or reduction of quality. This tends to assert itself over and through the apparent virtualisation which partially replaces the more obvious entropy (e.g. pollution) of early industrial society. Whenever capital is reproduced, there remains a counterpart in the form of degradation, it is simply less direct. For example, hedging, which seems to produce profit out of nothing, is really underpinned by the degradation of the environment and of livelihoods to which it attaches itself. But if finance capital is not really delinked from throughput, it is indeed delinked, more than in earlier industrial society, from *reality* (in the dual sense of losing contact with the real economy, and of failing to read information on approaching disaster). Consequently, signals of entropy are distorted, and embraced as a source of profit. The notion of risk (already central to capitalist economic discourse) takes on a wholly new and threatening meaning in the context of approaching ecological disaster, upon whose symptoms finance capital parasitises, and thus accentuates (for example in futures market speculation on food shortage).

In 'normal' economics, one might expect resource depletion to trigger a conservationist response, and something of this can indeed be discerned in individual business decisions (see our later argument). But it is neutralised at a whole-system level by the hegemony of speculative finance capital. The fundamental reason is, as Marx already spotted, the incompatibility between the circuits of capital reproduction and the cycles followed by nature.

Concretising this, a case study of food shows how every failure of dodgy science tends to be met with more of the same: instead of switching to low-energy approaches, more and more effort is thrown into the conventional paradigm, with increasingly absurd results, as in the case of biofuels. A decline in quality (for example, in nutrition) logically reflects the negative energy balance.

In a similar way, information about social degradation can't be faced up to. It must be 'spun' in such a way as to conceal the reality that poverty is produced by the same process as wealth. So more wealth is accumulated in the vain hope that it will 'trickle down'; or, in the livelihoods discourse, intervention serves to massage the tipping-points which might otherwise trigger unpredictable forms of emergence.

What really characterises the crisis is not so much objective limits, but rather the fact that the system tips into a state (or regime) where unpredictable or extreme events become more common. In the ecosystem this is clear, but we argue that something similar occurs in human systems, such as political economy. This is in turn linked with the environmental aspect through a range of factors, for example finance-capital speculation *on* these extreme events.

The chapter concludes by introducing the military dimension: the repressive shift around the turn of the twenty-first century responds pre-emptively to a shrinkage of the system's external energy supply, mediated through resource struggles. The notion of security, entirely losing its meaning as a common-property resource related to popular livelihoods, thus becomes increasingly privatised and fenced-in.

Chapter 5 then focuses squarely upon the repressive apparatus. The question again is how a system would respond to information of its own unsustainability. What is interesting is precisely why capitalism does not operate like some abstract model of a system we could construct, where such information would trigger a corrective response. The George W. Bush phenomenon is used as a case study, but first we place this in a wider historical context: the diseased response draws upon factors always latent within imperialism.

Systems of domination typically distort the notion of order (order should in principle be a good thing in the sense of proving one is in an open system which successfully resists entropy), into an argument to justify centralised or top-down rule as the only bastion against chaos. That is the more obvious tactic. But there is also a secondary theme whereby a system may be ruled through chaotic and decentralised forms. It is precisely the rise of this feature which we wish to emphasise. Thus, in some respects the central monopoly of violence is relaxed in favour of a more diffuse violence, as in the Iraq occupation with its shadowy networks of privatised military sub-contractors. Although the latter looks like just another form of neo-liberal outsourcing, the difference is that, rather than a creation of (exploitative) structure, we have rather a dissolution of it.

The chapter therefore analyses the hidden history of clandestine and chaotic military-political repressive networks, not just in the colonial context but even within the core itself. Once pluralist subordinate systems and civil society no longer seem reliable, it is tempting to bring the chaotic approach into the mainstream ... aided and abetted by finance capital, which embraces the security sphere as yet another opportunity to parasitise upon the descent into entropy.

The result is a wholesale attack upon the limited degree of human and democratic rights developed by earlier capitalism. Most obviously, the direction of attack comes from the tendency to re-centralise in response to crisis. But we should be aware that there is also a contradictory approach on the part of oppressive systems, namely to play the complexity card: the notion of the whole being than the sum of parts is twisted to assert an 'organic' societal interest to which the individual must be sacrificed. The chapter counters this, both by asserting rights as an attribute of the individual, and opposing the 'state of exception' notion, which is precisely not exceptional, but rather leads to a generalised repression.

We can for sure interpret the terrorism discourse as a rational pre-emptive strategy to beef up repressive arsenals (both physical, and legal/moral) in preparation for the popular struggles likely to be triggered by upcoming socio-ecological events; that is the instrumental side of the spectrum. But the chapter insists also on an irrational dimension, where the discourse becomes a projection or externalisation of the pathological development of imperialism itself: destruction is here pursued for its own sake, accompanied only by a mystical and delirious sense that it somehow heralds a transition to a new order.

Addressing the issue of a system which lurches towards disaster by processing signals so as (in place of corrective action) to accentuate the current trajectory, we introduce the notion of 'exterminism'. Already in Chapter 4 we showed how the coupling of energy and identity creates tendencies for a conflagration of existing resource stocks. We now discuss a complementary development in the military-political sphere, whereby a self-confirming 'logic' threatens to consume both society and the individuals that compose it. Sanctions, bombing, depleted uranium weapons and privatised military contractors are all part of this. Capitalism's traditional delusion of an omnipotent science controlling nature is projected into that of a high-precision, robotised war. Denial becomes crucial at this level. In the imagined model, where irregular repressive forces battle a self-propagating, rhyzome-like enemy, chaos would rule at whole-system level, with predictability maintained only within gated notes of privilege.

A key symptom of the system's decadence is the hollowing-out of its core: not content with continuing to devastate its periphery the ruling order seems bent on consuming its own civilisation in a kind of auto-cannibalism. Nevertheless, the chapter more optimistically concludes by hypothesising a 'great reversal' whereby the periphery becomes the upholder of a new generation of human and democratic rights.

Chapter 6 deepens the treatment of the international relations (IR) part of our model. Accumulation must be structured at a world level, in a way which reflects the role of states as fundamental units of capitalist organisation. The point is again that imperialism must not just extract energy from the system, but *rule* it. 'Security' (in the dominant defini-tion) thus means not only a predictable reproduction of capital, but also stable configurations of international power. The top-down and centralist definitions of power historically characteristic of the IR level must somehow be harmonised with an international form of that *sys-temic* power (i.e. emergent, as opposed to centralist) which this book has already discerned at several different levels. The problem was tem-porarily resolved by the state's surrender to neo-liberal privatisation agendas and to the value chains which cross national boundaries. But this is not such an attractive solution in a crisis situation, where the state remains an essential regulatory tool.

The core of any system tends to determine its fundamental logic, for its own benefit. In this sense, the world system's overall meaning remains fundamentally Atlantocentric. But the issue is that, as we have noted, the *dynamism* lies elsewhere. It is not just that, in a propaganda sense, capitalism requires the 'rise of Asia' discourse to conjure away the evidence of its decadence, but also that it *really* needs institutional dynamism from outside its own narrow circle. In fact, as we will see more fully in the final chapter, it must parasitise upon forces of renewal wherever it can find them. This issue applies more broadly to the regen-eration of human society from its margins, a process which in principle goes against capitalism, but which can in part temporarily be co-opted by it: yet another way in which capitalism's highest phase prepares the groundwork for an alternative mode of production.

Even at the level of IR itself, peripheral demands may be functional up to a point in disrupting institutional torpor: after all, grassroots struggles are historically sometimes co-opted to clear the debris of an old regime, so that it may be replaced by a new exploitative setup.

During capitalism's more triumphalist phase in the early part of the post-1980 accumulation regime it seemed that the state-centricity of traditional IR could be supplemented by an exploitative governance more appropriate for today's complexity, enlisting emergent relationships among those actors or processes whose character is precisely to challenge state-centricity.

But this all changes once environmental limits impinge, reinforcing the sense that there is not enough room for everyone to develop capitalistically. Emergent forces, of which migration is just one, appear impossible to manage. Habitual forms of dominance are then likely to reassert themselves and increasing energies (both physical and institutional) be diverted to maintaining them.

In order for the core to tighten its monopoly, not just over the remaining physical resources but over institutional experimentation and the definition of the world system's basic identity, it has to consolidate its own internal relations. In the military sphere, this is ritually enacted through joint military operations, as in Afghanistan. Economically, intra-core readjustment must maintain the USA's peculiar status as 'core of the core', which somehow not only draws benefit from the system but also (consistent with the decadent nature of an imperialism which it personifies) acts as repository for high amounts of entropy, notably in the social sphere. But this definition of consolidation requires single-mindedness both in rejecting inconvenient information, and more specifically in refusing to puncture the bubble of the core's own finance capital operations. The 2008 finance crisis was one result.

In a manner analogous to the more general issue of constrained emergence discussed in Chapter 3, wherever decentralisation is to be permitted (as for instance in the 'embedding' of local industry), there must be a corresponding strengthening of the centre to prevent a slippage of control. Addressing the issue of the scope and limitations of non-Eurocentric (non-Atlantocentric) capitalism, the chapter explains both why this tendency must arise, and also why it must be blocked, thus condemning the system to a limbo where it flutters perpetually between the two poles.

But this still leaves a deficiency in international structure, since nothing stable really arose to replace the Cold War. A new statist balance of power with a resurgent South appears a theoretical option, but the heritage of imperialism means that this is resisted at all costs. A less threatening alternative might be a rules-based order, since this would allow for a manipulated pluralism, and the early post-Cold War period seemed indeed to look in this direction with rules-based regimes addressing both trade and human rights, and populated with international institutions, NGOs etc. But ultimately the historic core rejects any rules which would restrict itself. The 'war on terror', with its rejection of all human-rights norms, confirms this.

While the consolidated core rules the system, peripheral elites are nevertheless essential for its functioning. This incentivises them at least to sell their allegiance dearly, which is not without posing some challenges. How is the core to respond? While rejecting norms, rights and rules as we have seen, it nevertheless plays with these issues whenever convenient, as an interventionist slogan: thus humanitarian intervention may threaten Southern elites and keep them in line. An arm-wrestling match ensues, in which some cards are certainly held by the South. Nevertheless, the book argues, effective rebellion by the periphery would require mass support, and could not therefore be conducted on a basis of capitalism.

Chapter 7 draws the threads of the argument together by assessing contemporary trends and suggesting future lines of development.

We now enter a phase marked by chaotic features, not just environmentally, but because the capitalist mode of production which organised humanity over a long period is losing its grip. Since disorder is there anyway, why not embrace it as an opportunity for change? The ruling system can still meet this challenge by playing a double game, posing as guarantor of order while actually promoting those chaotic features which stimulate a security reflex. The problem is, though, that it cannot even master its *own* chaotic features by creating a stable new accumulation regime: it lacks new institutional ideas or fresh energy sources of a kind which fuelled past efforts of regime-building.

Having once opened up (albeit in an exploitative spirit) the Pandora's box of self-organising systems, it is very hard to re-centralise; hence, when constructive (exploitative) emergence begins to fail, for example when subordinate plural socio-political systems become unmanageable, the tendency is to cultivate instead *destructive* – but still chaotic and decentralised – emergent properties. We describe a 'cold imperialism' scenario where the system would, after making a bonfire of the remaining resources, start adapting to a high-entropy world, one where information is sparse, predictability survives only within gated enclaves, and relations with the lifeworld beyond are merely repressive. In its global policy, there are strong tendencies for imperialism to follow this option, strengthening its hold on areas of key strategic importance. It must after all keep the resource inputs flowing, not least to provide the payoffs rewarding co-operation in the inter-imperialist subsystem, without which everything else would fall apart.

But chaos cuts both ways. While undermining livelihood security and thus making working people more vulnerable to control, it may also signal a weakening of the capitalist attractor and open up a bifurcation, where one pathway leads towards creativity in inventing a new mode of production. Capitalism cannot therefore shut its eyes to the lifeworld's developing response to crisis.

In the international dimension, Southern nationalism here plays an ambiguous role. Partly, it may pretend to take advantage of resource scarcity to challenge the historic core within the parameters of the existing mode of production, a dead-end because it conveniently forgets that it is the mode of production itself which is in crisis, not just the core. But on the other hand, there could be a creative pact with the grassroots in redefining security in a manner condusive to livelihoods. The imperialist response is to reactivate the social imperialism of a century ago, employing 'democracy promotion' (a definition of democracy negatively related to sovereignty) in a way more intrusive even than the 'war on terror'.

In the above sense, we might argue that the core's dabbling in the lifeworld is merely a negative spoiling tactic to prevent autonomy. But there is something else as well–in a crisis context, strong human traits which would push towards a co-operative response. One of the subtlest and most interesting adaptations of capitalism might be to parasitise *upon* the forces of human renewal, while attempting of course to downplay their post-capitalist features.

Although in one sense the 'systemic turn' of capitalism in the '80s was a precursor of this, because it drew precisely upon natural human modes of interaction separate from market capitalism, the qualitative difference is that today the human co-operative response is triggered in crisis mode. Although this looks threateningly post-capitalist, we would also have to recognise the definition of imperialism as 'parasitic': could it then parasitise upon these forces? Of course, any wooing of human responses (for example, localism) would be just one among the four scenarios outlined earlier and would find its place among the other more repressive forms of adaptation, which both contradict it, and serve to police it. The aspect where some such 'new parasitism' might succeed easiest would be those developments which seem to proceed from within capitalism itself: the physical productive experiments with metabolic and closed-loop solutions, treating waste as an input. But there is also an institutional dimension, whereby the crisis triggers a resurgence of commons regimes. Thus local communities might for example undertake responsibility for their own social reproduction, thereby maintaining the social fabric in a low-cost way and relieving capitalism of that responsibility. One tactic is to confine regime development within regions which are safe, and stop it 'invading' the political economy as a whole, thus harnessing its energies in a non-threatening manner, notably to offset the social entropy caused through pauperisation. Hence the 'sustainable communities' discourse.

Bolstered by a decade of the 'war on terror', the ruling order thinks it has enough repressive and surveillance capacities to keep this under control. But the fallacy is clear: the more repression is employed to *enable* exploitation of the lifeworld, the weaker the indirect, hegemonic mode of control.

Despite the co-optation risks, radicals must enter the 'sustainable communities' arena, since experiments with a new mode of production cannot be delayed; its building blocks must be assembled partly from what already exists. The case of local food is discussed. Globally, capitalism's position is actually quite weak, since ultimately the huge societal energy released by the 'deep' adaptation mechanisms of humanity in crisis mode exerts a counter-pull to capitalism's hegemony, drawing all the experiments (including those addressing closed loops, localism etc.) in the direction of a new attractor, a new mode of production.

As far as the Left is concerned, it is still waking up to the fact that it is no longer possible (if it ever was) to think of overthrowing capitalism from the centre or top. The fundamental point is that self-organising systems *should* be the terrain of the Left, but somehow (mostly due to the stance of competing with capitalism at being better at central planning), capitalism has been allowed to appropriate this sphere.

To move on from this situation is not wholly straightforward because were we to liquidate the 'old' left on the grounds that it is too centralised, this would obviously serve ruling agendas. Nevertheless, circumstances increasingly favour a challenge to capitalism's partial hegemony over networking: not least because of the contradictoriness, not to say panic, of capitalism's own response to crisis: strong authoritarian and exterminist tendencies tend to undermine its capacity to manipulate networks anyway. The more confident the Left becomes, the more able it will be to assemble the elements of a new mode of production.

While including as 'found objects' even those low-input systems which have matured within capitalism, the foundation will be grassroots regime solutions, such as worker co-operatives. Physical productive systems and institutional systems could then be united along common principles of low input and symbiosis.

Perhaps the key to the practical agenda for change will be to *link* experimental systems, and even more importantly to link *struggles*. The revolutionary movement in the largest sense is itself a complex system, whose emergent characteristics cannot be predicted from the individual parts, and will become clear only once the spaces of struggle begin to unfold a worldwide linkage and interaction.

CHAPTER ONE

UNDERSTANDING THE LIMITS AND DECAY OF THE CAPITALIST MODE OF PRODUCTION

"The next 50 to 100 years or so, beginning from now, will be a great era of radical change in the social system throughout the world, an earth-shaking era without equal in any previous historical period. Living in such an era, we must be prepared to engage in great struggles which will have many features different in form from those of the past." – Mao Zedong, 1962

"What shall I do with this new and coming hour, so unfamiliar to me?" – Garcia Lorca

Introduction and Core Hypothesis of the Argument

Although the current finance crisis is serious enough, it could be argued that we have seen its like before. But underpinning this is a deeper crisis of unprecedented scope. Most obviously, it is ecological: exceptional levels of unpredictability and extreme events. In a less easily definable sense it is societal.

In developing an explanatory model, we can begin by interpreting the symptoms. For about a decade since the end of the 1990s we witnessed a generalised shift towards repression and militarism. The thing to which this *claimed* to respond – terrorism – is not a convincing reason, and we should look for some deeper sense in which capitalism has come under threat.

Logically, this could include the following factors: an internal exhaustion within the mode of production itself, of its developmental potential; some external 'limits' which it confronts, and which distort its normal course of development; and some struggle against it (other than the enemy it has imagined).

Since our approach seeks to embrace complexity and shun reductionist single-cause explanations, we must take up the challenge of describing an interaction between all these causes. Internal decay and external limits feedback between one another. The system is indeed challenged by real struggles, completely different from the imaginary enemy: the class struggle, women's struggle, struggles led by indigenous peoples to safeguard humanity's harmonious relations with nature.... and, in a context of an order heavily imprinted with colonialism and North-South polarisation, these inevitably express themselves partly under the contingent form of national movements, which may question the Eurocentrism of the dominant order.

Capitalism has acquired experience of manoeuvring within this lattice-work of issues. Problems which are getting too acute in the social realm can be exported into the ecological sphere: economic 'growth' has, at immense ecological cost, enabled social contradictions to be kept at bay to some extent. Repression operates not just politically, but in a psychological sense (the denial mechanism, for example with respect to ecological degradation); radical struggles are sidestepped or their acceptable facets co-opted (aspects of feminism may be co-opted into consumerism, though without abolishing its radical core). To describe this faculty, we will use the term regulation.[1] Such manoeuvrings do not remove the fundamental problems but merely shift them around. Nevertheless they have enabled capitalism to surmount seemingly insuperable crises, and to continue fulfilling its historic mission of exploiting and accumulating.

But we will argue that the current crisis is different, and not resolvable by normal regulation.

In order to understand why, we will have to enter quite deeply into certain areas of theory, not for their own sake, but to guide the struggles which arise in this situation. In viewing capitalism as a complex adaptive system, the proposition of this book is that we can employ systems theory in a way consistent with Marxism and dialectics, thus revealing links between aspects of the crisis which are hard to understand by conventional thinking. For example, a system whose energy source is drying up will experience a narrowing of options. The 'war on terror', as a highly simplifying repressive discourse, is thus in a significant sense a response to the ecological 'squeeze' which global capitalism now experiences. While this endeavour involves us in trying to understand structure, we will seek to combat an excessive structuralism by continually emphasising agency. We must in particular guard

---

[1] Our usage is influenced by regulation theory, but we seek to develop this in a special sense which will be explained later, notably by a more consistent usage of the systems perspective.

against any assumption that the ruling order would collapse by itself. Of course, it might indeed collapse in some sense if it were permitted to damage nature and society to such a degree that these could no longer reproduce it, but such a scenario must be pre-empted in any case, because then capitalism would bring much of the social and eco-logical fabric crashing down with it. For the moment, it is very much the case that the more decayed it is, the more determined to hold on; we must therefore observe the principle, 'if you don't hit it, it won't fall' (Mao, 1969, p. 19).

Contribution of the Systems Perspective

The systems perspective is quite rich and multi-faceted, and in a sense the whole of this book will be an exercise in defining it. But let us begin with some simple definitions.

Firstly, the constraint: order tends to decrease, things tend to decay. In technical language this is expressed as the Second Law of Thermodynamics, which says that the entropy of a closed system increases with time (entropy is a rich notion, whose layers of mean-ing we will explore throughout our discussion). The famous repre-sentation of the 'arrow of time' is that a glass will break, but not reconstitute itself.

The reason we *can* develop is that our system (i.e. society) is not closed, but rather 'dissipative': it has an environment (surrounding system) with which it can exchange energy. In fact, there are two lev-els of surrounding system. Most fundamentally, it is the solar system. The decay of the sun, which degrades as it radiates its energy, supplies more than enough entropy to counterbalance any level of develop-ment: this is the only true definition of sustainability (Georgescu-Roegen, 1975).

But of course society is not inserted directly into the solar system, but only through the intermediary of the ecosystem, *of which it is part*. This requires several features: a particular condition of the upper atmosphere which absorbs the right amount of heat and protects against radiation, an equilibrium which is not merely static but which can evolve to absorb future shocks, sufficient biodiversity to provide material for this adaptive development, etc. At a whole-systems level, the operation of this is described in the Gaia model. That system is *complex*: De Rosnay's notion of the 'macroscope' is one way of identifying the wider interactions which might be lost if we define a particular problematic (e.g. mainstream economics) too narrowly (de Rosnay, 1979).

The only safe way of organising productive systems and society is to insist that they be low-input/low-output. The point is not just to avoid *importing* into the social system finite stocks, but more profoundly to avoid the *export* of waste (another representation of entropy) in a way which undermines the balancing mechanisms which should enable us to access solar energy safely (destruction of the ozone layer, excessive CO_2 etc.). Any attempt at a 'magical' solution which pretends to escape these constraints is likely to have a hidden cost which is exported somewhere or stored up for the future.

We should avoid a narrow and reductionist reading of energy. Thus, the reductionist analysis of the Iraq war as being 'about oil' is unsatisfactory, but in a wider sense we can validly see it as being 'about energy'. It is 'about' a situation where the institutional energy expended on controlling complex exploitative systems outstrips the physical *and human* resources they make available to the exploiter: in such a situation, the exploiter falls back on generalised repression.

We can understand this better by exploring a different facet of the systems approach: the notion of information. The definitions of entropy in thermodynamics and in information theory are equivalent (Lovelock and Margulis, 1974). Information requires differentiation: in its absence, the signals degenerate into mere noise, and this noise is another way of describing entropy. In this sense, a system with high entropy might better be described not as disordered, but as homogenised or uniform. This way of seeing things will be very important in addressing the globalising phase of capitalism, which precisely tends to remove diversity.

Nature presents us with various 'resources', i.e. materials which, because they are strongly differentiated from their background environment, are the opposite of an undifferentiated 'noise'. So we can represent them as 'negative entropy' (negentropy, or, the term we will often employ, exergy). In using them up, the matter itself does not disappear, but its orderliness or differentiation does. And according to the arrow of time, this cannot reconstitute itself (in fact, as we will see in a moment, capitalism does actually attempt such a reconstitution, but only by using up more energy than the process makes available, an absurd procedure, but nevertheless one which the current crisis has made increasingly prevalent). The advantage of exergy as a notion is that it unifies within a single concept fossil fuels as well as the other raw materials which nature has made available to humanity in a useful form. When consumed, resources turn into high entropy (waste). A social system premised on intensive resource use is unsustainable, not just in terms of its input, but of its output.

Of course, biological resources may be renewable, but their reproduction still has to be respected. Particular societies may have collapsed in the past by consuming their own ecological basis, for example Easter Island, but the impact was only local. Capitalism is the first such case where the impact is global. What we are witnessing at the time of writing is more or less the threat of a global Easter Island. The whole point is, of course, again the complexity: it is not just the reproduction of individual species which is sacrificed, but above all the complex whole wherein they interact.

So much for constraint. The opposite way of approaching the systems perspective is as opportunity. Order can 'emerge' (arise spontaneously). Emergent forms of order are more efficient (better at being low-input/low-output) than top-down, over-designed ones. By giving full play to this opportunity, we can minimise the constraint.

If we imagine a future society which, instead of repression, develops diffuse capacity and the spontaneous order generated by grassroots innovation, the innovatory capacity itself would supply a relatively 'free' source of energy (always conditional on the fact that the people who exercise the capacity can be fed, a big question which will form a major concern in this book!). Traditional systems were like this, making extensive use of knowledge and experimentation by the actual producers, organised through institutional structures ('regimes' in the special sense employed by institutional theory) to manage common-pool resources; not just physical ones like land, but less obviously intangible resources like knowledge and institutional knowhow about the management of society itself. This is a natural mode of human organisation which we can rediscover without turning the clock back to actual tradition. But to achieve this could only represent a development of human society in a larger sense, and not a development *of capitalism*. The actual trajectory of capitalism seems diametrically opposed to this sustainable direction: its social antagonisms can only (with difficulty) be managed at the expense of a high degree of physical environmental degradation, which can in a sense be seen as the dissipation of the energy expended in controlling society. But we will need to understand this trajectory in detail, because it governs the conditions under which we may contemplate shifting social development onto a different course. This is precisely our task in this book.

The Entropy Question within Marxism

The agent of change must be a social movement sufficiently radical in its ability to escape the pull of the ruling order. This does not mean that it rejects every feature of current society, because one cannot begin with a clean slate. But it must not be enslaved to the ruling order *as a system*. This is why Marxism is so important to us. A major focus of this work will be to establish the dialogue between Marxism and systems theory.

Marxism has always highlighted the destructiveness internal to capitalism, which drives its tendency to decay. The *Communist Manifesto* is full of a sense that the moment of capitalism's triumph, when it was very much transforming the world in its image – and above all, opening up the world market – was itself an expression of self-exhaustion, of the fact that it was ripe for abolition. Of course, we should avoid a catastrophist reading. Rather, the issue unfolds over a whole era, as we can see in the sense that the world market was not *fully* realised in Marx' day, but rather in more recent processes of globalisation.

In one sense, the fruition-decay relationship is simply logical: in Hegel's words, "The highest maturity, the highest stage, which anything can attain is that in which its downfall begins (Hegel, 1969, pp.611)." But while this is partly true, we must be a bit wary because the argument could be read in a deterministic way, in the sense that capitalism begun with a 'fund' of progressive potential which needed to be 'exhausted'. In answer to this, we emphasise that the 'mission' was *always* destructive … of nature and – we need only consider the colonial context – of society. It is therefore justified to struggle to halt this at any time; this was just as much the case with 16th century slave revolts, as with today's anti-globalisation.

Nevertheless, in interpreting the contemporary form of capitalism, it remains valid to see this as more decadent than its earlier forms.

At this point the concept of imperialism becomes essential. Imperialism was hotly debated around the beginning of the 20th century, debates which introduced a number of remarkably farsighted ideas, along with some weaknesses: weaknesses included a tendency to underestimate the historical dimension of previous colonialism, as well as the latent scope which the system still possessed to restructure itself and surmount particular crises – a scope which, we will argue, has now become exhausted, triggering an advanced stage of entropy. In what follows, we will analyse the imperialism debate critically. We will emphasise imperialism as a *period* of transition through which capitalism's contradictions are further revealed, and the struggle for something new begins to emerge.

The depletion associated with capitalism should always be seen under two aspects: that of its physical and social support systems; and the *self*-depletion of the mode of production's developmental options. How are we to understand the relation between the two? In a sense, it is the self-depletion, the increasing difficulty of maintaining the social and economic conditions for capital accumulation, which drives the system to destroy its external environments. As Marx (1954) puts it, "Capitalist production ... develops technology, and the combining together of various processes into a social whole, only by sapping the original sources of all wealth – the land and the labourer". The only way of overcoming the hindrances on reproducing *itself* satisfactorily – by which we mean not just reproducing *capital* (turnover, making a profit), but the complex system which makes this possible (its institutional features, management practices, structures of international politics, ideologies etc.) – is for capitalism to eat away at the reproduction of its physical and social underpinnings.

When we speak of the reproduction of nature and of society being interfered with or undermined, the systems perspective would emphasise the reduction of its 'immune systems', its reduced ability to withstand shocks (to be self-righting or self-repairing), and more specifically, to prevent dangerous positive feedback processes. Positive feedback is any process where the result magnifies the cause: an example is the screech which comes from a sound system when the signal from the speaker is itself picked up by the mic, which feeds it through to the speaker, forming a continuous loop. We can stop this by turning the sound system off, but what is more difficult to turn off is the positive feedback associated with global warming, for example: the melting of the ice-caps decreases the earth's albedo (whiteness), which in turn makes it less reflective (it absorbs more solar heat, therefore getting hotter), which in turn causes the ice-cap to melt faster, which brings us back to the beginning of the loop. Similar positive feedback processes occur in society: we will encounter many examples in the course of this enquiry.

The ecological crisis, even if historically the fault of capitalism, will be inherited by future society, however it is organised. In this sense it is apparently above class and independent of social system. But we have to consider this assumption critically. The only social forces which can take the lead in solving it are the classes and strata oppressed by the current system, and which have least to lose by overthrowing it. In this sense, the issue is not really above class.

Understanding the relationship between the social and ecological issues is therefore of key importance. Marx' thinking on this issue is quite complex, precisely because he understood – as must we, today – the necessity of guarding simultaneously against a number of mistaken positions (a one-sided critique of just one error always runs the risk of opening up another!). As Lenin (1915) said, the development of knowledge is a complex, spiral-like process where any fragment or segment can "be transformed (transformed one-sidedly) into an independent, complete, straight line" where it tends to become "*anchored* by the class interests of the ruling classes (p. 363)." There are a number of one-sided positions which, while they can be considered erroneous, nevertheless all precede from premises which are partly correct. Stripping the problem to its barest logic we can propose the following schema of four possible errors, bearing in mind that this is an oversimplification:

One, there are absolute environmental limits and no change of social system can do anything about this (the Malthusian position). *Two*, apparent scarcity is caused by maldistribution, and once exploitation is removed the environmental problem is revealed as illusory (a variant of utopian socialism, e.g. Saint Simon). *Three*, while capitalism is still in place it operates in a totally deterministic way, for example in squeezing every last drop out of the working population, and allowing no role for struggle (the Lasallean position in the German workers' movement critiqued by Marx). *Four*, the *essential* factor undermining capitalism is the feedback it receives from the depletion of its external (social, by extension, ecological) environments rather than its internal contradictions (not so clearly expressed in Marx' day, but can be derived from Rosa Luxemburg's position).

All of these are wrong, not because they have no relation to reality, but because they develop certain parts of it in one-sided ways. We can only answer these arguments through a complex response where we fuse what is true in the issues addressed by these positions in a dialectical and not eclectic way. Even today, this task is very difficult, but it was particularly so in Marx' day where these lines had not all had articulated themselves clearly or exposed their implications. In the circumstances, he made a heroic effort to act simultaneously on all these fronts.

One: Marx was consistent in seeing Malthusianism as a reductionist and deterministic ideology which served the power interests of the day. Nevertheless, the true point, 'maldeveloped' by Malthus, is that there are limits to what any social system can do in abusing its environment. As we know, it was not only capitalism which neglected this, but a certain form of 20th-century socialism heavily influenced by capitalism's modernist phase. When the first inklings of payback were experienced in the 1970s, the *Limits to Growth* debate (Meadows, 1972) as well as in the development of this debate by Malcolm Caldwell, articulated some basically correct ideas, despite the Malthusian tone of some of the pronouncements. Post-capitalist society cannot simply consider the issue of limits to be resolved by a change in the relations of production.

What we have just said is sufficient to expose the fundamental error in scenario *Two*, as expressed in some of the more simplistic contemporary Left critics of the *Limits to Growth* (Cole, 1973). For example, although it is objectively true that there is enough food to overcome hunger if poor people had the entitlements to buy it (as demonstrated by Sen, 1982), this statement leaves untouched the fact that the food system *itself* is unsustainable, as I will show in more detail later. Only the profoundest ecologically-conscious revolution can address this. Nevertheless, we cannot lose sight of the fact that *Two* proceeds from a certain correct premise: although distribution cannot *per se* solve the whole environmental problem, a change in the mode of production (from which a fundamental change in distribution is surely inseparable) will address the basis of the problem – *particularly in terms of its future thrust* – by removing the incentive for growth which proceeds from the need to expand profit at all costs. Although it is unfortunate that the Soviet system became trapped into demonstrating its superiority over capitalism by growing faster – which is a serious aberration – it remains true that growth is inherently an obsession of capitalism, both in general because it embodies the imperative of expanded reproduction, and more specifically because it is the only way of keeping some sort of control over pauperisation without sacrificing the *relative* power of the capitalist class, as I will demonstrate later.

Three (the deterministic representation of exploitation) is wrong because it neglects the role of struggle within capitalism: the social contradictions are *active* and not merely latent. We must understand struggle, firstly because we cannot otherwise understand the *regulation* of capitalism which operates essentially through a mixture of repression and co-optation of struggle; and secondly because struggle builds both the social forces themselves, and the institutional experiments, which will feed into radical change. Nevertheless, the true point underlying *Three* is that there is a strong tendency to degrade society by squeezing the last drop out of the working population, and this would reach a qualitative point (perhaps somehow analogous to the tipping-point in environmental degradation) which would call into question social reproduction.

The complexity of Marx' social and environmental thought can be explained by the fact that he was roughly aware of the broad picture we have outlined (some aspects of it more explicitly, others more intuitively), and in responding to one error, strove to avoid encouraging the others. Dialectics at the level of reason seeks to reflect the objective dialectics of the real world, and therefore necessarily shuns simplistic, reductionist, single-cause explanations.

This takes us to a consideration of *Four*. We must develop this a bit more fully, because it raises some crucial issues which will help to draw the foregoing threads together. *Four*, the position which focuses on the external restrictions at the expense of the internal contradictions, is wrong because it is the latter which actually *cause* the behaviour which leads to physical and social environmental degradation. The result is that limitations which are in essence internal, *are manifested as external*: the milieu has a finite capacity to absorb them. Nevertheless, there is something powerfully progressive in the argument that 'pure' capitalism could not function for a moment if it did not have the 'other': informal workers, semi-clandestine migrants, the household, the whole hidden economy, the sphere of non-monetary relations and reciprocity. It is precisely in these areas – strongly determined by gender and colour – that some of the major *struggles* against the system arise. Were it to neglect this fact and instead be fixated on the 'pure' mode of production, the Left would inevitably collapse into frozen forms of ideology which are typically Eurocentric, neglect the gender dimension, focus on the labour aristocracy and exaggerate the power of 'man' to dominate nature ... which is precisely what *has* tended to happen.

This is where Luxemburg's contribution sets us onto a very interesting course of enquiry. The *regulation* of capitalism as a system has always required this 'other', which we could see as excluded from full capitalist status by some visible or invisible boundary. Thus, "overseas, it [capital] begins with the subjugation and destruction of traditional communities, the world historical act of the birth of capital, since then the constant epiphenomenon of accumulation"(Luxemburg, 1972, pp. 59–60); accumulation then fuels itself from the "progressive breakdown and disintegration" of a *milieu* (she employs this French term, rendered in the usual English translation as 'environment', Luxemburg, 1913). Although the aspect she explicitly highlighted was the social, not the ecological surrounding system, implicitly this opens up the possibility of considering capitalism as a dissipative system in a wider, physical sense. The two are related, in the sense that the sphere of traditional social relations was not just 'space' which could be gobbled up in expanding the sphere of accumulation, they were also gatekeepers to the natural world, whose destruction opened the way to the depletion of exergy. This is the reason why capitalism has always been *intrinsically* linked to an act of colonisation: both an *internal* colonisation of the commons, and an external one, of the global South. Although Luxemburg (who was after all obliged to evolve within a fundamentally macho world of left-wing polemic) doesn't highlight the feminist angle directly, it is clear that the argument leads in the direction of Carolyn Merchant's 'death of nature' thesis; (Merchant, 1990) women occupied an ascribed gender role of special importance as guardians of the natural world.

The key lesson for today's situation is that the milieu which has enabled capitalism to continue expanding is now to a significant extent depleted. It is depleted in two senses. Firstly, a reduction of *scope*: both physical resources like oil, and also the un-monetarised social spaces available for the spread of commodification (the two are connected, since physical resources serve as an energetic source to *drive* globalised commodity society) run out. Secondly, a qualitative exhaustion, as social and ecological repair-systems are undermined. Information from impending exhaustion then begins to make itself felt.

This information modifies the behaviour of the system in ways which we will consider later. But the important thing to draw out of the Marxist critique of Malthusianism is both that exploitation produces struggle, and that it is always *worth* struggling. And in this respect, social struggles over distribution have never been entirely separable from struggles to defend nature. For example, only massive popular protest forced Uganda's President Museveni, an enthusiastic acolyte of biofuels, to halt the destruction of large areas of priceless rain forest for biofuel plantations (Byakola, 2007). Leaders try to sell the new agenda on the grounds that it will help development to pull the people out of poverty, but the masses are not fooled: they are once more becoming the gatekeepers of the natural world because their livelihoods are wrapped up in it, something far more real and tangible than promises of trickle-down which never deliver. The contradictions of capitalism are therefore expressed in its shrinking ability to export disorder, not merely (as would be assumed on a Malthusian argument) because of absolutely limited environmental scope, but because of the politics of resistance. In practical terms, environmental limits are therefore not merely external parameters to the human mode of production, but internal to it. Although resistance does not per se sort out the environmental problem, it does create unexpected tools for solving it. There is nothing utopian about this, because contestatory institutional experiments already exist within the interstices of the current order. I will return to this topic in more detail in the final section, but will now briefly introduce a conceptual framework for understanding it.

The Significance of Human Capacity

Our starting point is that there is a hidden potential within society which can be unleashed to substitute for *physical* energy.

The most straightforward way we can represent this potential is by calling it capacity. This refers to people's innate problem-solving ability; indeed we can go further and say there is an innate love of discovery, of posing and resolving problems. Peruvian potato-farmers love the challenge of growing their crops in difficult environments (Salas, 1991, pp. 211–222). As Samir Amin (1981) shows, it is perfectly possible for economic models to encompass grassroots innovation as a genuine resource. Capacity can in a certain sense be seen as a *free* resource because it is not dissipative. In reality, this is not entirely true, because the people who exercise capacity have to be nourished, and if there is a decline in the nutritional value of food this becomes a problem as we will see later. But the important point for our present argument is the following hypothesis, which will be central to our enquiry: on the basis of a given population, if you can discover a social system which unleashes capacity, you will have released a latent free resource; by expanding this, you can in parallel reduce ecological depletion without any overall loss of welfare.

And there is more. If we address capacity purely at an individual level this only takes us part of the way, because it neglects people's inherently *social* character: there has always been experimentation not just in particular techniques like potato-growing, but at the level of the social system itself. To understand this social dimension of innovation we can begin to employ the term 'institutional' in the special way it is used in institutional theory: here we refer not just to formal *organisations* but to informal structures, such as 'regimes'. Regimes (again used in a special sense) refer to non-compulsory structures which serve an accepted goal and operate through reciprocity and mutual benefit.

The link between this idea and systems theory is that the latter recognises a faculty called 'emergence'. Emergence is a self-forming type of order. Self-organising systems (such as commons regimes) tend to be more robust, adaptable and efficient than ones designed from above; too much control wastes energy and comes up with a less satisfactory result. The general deduction from this argument is that by unfolding a combination of capacity and emergence, social solutions can be developed which minimise the exported ecological cost.

Even traditional class systems, insofar as they were top-down, necessarily restricted capacity and emergence to some degree. But these societies did at least respect a certain autonomous sphere in which experimentation was conducted and knowledge developed and transmitted orally (Biel, 2000). Traditional exploiter-class societies can be described as 'tributary' insofar as they extract a tribute from this sphere, whose autonomy they nevertheless respect (except when it generates things like peasants' revolts!). There is a qualitative difference with capitalism, at least in the form of the latter's 'modernising' strand which is inherently distrustful of anything autonomous, and seeks to stamp it out.

In fact, as I will show later, a major adaptation of capitalism over the past quarter-century has been to attempt to shed modernism to the extent of recognising a tame 'informal' sphere, and reconstituting a kind of 'tributary' dominance over it. Nevertheless, this never permitted a true development of capacity, and the 'war on terror' threatens a return to the repressive reflex which fears any whiff of self-organisation.

Our hypothesis is that the more capacity is restricted, the more society has to fuel itself in other, unsustainable ways. There is an opposite, reciprocal movement of the two variables: as the scope of capacity (grassroots innovation, institutional experimentation) goes down, the scope of resource-depletion goes up. While this explains why capitalism cannot develop a green form, it also reveals something encouraging for the future: if capacity is restored, society automatically acquires a way of greening itself.

In order to concretise this argument let us draw some examples from the food system.

The most obvious expression of the Malthusian position seems to be the equation of population versus food supply. The issue of how to feed a large global population looks like a clear case of an absolute limit, in the sense that it would not be removed simply by a change in social system, for example by abolishing the concentration of wealth. Nevertheless, a change of social system *could* contribute to a solution in the following way.

Firstly, as Sen's work shows, (Sen, 1982) malnutrition would *partly* be resolved by redistribution, insofar as the problem is caused by deficient entitlements rather than by deficient production per se. It is therefore arguably true that redistribution would remove malnutrition on the basis of the existing food supply. We can add that there would be a beneficial feedback in the sense that it is now understood that a reduction in poverty, *and particularly in the insecurity which accompanies poverty*, would also lead to a reduction in the rate of population growth (Lappé and Shurman, 1989). This knocks on the head the Malthusian position.

Apparently, we could therefore argue that the current volume of food production – and more broadly, the supply of goods – is adequate to give everyone a decent living standard provided that distribution was changed.

But this argument, unfortunately, is insufficient. The problem is that the current system of production as a whole, and more specifically of food, *is itself unsustainable*. This is because of its reliance on excessive energy inputs, its effect on climate change and, in the case of food, its impact on soil structure and biodiversity and propensity to create massive hazard.

This takes us to the second step in our argument: The entire agricultural order would have to be redesigned on organic lines.

This could, however, be achieved partly by redirecting *existing* resources: for example, as Wolfe shows, only a tiny fragment of current R&D is devoted to organic agriculture (Wolfe, n.d.) Although there are tendencies within capitalism for organics to increase, they are unfortunately likely to be overwhelmed by the aggregate trend; but under a different social system, the priorities could easily be changed without consuming any new resources. This is an argument similar to the 'peace dividend'. As I will show in detail later, there are important reasons of path-dependency which explain why neither a peace dividend nor an 'organic dividend' is possible under capitalism; but if we remove the condition of capitalism, a redirection of *existing* resources could solve many problems without having to create something out of nothing.

Now we are getting close to the essence of the matter. The argument so far, though encouraging, still masks a key problem. We cannot simply redirect R&D in the sense of official, top-down science because this has evolved in such a way as *inherently* to restrict capacity and emergence. Nor is it sufficient to speak of organics unless we simultaneously say low-throughput: an agriculture which consumed a lot of fossil fuel and water, and produced a lot of greenhouse gas (for example, methane from the meat industry) could qualify as organic but still be unsustainable. Any change in social system, if it is to solve the problem, must therefore both address throughput and liberate capacity from the base. But this is perfectly possible: fortunately, we have the Cuban case to prove how a radical reorganisation towards a low-throughput economy can be achieved (Rosset, 2000). Cuba has been artificially – thanks to the US blockade – forced to anticipate a problem which is beginning now to confront the whole of humanity; the solution must be highly creative, but capacity from the base can easily supply this creativity.

Obviously, climate change will continue to be a problem because the temperature-deregulation initiated by capitalism cannot simply be put into reverse gear. However, human capacity and a plurality of different cultural responses have always created the possibility of adaptation. It was precisely the traditional strategy of keeping alive all possible genetic variety (seeds, animals) which provided a basis for doing this; (Shiva, 1988) the work of Fre with respect to pastoralists illustrates this strikingly (Fre, 1990). This adaptive capacity can be rediscovered.

Capitalism is also adaptive, but its adaptation is exclusively focused on preserving *itself* as a system, i.e. the control of the capitalist class over the means of production – nature – and over people. The answer to whether it could suddenly begin to act on behalf *of humanity* is a bit like the old Irish Republican slogan "there can be no British solution" – intuitively, it is hard to see how the cause of the problem can also be its solution, or (as in a well-known quotation attributed to Einstein), "We cannot solve our problems with the same thinking we used when we created them". The adaptation of human society to address these issues cannot therefore be an adaptation *of capitalism*. This is the reason why agency is manifested not just as problem-solving (if by this we understand a politically neutral adaptive response to particular issues of living with climate change, etc.) but primarily as struggle against the system which is preventing humanity from responding to these challenges.

In our hypothesis, since it is the extraordinarily intense social contradictions which cause capitalism to export its problems onto the environment, a different system could reduce its ecological footprint.

As an abstract thought experiment we might envisage a society which fuelled itself only by exploiting either the environment or society. Saint Simon's version of the utopian socialist vision may have had some aspects of the former, a society without social contradictions advancing through more intensive 'mastery' of nature, but this is not realisable in practice. Traditional exploiter-class societies possessed aspects of the latter, and in this case the model seemingly *is* viable, because such societies really existed and could sustain their environmental milieus for millennia, something capitalism has proved incapable of achieving.

Even so, it is a hypothesis worth considering that the surplus generated to support the ruling order of pre-capitalist agricultural class societies was achieved by introducing some ecologically questionable practices, notably deep ploughing and irrigation. We have to understand that there are alternative, viable and productive agricultural systems which avoid these practices (Koponen, 1991; Belshaw, 1980; Richards, 1985). *Their flaw, from an exploiter-class perspective, is that they are not conducive to central control.* It is therefore arguable that a positive feedback relation exists between class dominance and unsustainablity. Drawing upon indigenous experiences, progressive current thinking is increasingly emphasising that the agriculture of the future should look to no-till principles and the minimisation of water loss (significant in the context of a post-capitalist society having to grapple with the legacy of climate change). Modern agricultural systems which depend on irrigation are becoming extremely vulnerable, for example, Australia has suddenly woken up to a drought so severe that irrigation may have to be sacrificed in order to keep enough to drink (Marks, 2007). Future adaptation to the challenges of anthropogenic climate change will therefore have to look back to more ancient methods.

As Marx points out, capitalism's control over nature is the foundation of everything, but this is hidden: "The bourgeois have very good grounds for falsely ascribing *supernatural creative power* to labour", (Marx, 1970) precisely in order to hide the fundamental issue of control over the natural conditions of production. In the 19th and even most of the 20th centuries, damage to the physical environment could be neglected, or where it manifested itself in deterioration of the immediate urban living environment, such as smogs, mitigated through legislation. The social contradictions were thus the most obvious, but even in this case, their intensity was underestimated because they could be exported onto the physical environment, through 'growth'. In this sense, there was a 'sequestered' form of ecological decay, itself in a sense a transmuted form of social contradictions, which is now exacting its payback in the form of climate change, massive hazard in the food system etc. All of this is, in a way, a result of capitalist society turning its back on the only free resource: the interaction between the natural world and human capacity.

A Trend towards Absolute Poverty

Mainstream development discourses now talk obsessively about poverty, but this is really a smokescreen to hide *exploitation*.

What restricts capacity is not poverty but the system itself. If entropy can partly be represented as waste, then we could look towards some social representation of entropy as the human capacity which goes to waste, generation after generation. There is a sense in which human society is, under capitalism, depleting not just nature *but itself*. Arundhati Roy speaks of contemporary India living by consuming its own limbs, (Roy, 2007) and this striking image could apply in a wider sense to an entire 'autophrage' world system.

Inherent to the notion of entropy is an arrow of time, and this would lead us to look for a *trend*. It is in this context that we should consider the pauperisation thesis of Marx.

Current anti-poverty discourses address the systemic dimension up to a point, at least at the level of *symptoms*: the 'sustainable livelihoods' approach highlights a restriction on the ability of systems at a grassroots level (i.e. people's social networks) to reproduce and to withstand shocks. But what the discourse totally cannot encompass is *cause*: the increase of poverty is seen as a puzzling anomaly because wealth is being accumulated which looks like it should provide the solution, but for some mysterious reason it obstinately refuses to 'trickle down'. Sooner or later we should wake up to the fact that if wealth has been accumulating for centuries without alleviating poverty, then Marx was probably right that the supposed solution to the problem is actually its cause. This is not to say that all wealth is necessarily extracted *from* the masses, because its source is fundamentally nature; the more accurate formulation is that the process of its accumulation is *inseparable* from processes which deplete society, under conditions where nature is monopolised and the masses excluded from it.

Poverty is often classified as 'absolute' and 'relative'. But neither of these terms is straightforward. I will define absolute poverty as the self-consuming facet, the tendency of the mode of production to undermine society's own reproduction. The entropic feature of this is the arrow of time in the direction of decay. Capitalism here appears as a parasite which (in defiance of the criteria of an ecologically rooted parasite!) exhausts the life-blood of its host. Marx' and Engels' great early work the *Communist Manifesto* is deeply imbued with such a feeling, as for example in the statement that the bourgeoisie "is unfit to rule because it is incompetent to assure an existence to its slave within his slavery, because it cannot help letting him sink into such a state, that it has to feed him, instead of being fed by him", (Marx, 1969, p. 119) a statement which strikingly anticipates the issue now facing capitalism at a world level, as it desperately grapples with a potentially disaffected population which it doesn't really need but has to keep alive somehow.

Let us now consider the relative dimension. Relativity theories remove absolute frames of reference. Now, as Sowell argues, Marx' later discussions of poverty tend increasingly to address it in a relative sense (Sowell, 1960, pp. 111–120). We need to explain this shift, because it looks at first sight like a weakening of the clarity of the earlier statement, in particular with respect to the entropy issue.

The Victorian approach to absolute poverty was in a way the response of an autophrage system which threatens to deplete its own basis, i.e. if workers cannot access the bare necessities, it will be impossible to go on exploiting them. This way of defining absolute poverty serves the establishment in two interconnected ways: it is open to a Malthusian interpretation (which confines history to rigid, deterministic laws), and it sidelines the issue of distribution. On this basis, we can similarly identify two linked reasons why the more radical social historians, beginning with Marx, have tended to emphasise relativity. We can understand this by considering, respectively, two of Marx' key works, *Wage Labour and Capital* and *Wages, Price and Profit*.

The argument we can derive from the former takes as its starting point the simple fact that the logic of accumulation makes wealth flow to those who already control it. Here, Marx shows that an increase of capitalist power over the masses is perfectly compatible with an absolute improvement of the latter's material conditions (Marx, 1969 b). This is particularly relevant in the context of today's globalisation discourse. If we take the most optimistic capitalist vision where the size of the cake grows (forgetting for a moment any environmental constraints), this would indeed permit the *absolute* standard of the poorer segment to improve, but could well be compatible with a decline in their class status: for example, if the cake (which we could represent in the form of total national income) doubled in size and workers' share shrunk from 8% to 5%, the latter would be materially better off and at the same time more subservient! Subsequent research, notably that of Portes and Walton in the United States, provides empirical confirmation (Portes and Walton, 1981). Moreover, a detailed sociological analysis using the relative poverty approach, as in the work of Townsend, (Townsend, 1979) can reveal how imperialism operates to neutralise dissent by buying off certain segments and marginalising others.

The second argument, the more dynamic one, is linked to Marx' critique of Malthusianism. The living standard of the working class is a reflection of the *value* of the labour power they sell to the capitalists; this value is, however, not fixed by any absolute ('iron') law. As Marx showed in *Wages, Price and Profit*, it is simply an invitation to struggle (Marx, 1969 c). The class struggle is a natural and endemic response to exploitation, a just struggle and one which forms the bedrock for subsequent, more politicised forms of action. This position is of course compatible with an ecological perspective: if we accept that for ecological reasons the cake can't be permitted to grow, class struggle comes into its own, as the only way to change the relative size of the slices. The radical potential of this line of argument is pretty clear: we can simply say to all the mainstream forces who claim to be concerned about poverty: if you are serious about eliminating it, you need to support radical, grassroots and socialist movements!

As one might expect, the establishment poverty discourse would recoil in horror at such a conclusion; it must therefore tamper with the logic which leads inexorably in such a direction. To neutralise the dangers of the relative approach it therefore *anchors* ('anchors' in the sense of the Lenin passage quoted above) the issue within Victorian-style definitions of absolute poverty, as encapsulated in the introduction of the Millennium Development Goals in 2000.[2] But this is balanced, notably within World Bank ideologies, (Ravallion, 2003) by a phoney debate with an antiseptic form of the relative poverty idea. The latter is twisted into a form which actually responds to the dilemma signalled in our quote from the *Communist Manifesto*: unable to feed its own slaves, and certainly unwilling to sacrifice its own share of the global cake to do so, the discourse hypocritically urges the Southern ruling class to accept the full burden of a redistribution which the rulers of the core would never accept even within their own countries, still less internationally. We will discuss the practical implications of this attempt later.

It is clear from the above argument why in today's situation it is more important than ever to uphold the relative position, and more specifically its radical form.

Nevertheless, and having said all this, I would argue that today's situation is in some respects new; and that the key task now is actually to shift the emphasis onto the *absolute* definition of pauperisation, and to rediscover the radical potential of this notion. The early Marxian discussion of pauperisation as an absolute trend holds within it an understanding of the intrinsically autophrage nature of the capitalist mode of production. This problem was masked during the 20th century by a devastatingly simple, and in its long-term implications devastatingly dangerous expedient: it was shifted onto the physical environment (Biel, 2006). If we take the notion of 'feeding' the slaves literally, the growing food crisis now demonstrates its limits; if we take it in an extended sense and speak of, for example, providing adequate warmth, we now confront a fuel crisis. In all these ways, the feedback from the ecological dimension within which the *seemingly*-eliminated entropy was temporarily stored, is now beginning to restrict all the room for manoeuvre formerly available to a system which fallaciously preached that it could without limits expand its boundaries, its 'cake'. As we will see later, for a system so obsessed with poverty, meaningful statistics are surprisingly hard to find; but empirically, what looks like an absolute immiseration of large sections of the population occurs in tandem

---

[2] United Nations General Assembly A/RES/55/2, *United Nations Millennium Declaration* September 2000, on http://www.un.org/millennium/declaration/ares552e .pdf

with what is called 'development', and it is not rocket science to hypoth-esise a link between the two.

Imperialism and the Entropy Question

The concept of imperialism as the *'highest'* stage of capitalism (Lenin's phrase) provides another possible representation of entropy, as some-thing which has in some sense exhausted its 'fuel', whether we define this in a literal, physical sense, or in some extended sense of social or institutional scope.

As I will now argue, this representation does not deny the possibility of *development* within imperialism, but any such development must be a playing-out of the contradictions which ultimately exhaust it.

Around the turn of the 19th–20th centuries, there was a certain consensus about the existence of something called imperialism: the term was used both by those who advocated it and those, on the left, who opposed it (as well as intermediate trends like Hobson who strongly critiqued the existing *form*, while being open to supporting a reformed version of it). A further common theme was a recognition of some sense of limits, the difference being that the Right would see the limits as deterministic, Malthusian ones (thus encouraging violent struggle to monopolise scarce resources), whereas the Left tended to believe that the limits were those of capitalism itself, and could be tran-scended through a change of social system, and only in this way.

In the '60s, Harold and Margaret Sprout performed a major contri-bution, in introducing an 'ecological' view of international relations (Sprout, H. and Sprout, M., 1965). Here, 'ecology' is employed in a somewhat unusual way, but one which adds something to the more conventional usage. Translating this usage into our own terminology, we could define this as relating to *the behaviour of a system under con-ditions of immediate and impinging limits*. Let us consider how this might apply to imperialism. In the early 1900s, I would argue, the lim-its appeared more immediate than they were in reality, and subse-quently, particularly during the second half of the 20th century, the system found a way to repress the sense of limits through technological and institutional developments which sustained the growth illusion. The entropy was still there but was simply transposed, for example many new 'resources' (i.e. forms of exergy) were discovered (petro-leum, bauxite), so the limits were not the absolute availability but rather the carrying capacity of the ecosystem to absorb the effects unleashed by liquidating the negative entropy they contained (as in the CO_2 emissions made when transforming bauxite into alumina). Today the fundamental issues are once more coming to the surface, but now they really *are* immediate. This is precisely why the issues debated a century ago have never been more actual.

Nowadays the establishment would (despite a not insignificant right-wing backlash in favour of a renewed colonialism) mainly deny that they are imperialist. Some progressives like E.P. Thompson would also reject the continued relevance of the concept. However I disagree: the notion of imperialism as a tool in our analysis becomes more and more important with each new ingredient in the crisis.

The strongest part seems to be the understanding of structural changes within capitalism, such as the rise of oligopolies, militarism and the state, and these things are still very much with us. The aspect which appears to be more outdated is the fact that semantically the term relates to empires. But in this book we are seeing 'empire' as an expression of the drive for a periphery into which to dissipate, a sink (or, source of exergy which is the opposite way of saying the same thing), as well as the psychological dimension of being able to carve out spaces of predictable order (not the higher 'civilisation' the core claimed to be building within itself, but a kind of low order, conducive to exploitation). This quest did not come to an end with formal colonialism, quite the contrary, it only intensifies today as we will see in the final chapter. Stating this more generally, we could define imperialism in the broadest sense as the projection of the contradictions of capitalism into the problem of how such a system can, at a global level, be *ruled*. A specific aspect of this (not the totality but nevertheless extremely important) is the projection of contradictions into the system of international relations, an issue which we will consider in Chapter 6.

When we speak of the 'rulers' of this system, we must accept a partially 'racial' determination. The issue of Eurocentrism is therefore fundamental to an understanding of imperialism. The most dangerous misunderstanding to which classic imperialism theory sometimes laid itself open was a tendency to ignore the fundamental importance of the exploitation of the South's human and ecological resources to the *whole* of capitalism, from its origins. If one fails to understand the continuity, one can't correctly understand where, in another respect, imperialism *breaks* the continuity. This is why the contribution of W.E.B Du Bois to the 1900s imperialism debate, though marginalised at the time, should now be recognised as central (Du Bois, 1970). As I will argue, the Black Marxist perspective is essential if we are to acquire an all-round, and not merely selective, understanding of systemic degradation. It is also essential to understanding how the imperialist order has been able to stabilise itself by generating a certain social solidarity within the core. Thus the class contradiction was institutionally managed through a development known as social-imperialism, which introduced several elements which have remained in force ever since: a partial political liberalisation to bring the labour aristocracy into the political fold, spending a small amount of the accumulated surplus on public services, on education and on media which, instead of ignoring the masses, began actively to work on brainwashing them.

In early imperialism, as yet relatively uncorrupted by phoney 'growth' ideology, the substratum for this management of contradictions was a fairly transparent recognition of limits. In its social-Darwinist form, early social-imperialism was very much tied to the Malthusian premise that you had better line up behind your own imperialist power in order to grab as much as possible of the (finite) resources, which can then be shared out within that particular national society. Although this is not explicit today, the hidden agenda is still that, if there are insufficient resources for capitalist development of both core and periphery, the core wants to ensure that *it* is the one to develop.

But what interests us particularly is the dynamic aspect, the entropy dimension which caused the system to change *structurally*.

Such a line of argument is perhaps most clearly expressed in a paper by Halford Mackinder, widely recognised as a key point of departure for the geopolitics school. As with some other contributions to the imperialism debate (notably the work of Luxemburg), Mackinder was forced to invent, in a truly astounding way, a systems vocabulary which did not yet exist: "Every explosion of social forces, instead of being dissipated in a surrounding circuit of unknown space and surrounding chaos, will be sharply re-echoed from the far side of the globe, and weak elements in the political and economic organism of the world will be shattered in consequence" (Mackinder, 1904, pp. 421–437). Superficially, this resembles Lenin's point that, with the impingement of *territorial* limits, the world could only be re-divided. But territorial limits are only shorthand for something more profound: limited scope for dissipation. This could apply equally well to the carrying capacity of society or of the physical environment. The important point was that this was taken as an invitation for adaptation. Given the climate of thought at the time, this was seen as an *evolutionary* form of adaptation. Loosely seen as social-Darwinist, it may be more accurate, as O Tuathail has argued, to see the evolution as Lamarckian, in the sense of emphasising a speeded-up developmental process with the transmission of acquired characteristics (O Tuathail, 1996). This difference is important because it looks in the direction of institutional learning.

One of the main weaknesses of left-wing imperialism theory was its failure to take on board the possibility of such an evolutionary adaptation. This in turn springs from its failure to develop the potential of Marxism's ecological insights: there was a poor understanding of how capitalism might actually evolve – albeit, and this is the important point, in a high-entropy way.

Thus, for example, Mackinder foresaw the possibility that the system, faced with such catastrophic feedback, would bring about a change "from territorial expansion to the struggle for relative efficiency" (Mackinder, 1904). One way in which we could interpret this is in the sense of a shift from *extensive to intensive* modes of exploitation of the environment. This raises some very interesting issues. In fact, the possibility of a national-level intensive development was already anticipated in the theory of mid-19th century German economist Friedrich List, which emphasised the potential of human resources, of capacity (List, 1983). Capacity is, as we have seen, a genuinely renewable resource, and in this sense List was far ahead of any capitalist economist, at least prior to the systemic turn of the 1980s (when the system tried for the first time seriously to explore capacity in an exploitative framework, and List's work experienced a certain revival).

But in a deep sense, a capacity-intensive line of development is impossible under capitalism. Instead what tended to happen was an increasingly intensive exploitation of the *physical* environment. This was particularly the case when the national model of development (with a significant degree of local self-sufficiency) was replaced by free trade.

This analysis has begun to lead us in the direction of addressing adaptation. In the next chapter we will develop this line of argument, more particularly with respect to the specifics of imperialism. But first, let us consider the adaptive nature of capitalism in general.

CHAPTER TWO

CAPITALISM AS AN ADAPTIVE SYSTEM

We have explained in a somewhat static way the fundamental contradictions of capitalism, and of course the merit of such an approach is to highlight what *doesn't* change. But the other side of the picture is that these contradictions must always be managed in some way: it is precisely the fact that they won't go away which demands acceptance, when necessary, of radical change in the *way* they are managed.

The fundamental problem underlying all efforts at management and regulation is still dissipation. But once we begin to view the mode of production in a dynamic sense, we must introduce a number of other insights from the systems perspective.

Simplicty and Complexity

Taking the whole span of human history, adaptation has meant resilience to shocks, capacity to improvise and to explore a plurality of different options; traditionally, humanity's survival was understood as inseparable from that of its natural environment, and the problem with capitalism is that it departs from all these criteria: it stifles capacity; and its developmental forms tend to be fuelled by depleting the environment, rather than preserving it. Nevertheless, it does adapt ... but with the sole criterion of preserving *itself* as a system, in terms of its core characteristics, most notably the expanded reproduction of capital. Efficiency in a thermodynamic sense means minimising throughput; efficiency in an exploitative sense means realising profit by converting exergy into waste, monopolising capacity within narrow regions in the centre and at the top, and expelling disorder among the excluded. Under capitalism, it is thus entirely the exploitative definition which prevails: entropy, both in the physical and informational senses increases.

This takes us to the issue of simplicity and complexity. In which of these directions is the system moving?

Entropy is sometimes defined as a descent into disorder. However, the order which truly resists decay is one characterised by the constructive *variety* upon which future development can occur. In some of the literature, entropy is therefore defined not as disorder but as equilibrium; (Swanson, Bailey and Miller, 1997, pp. 45–65) this makes sense, if we consider equilibrium here to signify 'order-as-uniformity', a condition which has lost its plurality and differentiatedness, and hence its developmental potential. This is precisely how contemporary capitalism reveals itself as a dead-end, as the enemy of future human development. So in this respect, the entropy of the system is expressed in its becoming more simple. With respect to living systems, 75% of biodiversity has already been lost.[1] Species show a steady decline (Baillie, Hilton-Tatlor and Stuart, 2004).

The social equivalent of biodiversity is cultural variety, and of course for the development of humans themselves (as distinct from the natural ecosystem upon which they depend), the cultural, as opposed to biological, dimension is primary. Here, as Goonaltilake points out, the process of 'hegemonic cultural blanketing' restricts the scope for future development (Goonatilake, 1982). And traditional cultures are of course not merely an asset of humanity, but an asset with respect to the preservation of the natural environment. Contrast the diversity of tradition with the highly simplistic dogmas (modernisation, market fundamentalism, export promotion, 'tame' forms of institutional theory) which have embodied the accumulation imperative at different phases of the international political economy.

Establishment versions of systems thinking come up with weird results when explaining the *trend* in relation to complexity. Thus, Kenneth D. Bailey proposes that, in the US context, "maximum entropy would constitute pure equality" (Bailey 1996). On this basis, we might suppose that all the US has to do to resist entropy is to ensure it doesn't become too egalitarian … which fortunately is not too much of a problem! But of course we can demolish this argument by saying that the true sign of entropy is the stamping-down on capacity and variety, a result which is obviously accentuated by the deprivation associated with inequality.

But if the response-vocabulary is becoming too simplified, the complementary opposite of problem is that *challenges* are becoming more complex. Species in the ecosystem are interdependent so a problem in one area can have unexpected results in another. For example, bees are

---

[1] *Guardian*, Feb 10 2007

crucial in pollination, upon which the whole plant world relies; however the bee population is increasingly dominated by commercially-farmed bees which employ unnaturally-proportioned combs and many chemicals, and the beginning of 2007 saw the emergence of a phenomenon known as Colony Collapse Disorder (CCD). Many different possible causes are debated, but what seems most likely is that the bees are stressed by intensive methods, and this in turn renders them vulnerable to attacks (whether of fungus, parasites etc.) to which they would otherwise be resistant.[2] Both in its causes and in its effect, CCD cannot be reduced to single explanations; and this is in turn part of a wider complex environmental crisis.

In the ecological sense, it is therefore easy to see how complex challenges may swamp capitalism's increasingly simplifying response-faculty. But our argument is that complex *socio-political* challenges can do the same.

An extremely interesting relationship between simplicity and complexity now appears. When complexity is excessive, a simple *dismissive* response may follow. In Michel Baranger's explanation, complexity becomes chaos in certain regions of the system, (Baranger n.d.) ones where perhaps the chaos has become fractalised; if a residual order still exists within such regions, it cannot *usefully* be said to exist, since it cannot be comprehended. Henri Atlan profoundly defined complexity as the "property to react to noise in two opposed ways without ceasing to function": (Taylor, 2001, p. 137) disorder is at the same time plurality, the very thing from which development proceeds, which could be viewed either as threat, or embraced as opportunity. What seems to be mere noise can actually be emergent order, and can thus be converted into information. Alvaro Malaina speaks of the development, today, of a 'restricted' complexity.[3] It is partly restricted by the categories we use to comprehend it, but the restriction can also be imposed in an instrumental way by a hegemonic order, to contain development within parameters acceptable to it.

---

[2] Organically-farmed bees kept in normal sized combs appeared to escape the danger: c.f. Peter Dearman, "Please Lord, not the bees – Everything you didn't want to know about Colony Collapse Disorder", GNN, Wed, May 2 2007 on http://www.gnn.tv/articles/3063/Please_Lord_not_the_bees

[3] Malaina, Alvaro, *Edgar Morin et Jesus Ibañez : la sociologie et les théories de la complexité*, duplicated

Since capitalism has subsumed the general question of adaptation into the narrow one of its *own* adaptation, and thereby ruins the capacity and plurality required to respond to complexity challenges, the normative issue arises of returning to a situation of adaptability at the level of the human social system. The 'positive' (as distinct from normative) dimension is that, particularly in order to appreciate the political context for change, we must understand how the system functions while it is still in place. Since capitalism's vocabulary for comprehending the real world is restricted, when standard methods fail it will write off whole regions of the system as being beyond comprehension: in Baranger's term, 'bagging the mess'.

As we will see, the repressive shift of the turn of the millennium was more specifically a backlash occasioned by a collapse of confidence in an earlier attempt to work *with* rather than against complexity.

The Critique of Modernism

We will consider in more detail the experiment with complexity in the next chapter, but it will be important to set the scene here. The simple mode of governance is the top-down one, and surveying the history of capitalism as a whole, it seems the main line of development has been toward imposing simple definitions upon real-world complexity and siphoning the power to determine order from the top. But the issues addressed by Gramsci and Foucault suggest that there was always a diffuse power running alongside the more obvious top-down kind. Power can operate through networks, and arguably is then at its most effective.

The mode of production has both static and dynamic features: while the basic contradictions remain (the inherent difficulty of expanded reproduction, the manufacture of poverty etc.) and continue to circumscribe capitalism, the system evolves, sometimes radically, in its manner of responding to these. There is however a hybrid position between the two extremes which may be of key importance: path-dependency. The system acquires certain modes of operation which are not necessarily the 'best' in the abstract, but become embedded and reproduce themselves. Some of these may be impossible to slough off: for example, the really-existing IPE is profoundly ethnocentric in terms of dominance by the white world, and since the latter holds the economic and military power, it is difficult to select an alternative strategy (such as the displacement of the fulcrum of development to the South) even *if the latter were better for capitalism* in the abstract. I will examine this particular example in detail in Chapter 6. But we could have been forgiven for thinking that modernism was similarly embedded: the old Soviet orthodoxy was fooled into thinking that capitalism had initiated an inexorable trend towards top-down organisation (in the shape of state capitalism or the strategic decision-making of oligopolistic corporations), which it could not however bring to fruition; thus, for the Soviets, socialist development inherits the mission of carrying on where capitalism had failed. But this, whether in its capitalist or socialist form, was a dead-end. In the 1980s, capitalism proved itself capable of kicking aside this particular path-dependency, and beginning to explore emergent order. At this point, socialism, which should really be about spontaneous emergence, was (at least in its Soviet form) suddenly revealed to be more top-down and sclerotic than capitalism, making the latter appear dynamic by contrast. This was enough to put paid to the Soviet system. It will not however be enough to save capitalism. As we will show, the contradiction of a contained emergence, uniquely confined to exploitative forms, *itself* soon began to unravel.

Burkett and Bellamy Foster made a great contribution in producing a well-researched vindication of a thermodynamic interpretation of Marx, (Burkett and Ballamy, 2006) and if we read Marx thermodynamically, this opens up fascinating new doors to a different conceptual world. The capitalists are trying to expand the quantity of *work*, and work is a thermodynamic process which capitalism is *harnessing*. So far so good. The problem, however, is that the Burkett and Bellamy Foster analysis produces a somewhat mechanistic version of this process. The key weakness is a failure to realise that thermodynamics is not the whole of systems theory: we also have to understand the principle of emergence and the crucial role of information. Capitalism controls information, and its disempowerment of the workforce at the level of knowledge is an absolutely fundamental condition for controlling 'work'. In fact, in the pre-capitalist situation 'work' was inseparable not only from individual knowledge (properties of plants, craft-skills) but from a social and *institutional* dimension (gender roles, regimes for the collective management not just of physical resources but skills). The destruction of this autonomous sphere was from the beginning fundamental to the rise of capitalism, a reality of which a narrow, purely thermodynamic reading would remain ignorant. It is true that in Marx' day and for some time thereafter, the focus was wholly on siphoning capacity away from the grassroots productive sphere and centralising it among the elite, so in the sense everything beyond the sphere of dominated information was regarded as mere *mechanical* 'work': hence, the empirical fact of augmenting profit by getting people to work longer hours. But this narrow, mechanistic vision which Burkett and Bellamy Foster tend to regard as the correct (albeit intrinsically thermodynamic) reading of Marx, although it makes superficial sense of *industrial* capitalism and even early imperialism, is insufficient to explain the system's subsequent development and adaptation. In its more recent development, while continuing to control *knowledge*, capitalism could tune into the principle of emergence, concentrating much more on an exploitation of capacity than on pure, mechanical 'work'.

As in the passage from Lenin we quoted earlier, the development of understanding is a complex, spiral-like process where any fragment or segment can "be transformed (transformed one-sidedly) into an independent, complete, straight line" where it tends to become "*anchored* by the class interests of the ruling classes" (Lenin, 1915, p. 363). This can be applied to systems theory itself. The notion of emergence is a brilliant insight, but it can be developed one-sidedly in such a way as to serve the ruling interests. The fascinating discovery is that capitalism *can enlist in its favour the valid systems critique of modernism.*

It is only possible to see through this trick if we take a dialectical view of modernism itself. There was class struggle involved in its definition. The progressive modernists like the Bauhaus school of architects had a social conscience, whereas post-World War II modernism largely fitted in with the consumerist culture underpinning the Fordist accumulation regime. The point is to hold onto the progressive social orientation, and critique modernism in a progressive way, different from the manipulated capitalist perspective. There is indeed an element in post-modernism where it can link with the systems approach and dialectics in order to emphasise the superiority of emergence (Heylighen, Cilliers and Gershenson, 2006). Seemingly chaotic forms of emergent self-organisation by working people are more rich, robust, creative and developmental than anything which planners could design. It is a very good thing that social systems possess a faculty for a self-organisation, which is precisely what socialism could be like. In this sense, the break with modernism was part of a progressive development of knowledge, but one which developed one-sidedly and became anchored in the dominant class interests. For them, the *immediate* instrumental agenda in getting rid of modernism was to crush the socially-progressive aspect and to remove the possibility for the state to be fought over by progressive forces to push redistribution; the more strategic aspect was to create a post-modern form of capitalism, every bit as exploitative and actually more efficiently so than the modernist form, in the sense that exploitative systems now partially design themselves without capitalism having to waste the effort in doing so.

This takes us our next major conceptual challenge, the structure-agency issue. This is fundamental to an understanding of development, and also brings us back to the tricky subject of evolution.

Issues of Structuralism and Evolution

Our enquiry could be wrecked by being lured onto either of two rocks: on the one hand structural determinism which completely neglects agency, on the other conspiracy theories. We must try to avoid both.

Structuralism, for example structural anthropology, (Levi-Strauss, 1958) characteristically describes an emergent order at a whole-systems level which is not sought by, or even understood by, individual actors. The weakness is a strong tendency towards determinism and neglect of agency, as we see particularly in the gender dimension: structural anthropology, as in the work of Lévi-Strauss, had a lot to say about oppressive gender relations, and in this sense it looks like it should be progressive. But in reality (for example, in the discussion of exogamy), the strong tendency was to view women only as passive victims of alienation, and not at all in terms of any autonomous role (Lerner, 1987). In a theoretical sense, this representation of emergence is indeed not entirely demarcated from that of economic liberalism which similarly posits an emergent higher-level order over which we have no control. Nevertheless, structuralism's merit, as distinct from liberalism, is to recognise that the emergent order may well be alienating; even though, as Cavanaugh points out, this is a somewhat pessimistic version of alienation which offers few possibilities of escape, unlike the way alienation is treated by Marx (Cavanaugh, 1976, p. 158).

Classic liberal economic theory is reductionist and mechanistic (Newtonian, in a way) in that the overall order, although emergent in the sense of not being *sought* by individual choices, is nevertheless predictable from them. Its key role in 'anchoring' the debate within ruling

class interests lies simply in its characteristic statement that any intervention to change the result generated by laissez-faire would necessarily make things worse. With one stroke, social projects are written off.

But the modernist form of capitalist mainstream economics which
developed during the 20th century had begun to admit more and more
areas where public policy should intervene to correct market failures
and externalities. This discourse is itself deceptive, in the sense of con-
cealing the fact that the bad features of capitalism are actually *intrinsic*
products (rather than failures) of the market, and should really be
addressed as 'internalities'. Nevertheless, this trend created the possibility for social and ecological issues to be regulated – albeit in a top-
down and disempowering way – through the state, as in the work of
Pigou. It is at this point that the neo-liberal counter-attack intervened,
attempting to overthrow this whole lineage of capitalist economics.
In particular, Friedrich von Hayek, the godfather of neo-liberalism,
invented a highly fatalistic structuralist reading of the liberal argument, which effectively employs the notion of spontaneous order to
sanctify the status quo, (Hayek, 1964) and rule out Pigou-style intervention. This is the most corrupt form of structuralism in the sense
that, although like structural anthropology it undervalues agency,
unlike the latter it doesn't at all admit the alienating nature of the established order.

The non-interventionist argument could in theory develop in a lib-
ertarian direction, but in the real world, from Pinochet to George Bush,
neo-liberalism has accommodated itself very well with the most
extreme authoritarianism, one accompanied indeed by a strong cru-
sading tinge: deluded opponents of the one true order (for example
anti-globalisers) must forcibly be converted, or if they persist, crushed.
The paradox is that neo-liberalism is itself one of the strongest demonstrations of the role of agency in its extremists form, because it really
was a conspiracy: neo-liberals in the 1970s had a very deliberate agenda
of capturing outposts in the media in order to prepare opinion for
attacking Keynesianism and organised labour. In the following argument we will examine many instances of conspiracy. Nevertheless, in
our own endeavours to construct a progressive line of argument, we
must be careful, while avoiding structural determinism, to avoid also
sinking into the opposite error and becoming a prey to the conspiracy perspective. It is crucial to recognise that the latter is, just as much
as structural determinism, anchored in the interests of the ruling
classes (we only have to think of the confusion created by eclectic

trends ranging from the US extreme right to Da Vinci code-style fantasies to off-the-wall theories about the World Trade Centre). In opposition to the conspiracy perspective, we must be careful to retain a consciousness that it is in some sense the mode of production *itself* which is adapting, not necessarily according to the conscious plan of certain individuals. But then, we have to understand how.

The kind of determinism we've critiqued so far is a static form, for example in structural anthropology the weight of tradition appears so strong as to make alienation inescapable. But systems are not static: they evolve. As Gould points out, the exciting thing about evolution is that it is not determinist. However, the notion of evolution, though a key part of the development of knowledge, can as such be developed one-sidedly to become anchored in the dominant interests by itself assuming a deterministic form and undervaluing agency. Then, any status quo can be justified simply on the grounds that it *has* evolved. This can happen in two ways: in the biological reading, we are fatalistically imprisoned by our genetic makeup, as in sociobiology, a school of thought with strong associations with racism and fascism. (Cracker, 1983) In an extended reading, evolved social and economic institutions are sacrosanct.

I will develop more fully the critique of evolution in Chapter 7, but the point to note here is that the basis for such distortions is usually reductionism. In a complex system, "Each level is both characterized and governed by emergent laws that do not appear at the lower levels of organization."(Mazzocchi, 2008) The term hierarchy is often employed as a representation of this 'multi-leveledness'; but of course when we consider human socio-political systems, the notion of hierarchy becomes less neutral: *the higher levels can control the lower ones* because the understanding of order may be deliberately siphoned away from the lower-level actors. Either a general politico-cultural hegemony of the type described by Gramsci could result, or something more specific like the operation of global value chains, which we will consider in detail in the next chapter.

Having made this point, we must recognise an aspect of development where the higher-level emergent order is not targeted by the individual actors. Thus, for example, in the Marxian explanation of the falling rate of profit, competition forces capitalists to mechanise production even though the *general* result is to diminish the proportion of labour within the total capital outlay. This could be extended into an evolutionist approach to the *institutional* dimension of capitalist development, as in the work of Hodgson: (Hodgson and Knudsen, 2006) spontaneous order and self-organisation really do prevail at certain levels of the system. This is an important point, because the development of capitalism into its current globalised form must be explicable on an assumption that the basic units, i.e. firms, acquire new characteristics such as flexibility, readiness to interact through subcontracting and clustering etc.; the *large-scale* development at the level of the regime of accumulation which began around 1980, with its global value chains and new management systems etc., could not have occurred without this more basic adaptation.

A favourite theme of the old Soviet discourse was to accuse capitalism of being 'anarchic'. There is a valid point insofar as the real cost of boom-bust business cycles (intrinsic to the mode of production) is experienced in the form of human cost by the working population. But if we shift the level of analysis from the business cycle to the more significant *long* cycle or regime of accumulation whereby capitalism is structured over significant periods (perhaps 30 years), the issue of 'anarchy' now appears very different: chaos is highly beneficial to capitalism, in the sense that its phase transitions between long cycles can only occur through a process of creative destruction, in the terminology introduced by Schumpeter. It remains of course true that the destruction (of livelihoods etc.) is experienced by workers, the creativity by capitalists, and under an alternative social system this could be avoided. But disordered phase transitions will be a part of *any* social development, and are nothing to be afraid of, quite the contrary. The weakness of the Soviet critique was to forget – in contrasting a smooth and predictable socialism to chaotic capitalism – that a smooth and predictable society is neither workable, nor indeed attractive! An evolutionary view of capitalism might joyfully assume the epithet which was supposed to be an insult, and see the chaotic state as a necessary precursor of order. The order which is the complementary opposite of anarchy or chaos is in this definition not necessarily top-down order-as-control, but on the contrary *emergent* structure. If we take this issue seriously, we would have to define the whole socialism-capitalism antithesis differently. The problem with capitalism is not per se that it is lumpy and unpredictable, but that its developmental basis is extremely narrow, it is uniquely concerned with preserving exploitation, and that it has painted humanity (and itself) into a corner where we are imprisoned by feedback loops of repression and environmental degradation. Socialism will be able to develop creativity in a manner unrestricted by these narrow constraints ... but, for this very reason, it will be even more lumpy and unpredictable! Socialism's argument should never have been to impose *rule* on society.

If we could just liberate evolutionism from its instrumental role in sanctifying the status quo, we could push it in a direction which addresses the development of human society beyond capitalism. In this enterprise, there are many pitfalls. For example, in Jeff Vail's theory, (Vail, 2004) the alienation is caused by non-biological forms of evolution (i.e. culture, economics) having come to conflict with the biological ones, the latter model being derived from the reductionist single-gene evolutionism of Richard Dawkins. Nevertheless, the interesting deduction from Vail's premise is that hierarchy is unnatural. The notion that networks are a natural mode of interaction both of matter in general, and more specifically of society (because we evolved in this way and capitalism has been around for only a brief half-millennium), is a notion to which we will return. The key point for our current argument is that the ruling order has undergone an unexpected adaptation (or evolution): it has itself, partially, *learned to assume a networked form.* This adaptation will form one of the fundamental themes of the analysis developed throughout this book. Actually, this fact in no way undermines the argument that networks are a better mode of organisation, because capitalism's use of networks takes a highly stultified and limited form, serving only to prolong the existence of a mode of organisation which remains essentially hierarchical.

The Role of Agency

As soon as we begin moving beyond the mechanical rational-actor model, ethics are necessarily present, (Heylighen, et al., 2006) simply because there are choices to be made. The central issue therefore remains the social projects which reflect upon, and seek to change, society as a whole.

The systems approach does not detract from the role of agency, it simply suggests ways of liberating ourselves from rigidly counterposing structure and agency. For example, the contribution of cybernetics is to recognise that adaptation requires some 'information' about the acceptable states which the system *could* develop into. In this way we are free to choose, but on the basis of respect for existing laws.

This is fully in conformity with the indigenous approach to respect for nature ... and in conformity with Marxism. For Engels, the goal is "existence in harmony with the laws of nature", the degree of control exercised over nature being strictly "founded on knowledge of natural necessity" (Engels, 1969, pp. 137–138).

The argument which really challenges any mechanical counterposing of structure and agency is the realisation, firstly that information is the *objective* mode of organisation of biological systems; secondly that we must then go further because there is something special about human systems: in Roederer's phrase, *information about the future* (Roederer, 2003, p. 3). For example, the recently-formed Transition Towns movement, which can be seen as a progressive type of network in the sense addressed above, envisions a low-input, ecologically sound future and then backcasts from this to the present (Lawrence, 2007). Although at a certain level information about the future could be identified with *prescience* – and this is not a negligible issue, as is clear from the debt we owe to the farsightedness of early imperialism theorists like Hobson and Luxemburg – in the last analysis prescience is a rather poor and partial characterisation: in the fullest sense, information about the future is inseparable from normative intervention. The only way to obtain feed-forward from the future is actively to intervene in *creating* it.

In this context, Ahearn has highlighted an issue central to our understanding of the relationship between evolution and agency: the distinction between actor and agent. Whereas the actor's mode of operation is purely rule-governed or rule-oriented, the agent has the attribute of power in the sense of action to (re)constitute the world (Ahearn, 2001). We can further dissect this notion of power. Power is a thermodynamic category, and a concept of power as 'capacity to produce effects' becomes exciting when it highlights the interlocking between social and thermodynamic aspects (Gale, 1998). In the real conditions of the present and future, the recognition of our ability to re-shape the world is not purely voluntarist, because it must be rooted in ecology. Here, the systems approach has the advantage: this comes naturally, due to its ancestry in thermodynamics.

The hegemonic system imposes its own information about the future: a fatalistic globalisation where, in order to survive, you must seek niches within which to be exploited. But this vision is questioned and critiqued from below, on the basis of a vision which recognises the thermodynamic unsustainability of this model. Whereas capitalism's version of the future is limited to an information-set about possible future states of a system consistent with the rules of capital accumulation and exploitation, a critical vision is not so constrained.

Of course, if the agent were an isolated individual, our perspective would remain vulnerable to a neo-liberal version of emergence. But what we are talking about is social *movements*. It is important also to critique the notion of the movement as a 'blind-watchmaker' product of individual agents who don't target the higher order. As Guha importantly points out, insurgent movements do have a vision of the future they are aiming to attain (Guha, 1983). They obviously cannot predict completely the future arising from their actions (otherwise we would be into a Newtonian form of reductionism and neglect the lessons of complexity), but they can envisage it. The exciting thing about emergence is precisely that, consistent with an overall orientation of a future which unleashes human capacity, there is much open-endedness about the *forms* which this capacity might take. This is precisely the attractive part of socialism. Marx was on the whole more interested to observe how the working class was actually organising, as in the Paris Commune, (Marx, 1969 d, p. 178) than in making utopian predictions.

This does not mean the future will be formless. You could not have predicted all details of capitalism's subsequent development as an adaptive system, either from Marx' theories or Lenin's analysis of imperialism, but you could be sure that this would have to be compatible with the expanded reproduction of capital. Similarly, when we seek information about the future social system, there will be order, but we simply have to conceive of order differently from predictability. Drawing on dialectics, our information about the future might apply the principle of the negation of the negation (communitarian forms of social organisation negated by capitalism are 'carried forward' in this negation because capitalism defines its own identity negatively with respect to them, and will probably be restored in a changed form once capitalism is itself negated). Approaching a similar argument from the perspective of systems theory, we can recognise that chaos is only a limited category of complexity: in many areas or phases of complex systems there is typically a constrained set of types of interaction, for example, in the system constituted by language, meanings may be infinite but are also bounded (Ahearn, 2001, p. 112).

Phase Transitions and Acquired Momentum in
Capitalist Development

While holding to such a normative vision of a future society, we also
need a good understanding of what the reality is today: both what is
wrong with the present setup and needs to be struggled against, and
also the openings within which a progressive change can be constructed. This is the 'positive' (as distinct from normative) dimension
of our research. Its task includes an understanding of those characteristics the system has acquired 'on its way', which were not immanent,
except perhaps as possibilities, in its original definition. As we have just
seen, the 'lumpiness' of long cycles reveals that capitalism, while it
cannot overcome its basic contradictions (for example pauperisation),
can evolve temporary structures for managing these. At this point it
will be useful to address the issues raised by the school known as regulation theory.

Much of regulation theory is so much anchored in the 'positive' side
that it is hard to escape the feeling that it is not just analysing capitalism
as it is, but somehow telling capitalism how to do its job better;[4] however, there is an aspect which is closer to the contestatory social movements, particularly in the work of Lipietz (1987). Potentially, the
strength of the regulation approach is that it does take on board the
whole-system dimension, at least within the confines of the socio-
economic sphere. An accumulation regime (AR), the key category in
the regulationist approach to the 'lumpy' regularisation of capitalism,
cannot be fully explicable on the basis of agency. It must to some extent
just 'happen', the different elements in the system coalescing around a
set pattern of relations which acquires a definite stability. For example,
in the response to the inter-war crisis, trades unions were co-opted into
tripartite bargaining with management and the state, in the context of
an economic model which used Keynesian feedback loops (investment
→ employment → consumption, leading to a new cycle of investment etc.) to sponge up unemployment and win the allegiance of the
working class through consumerism. This was closely associated with
modernism, and created certain roles, norms and expectations. The
Keynesian 'multiplier' caused the illusion that value was creating itself

---

[4] See for example the journal *Issues in Regulation Theory*, see http://web.upmf
-grenoble.fr/regulation/Issue_Regulation_theory/index.html

out of itself, in violation of the Second Law of thermodynamics. Actually, in this case agency looks deceptively strong because of the role of leaders like Franklin D. Roosevelt and Keynes himself in finding a way out of the crisis, but what is precisely interesting was the unacknowledged, parallel universe underpinning modernism, to which the dominant discourse shut its eyes: the whole world of super-exploited and informally-exploited women and peoples of colour. The thing which is left unsaid, but which no-one questions, is as important as the surface discourse. These different elements hung together coherently for a time, but later the ensemble was discarded when neo-liberalism took over.[5] As we will see in the next chapter, the neo-liberal AR both had to be even more emergent than modernism, because of its greater complexity; and actually *used* complexity in a way which would be inaccessible to a top-down and controlled system of the modernist type.

Complexity analysis (where the emergent properties of an ensemble cannot be reduced to its constituent parts) is thus relevant even within a purely socio-economic framework. But of course we will only get a complete picture if we encompass also the ecological context. After all, regulation is a property of physical systems ... perhaps its key property, if one thinks of the importance of temperature in the earth-system model. An accumulation regime must therefore be sustainable not merely in a purely institutional sense (its ability to orchestrate production and social relations according to a set of rules which prevail over a particular 'lump' of history), but must establish some characteristic set of relations with its environment. Either it would be a low-energy mode (which is impossible under capitalism, as we will see in a moment), or it must establish a characteristic mode of *dissipation and depletion*, which probably requires the availability of some major resource or sink. This has very much been the case with past accumulation regimes.

Let's now connect the notion of phase transitions to that of imperialism. The reason for affirming the continued validity of imperialism as an idea is that the fundamental features – militarism, repression, parasitic finance capital – have never been cancelled out in any subsequent phase; therefore the new forms of stabilisation (in 1945, 1980) should be regarded as phases *of* imperialism, rather than as something new or different. Nevertheless, we are not in a teleological situation where the

---

[5] for a discussion of why this change occurred, see Biel (2000) op. cit.

subsequent forms were immanent from the origins. Rather, the system has, with respect to its basic contradictions (conflict within the North at an international-systems and social level, the contradiction with the colonial world, poverty and social decay etc.), developed a set of regulation practices. These have become embedded, or we could say institutionalised, using this term in the sense employed in institutional theory where it encompasses informal rules or structures.

In this context, the notion of feedback is important in avoiding single-cause reductionism and sterile 'debates' between one-sided positions. Let us consider this proposition by taking the case of the Cold War. Was militarism an economic response to maintaining the armaments industry (which had extricated America from crisis via 'military Keynesianism'), or alternatively was its fundamental purpose to create a new *political* world order conducive to US interests (allowing that these were fundamentally economic, such as the extraction of raw materials from Asia, but that a political grand design was essential to achieving them)?(Leffler, 1994) Although my tendency is to prefer political explanations to economistic ones, *as initiators* of the loop, this is fully compatible with recognising that economic accumulation became coupled to militarism and that the military-industrial complex has assumed an autonomous role.

Now, this general approach acquired certain specific forms which have left a lasting imprint upon the IPE. To further concretise this, we can consider how the Cold War expressed itself in the world food system: the so-called Green Revolution. The latter was one expression of a general strategy to use the East-West conflict as an excuse by imperialism to enslave the South, in this case by conning or browbeating Southern farmers into using hybrid crops; since these crops do not reproduce true to type from seed, the imperialists had a monopoly of supply. I would argue that the principal motivation was political, but this in no way denies a powerful interlocking with the economic interests which, for example, supplied the artificial fertilisers and machinery which the hybridised crops were deliberately designed to demand (Delpeuch, 1985). The *natural* cycle of agriculture was broken, to be replaced it by something extraneous. Most obviously, we can say that this 'something' was the circuit of capital accumulation, uniquely concerned with expanded reproduction. But we are now in a position to add an extra layer: a feedback loop between economic and political interests. What is interesting is the path-dependency which this creates. Although the Cold War and Green Revolution are no longer present in their original form, *the loops which they initiated are still active*: with the creation of the WTO combined with the introduction of GM, the ruling order has replaced hybridisation with new tools of control such as intellectual property rules and 'terminator genes'. Henry Kissinger's statement that food in US hands is a more powerful weapon than the H-bomb (Linear, 1985) is still apposite: in the last analysis, politics is probably primary. But at the same time, the economic interests spawned by this path-dependent line of development (seed corporations, global companies which now control the water industry in many countries) have an extremely strong autonomous role in promoting it. If we consider more generally the significance of the 'war on terror' as successor to the Cold War,[6] then the interplay with economic interests has even increased, perhaps qualitatively, with the unprecedented privatisation of 'security'.

In this way, the systems notion of feedback can be very helpful in balancing an acknowledgement of the fundamental importance of the economic base, with an avoidance of economism and reductionism.

The self-organising property of matter, when we apply this to society, necessarily works through information. Knowledge, which is a higher level of information because more reflective, is central to this, as we will see in the next chapter in our case study of how the mainstream discourse has enlisted industrial clustering and embedding. Information about the future is a more normative and forward-looking variant of knowledge, and guides agency. In order to be effective, it shouldn't be purely voluntaristic, but should take account of real possibilities, for example latent but unexplored developmental tendencies. The class/social struggle runs through everything: the ruling order tries to develop latent systemic tendencies in an exploitative way, whereas oppressed groups unfold agency in the form of struggle, which can in turn encompass both resistance, and, normatively, cultivating alternative futures.

In the real world, ruling-order structural development could not occur at all in the absence of grassroots struggle, with which it interacts as part of its process of regulation, seeking to repress, outflank or co-opt it. On the other hand, it is an essential principle of Marxism that

---

[6] The successor was supposed to be the New World Order, but it lacked a manufactured enemy as an excuse to suppress the masses, which the 'war on terror' then supplied.

struggle can act to hold depletion *at bay*. Community struggle (as the environmental justice perspective shows) curtails specific forms of depletion; or, national-level struggle could push up commodity prices. If we imagined a system without struggle, capital might deplete the whole of society and nature in a generation. Of course, such a situation of 'non-struggle' is a non-possibility, a purely imaginary condition serving to make a logical point: the propensity to struggle against oppression is an inherent human trait. It still needs to find direction, which is the purpose of political movements; what Marx polemicised against was mostly so-called leaders of such movements who failed to *recognise* struggle.

The Adaptive Problem Faced by Imperialism

In thinking of adaptation by imperialism, we have a useful term to play around with: ultra-imperialism. It could mean several things, since there are a number of contradictions involved. However, in the early imperialism debate, one issue predominated: acute conflict amongst imperialist powers. This was so important at the time because it made the other contradictions hard to solve: if capitalist powers wasted energy fighting each other, it was harder for them to crush social or national movements. Now, the system had adapted to this reality: initially, faced with the 'shrinking world' addressed by Mackinder, the powers made the best of this by turning competition into an argument to enlist their own working class behind the endeavour of grabbing for *their* nation the scarce resources which remained. The old imperialists loved quoting a passage by Goethe: you must climb or sink, rule and gain or serve and lose, suffer or triumph, *be anvil or hammer*.[7] This perfectly expresses a zero-sum situation where one party's gain is exactly the other's loss ($+1 -1 = 0$).

But the gain in social cohesion realised in this way scarcely compensated for the loss of a much greater *potential* benefit, which could be accessed if the competitive energy were conserved.

The notion of a development towards 'ultra-imperialism' was proposed by Karl Kautsky, and vigorously refuted by Lenin. Now, while it was precisely the issue of inter-imperialist strife that Kautsy's *explicit*

---

[7] Du mußt steigen oder sinken, Du mußt herrschen und gewinnen, oder dienen und verlieren, leiden oder triumphieren, Amboß oder Hammer sein. Goethe, Cophtische Lieder no. 2

argument addressed, (Kautsky, 1914) in fact Lenin's critique seems intuitively to have focussed on some deeper issue which he sensed as underlying the surface debate: whether capitalism could strategically move into a new phase where it became somehow more harmonious and stable. Lenin was absolutely correct in refuting this assumption because, whereas capitalism could stabilise itself temporarily in the form of regimes of accumulation, these really in a sense *embody* the contradictions, rather than solving them. Imperialism has never stopped manufacturing poverty and war, and the underlying issue would therefore never be resolved either by success, or indeed by failure, to regulate inter-imperialist contention. This shows the strategic far-sightedness of Lenin. Nevertheless, Kautsky was right to signal the importance of the inter-imperialist issue, because it is hard to see in practice how the system would have survived without addressing it: it is impossible to envisage the great capitalist structural creations of 1945 and 1980 under conditions of fragmented national economies.

In the early imperialism debate, this question was posed in an extremely far-sighted way by J.A. Hobson, who coined the notion of the Federation of Western States, (Hobson, 1902) which reads like a blueprint for everything which happened after World War II: NATO, OECD, G7 etc. He believed that such an equilibrium *might* be envisaged, but under what conditions?

Game theory – "a theory of interdependent choice"(Zagare, 1984) – is a useful tool here, because it critically examines the notion of equilibrium. A key contribution of game theory is the so-called prisoners' dilemma (PD) model. The original image concerns two prisoners who are being interrogated separately: their objective interest would lie in neither confessing, but it is impossible, rationally, for them to arrive at this strategy because each will assume that if s/he confesses and the other doesn't then her/his situation will be overwhelmingly bad; therefore, both are likely to confess. I will now translate this into an 'imperialism game'. If all imperialist powers are fighting each other, they will be stuck at an equilibrium in the bottom right-hand corner of the 'matrix' (the framework used by game theory in visualising choices). The problem is that if any of them unilaterally drops its guard by shifting to a co-operative and non-conflictual stance, it will risk annihilation by its rival (who might grab its colonies, territory etc.). Therefore, it appears almost impossible that they will move to the ideal equilibrium, in the opposite corner. But if they did achieve this, the new equilibrium would itself probably become stable because no-one would have an interest in changing it.

A

	Co-op	Hostile
Co-op	10, 10	5, -10
Hostile	-10, 5	-2,-2

B (row label)

Figure 1: Inter-imperialist co-operation as a prisoners' dilemma model.

What game theory doesn't usually do, but we can now attempt, is to consider this problem thermodynamically. We can approach this in two complementary ways. Firstly, we can say that any displacement requires effort, so in this sense an input of energy is required to *shift* to the new equilibrium; secondly, we can ask what fuels the massively *positive sum* in the top-left corner, the nirvana of co-operative imperialism. This is a very interesting way of posing the issue, because it shows the unexpected insights which arise once we begin to develop a thermodynamic theory of imperialism not just in the more obvious sense that there is an attempt to grab resources, but from an institutional perspective. It similarly critiques the PD model in an important way, because a key assumption is that the problem is the *initial* shift away from the 'bad' (lower-right) equilibrium, and that if the 'good' equilibrium is attained, it will become stable; all the thermodynamic tools we have developed up to this point would make us suspicious of this assumption: the new equilibrium may instead require *continuous* fuelling.

Now, if we consider the PD problem outside the context of imperialism, there is indeed a solution to this question: if conflict is reduced, capacity can increase. For example, Ponna and Wignaraja have importantly shown how, in a conflictual region like South Asia, a massive flowering of human capacity could result from co-operation (Wignaraja and Hussain, 1989). An apparently intractable zero-sum conflicts over scarce resources like water, for example, could give way to innovative grassroots-based stewardship regimes, with a huge net gain in human capacity; and not only is there no ecological cost, there is actually an ecological gain too, in the form of improved conservation. This scenario is entirely realistic, and co-operation is established with no exported cost. But it is a completely different question whether it is realistic *under capitalism*.

We are, after all, talking about a movement from disorder in the direction of greater order, so the question always arises in the context of a dissipative system, where is the disorder exported to? This question is already anticipated in Rousseau's excellent analysis of IR, (Rousseau, 1964) where, if we translate it into systems concepts, conflict is reduced *within* individual societies while reciprocally increasing at the level of the international system. The progression to greater order is merely illusory if it is never eliminated but merely shifted. Now, if we take this one step further and the disorder is reduced at the level of the great-power subsystem, where does it go then?

The answer has got to be the physical environment. What happened was that the new situation of co-operative inter-imperialist relations created conditions for a much more intensive exploitation. Conflict under conditions of scarce resources, though the old imperialists partly believed it, had not been premised on a genuine acceptance of environmental constraints, but merely on the fact that the system could not work out *how* to deplete the environment more intensively while energy was being wasted on competition. The fact is that a massive increase in depletion occurred exactly in 1945 when the co-operative inter-imperialist regime was established; and – this is the important point – *continued thereafter*, in a path-dependent way because maintained by the feedback loops running between politics and capital accumulation. We can for example represent the ecological cost in terms of energy consumption.

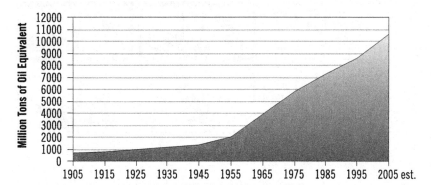

Figure 2: World energy consumption, 1905–2005.

Source: Biel R. "The interplay between social and environmental degradation in the development of the international political economy" *Journal of World-Systems Research*, xii, 1 July 2006, p. 127; source of data: *BP Statistical Review of World Energy 2004*; Energy Information Administration, *International Energy Outlook 2004*; Jancovici J-M, *l'Avenir climatique*, Paris (Seuil) 2002.

Of course, the entropy measured in the depletion of stocks could also be represented in the ejection of disorder, i.e. pollution and greenhouse gas emission.

The postwar system introduced a further element of path-dependency in the shape of high mass consumption. When the next regime-shift occurred around 1980, although it reversed many things like modernism and Keynesianism, it not only continued with consumerism, but (through globalisation, both of commodities and of consumer culture) took it to levels unimagined even by the postwar modernisers.

Our argument that it was environmental depletion which underpinned the new regime of co-operative imperialism can be confirmed from a slightly different direction by considering free trade. Here too, highly positive payoffs are supposed to result from a co-operative equilibrium, and in the case of trade theory, these are supposed to be self-generated by the very act of abandoning nationalism and protectionism. In David Ricardo's model, the political effect is to "bind together by one common tie of interest and intercourse, the universal society of nations throughout the civilised world [i.e. the inter-great power subsystem]" (Ricardo, 1951). The source of the payoffs is the efficiency gains arising once countries give up trying to maintain diverse socio-economic systems, and instead specialise in what they 'do best' (or more strictly, in the activities for which they have the greatest comparative advantage).

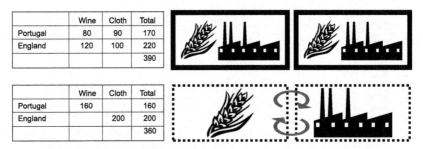

	Wine	Cloth	Total
Portugal	80	90	170
England	120	100	220
			390

	Wine	Cloth	Total
Portugal	160		160
England		200	200
			360

Figure 3: Ricardo's theory of free trade.

At the top, we have two self-sufficient closed economies, at the bottom a situation where free trade has led to specialisation. The figures refer to the number of hours used in manufacturing the different commodities, therefore the lower the number, the more efficient. Even though Portugal is more efficient in both commodities, it still has an interest in specialising in that for which its comparative advantage is higher.

Effectively, the positive-sum payoffs in the top-left corner of the PD matrix (Figure 2) are equivalent to the saving of 30 hours which, in the Ricardo model, reward countries for abandoning the protection of complete economies. Attempts have even been made to quantify this 'dividend'. Thus, in 1993 the World Bank produced an actual figure of $200–275 billion to quantify the alleged gains from free trade, and thus overcome resistance to the ongoing GATT negotiations which led to the formation of the WTO (Biel, 2000, p. 263). Among other things, this figure served to gain acceptance for the notion that the system 'could' relieve poverty 'if only' certain anomalies could be removed (for example, 'corruption').

There are many interesting lessons we could draw from a critical analysis of this model. Amin develops it to show how – even if we accept its basic logic – the benefits of specialisation will accrue to the countries who start from the strongest position, i.e. the North (Amin, 1970). But the main issue we want to emphasise here is the environmental cost: it is obviously things like transport and the environmental cost of the consumer economy which really bear the hidden cost of the supposed gains from efficiency. Of course, in Ricardo's day, wind power was employed for transport, but it is difficult to envisage the clock being turned back to this, with the frantic pace of globalisation. Escalating environmental costs have all the hallmarks of a path-dependency which looks unlikely to change.

Nevertheless, we must be prepared to examine our assumptions critically. The system is for the first time facing extremely serious ecological feedback from its depletion. This is qualitatively different from the kind of feedback resulting merely from depletion of colonial *space*, as for example discussed by Mackinder. If capitalism is truly adaptive, *might* it adapt to this reality?

Actually, there are two ways this could be imagined. One is a triumphant green capitalism which continues gloriously accumulating, the second a 'cold' imperialism which viciously rules, Mad Max-style, a post-apocalyptic shrunken landscape. I will develop the second of these images later in this enquiry, but for the moment let us consider the first scenario.

Even if successful, such a scenario would only postpone, rather than hastening, a serious green restructuring in the interests of humanity and of the ecosystem. In this sense, there is no human or ecological interest in prolonging the capitalist mode of production. But we can also argue this the opposite way round: if capitalism is going to survive for a given period anyway, the less devastation it leaves behind it, the better, and on this reasoning, a 'greening' should be supported. But this still begs the question of whether such a thing is possible.

Why Capitalism Can't Adapt to become More Green

On the surface it seems that existing resources might permit capitalism, in a crisis of the kind developing now, to rearrange its priorities in a 'green' sense. For example, debates in the mid-2000s highlighted the fact that, by coincidence, the cost of renewing Britain's nuclear missiles was exactly the same (£76 billion) as that of cutting down from today's 150m tonnes of annual carbon emissions to a target figure of 60m tonnes by 2030 (Vidal, et al., 2006). Similar calculations are often made with respect to the possibility of reducing militarism and using the 'peace dividend' to alleviate the symptoms of poverty. Such a readjustment would not mean defying the entropy condition, because it would use existing resources rather than conjuring them from nowhere.

But in reality it seems as though solutions like this never *are* adopted: instead of greening itself to consume less resources, the system militarises in order to grab the shrinking stock which remains. Why is this? The issue is complex, and to answer it in a general sense is the overall task of this book, but we can introduce a few key arguments here.

Although in its escape from the crisis of the 1970s the system gained vitality by becoming more genuinely evolutionary, it achieved this, in some Faustian pact, at the expense of abandoning the modernist tools of planning. Perhaps in 1968–72, when multinational corporations sponsored the futures modelling exercise known as the *Limits to Growth*, (Meadows, 1972) this was the last gasp of an aspiring centrally-planned, technocentric and 'green' ultra-imperialism; today, that era is long gone.

In an evolutionary model of capitalism, any aggregate trend must be explained on the basis of decisions by individual actors, and this raises some extremely interesting issues. The orthodox argument of environmental economics would be that the individual decisions of micro-level actors are short-sighted, or perhaps even daren't follow ecological goals for fear of losing competitiveness, so that externalities must be corrected from the top. But we could argue the opposite: under conditions of crisis, the individual capitalist, acting from self-interest, might perceive that throughput is costly: if scarcity pushes prices up, raw materials cost too much money, and a similar point could be made about waste-disposal (an important manifestation of entropy being the shrinking space available for dumping). One would be more competitive by reducing both. An airline in China asks passengers to use the toilet before boarding the plane because to use it while in the air consumes as much energy as driving a car 10 km! This reasoning may extend not just to the individual actions of green entrepreneurs but even to progressive solutions which themselves begin to think systemically, by creating a cycle where waste from one process becomes an input into another, as in the industrial ecology model.[8] Similarly, some commercial farmers are becoming increasingly interested in the principles of 'no-till agriculture', a response which *substantively* represents an extremely radical challenge to the entire capitalist mindset on food (and one essential for a radical overhaul of the entire global food system); but which they adopt not really from ecological consciousness, but simply from a realisation that it makes sound economic sense not to waste money on herbicides, fuel, fuel-based fertilisers etc.[9] The weird thing is that 'green' capitalism can actually be highly successful at the level of particular businesses or even (as in the industrial ecology model) districts, and as the crisis begins to bite more and more, the viability of such decisions may be expected to increase.

This gives rise to the illusion that the solution can be 'scaled up' in the shape of an entirely restructured capitalist mode of production. The most vocal proponent of such a thesis has for decades been Amory Lovins, notably in the book *Natural Capitalism* (Hawken, Lovins and Lovins, 1999). As Robert Bryce very well points out, Lovins' optimistic (i.e. optimistic for the green capitalism thesis) predictions have consistently been proved wrong since 1976, without apparently undermining his guru status (Bryce, 2008).[10] The fallacy is firstly to give the impression that capitalism can be anything other than *un*natural, and secondly to ignore the fundamental line of development at a whole-system level, particularly imperialism. The crucial point is not to confuse adaptation by the human social system with adaptation by capitalism: the former can adapt by returning to its 'natural' line of development, the latter can't. Capitalism's inability to respond to the challenges humanity now faces is ingrained from its foundations in the

---

[8] See for example the resources page of the *Journal of Industrial Ecology*, on http://www.yale.edu/jie/

[9] See for example http://www.fairfaxcounty.gov/nvswcd/newsletter/notill.htm. This model is qualitatively different in some respects from the high-productivity, small-scale approach we discuss in the final chapter, but it fascinatingly incorporates major aspects of the latter.

[10] See extract, 'If We All Started Driving Priuses, We'd Consume More Energy Than Ever Before' on http://www.alternet.org/environment/84982/?page=3

appropriation of nature and its war against of the cultural systems (knowledge, experimentation) evolved by humanity to manage its relationship with nature sustainably: hence, the 'Death of Nature', colonialist resource-plunder and 'dominating knowledge'; while this same fixation with appropriation makes capitalism inherently hostile to the only viable *institutional* solution, namely common-pool resources and the regimes which naturally evolve to manage them.

Although the replacement of the capitalist mode of production is an essential condition for a *general* adaptation by humanity, this does not mean that the adaptive faculty goes into sleep mode for the moment. Experimentation is proceeding, and it is natural that some such experiments occur currently under the guise of an adaptation *of capitalism*, simply because they must be able to survive under conditions where that mode of production still prevails. But at the whole-system level, the line of capitalist development has been subsumed by imperialism. The state and finance capital here interact to distort the price signals which might be picked up by a theoretical purely *market* capitalism, while militarism provides a tempting 'entitlement' to grab the scarce resources which remain.

Capitalism brought huge developments of science and technology. The limitation is that it is imperialism which really governs how they will be applied, but this is easily forgotten: hence the assumption that scientific miracles will be able to resolve future problems, creating a dangerous illusion that current consumption can continue unabated. The miracle cure might for instance include some mixture of nanotechnology and 'hydrogen economy'. A typical example,[11] reveals the shortcomings of this approach: what notably constrains it is (a) unwillingness to accept a change of lifestyle, or of calling into question the American way of life as a global model, e.g. the dream of hydrogen cars made of ultra-light nano-engineered materials accepts that the car is sacrosanct; (b) 'security' issues (i.e. undermining the power of Southern raw material producers to set prices high enough for them to channel the value into their own development) are the main motivation, rather than sustainability per se; (c) the core concerns of R&D are effectively controlled by the military.

An important issue nevertheless remains. During most of capitalist history, the reproduction of capital has been linked to industrial

---

[11] James A. Baker Institute of Public Policy, Rice University, *Energy and Nanotechnology – Strategy for the Future* 2005, on http://www.rice.edu/energy/publications/docs/NanoReport.pdf

production and could thus reasonably be considered coupled to environmental degradation. But with more recent qualitative changes, reproduction seems to have become 'dematerialised'. Under classic capitalism, the manufacture of a physical commodity typically intervened, but this is less obvious today (as Magdoff, 2006 points out, the expansion of capital tends to take the form M-M' rather than M-C-M'). The values involved in financial operations appear increasingly fictional. If capital can multiply itself more effectively through speculation on, for example, a subprime mortgage, rather than by a direct act of smelting ore and pumping out fumes, does this mean that the essential relationship with entropy has been lost?

In general, the systems perspective would make us suspicious of any suggestion that the arrow of time is being put into reverse: accumulation may still be coupled to environmental degradation, merely in a less obvious way. In later chapters I will address this in more detail, with particular emphasis on hedging, but it will be interesting at this point to introduce some important elements in our argument, via a critique of 'virtuality'. Let's first create an ecological expression of Marx' model of the expanded reproduction of capital.

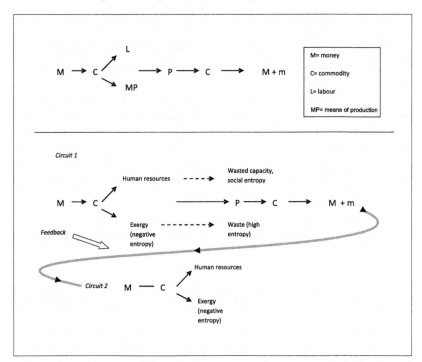

Figure 4: The expanded reproduction of capital.

The top diagram is the standard Marxian expression of expanded reproduction, the bottom one a development designed to highlight the systemic dimensions, and in particular the less obvious destructive side of the process.

In a conventional reading of exergy, (Dincer, 2002) raw materials present themselves as a 'given', a concentrated form of negative entropy strongly differentiated from its environment. In this case, our responsibility is expressed in the fact that we shouldn't use them up thoughtlessly (exhaust stocks, or convert them into high-entropy waste, for example in the form of greenhouse gas). But it should be clear that this statement is not adequate. There is first of all the socio-political dimension. Before you can access minerals you have to be prepared to destroy not just the physical environment, but, as Carolyn Merchant's 'death of nature' thesis shows, (Merchant 1990) the social systems which have evolved to protect the resources. This remains the case today. As we will see, there is a huge expenditure of energy on the militarism which serves to grab the resources.

Less obviously, there are also apparent technological fixes. Of course the creation of exergy is an absurdity because at some level it would seem obvious that more effort would have to be expended (or destruction caused) than the useful potential which is generated. Nevertheless, capitalism can embrace many forms of absurdity so long as the payback is concealed or postponed in some way. This is all part of its doomed battle against entropy.

Thus, one of the most important raw materials for the postwar economy was aluminium. Here, most of the input of energy is involved in creating the raw material itself, rather than in making something useful with it: 2–3% of *total* US industrial energy consumption has been expended simply in making aluminium as a material[12] (so in this case it is the 'order' of the material itself rather than of the product which is being made). Similarly, a serious structural weakness in the Chinese economy has been attributed to global demand for materials which are highly energy-intensive at the *primary* phase.[13] I will develop the notion

[12] United States Government, Energy Information Agency, *Energy Use – Aluminum Industry Analysis Brief* on http://www.eia.doe.gov/emeu/mecs/iab/aluminum/page2.html
[13] *People's Daily Online*, "94 pct of China's energy consumption self-supplied" September 22, 2005, accessed March 2007 on http://english.people.com.cn/200509/22/eng20050922_210070.html

of exergy-creation later with respect to what is surely one of the weirdest recent developments, the biofuel agenda. It may seem reasonable to hypothesise that, as a manifestation of the entropy of capitalism, such 'manufacture of exergy' is condemned to increase.

This line of analysis will help us critically to examine today's supposed dematerialisation. Let us consider the IT sector. Not only is it a significant basis of accumulation in its own right (the $140 billion semiconductor industry having enjoyed an average growth rate of 16% p.a.), but it forms the basis of the apparent virtualisation of the socio-economy as a whole.

Now, it is known that the energy consumption of IT is actually very significant. One remarkable calculation throws this into sharp relief: on the networking site Second Life (powered by 4,000 servers), each avatar (a computer-generated figure representing a participant) consumes more energy than a real citizen of a developing country (1,752 kWh per annum compared to 1,015 kWh) (Carr, 2006).

But less obvious and more fundamental issues are revealed if we adopt an exergy perspective. Very important evidence is provided by an academic study published in 2002 by Eric D. Williams et al.

Concretely, the key starting point is that *all materials employed in the semiconductor industry must be exceptionally pure*. This applies to the silicon itself which goes through six stages of purification, to the water used (in large quantities), and to the large number of chemicals employed. Purity rates of 99.9999% may be required, far higher than for 'old' industrial processes. These successive stages of purification require (presumably according to some issue of diminishing returns) massive energy inputs. The ratio between the mass of the final product versus the mass of secondary materials used in making it is 1:630 in the case of microchip production, as against 1:2 for an 'old' industrial product like a car. Williams et al explain that the massive energy inputs are due to the fact that you are moving from a relatively high-entropy form of matter into an extremely low-entropy form (extremely pure and highly organised). When technology *appears* to dematerialise production by reducing resource use, purification processes are rarely accounted; the notion of a 'secondary materialisation' can therefore be proposed (Williams, E., Ayers and Heller, 2002, p. 5509).

On this basis, it is surely worth hypothesising that, with each stage in capitalist development, the resources typical of that stage are decreasingly encountered in a sufficiently low-entropy state, necessitating an increasingly Sysiphan expenditure of effort to reverse the arrow of time. The fundamental entropy may merely be obscured by the fact that finance capital typically mediates its relationships through a long 'chain' where risks are hedged; but it cannot be eliminated.

In this chapter we sought to confront some of the key problems in understanding adaptation. We have outlined these only in a general way, seeking nevertheless to concretise them in relation to real-world issues. Our basic challenge in this book is to apply this framework to the very specific issues arising in relation to the current transition. Let us now begin this task.

CHAPTER THREE

THE 'SYSTEMIC TURN' IN CAPITALIST POLITICAL ECONOMY

Defining the 'Systemic Turn'

Our argument so far raises serious doubts about the viability of what is perhaps the most obvious adaptation which might prolong the capitalist mode of production, namely 'greening' it.

But there is one other line of development which might hypothetically serve to counteract its entropy, in other words a 'missing ingredient' upon which capitalism might draw.

This ingredient can be understood from two complementary directions. The first is the angle of capacity. Our argument has revealed a massive waste not just of natural resources, but of human capacity. But capacity is a free resource: as long as people receive enough energy to live at a reasonable level, they can create a lot of order (innovation, institutional self-organisation). All exploitative systems have restricted this potential to some extent, by concentrating knowledge in an elite and being too hierarchical or centralist to permit a full flowering of self-organisation. Nevertheless, they usually allowed self-organisation within a restricted region of society, and extracted a tribute from this region (for example, the village economy under feudalism). During most of its career, capitalism failed to do enough of this. The increasing role of the state and of bureaucracy created little promise that this failure could ever be redressed.

The vision of a sustainable future could envisage a reciprocal reduction of physical environmental depletion, counterbalanced by a vast increase of capacity. The limits currently facing us would thus be revealed not as absolute Malthusian ones, but rather as limits on the ability of our social order to access the human resources which could act as a substitute for depletion. Ideally, conservation of energy would be pursued in parallel in both physical productive systems and in human resources management, as implied in the work of Göran Wall (Wall, 1993).

As I will argue in the final chapter, this is really an agenda for post-capitalist transition. Nevertheless, the question arises whether capitalism could prolong itself at least for a time by anticipating such an evolution under its own auspices. Establishment theory has been moving for some time, at least tentatively, in a direction of recognising capacity. Krugman says that the only notion of growth which makes any sense is one premised on capacity, (Krugman, 1994) while Amartya Sen's work too has been drawn more into the mainstream and Friedrich List's precocious interest in human resources has undergone something of a revival.

The second direction from which we can picture the 'missing element' is the notion of self-organising systems. Top-down or centralised systems forsake the benefits of emergent, spontaneous order.

Conventionally, with the advent of imperialism, capitalism seemed to be developing in exactly the wrong way, by becoming *more* top-down. But if we employ dialectics, we can see things in a less linear way. More specifically I will draw upon an intuitive formulation by Lenin, namely, that imperialism "drags the capitalists, against their will and consciousness, into some sort of new social order..."(Lenin, 1939) This notion will be extremely important in our subsequent argument.

In representing this future towards which capitalism is 'dragged', Lenin uses a concept already familiar from Marx: 'socialisation'. A modernist and unilinear reading would assume socialisation to mean the system becoming increasingly organised at a societal level, in a controlled and top-down way; this could be interpreted either in a structuralist sense, or, in a different linear reading,[1] as the *deliberate* planning of production. Once the classic capitalism of small firms was irrevocably swept aside by oligopoly and strategic decision-making, all initiatives by, or emergent relationships between, small actors would disappear. This in turn would open up the possibility of a planned and organised economy. At this point, there would be two possible deductions. Either, in the ultra-imperialism scenario, the top-down rational order will be introduced by capitalism itself, under the auspices of the corporations and the state. Or, in the mainstream socialist *critique* of ultra-imperialism, the possibility of organisation, although opened up by capitalism, could not be realised by it, mainly because it is still

---

[1] This seems, for example, to be the view expressed in Merk, J. "Regulating the Global Athletic Footwear Industry – the Collective Worker in the Production Chain" in van der Pijl K. et al (eds.) *Global Regulation – Managing Crises after the Imperial Turn*, Basingstoke (Palgrave Macmillan) 2004, pp. 132–3

competitive: the task therefore falls to a 'socialism' (as defined as a prolongation of this mechanistic understanding of socialisation), which would remove the obstacle of competition by instituting a centrally planned economy. This shows quite well how a mechanistic socialist ideology dovetails with a mechanistic capitalist one, and is effectively the interpretation which became orthodox in the Communist movement in the inter-war years. But this produces a strange definition of socialism, inconsistent with the Marxian vision.

As a critique of this linear reading, we can use elements of both dialectics and systems theory to develop Lenin's proposition in a totally different way.

Development is not predictable, but we can guess at certain aspects through the application of the negation of the negation: earlier steps in a developmental process are not mechanically cancelled out, but rather 'preserved in the act of being negated' (sublated, in Hegel's term). Thus, if the modernised form of capitalism had negated the networking and emergence characteristic of natural human modes of interaction, what would happen if modernised capitalism itself were negated? We would expect the natural modes of interaction to reassert themselves. If the capitalist mode of production had come to an end at the same time as modernism, then networking and the new social order would appear simultaneously. But this is not how things happen in the real world, where the embryonic forms of a new setup develop within the framework of the old. Networking and emergence therefore begin to raise their head *within capitalism*, as the latter tries to cultivate them in a tame and exploitative form. But the reason why it cannot carry them to fruition is that emergence must by definition be constrained within the ground-rules of capitalism itself ... and the more it is constrained, the less it is true emergence. This is a fundamental premise of the remainder of our argument.

If capitalism needs to be overthrown not because it is a restriction on central planning but because it is a restriction on networking and grassroots capacity, then we arrive at an understanding of the post-capitalist future fully consistent with the Marxian vision, one where small local cells of society and economy could create higher-level order, knowledge and innovation, only through networking and emergence. The nature of this order can't be predicted fully, but non-linearity is not the same as random or chaotic development: we can understand a certain logic without predicting it in detail.

Capitalism Learns to Act with Systemic Processes

Around 1980, capitalism suddenly discovered an approach which could, without abolishing the fundamental contradictions causing exploitation and dissipation, *organise* them in a more efficient way by exploring both the advantages of capacity and the emergent properties of self-organising systems. Because the Soviet world had committed itself to competing with capitalism on precisely the wrong terrain – i.e. being more efficient at top-downism – it was quickly defeated. But in the moment of its triumph, capitalism was at the same time unleashing a development whose long-term tendencies imply its own destruction.

Let us now consider in more detail the characteristics of this new order. It is not just about accessing capacity at an individual level, but about the creativity which emerges from within a complex system.

In its purest form, the unleashing of capacity would be too dangerous to spread to the grassroots, so it tends to be ring-fenced within the elite. A common representation is 'network capitalism', (von Tunzelmann, 2003, p. 369) but for a more provocative and interesting formulation we can look to Michel Bauwens' formulation, "The Communism of Capital". (Bauwens, 2007, p. 14) This seems very much in line with the spirit of Lenin's quote, whereby, on the basis of socialisation, capital opens up something fundamentally in contradiction with its own mode of appropriation. Networking and peer-to-peer (P2P) relationships thus demonstrate the superiority of socialised modes of production of information systems; and progressive IT geeks can take this to the next logical step by arguing that the products themselves should be free, not merely the modes of interaction: this would apply in different ways to both free software and open source. In some respects this very clearly pushes in directions contradictory to capitalism. Within part of capitalism the approach to IT remains very hierarchical, centralised and appropriated, but the system cannot afford to destroy the alternative mode of organisation completely, because it relies on this for its creative edges. Nevertheless, just because IT is the leading edge of current development does not mean that the revolution in a larger sense will be conducted by geeks. The international political economy still rests on the shoulders of sweatshop operatives, plantation slaves and migrant domestic workers etc., and capital's goal is still to prevent *them* becoming networked.

Or at least the more autonomous and unconstrained aspect of networks cannot be spread to the grassroots. But a certain form of networks could also themselves act as a control mechanism. Just as it is questionable whether technology is a 'neutral' productive force which capitalism merely *misapplies* (and which could therefore be employed in a progressive way by a different social system), (Bahr, 1980) there is a similar limitation with networks. A systemic dimension of power has always been latent within capitalist society. This is already clear in the work of Gramsci: power is embedded within structure. More recently, in his work in the mid-1970s, Michel Foucault seems to describe a system which was only fully to become established in the next decade: power is "exercised through networks", and "functions only when it is part of a chain" (Foucault, 2003, p. 29).

One of Foucault's interesting insights was to question the assumption of Hobbes that intra-societal war is abolished by the formation of the state (Foucault, 2003, pp. 16–17). This questions the assumption that modernism really had siphoned power to the top: there was a hidden, more diffuse and structural form of repression which could spring out to become the dominant form. Nor is systemic power necessarily 'soft'. Violence is intrinsic to the system: simply, where it is employed by those higher up against those lower down the hierarchy, it is either concealed or legitimised (Jensen, 1960).

In Chapter 5 we will examine this issue of the diffused, parallel power in its military dimension. But the interesting point for our present argument is that networks as a control mechanism could become part of the *economic* paradigm. The techniques whereby society treats the excluded, marginalised, imprisoned or abnormal are diffused within the system, developing as practices in a localised and specific way, and at a particular point become co-opted into the governance mechanism when they are profitable or politically expedient.

So we have two seemingly conflicting perspectives on networks, one in which they are borrowed from a future, natural mode of human interaction, and another where they come from a dark shadow-world intrinsic to capitalism itself. In the story which will unfold in this book, we will be able to trace many real-world examples of both, but the relationship between them remains difficult. On the one hand, there is the faculty of emergent order within complex systems, which is creative and draws upon capacity: this is the aspect which was genuinely stifled by modernism, and which looks towards a new social order. On the other, there is a *structural* form of repressive power, hidden within the Hobbesian or modernist order, which conveniently claimed to have centralised more power than it really had. At a particular stage, capitalism needed to unleash the first aspect, but it had to be contained within a framework which would serve exploitation, and restrict any subversive leanings. This is where the repressive form of networked power could be pressed into service to provide precisely this kind of containment.

Where Foucault's work is less helpful is in explaining how the latent repressive reality sprung out to overtake the whole of social development. I will argue that there are at least three watersheds: in the 1980s with the adoption of the explicit networked model, in 1997–8 when the ruling order began to despair of complexity and switched to repression, and in 2006–7 when serious feedback from entropy began. Only a developmental model can take account of these.

Here, the issue of energy addressed in systems theory becomes relevant: the creative energy unleashed must be more than that ploughed into the *encadrement* (containment) of the networks. Up to a point, the two aspects of networking could develop symbiotically and acquired a certain equilibrium. But then, complexity would outstrip the possibility of containment and the equilibrium would no longer be sustainable. At this point, the repressive aspect of networked power takes over, growing out of the hidden margins to engulf the whole of society.

The extreme free market discourse would claim to remove all restrictions on the free play of forces and sit back and embrace *whatever* emergent order results. A handful of maverick right-wing libertarians indeed argue exactly this, applauding the fact that the global economy has become uncontrollable, and the more so the better (North, 2006). But within the establishment, they are only a tiny minority; the mainstream has gone the opposite way. Neo-liberalism in its real (as opposed to propagandist) form was inherently authoritarian from its origins (think Pinochet, Thatcher, Structural Adjustment). This is not in contradiction to the fact that there was a certain element of genuinely unleashing (exploitative) spontaneous order, on the contrary, it was precisely the commandism which served to contain it, to impose draconian restrictions on its permitted lines of development. But there is a qualitative difference between on the one hand a situation where emergence operates under the auspices of commandism and repression, and on the other, one the system becomes *swamped* by commandism and repression. A major argument of this book is that the latter increasingly began to take over from the 'normal' form of neo-liberalism, particularly since the 1997–8 watershed.

Of course, as we might expect in a system with a complex topography, the loss of control is uneven. At present, the 'recognised' networks such as industrial clusters and value chains still exercise their self-exploitation in a reasonably reliable way and a 'soft' touch therefore suffices to police them. Where we really see the 'hard' side is when imperialism clamps down on attempts by the excluded to form parallel networks, for example in use of the 9/11 discourse on terrorist funding to clamp down on all autonomous funding networks: an *Asia Times* investigation of exchanges at the border crossing between Brazil, Argentina and Paraguay revealed how the US Southern Command (Southcom) was intervening furiously under the rationale of tracking down the funding networks of Hizbollah and Hamas!(Escobar, 2006) In this way, repression is seemingly focused against a group of outsiders and the majority think it doesn't affect them.

In this chapter we are primarily concerned with the first of the three watersheds, i.e. the origins of the 'normal' mode of controlled networked capitalism around 1980. We need to understand this well before we can then understand the more recent developments which occurred when this model began to come unstuck.

I am defining as the 'systemic turn' the change which occurred round at that time whereby capitalism began to adapt to working with complexity, and parasitise upon emergent properties rather than ignoring or resisting them. The approach to capacity in the management doctrines has two interlinked aspects: at the level of the individual human being; and the institutional dimension, which addresses emergent properties of systems. Thus on the one hand: 'Japanese' management systems emphasise a need to spread problem-solving capacity to the shopfloor; on the other, global value chains generate, via networking, a 'spontaneous order' far more effective than anything which could be designed in a top-down way by TNCs. Together these define a structure whereby the mode of production could access the benefits of self-organisation without the inconveniences, since a tight repressive structure could contain them.

Fundamental Contradictions Still Drive Capitalism

What is it within capitalism which drives this change? The mode of production harbours an intrinsic self-destructiveness, which we could variously represent as limitations, tendencies towards disorder, contradictions etc. Just one example would be a tendency to overproduction, ingrained within the very logic of accumulation itself, as indicated by Marx in his critique of Ricardo; (Marx, 1969 e, p. 470) other such issues of particular relevance to our discussion are the falling rate of profit and pauperisation. These contradictions cannot be disposed of, any more than entropy can be disposed of. But they can be shuffled around. In its instituted form, capitalism is a *regulated* system, and in this sense regulation is a kind of structured way of shuffling entropy. Therefore, although the contradictions are not eliminated, and somehow retain an indirect presence, they are not manifested in a pure form. The pauperisation generated by core capitalism was partly exported to the periphery – initially by exporting the 'unruly' poor themselves to the colonies, then by an increasing relative rise of poverty in the South – and partly to the physical environment (food costs artificially reduced through unsustainable farming practices as we will see in the next chapter). Various forms of environmental and social degradation can thus be seen as 'transposed' representations of the central contradictions of capitalism.

The important point of this argument is that we should not always expect to see the basic contradictions occurring as purely as they would in a non-regulated form of capitalism, which would in any case be a totally imaginary construct which cannot really exist. Much of the argument of this book will be an attempt to trace these indirect or transposed expressions of entropy.

Having made this point, it still remains an important challenge to see how far the basic contradictions are manifested in a direct form. What, for instance, has been happening to the rate of profit? Capital is for the moment continuing its expanded reproduction, but in the US at least, profits in the old industrial sectors have been in decline.

This could merely reflect a change to new sectors where the profit is higher. But in the US, an unprecedented proportion of GDP has been paid out to investors as dividends, (Norris, 2007) suggesting that future investment is being neglected in favour of sustaining the appearance of economic health here and now.

Another significant development has been an increase in the proportion of US corporate profits originating from overseas operations; it looks as though this is required to compensate for a declining profitability at home. The early postwar contribution of external profits was much lower than we might expect from a mechanical reading of imperialism, but the subsequent development is quite striking, climbing

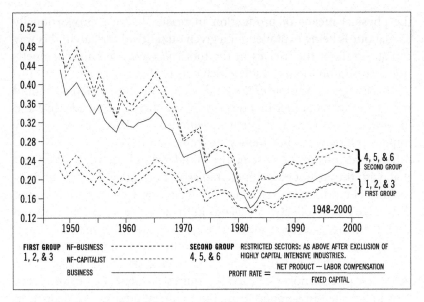

Figure 5: Case study of the rate of profit in US industry.
Source: Duménil, Gerard, and Dominique Lévy, "The Profit Rate: Where and How Much Did it Fall? Did it Recover? (USA 1948-2000)" Review of Radical Political Economics 34, 4, 2002, p. 448, re-illustrated by Eric Titolo for Biel R., "The interplay between social and environmental degradation in the development of the international political economy", Journal of World-Systems Research, Vol. 12, no. 1, 2006

from 10% to nearly 30% between the beginning of the '70s and the late 2000s.[2]

This could be an expression of diminishing returns within the core, an issue to which we will return:

The question then is, how does the rate of profit push adaptation? Traditionally within Marxian thinking this question has been linked to the impact of technology, in the following way.

Even if we make abstraction of external ecological limits, we would expect to find diminishing returns due to factors purely internal to the accumulation process. In its simplest expression, the rate of profit would fall whenever the proportion of total capital outlay invested in

---

[2] *New York Times*, August 3 2007, based on US Treasury statistics, on http://www.nytimes.com/2007/08/04/business/04charts.html?_r=1&oref=slogin

the physical means of production increases, because proportionally less labour is being exploited for a given quantity of capital. In this way capitalists shoot themselves in the foot *collectively*, because competition forces upon them a result which cuts profits.

This is a good example of the kind of contradiction which we should not expect to encounter in a pure form. Capitalism as an adaptive and instituted system can regulate it ... which, as we have said, in no way implies removing it, but merely dissecting and exporting bits of it to different regions of the system. The *initial* form of such regulation was that, with the advent of oligopoly (an aspect of imperialism), decision-making could become strategic. The giant corporations could – and did – take many collective decisions in their mutual interest, aided and abetted by the state, for example to buy up patents for things like long-lasting light bulbs and suppress such profit-damaging technologies; it is interesting that in many such cases the ecology indirectly bears the brunt because turnover of capital requires obsolescence of products. This looks like ultra-imperialism, but Lenin refuted such a deduction by saying that competition was not fully abolished, but rather 'hovers over' the oligopolies. This is fair enough, but only takes us part of the way. The systems perspective shows that the solution of 'organised capitalism' would fail *not just because of residual competition, but more profoundly because it is top-down and does not allow for self-organisation*. If this were the only possible course for capitalism it would have gone rapidly to its doom (as maybe seemed likely in the late 1960s and early '70s). Some were predicting 'convergence' with Soviet-style centrally-planned economies (CPEs), (Schmitter, 1990) but in fact 'organised' capitalism is actually less efficient than market capitalism, not better as that theory alleges.

The non-solution of 'organised capitalism' – an evolutionary blind-alley in the history of adaptive imperialism – applied to an era still not fundamentally different from the Victorian situation where Marx wrote: qualitative technical improvement was roughly synonymous with investing in expensive machinery, with the result that the proportion of labour in total capital outlay, and thus also the rate of profit, would fall. Today, with technology focused more on software, the impulse to increase labour productivity would not automatically mean investing in weighty industrial plant. Even so, if technology were used to *replace* labour, the issue would remain of a shrinking proportion of the thing which permits value to increase, namely labour. So this does not really get capitalism off the hook; the rate of profit problem would to some extent survive the software revolution.

But it would be different if the technology was used not to *replace* labour, but to *control* it. In such a productive setup, exploitative labour-intensive processes would run in parallel with high-tech ones. The point is that to make such a system work efficiently, it would be totally counter-productive to try and organise it too much. It is inherently a complex system which *must* make use of emergence and self-modifying structure.

If we attempt to research this in concrete terms, we indeed find that technology is not introduced in a wholesale way across the board, but selectively, and in a sense *politically*.

We can for example consider this in respect to robots. Significantly, the robotics sector is increasingly dominated, not by industry, but by the military: one specialist told the *New Scientist*, "If I don't work for the DoD [US Defense Department], I don't work."[3] In later chapters we will see where this leads in terms of adaptive-chaotic forms of warfare, but the point to emphasise here is that the growth of robotics in manufacturing has been relatively modest. Industrial robot sales experienced lean years in 2001–2, and although they took off again in 2003–4, uptake was driven by their falling price, in conjunction with increasing quality.[4] According to a UN report, by 2004, the price of robots, as a proportion of human labour costs, had fallen from an index of 100 in 1990 to 15 in Germany and to 12 in North America. (United Nations, 2004 b) This may imply that the organic composition of capital was if anything falling rather than rising. According to another set of UN figures, the projected increase of industrial robots during the first decade of the 2000s was to be very modest.[5]

This is not to deny that non-military robotics has been significant, but there is a sense that its uptake has been very selective, and driven above all by the function of controlling *labour*. This might help to explain why robots crop up in the most unexpected areas. One would scarcely have expected to encounter them in a quintessentially

---

[3] *New Scientist*, March 29 2008, p. 26
[4] United Nations Economic Commission for Europe Press Release ECE/STAT/05/ P03 Geneva, October 11 2005 on http://www.unece.org/press/pr2005/05stat_p03e.pdf
[5] United Nations Economic Commission for Europe Press Release ECE/STAT/05/ P03, p. 4

labour-intensive sector like fruit-picking, but it turns out that "California navel orange growers are developing an eight-armed robot to harvest their fruit. 'Farmers are now looking to robotics as a hedge', says Vision Robotics Corp CEO Derek Morikawa" (Slaughter, 2006). Presumably the risk being hedged is either that labour will demand its rights or that North America will collapse inward into autarky and limit immigration (a scenario which we will analyse later). In general, technology always acts as a hedge to prevent the exploited playing their strongest cards. The introduction of technical substitutes for raw materials (for example, fibre optics in place of copper), which in a fictional world might be used to 'green' capitalism, is concretely employed to undermine producers' cartels, and therefore keep prices down so that the 'old' resources like copper can continue cheaply to be depleted. Similarly, robotics are used not to provide leisure but to show workers that capitalism can do without them, with the result that wages remain low and labour-intensive production continue.

Basic Principles of the Systemic Turn in Management

Having seen what is driving it, we need to understand in more detail how such a system is organised.

The basic proposition is quite simple: less is more. Social systems have a property of emergent order, and the more scope you allow for this, the better they work.

Ideally, if you relax the top-down organisation of manufacturing industry, which used to be reflected in the tight control of a highly centralised corporation over its subsidiaries, then something will 'emerge' which spontaneously creates a much more efficient exploitative system. New modes of organisation such as networks will generate themselves. A phrase like 'network capitalism'(von Tunzelmann, 2003) expresses this. Examples are clusters and global value chains. Clustering, which sounds like a process in astrophysics, can be defined as the co-location of firms in a particular sector of production (perhaps specialising in different tasks within that sector) and in a particular region, and often integrating a range of functions from design up to finished products (Humphrey and Schmitz, 2002). By analogy with star-formation, these structures are genuinely self-organising and un-designed, but something un-designed can still generate order. An alternative social system could explore the potential of this emergence in undreamt-of ways, but capitalism can still explore it a bit, so long as it can control the process overall, and stamp out those forms of emergence which are too threatening (for example, workers' self-organisation). New technical developments such as IT obviously facilitated this shift. But the main method is probably that the large-scale emergent structures like global value chains could be used to contain the small-scale ones, thus forcing all local initiatives into the mould of self-exploitation in the wider interests of capital accumulation.

Whereas up to now we have been using systems thinking as a tool to *critique* capitalism (because it highlights the fragile thermodynamic basis and shows that grassroots organisations in tune with nature could run society better), now we are beginning to enter a situation where capitalism *itself* claims to think systemically. The ruling discourse is saying some things which are true, but nevertheless in an instrumental and twisted form, so we have to be aware of both the truth and the distortion.

The first point to make clear is that we should not take all the systems jargon at face value. If we consider, in a case like Britain, the dismemberment of public sectors like health and education, it is true up to a point that these sectors used to be centralist or top-down, and if such control structures are disrupted the result might theoretically be to clear the way for self-organisation. But in reality, since what replaces modernist control is merely a hollow management-speak about outsourcing, 'public-private partnerships' etc., it is far from clear that there really are efficiency gains. Rather, such measures look suspiciously like window-dressing for tossing the sectors to the piranhas of predatory private accumulation.

Even so, it is important that we hold to a perspective that there is a certain sphere where the systemic turn creates a *genuinely* more efficient (exploitative) system. This is particularly the case with manufacturing industry, which forms the original paradigm for the systemic management later abusively extended into other spheres like public services. Only on the premise that the systemic turn was partly genuine can the adaptive imperialism of the last couple of decades of the 20th century be explained, and indeed the background to its more recent collapse into a semi-chaotic state. But this has nevertheless been a highly *selective* form of systems approach, one which grabs only those aspects suitable to the accumulation of capital.

In analysing this, it will be helpful first to recognise that there are two aspects to the systemic turn: self-exploitation and innovation. Both are related to capacity but express it in significantly different ways. Self-exploitation is the easiest to understand. Here, the systemic phase builds upon earlier exploitative categories, while dialoguing with them in new ways.

Let us begin by considering the issue of boundaries, fundamental to any systems perspective, inasmuch as the relationship between a reference system and its environment or periphery is crucial to its dissipation. The new management systems use the notion of flexibility in an instrumental way, either (in the case of 'functional' flexibility) to break down job demarcations negotiated with unions under the Keynesian dispensation, or (in the case of 'numerical' flexibility) to scrap whole legions of workers (employed outside the boundaries of the core firm) when the order book dries up. But underlying this instrumental usage we can detect a more objective definition of flexibility: a sudden realisation that boundaries can be permeable.

The boundary most obvious to conventional economics is that between managed capitalism and the market. Less obvious but more fundamental is that between capitalism as a whole (whether managed or not), and the informal sphere, which lies partially outside the monetary economy but can still be exploited by it. In Coase's theory of the firm (an important tool of mainstream economics) (Hymer, 1990) he concentrated on the first of these aspects, interpreting the division rigidly: the intra-firm (controlled) sphere and the market sphere are opposites, the boundary between them being flexible only in the sense that it can shift, *but is not permeable*. This perspective was very limiting and reflects neither the reality nor the potential of exploitation. The new management doctrines overcame these limitations, by recognising both the scope for informal exploitation *anywhere* in the system, and the importance of non-market relations within a wider complex system evolving under the overall auspices of capitalism. Thus, on the one hand the firm is no longer synonymous with the managed sphere, but rather quasi-market relations could be introduced within it; on the other, the area beyond the firm's boundaries is not just composed of structureless economic transactions, but could cluster into local systems whose somewhat resilient sense of identity is 'glued' through non-market relations, such as trust or reciprocity. Unlike in Rosa Luxemburg's theory where the entropy of capitalism occurs merely as a progressive *depletion* of the non-market sphere (as a kind of finite resource analogous to fossil fuels laid down over millennia), we would encounter something more unexpected and complex: a continuing exploitation of a sphere of diffuse initiative and natural human interaction such as social networks, which can reconstitute themselves. In this case, entropy would be expressed in the paradox of a controlled emergence, i.e. the tendency for the energy consumed in controlling an emergent order to outstrip that which it supplies. There are clearly links between the two levels of permeability: in order to make the informal (emergent) aspect *of capitalism* function better, you import some modes of interaction from *beyond capitalism*.

Because of their connection with natural modes of interaction like reciprocity, the emergent networks in some sense reach towards a new social order. But the exploitative form which develops under capitalism holds this potential at bay by tying them to something else imported from the past: dualism. It was the feminist analysis which pointed out that dualism, as an ingrained mode of operation of exploitative systems, predates capitalism (Biel, 2000). Here, the household is the fundamental category which, in a systems interpretation, could be identified as an environment or 'sink' into which many of the problems generated by capitalism could be dissipated: aspects of pauperisation, the disorder expressed in unemployment when there is a downturn (Biel, 2003 a). Being hidden from history, this periphery could be excluded from the sphere of officially-acknowledged institutional development (Harstock, 1983). These dualistic approaches were taken on board and adapted by capitalism. Then, with the advent of colonialism, racism adds another determinant, with 'racial' divisions being used in order to demarcate particular categories of super-exploited labour (Fevre, 1985). The 'new' management systems are in this sense 'old': they turn dualism into an even more pervasive principle of organisation. Kopinak is right that the different ways of relating to labour represent not stages (along a time continuum) but 'moments' which exist side by side (Kopinak, 1995, pp. 68–94). They supply a variety of textures which successive stages of exploitative society can orchestrate in different ways. The more primitive forms of exploitation receive a new lease of life, precisely as the mode of operation of the most modern ones. In the 'Japanese' subcontracting model, employment is relatively stable within the core firm at the top, and as one descends the subcontracting chain, conditions become more precarious and wages lower; (Sumiya, 1989) and this is what provided the paradigm for the whole restructuring of industry in the '80s (Oliver and Wilkinson, 1988).

An understanding of this relationship – the overlapping of ancient and modern exploitative forms – was partly foreshadowed in the notion of articulation of modes of production, central to dependency theory. As Frank put it, "insofar as primitive accumulation refers to accumulation on the basis of production with noncapitalist relations of production, it need not be prior to, but can also be contemporary with capitalist production and accumulation" (Frank, 1978, p. 241). What was not yet clear at that time was the institutional form whereby subordinate economic actors could *spontaneously* organise their own exploitation under the capitalist auspices, but a basis for such understanding existed in Chayanov's important theory of self-exploitation (Chayanov, 1966). The peasant household, which organised its resources internally according to principles which were not capitalist, (Thorner, 1971) was a kind of 'institution' which interacted with a wider, monetarised economy. We could see self-exploitation as a form of self-organisation, and by extension, this could apply not just to the peasant economy but to the whole informal sector. Crucial in teaching global capitalism how to do this was the work of de Soto: (de Soto, 2000, 2001) under the guise of empowering the informal sector, he gave the dominant forces clues about how to exploit it, hence the enthusiasm with which his ideas were embraced by the World Bank. Modernism used to hate informality and pretend it didn't exist, but the ruling order now rehabilitates it as a powerful tool to generate emergent, self-exploiting structures.

From this perspective, recent capitalist development has merely dredged something exploitative from the past and generalised it. But we should not lose sight of the other aspect of the new systems, innovation. Here we are on less familiar terrain. Although it can be argued that Amin's excellent treatment of socialism in China anticipates the notion of capacity as a free resource, (Amin, 1981) the dependency perspective was in general always better at understanding labour as a motor of production than as a force possessing a creative and innovative potential, which might be explored *even under capitalism*.

This was in a sense excusable because until recently capitalism has shown little interest in doing so. A consistent theme throughout its history of has been 'dominating knowledge', (Marglin, F. and Marglin, S., 1990) and the easiest way of doing this was simply to monopolise design, innovation etc. at the top. This has been the default mode since earliest capitalism, and if development were merely linear, this feature would presumably continue to intensify. The rationale is clear: if you deprive working people of knowledge, they are easier to exploit. But this conflicts with strong arguments which go in the opposite direction: in a complex system, innovation should be diffused, and the further you are removed from the shop floor the less well you understand the real problems which need to be resolved in production!

More specifically, we can understand the limitations of the old (modernist) industrial model at two levels: in the workplace, and in the wider, notably international, division of labour. At the workplace level the Taylor system of labour management centralised all thinking and planning at the top (Braverman, 1974). Anyone with direct experience of Taylorism knows a thousand stories about a situation where the worker could see where a production-problem was developing, and identify a potential solution, but was actively discouraged from pointing it out: 'I'm only paid from here down' (indicating a boundary in the region of the neck). By extension, all modernist and Fordist approaches to the division of labour *between firms*, both nationally and internationally, would tend to do the same. A hierarchical system is a bit more sophisticated, but remains linear: in the product cycle version of the international division of labour, knowledge would spread downwards, but in a merely imitative form. The core would hold onto innovation, as for example in the Japanese version of the product cycle, the flying geese model, (Kojima, 1977) where the leading goose of the formation is (unlike in nature!) always the same.

This regime not only promoted alienation and cut itself off from capacity, but rejected the reality of *diffuse* innovation within a complex system. When capitalism needed to come up with something new to escape from the crisis of the 1970s, Schumpeter's ideas suggest that this could be achieved by some creative destruction, and a prime target for such destruction would be the vertical division: if it could be weakened (or rendered at least permeable), the reward would be exploitation of the capacity to think, which has far more potential than mere muscle power.

The only problem then would be to contain the innovation within acceptable parameters: if workers are allowed to think creatively, the thought might occur to them that they can manage perfectly well without capitalism. Based on what we have already seen, the solution to prevent this would be to create a reciprocal relation between on the one hand a diffusion of capacity, on the other an increase of dualism, the latter serving to prevent the former getting out of hand.

Systemic Consciousness and the Issue of Development

We have presented the systemic turn under a guise which makes it look quite neat from capitalism's point of view. But in practice it is far from that straightforward.

A few pages back we posed the question of how far the systemic turn represents a real mode of operation, and how far mere propaganda. But actually, there is something which lies between these two extremes and which may be the key thing we need to understand: self-image. Capitalism has stumbled upon this line of development and tries to bolster its confidence that it is in control and that the future line of development is sound. The point is not just to deceive the people (though this is of course necessary), but also itself. It needs to believe it has a future, and to censor out the direst information it is receiving.

An important role in this self-consciousness is played by institutional theory,[6] an ideological development strongly related to the systemic turn. An economy is 'instituted' in the sense of being populated by structures of the type we have considered (networks, clusters etc.). We can say that such an economy is 'organised', but then organisation itself has to be understood in a new way, not synonymous with central or top-down control, but rather with self-organising emergent properties. Although institutional theory is saying something important and true about self-organisation, at the same time its purpose is to help capitalism grapple with its self-image.

A substantial literature has thus grown up around value chains, clusters etc., and because capitalism *really* needs to understand these things, the literature is allowed to raise some genuine issues relevant to the mechanisms of exploitation (since it's largely academic, there is not so much risk of this knowledge percolating to the mass movement). Up to a point, it needs to describe reality 'warts and all'. But at the same time, there is a fine dividing line between self-consciousness and self-delusion.

In understanding how the two relate, it is useful to identify two aspects to the systemic turn: the mode of organisation during any particular slice of time (i.e. the type of institutions and patterns of relations between them: subcontracting, 'empowerment', production

---

[6] I am very grateful to Kho Mu-Jeong and Michael Walls for several discussions of institutional theory.

chains etc.); and development *through* time. It is with respect to the latter that self-delusion particularly creeps in. Symptoms of renewal seem to be there: a host of new products, the rise of manufacturing in Asia. But does this mean that capitalism is, in its development through time, going somewhere? *Really* to answer this question you would have to ask firstly whether the fundamental contradictions *internal* to capitalism can ever really be resolved, secondly whether the mode of production could in any case survive the drying-up of its external energy sources. The fact that these issues are taboo to the mainstream debate, severely limits the value of institutional theories, particularly when they address issues of progression through time.

Thus for example we find one model referring to three successive steps wherein governance is exercised respectively through markets, hierarchies and networks (von Tunzelmann, 2003). Another subdivides the globalisation era into investment-based, trade-based and digital phases (Gereffi, 2001). Each phase may have its own characteristic actors, for example the transnational corporations, typical of the centralised, top-down governance initiated by early imperialism, arguably reached their heyday within a 'hierarchical' phase, to be superceded (not entirely, but as *characteristic* actor) by the 'global network flagship' (Ernst and Kim, 2002). Such conceptualisations are useful to our understanding insofar as hierarchy, flagships etc. are indeed relevant categories. We can learn to use them critically, for example, in discovering that market, hierarchy and network are not related merely as a linear succession, which would give us simply a prolongation (with the addition of further stages) of the old Rostow model, (Rostow, 1960) but also overlap. Similarly, we must recognise that the characteristic actors addressed by imperialism theory are still present: in Gereffi's 'digital phase' where major auto-industry producers collaborate in sourcing components, (Gereffi, 2001) the corporations are still the effective actors. State and corporate interests are still wedded together, as in classic imperialism, the point is simply that they are not wedded in promoting top-downism, but rather in a different way: as co-conspirators in encouraging self-organisation, with the state acting in an 'enabling' role: for example, it may intervene to 'trigger' processes, such as clustering, which are then supposed to become 'self-augmenting' (Brenner and Fornahl, 2003). This would define a new role for agency: not less important than before, but qualitatively more systemic, development being defined as a progressive exploration of systemic forms. In this way, through a critical dialogue with new institutional theories of industrial organisation, we introduce insights which enrich a systemic model of imperialist political economy.

So far so good. But we must constantly remain aware of the limitations. Most obviously, the fact that capitalism is driven to explore these new methodologies does not prove its validity as a mode of production. While it is perfectly true that the governance (organisation) of a complex system *must* rely on self-modifying behaviours,[7] it is an entirely different question whether capitalism can achieve this on behalf of human society. On the contrary, the latter may have to overthrow capitalism in order to bring to fruition this breakthrough.

A Critique of Evolutionism

Since an important function of institutional theory is to kid the mode of production that it has a future, a key point of reference is evolution. This has the advantage of making the development process itself appear systemic, not just the particular forms which make it up. An "evolutionary theory of economic change"(Ernst and Kim, 2002, p. 1418) is thus sought. This would open up limitless *future* options, capitalism having in some sense become more 'organic'. It is here that propaganda and self-delusion begin to take over (as we will see in the next two chapters, an efficient exploitative system would distinguish rigorously between the two, cultivating the first while resisting the second; however, this distinction becomes increasingly difficult to maintain as information from the future becomes increasingly dire).

At several points in our enquiry we will confront evolution, our orientation being to highlight the correct core meaning of open-ended development, while critiquing the distortions which turn it into a justification for the status quo. Arguably, Darwin himself opened the way to this perversion in his discussion of the genocide of Australasian aboriginals, (Darwin, 1959, p. 430) where effectively the argument is that whatever exists is justified by the mere fact that it *has* developed. This could fit in neatly with other forms of instrumentalised systems thinking, as in the anti-Communist work of Hayek, one of the first thinkers to deal with spontaneous order, but from the point of view that any attempt to improve the order which *had* evolved spontaneously – i.e.

---

[7] c.f. http://en.wikipedia.org/wiki/Self-modifying_code accessed January 30 2008

the capitalist status quo – was by definition doomed (Hayek, 1973). This seems merely to update the notion of the 'best of all possible worlds' once satirised by Voltaire, (Voltaire, 1968) although actually, to be accurate we are talking about the 'second-best of all possible worlds'! Social-Darwinism does not necessarily say that the current order is good, merely that it exists. Similarly, 'second-best' economic theory has been twisted to justify neo-liberalism, (Toye, 1987) in the sense that the different elements in a system co-evolve to acquire a certain equilibrium, so it is counter-productive to intervene in order to establish the optimum in just one parameter. In the case of industrial organisation, as Young has shown, the existing division of labour was made to appear sacrosanct because it was 'organic'; (Young, 1990) the justification for today's division of labour – called 'globalisation', an emergent order arising on the basis of deregulated markets – could be considered a rehash of this same argument.

The existence of such distortion does not, however, mean that we can dismiss as pure nonsense the notion of evolution within the capitalist political economy. We simply have to see it as a 'contained' form of evolution. The large-scale system of the international political economy partly evolves, but with a strong input of agency from the historic core which defines the parameters instrumentally in accordance with its hegemonic interest, and this large-scale structure in turn creates a context within where local initiatives evolve, but in a contained way. Such a model is consistent with Dos Santos' formulation of dependency, (Dos Santos, 1970) but develops it in a more complex and sophisticated way. We can illustrate the reasoning with an example. In Kenya, the early 21st century opened a brief window of opportunity with the passing of the US Africa Growth and Opportunity Act (AGOA). In 2005, ten years after the beginning of the WTO, the special regime on textiles (the Long Term Arrangement) would expire, creating a competitive market which would be difficult for African producers, but between 2000–5 they would have preferential access to the US market, and even for a time beyond this there would be exemption from Rules of Origin (RoO) enabling them to act as intermediaries for textiles produced in Asia which the US market would normally exclude. On the basis of this institutional framework, a Kenyan textile industry rapidly evolved (Kindiki, 2007). In a sense, spontaneous evolutionary order unfolds only within these confines, and concerns itself only with exploring the most efficient structures of self exploitation. Although AGOA is a pure product of agency, the global value chains, within which such locally specific development is inserted, must be partly emergent.

If we take seriously the notion that capitalism is, a least partly, a *really* evolutionary (adaptive, self-modifying) system, there must be a sense in which development is to be explained in terms of the motives of the lower-level actors, i.e. firms, which experiment with certain management practices, some of which increase their 'fitness'. It therefore makes sense for Hodgson and Knudsen to apply a Darwinian approach to firms' institutional development (Hodgson and Knudsen, 2006). Similarly, Jessop rightly highlights the fact that the institutions of capitalism are themselves emergent; (Jessop, 2001) they develop in a way which cannot be predicted a priori. But the risk in this line of argument is that it may fall into a kind of institutional variant of neo-liberalism where the higher-level order is *only* the product of 'blind', non-targetted action by the individual actor, because then we would not understand the instrumentality of the WTO etc.

Even so, and allowing for the level of instrumentality driven by the historic core's self-interest, the regime of accumulation is not, in its complex totality, planned. This implies that the higher-level system too is, at least partially, evolutionary. But how then does selection operate? It is interesting here to consider Claus Offe's version of institutional theory, which emphasises a notion of 'institutional gardening', as opposed to 'institutional design': (Offe, 1996, p. 52) in his development of the concept, the large-scale structure is not predetermined, but selectively determines itself in a particular form once it is underway, because the cost of change is too high. But the 'gardening' metaphor could have a wider relevance, which we will explore in the course of our enquiry. After all, gardening works deliberately with an evolved and evolving genetic material, certain forms of which it selectively emphasises, and there are important choices about whether you seek to understand and work with issues of higher-system symbiosis (for example, sympathetic planting) or, by the use of chemicals, imagine you can override them. This could suggest some important insights on the structure-agency relationship, as well as its ecological context. In Chapter 7, weed killer will supply a useful metaphor!

Although the 'environment' wherein individual actors thrive or perish can be seen purely in terms of the internal workings of capitalist economy, such an institutional level of analysis will come up with totally nonsensical conclusions if it neglects to ask whether capitalism, both in general, and as embodied in its specific developmental 'paths', is viable in relationship to the *physical* environment, i.e. nature. From this

standpoint, we can for example easily refute Darwin's spin on the genocide of aboriginal peoples in the following way. Aboriginal society was
'fit' because it fulfilled the primary evolutionary criterion, namely to
operate in harmony with nature, whereas colonialism set human development at odds with nature and on a course leading to extinction: the
aboriginal peoples were 'unfit' only by the yardstick of a system which
is itself, in a larger sense unfit. Since much evolutionary theory concerns large-scale extinctions, if we take evolution at its word there
should be no problem in speculating about the extinction of capitalism
as a whole. But this deduction would be anathema to mainstream institutional theories: they are comfortable only with firms, clusters and
global value chains, oblivious of the fact that the evolution of such
things cannot go beyond the parameters of the mode of production of
which they are merely an expression, and whose own development is
beginning to be overwhelmed by entropy.

Of course, if capitalism continued on its destructive course we could
argue that it would become extinct because the energy conditions (and
carrying capacity for waste) would be exhausted. Such views are indeed
current within radical environmentalism (though usually speaking of
'industrial society' rather than capitalism). But the point about the Left
perspective is to say that we can exercise agency to overthrow the mode
of production *before* it destroys the conditions of human existence.
So long as the entropy condition is fulfilled, we can envisage futures
where we are fully liberated from the stultifying reading of evolution
which justifies existing injustices merely because they exist. Pursuing
the 'gardening' metaphor, where capitalism has gone wrong is precisely
in expunging diversity, narrowing down the vocabulary for future
development, and applying herbicides indiscriminately to exterminate
anything not perceived as fitting the dominant paradigm. A similar
form of gardening applied to institutions (and, given the dominant
mindset, it is likely to be similar) would likewise expunge any readiness
to accept the spontaneity of true evolution. And it would not be fanci-
ful to suggest that this has a wider relevance, for example to one of our
central task in this enquiry, an understanding of the 'war on terror'.

A Largely Phoney 'Empowerment' of Workers

In seeking to limit its entropy, the mode of production is on the look-
out for a free lunch, and institutional self-organisation is the nearest
thing to supplying this, because capacity seems to create something out

of nothing. Managerial energy is conserved. Theoretically, we could even posit a unified approach to energy-conservation where we would address 'effort', a concept derived from thermodynamics but which can be used more broadly to pinpoint areas of loss (or of potential gain) within a canvas of social organisation which unifies formerly-disparate disciplines such as economics, human resources and management of the actual productive process (we have just discussed the limitations of Göran Wall's attempt to create such a model). We will discuss in detail in the next chapter the limitations on capitalism's ability to conserve *physical* energy. But a similar restriction applies to human capacity, as we will now show.

Selectively, capitalism can open up to a perspective where labour is "no longer seen as a cost of production which should be minimized, but as a resource which needs to be augmented."(Kaplinski, 1995, p. 63) Some case studies do indeed show this in action: workers have been known to save a company millions by proposing innovations, and thus making an effective input into management decisions (Psoinos and Smithson, 2002). The *potential* of labour is such that this should in no way surprise us. But when addressing practice, we start confronting the realities of a system geared not just to efficiency in the abstract, but to efficiency of exploitation. This is always what limits it.

In theory, by manipulating dualism, the system could use divide and rule by making the workforce of the core firm relatively more 'empowered' and disalienated, rewarding them with a 'functional' form of flexibility (i.e. multi-tasking); if they were sufficiently scared by the prospect of being cast into the peripheral wilderness (where they would experience the other, more savage definition of flexibility, i.e. being thrown out of work when orders dry up), capitalism might exploit their creativity and initiative, while assured that empowerment would not spin off in dangerous directions. That is more or less the idea behind the management systems, but when we look at the real world, we would have to question whether capitalism is really able to make this work. Empowering workers is fraught with risks. Although it may be true that capitalism would like to 'augment' labour in this way, in the absence of a Freirean approach to education – which by definition capitalism cannot employ because Freire's whole approach is to liberate you from the limitation of futures which are merely a carbon copy of the present (Freire, 1972)! – the attempts at training and capacity-building tend to fall flat. Significantly, the optimistic appraisal of workers' decision-making input which we have just quoted was based on interviews with bosses; (Psoinos and Smithson, 2002) in a different study where *workers* were interviewed, what comes across is mainly the oppressive aspects, for example the compulsory devolution of additional responsibilities (Lewchuk and Stewart, 2001). And the methods used to keep workers on their toes are in reality so oppressive as to undermine even a highly constrained empowerment. In earlier work, I highlighted the significance of a remarkable incident in Canada in January 1995 when an unconfirmed rumour of job offers by General Motors caused 15,000 job-seekers to converge and wait anxiously outside the factory overnight in temperatures of minus 20° C (Biel, 2000, p. 171).[8] This looks like a spontaneous emergent process. But more recent research reveals that the rumour was started deliberately by General Motors bosses; (Butz and Leslie, 2001) there was never any intention of offering jobs, but the sight of 15,000 freezing job-seekers was an effective deterrent to prevent those *inside* from organising. So much does capital fear organised labour that its draconian control mechanisms surely inhibit even any meaningful *exploitative* access to capacity. The claim to liberation (which Boltanski and Chiapello rightly see as a major selling point for neo-liberalism (Boltanski and Chiapello, 1999) stands revealed as another form of servitude!

With respect to workers, therefore, nothing could safely be left to self-evolve. Indeed, arguably things have got worse, not better, under the systemic turn. Earlier forms of imperialism had effective structural ways of co-opting workers' organisation, such as the tripartite bargaining promoted by the ILO after World War I or the corporatist elements in Keynesianism. The equivalent in IR terms was the East-West power balance, wherein the Soviet bloc, again highly bureaucratised, helped stabilise the system. But then neo-liberalism came along, deciding that, rather than submitting to the constraints of structure, it wanted undivided and unfettered power over the institution-world, leaving no institution-space whatever for workers as a social category. This is in fact the key contradiction of capitalism over the past 30 years: it explores emergence, yet insists on a profound unipolarity, an unfettered power which brooks no rival. Specifically, no networked form of labour movement was permitted to 'emerge' to replace the bureaucratic form which was the image of modernism. In the long term, one of the

---

[8] c.f. *The Independent*, January 12 1995

current order's key weaknesses may be its inability to generate a co-optable institutional form for labour.

In a sense, the main instrument of tyranny is something which will be of fundamental importance in our enquiry: security. There is one way we can define security where it describes things precious for working people like job security, access to pensions and healthcare, opportunities for one's children etc. But under capitalism, livelihoods will never receive this degree of structure or predictability. By increasing security in its own accumulation circuits, capital reciprocally reduces it in the lives of the working population. This is functional, but if livelihoods get too bad, people might rebel. So it is not enough for the dominant definition of security to mean stable accumulation: it must increasingly also have a militaristic and repressive definition, which speaks volumes about the system's real willingness to tolerate self-organisation.

But if creativity and networking are largely phoney with respect to the workforce, capitalism can still unfold these things within the sphere it more closely controls. What we do find is an extraordinary development of horizontal networking, but in a form which arguably strengthens the vertical division. As we saw at the beginning of this chapter, peer-to-peer (P2P) networking is the way forward, and although there is a certain dynamic in this direction, it is mainly encouraged *within* the core/apex rather than at any other level in the system. Thus, Pyka shows how corporations are suddenly happy to abandon the introspective guarding of secrets which once characterised the discrete and competitive firm: their researchers now routinely network with their 'rivals' (Pyka, 1999). By consolidating this elite community of interest, you could simultaneously explore the benefits of the systemic turn, and prevent them 'leaking' too much. It looks very different from the furiously competitive relations conventionally expected from imperialism, but if we think about it, maybe it re-establishes the *essentials* of imperialism by casting away the old shibboleths.

Such 'networks from the top' can bring important benefits, but the problem is that if the only boundaries to be broken down were horizontal ones, this might actually strengthen top-downism and thus outweigh any possible gains from the standpoint of emergence. A complex system would require *diffusion* of innovation, and if the empowerment of workers is largely phoney, where can this input come from?

The answer is to explore the capacity of *firms*. This would be a relationship between different parts of capitalism, so it would be safer.

What then is the basis for such a diffusion of innovation at the firm level?

Knowledge as a Basis for Selective Diffusion

In Chapter 7 we will further explore the relationship between the ideas of Karl and Michael Polanyi, but the point we wish to explore here is that, ignoring Karl Polanyi's correct point that the self-regulating market it incompatible with natural human self-organisation, the ruling order is relatively comfortable with Michael Polanyi's discussion of self-organisation on a basis of knowledge. By confining discussion to the level of firms, innovation will be safely contained within the orbit of capitalist production relations. What concretely interests the management literature is Michael Polanyi's categorisation of knowledge into two forms: 'codified' – the aspect which can easily be transferred and appropriated – and 'tacit', the less tangible ability to solve new problems ... which crucially tends to be embedded within networks. It is this important distinction which the current form of capitalism seeks to 'tame' and, within a limited framework, encourage to evolve. Tacit knowledge, which is creative, is precisely the faculty which the Taylorist and modernist approaches never understood, and therefore stifled.

At first sight, we might think that globalisation increases the scope of the codified form; as the new management literature recognises, this is the form which is associated with increasing modularisation, separability and specialisation (Malerba and Orsenigo, 2000, p. 289). But in a sense, this only highlights the irreducible importance of the tacit form. The latter is not susceptible to being codified; (Isaksen, 2001) it is less transferrable beyond the context in which it is immediately embedded, a fact which improves its internal circulation, but impedes external accessibility (Keeble and Wilkinson, 1998). This is precisely why it is embedded in networks, a fact which the ruling order cannot circumvent, but must instead embrace.

It is clear that such an understanding opens new possibilities for a decentralised system with a higher degree of emergence, but then, how can this be controlled? The issue is not straightforward. While both forms of knowledge create value which capitalism could appropriate, both also have subversive potential. The tacit (creative) form is simultaneously less specific (in the sense that it represents not a response to a particular problem but a generalised ability to solve any problem), and also more specific, because it implies a social context, drawing upon faculties in a local knowledge community which cannot simply be scattered indiscriminately over the globe; interestingly, on the other hand, the codified form could also have a subversive aspect as in the case of Open Source Free Software, which represents a reconnection with the traditional approach of knowledge as a common-pool resource.

Either form of knowledge may therefore go in two directions, either radically challenging the current order, or subservient to it. It depends under whose auspices they develop. What kind of 'information about the future' (Roederer, 2003, p. 3) do we espouse, a future within or beyond capitalism? In some of the debate about knowledge we might think of a ladder, proceeding from data at the bottom, through information, then knowledge, and finally to wisdom; it is wisdom which looks to the future (Bellinger et al., 2004). So what the ruling order needs to do is to control the definitions of future. If the future can *only* be some variant of capitalism, then the latter can theoretically be free to explore emergence, become an open-ended system and embrace radically unexpected forms. Such a hegemonic definition of 'future' is just what the 'end of history' discourse, and its embodiment in globalisation, sought to impose.

The North-South Issue within the New Management Models

How are we to understand the new management notions in the context of the established North-South divide? The model of subcontracting to small enterprises and rationing security/enslavement could work perfectly well through co-location within the core, as in the Japanese Toyota model, and indeed one could ask whether the core states, in aggressively developing their own internal form of super-exploited economic actors (vulnerable labour, and the struggling small firms who employ it) are trying to stop the South exploiting their own competitive advantage; growing South-North labour migration may also fall into this pattern by increasing the exploitable 'periphery within the core'. At best, it may seem, the Southern 'threat', if it did not exist, would need to be invented as an excuse to browbeat core workers by threatening to outsource their jobs to Mexico or Asia.

Despite this, I will argue that the South has a qualitative, and perhaps increasing, role within the systemic phase.

From the beginnings of imperialism more than a century ago – we know this because Hobson explicitly posited it in a brilliant and far-sighted passage (Hobson, 1902) – the North faced the problem that, in order to exploit cheap labour in the South, it must transfer some industrial functions there, *partially de-industrialising itself in the process.* How could one stop this slipping out of control? Of course, an important part of the answer is political and military. This is actually the aspect Hobson concentrated on, by introducing the notion of a Federation of the Western States, which has since materialised in the shape of the Marshall Plan, NATO, OECD, G7 etc. Still, this would not be enough if there was not also a separate regulating mechanism within the *productive* sphere (to rely on only one mechanism would be risky). After World War II, this was typically achieved by the import substitution model, where supposedly local industries in the 'developing' South were often actually subsidiaries of transnational corporations. The South was kept happy by product cycle theory, which promised that the core would eventually divest itself of *complete* industries, and thus allow developing countries a foothold on the developmental ladder.

Such an assumption was critiqued in the late '70s by the famous 'new international division of labour' (NIDL) thesis of Fröbel, Heinrichs and Kreye. That important critique made the point that the division of labour has, since the early days of industrial capitalism, pushed in the direction of the *fragmentation* of productive processes, rather than maintaining their unity. Such an approach could easily be internationalised, as core capitalism de-located the less strategic *parts* of a productive process, in pursuit of the cheapest labour available to execute each of them (Frobel, Heinrichs and Kreye, 1980). Other studies based on '70s data confirmed this (Clairmonte and Cavanagh, 1981).

The problem is that the highly centralised control of this system by TNCs, characteristic of the postwar regime of accumulation, inhibited future development. It needed to be relaxed ... but what would it be replaced by?

Some aspects of the NIDL could easily be salvaged and incorporated into a new setup. The basic thesis of a fragmentation of the productive process is fully compatible with an emergent, rather than 'directed', division of labour; indeed, it would arguably flourish *better* under the latter. This is to a large extent what actually does happen in value chains.

But there is one crucial area of weakness in the NIDL theory: the assumption that the only thing which interests capital is cheap labour. This is all the more surprising in that the early 19th century pioneer of the 'scientific' division of labour Charles Babbage, frequently cited in the Fröbel book as evidence for the fragmentation of the productive process, is very clear that the changing division of labour results from advances in *knowledge* (Babbage, 1832, p. 8). As we have just seen, any system which aspires to be dynamic and evolutionary would need to maximise the knowledge embedded within it, and, in an important sense, this means *diffused* within it.

Would it be sufficient merely to diffuse innovation within the core of the global system, and keep it away from the periphery? This is the big question. Undoubtedly there are tendencies for diffusion to be limited in this way, but there are important reasons why it cannot be the unique mode of conduct. To explain this, let's introduce a variant of our earlier hypothesis. Employing the concept of the negation of the negation, we suggested that the 'old' features of human interaction (networking, reciprocity) are also the most advanced, the ones which harbour true dynamism. We can now extend this as follows: if the truly creative faculties are precisely those which are not intrinsically capitalist, then the 'complete' capitalist regions of the world might actually be at a disadvantage. The most creative region may be the periphery (one is reminded of the notion in the permaculture system of land management that the areas with most potential and energy are on the margins: for example the *lisière*, the forest margins). This pushes into an unexpected direction our interpretation of Lenin's idea that imperialism drags the capitalists towards a new order.

Such a perspective is quite challenging to accepted notions. Classic dependency theory indeed highlighted the issue of 'completeness': the global core was relatively 'complete' in its capitalism, i.e. more simple, whereas the periphery had complex social formations characterised by the articulation of elements of different modes of production under the auspices of a dominant mode (capitalism). Already foreshadowed in Baran's theory, (Baran, 1973) and later in the work of Amin, this concept not only marked an important step in the development of a non-Eurocentric Marxism, but implicitly also opened up the notion of institutional complexity as a key category of analysis. But the usual dependency interpretation of this important finding tended to be mechanical and modernist: *completeness (simplicity) was seen as a source of strength, and complexity a source of weakness.* The systems perspective would always suspect that this is wrong, and that the true relationship is the opposite. In the period when dependency theory originated, this limitation was not so obvious, but one can validly critique the dependency literature for not grasping the issue of ecological limits – at a time when it was already well understood by Malcolm Caldwell, for example (Caldwell, n.d. [1970]) – which partly *forced* the system to investigate the free lunch offer offered by capacity. Interestingly, even the adaptation of dependency concepts to the Asian context by Kim Young-ho sticks anachronistically to the modernist view of tradition as something which *inhibits* 'spreading', (Kim, 1987) rather than looking for aspects (such as those addressed by Michael Polanyi) which might promote it.

In the reality of dynamic Asian capitalism is revealed a capacity – as for example in Lam and Lee's research (Lam and Lee, 1992) – to access past/future principles of reciprocity more intensively than might be possible in the more 'purely' capitalist core. In a cluster or network, a handshake is more important than a contract, informal tacit knowledge indicates who can do which task reliably, and perhaps most importantly, relations are not zero-sum: the firm which loses a tendering process may still win because the successful bidder will then subcontract to it, a favour which it may be in a position to return later. But while the modes of interaction are not capitalist, the actors are, so in this way, it may be possible to ring-fence the creativity within capitalist parameters. It is this relationship which is the real basis of the dynamism created by globalisation. To affirm this is not to espouse crude notions about 'Confucian' societies or Asian exceptionalism, but simply the dialectical view of the negation of the negation: the greater creativity is found in the more complex regions where past/future faculties can more easily emerge. As research suggests, closed and self-referential networks are limited in their capacity for innovation, or the generation of radical new ideas, (Keeble and Wilkinson, 1998) which is exactly what we would expect from cybernetics or evolutionary theory. At a certain point, global capitalism may be forced to tap the hidden reservoir of capacity in order to overcome the limitations of the relative stagnancy of the historic core. One of the ways capitalism is 'dragged' towards a new social order is by having to think outside its own narrow frame of reference.

But the problem for the core is of course to control all this. This should be the function of governance. Some research indicates that the lead firm selects participants and builds the network's culture (Palpacuer and Parisotto, 1998). Here, 'selecting' again suggests a manipulated Darwinism, a kind of 'gardening' whereby institutions conducive to capital accumulation could be given a leg up the evolutionary ladder, and others switched off. But even more important perhaps is the sense that culture signifies the 'environment' within which the actors are permitted to evolve. Gereffi speaks of rents arising from an advantage within the chain, which include not only the more obvious things (technology, brand identity), but also *an understanding of the structure itself* (Gereffi, 2001). This suggests a particular, institutional form of knowledge. Drawing upon Sen's (1981) concept of entitlements, this knowledge may be seen as an entitlement to draw benefit from the chain.

But this benefit is ultimately fragile. Most fundamentally, this is because of thermodynamics: if the *physical* energy source dries up, so will globalisation. We will introduce this argument in detail in the next chapter. However the entropy of capitalism is measured not just in external limits, but in the inability of its social and institutional system, firstly to develop in such a way that it doesn't *have to* keep depleting the physical environment, secondly to find solutions to the environmental problem once it begins to materialise. In this sense, the institutional dimension of the limits may be primary. A key expression of this is the inherent difficulty of simultaneously unleashing and containing emergence. Although it might be easier to control and channel the initiative of *firms* (clusters, etc.) than of labour (because the former is an internal relationship between different parts of capital), the issue remains that the more one unleashes genuine spontaneous order, the more control is needed to channel the emergence in acceptable directions. And because the system is complex, the governance system must mirror this complexity … which is possible, but only up to a point.

The Notion of 'Embedding' and Its Contradictions

The link with tacit knowledge is that the pre/post-capitalist faculties which the system needs to access are embedded locally. Unsurprisingly, mainstream industrial governance literature increasingly draws upon not just institutional theory, but geography and cultural studies: embedding is a notion which requires all these dimensions if it is to be considered in a unified way.

Dependency theory was always aware that, in order to develop, capitalism must play around with the possibility of 'spreading', (Dos Santos, 1970) so if, as we have argued, development means an ability to adapt via the discovery of new institutional forms, the question arises:

what is the relationship between spreading and embedding? Simplistically, one might assume, as for example Felker appears to argue, (Felker, 2003) that the recognition of embedding would herald the era of a non-dependent form of spreading, in which case of the dependency dilemma would be at an end. But this deduction is incorrect. To understand why, let's consider how embedding works concretely.

Spreading in the sense addressed by Dos Santos is actually a *manifestation* of dependency, rather than its opposite, and it is plausible to assume that the same could be said about embedding. Nevertheless, the two situations are not identical because the system has developed in a new way, for which I will propose the term 'complex dependency'. Here, governance is embodied or instituted within structures (e.g. networks). The core still wants to *extract* something, which in the last analysis is still the thing Marx talked about, surplus value. But the advantage of the systems perspective is to open up less conventional ways of understanding the mechanisms or flows which realise its extraction. We are now dealing in categories like order and risk. The contradiction is that risk in the creative sense is good because emergence always has an edgy dimension, and there must be innovation or the system ceases to develop and dies. But in the capital-reproduction sense there is a need for predictability, expressed particularly in the successful orchestration of many outsourced processes. The exported risk would be absorbed by small enterprises and their labour-force, which can be cast adrift at will, or more fundamentally the unemployed and the household which constitute the true social sink. Profit (the positive transfer, or 'flow') is driven up the chain at the same time as risk is pushed down it (the lower the level, the more insecurity faced by the workforce), and the two processes look as though they may be reciprocal.

This would help to establish order in the sense of *control*, but is not completely in harmony with order expressed as *predictability*. Today's management employs concepts like Total Quality and Just in Time (TQ and JIT), which seek to establish some relationship between these two aspects of order, being simultaneously principles for smoothly reproducing capital (for the benefit of the core) and instruments of control, of enforcement. It is precisely the process of policing TQ and JIT standards which encourages 'quasi-hierarchical' forms of governance (Humphrey and Schmitz, 2002). As Kaplinski shows, small firms, more specifically in less-developed parts of the South, find it hard to meet time and quality criteria (Kaplinski, 1995). This keeps

them subordinate because it reduces autonomy, but the problem is that
the standards must nevertheless be made to work somehow, otherwise
capital could not reproduce. A compromise is therefore needed. Not
surprisingly, it is a hierarchical compromise, but of a special type.
Instead of risk and uncertainty increasing incrementally at each step
down the chain – as in a simple hierarchical model – the top-tier supplier tends to be stabilised to a disproportionate degree; in fact the core
firm may itself operate at a higher level of risk than its top-tier supplier,
in a sense pulling upwards (rather than exporting down) some of the
risk: research suggests the top-tier supplier's rate of profit to be more
stable than that of the core firm (Okamuro, 2001). The most successful
networks are therefore "characterized by an *evolving tiered structure* in
which a first-tier of selected, stable partners are surrounded by a more
mobile row of second-tier suppliers (Palpacuer and Parisotto, 1998)."
A United Nations Industrial Development Organisation report confirms the preferred strategy of maintaining long-term relations with a
supplier who meets the required standards.[9] By this means the lead
firm can presumably free itself to concentrate on the entitlements it
derives from its understanding of the overall structure or culture.

This shows concretely how control can be embodied within a network while at the same time accessing the benefits of *relaxed* control so
as to permit emergence. But this occurs at the price of an increase in
embedding, which might create tendencies toward autonomy. How
could these be minimised?

One solution might be to accept that some slippage is needed to
access tacit knowledge, but to compensate for this by aggressively
siphoning *codified* knowledge into the core. This is certainly happening
with the Trade Related Intellectual Property Rights (TRIPS) regime of
the WTO, and since this development occurred at the same time as an
increase of embedding, we can reasonably regard them as reciprocal
motions, the gain of control in one area balancing the potential loss in
the other. It can also be noted that the enhanced security of the 'local
poles' is not totally a sacrifice by the core, since security under capitalism is double edged, as we have just seen in the General Motors case
where security of employment is equivalent to virtual slavery. In the
context of global value chains, the secure components would lose the

---

[9] United Nations Industrial Development Organisation (Unido), *Inserting Local
Industries into Global Value Chains and Global Production Networks: Opportunities and
Challenges for Upgrading*, Vienna: UNIDO, (2004) p. 16

'freedom' which comes with lack of attachment, with the latitude to 'unplug' oneself or use flexibility to one's advantage. Embedding would here signify the modern equivalent of a 'tied cottage' or company town!

But if knowledge and in particular innovation were drawn too much into the core, the benefit of a decentralised system disappears. Consequently, research suggests a tendency for the practice of displacement to the periphery and accommodation with the top-tier supplier to be extended into the sphere of innovation too. This may involve, for example the co-location not just of production but also of R&D; (Felker, 2003) or even the deliberate transfer of technological capacity (Ernst and Kim, 2002). Therefore, while the global production system is indeed fragmented, it is fragmented into *large* bits, shifted to selected areas of the South, *but co-located there around a pole* which is in effect the equivalent of the stabilised top-tier supplier. This has been the focus of much of the organisational innovation of the last few years. The phrase "concentration of dispersion" sums this up in a useful way (Ernst and Kim, 2002, p. 1420). Although this development looks at first sight risky for the core, it might be worth the risk to experiment innovative institutional structures to convey control. Brazil was a laboratory for the experimentation of new methods of 'modular' production, conducted under the auspices of TNCs, (Tacsir, 2005) which look very like an attempt to capture the clustering phenomenon under the core's auspices.

Nevertheless, there is no denying that embedding poses challenges to the core's power. From a systems perspective, dependency is always in some sense *mutual*, and indeed any core system is always more dependent on its periphery (which fuels it) than the periphery on it (humanity depends on the ecosystem, accumulation in the North depends on the South)! Against this background, the regulatory mechanisms which balance conflicting demands (the benefits of 'enclosing' initiative within the core, versus the benefits of diffusing it etc.) are above all arenas of struggle: the regulatory (balancing) faculty can never be separated from agency. Through negotiation, the periphery might unfold its own agency to establish a definition of embeddedness closer to their interests.

At the simplest level, public policy in the South might emulate the core's pump-priming of 'self-augmenting' clustering processes, by encouraging a clustering which induces more clustering (Lecler, 2002). But in the South, the impetus to any self-augmenting industrial development would not be merely endogenous, but also linked to foreign

direct investment (FDI) ... or in the terminology of imperialism theory, the export of capital. Public policy could therefore seek to embed
this. But then another problem arises. Capital has two aspects, a productive form and a merely predatory form. The latter, which shuns
embeddedness, is sometimes called 'footloose'. You may find a situation
where the Southern states desperately seeks to 'facilitate' embedding,
only to wind up facilitating a footloose, purely predatory capital instead;
this picture seems to come across in interesting research in Botswana,
for example (Good and Hughes, 2002). On the other hand, because
embedding encompasses aspects of culture and the local state, as well
as the issues of tacit knowledge and networks, this yields a complex
local environment in which the spreading facet of capitalism may arguably, in favourable situations, be 'entrapped'. Some studies of the
Chinese case could be read in this light (Sit and Liu, 2000).

On balance, global capitalism can still 'ride' the embedding phenomenon. But if the economic control mechanisms were watertight we
wouldn't need imperialism theory: core capitalism could control the
global system without needing politics and the military! This is certainly not the case; and it may not be accidental that militarism and
repression are growing at precisely the same time as the complex governance system begins to reveal its shortcomings.

The industrial management system we have just described is the
most successful part of capitalist governance. As such, it has acquired a
paradigmatic role for wider issues of social organisation. Increasingly,
it invades a public sphere, which in the old governance model was supposed to be external to (and benevolent towards) the realm of profit.
All areas of government, education, health etc. etc. have now become
arenas of accumulation, together with the repressive function: prisons,
the military. This represents a generalisation of the systemic turn, but
also a dilution of it. Whereas in its most authentic form the systemic
turn was a genuine attempt to unleash (exploitative) emergence, in its
degenerate form (characterised by a general augmentation of surveillance and repression and an increasingly invasive penetration by predatory finance capital of all spheres of life), real emergence has largely
disappeared. Amid this wreckage, industrial governance for the
moment retains its force as a real (albeit highly contradictory) tool of
emergent exploitative order. It does nevertheless experience its own
particular entropy. In its general expression this has two main features which are shared by all forms of capitalist governance. Firstly,
there is the drying-up of physical energy: however sophisticated the

institutional solutions, they will collapse like a house of cards once it ceases to be possible to ship products around the world at effectively zero cost! Secondly, there is a sense in which some definition of 'managerial energy' also moves into deficit: complexity outstrips the ability to channel it, or to put it slightly differently, the managerial energy ploughed into containing emergence outstrips the energy supplied.

These two general issues are manifested concretely in relation to a third contradiction specific to the industrial sphere. Capitalism's path-dependency from the earliest times has marked it as a racist, Eurocentric system. But the development of capitalism as an adaptive system, which seeks to prolong itself and its characteristic relations, is pushing in a direction with real tendencies to subvert this path-dependency: in other words, the only way to save the mode of production may be for it to develop a non-Eurocentric form. I will explore this hypothesis in detail in the last two chapters. I will argue that such a non-Eurocentric form cannot exist as a real thing, both because the physical energy is lacking and because the social contradictions, which Eurocentric capitalism has always exported to its periphery, would have nowhere to go. But this in no way diminishes the practical significance of embeddedness, because the coming phase will increasingly be characterised by a savage attempt of the historic core to resist its implications for a redistribution of power.

The Political Equivalent of Network Capitalism and Its Limitations

For the moment, the centre controls the Southern economies by controlling their politics. But this sphere too has sought to access some of the innovations of the systemic turn, a development which supplies the final piece in the jigsaw we are describing in this chapter.

We have said that a key feature of capitalist adaptation over the past 30 years was to co-opt the faculties of self-organising systems into its own modes of governance and intermediate-range structures. If we consider the special form this takes in politics, it immediately suggests the issues addressed by Gramsci. More specifically, the notion of civil society, which used to belong in radical theories, has been co-opted in a big way by the dominant discourse, to a point where it could become effectively the political equivalent of network capitalism. But there remains the issue that an emergent civil society would have to be tightly controlled, which in turn suggests that the dominant system keeps a repressive option up its sleeve. Against this background, the repressive shift around the turn of the millennium (to be analysed more fully in Chapter 5) may suggest a response to a tame civil society paradigm which somehow 'failed', in other words a situation where it was no longer possible to control society through indirect means. This is what we need to understand.

In imagining the organising principle which represents the political equivalent of network capitalism, it will first be useful to refer to a concept whose significance was signalled in research by William Robinson: the notion of 'polyarchy' (Robinson, 1996). The term arose within a school of '70s United States development sociology. It emphasised a kind of subordinate pluralism (more primitive than that enjoyed in the industrial world, but supposedly good enough for the more primitive South): by manipulating 'civil society', the North could rule much more effectively than through military dictatorships (the typical form during the heyday of the Cold War). Interpreting this theory in a systemic sense, it seems to imply a self-engineered form of subordinate political order which would be more effective (and consume less institutional energy) than one imposed from the top.

Robinson's weakness in *interpreting* polyarchy lies in a failure not only to appreciate the systemic dimensions, but also, more surprisingly to situate it within the wider context of US imperialism. Imperialism imparted a certain path-dependency to capitalist development which even the extraordinary experimentation of the systemic turn could not really shake. I would particularly emphasise the Corollary to the Monroe Doctrine adopted by US president Theodore Roosevelt in 1904, which has in a sense hovered over the whole of international history ever since (Biel, 2004). Roosevelt here replaces formal colonialism with a new approach, allowing the South independent states, but only to the extent that those states fulfil what the USA defines as being their duties: "If a nation shows that it knows how to act with reasonable efficiency and decency in social and political matters, if it keeps order and pays its obligations, it need fear no interference from the United States. Chronic wrongdoing, or an impotence which results in a general loosening of the ties of civilised society, may in America, as elsewhere, ultimately require intervention by some civilised nation…"(Roosevelt, 1904) This clearly foreshadows the twin categories which have crystallised within the new, 21st century discourse: 'failed states' which are too weak to fulfil their 'obligations', and 'rogue states' which are too sneaky to do so. In response, the Corollary assumed what it called an "international police power". Although originally applied to Latin America, the Doctrine had, by the time of early-20th century imperialism, become "world doctrine" (Queuille, 1969).

The Roosevelt Corollary thus established a framework within which political development of the subordinate entities was considered acceptable, and this, *up to a point*, could make dominance more concealed and indirect than under colonialism. To present police power as a power of last resort, employed in exceptional circumstances when a country seriously steps out of line, creates the illusion that when it is *not* exercised you are not being dominated, thereby hiding the reality of another kind of power which exists *endemically* as a 'background hum', within the networks (c.f. Foucault) and as a self-censoring of behaviour, an internalisation of dominant norms. The old dictatorships made it difficult to develop the full potential of such indirect control; under the Brazilian dictatorship, for example, civil society could only grow in opposition to the ruling order, (Landim, 1993) which had no basis for dialogue with, or co-optation of it. Pluralism on the other hand facilitates diffuse power. The historical background of polyarchy is therefore that it rose as the top-down Cold War dictatorships waned; effectively serving to hijack the energies unleashed by pro-democracy movements, and convert them into institutional superstructures for a new capitalist regime of accumulation. This in turn suggests a link with the notion of regulation: pluralism provides an arena for a kind of 'balance of power' where civil society acts as counterweight to the state, weakening the latter's potential as a tool of progressive nationalism. In this context, seemingly innocent notions such as participation and decentralisation acquire a sinister double meaning. And it is easy to see why the Roosevelt Corollary could be re-born in the era of neo-liberalism: a failed state can be a failed *enabling* state.

Here we have a beautiful example of systemic power … but also a very limited one. While the new paradigm works with complexity to some extent, entropy begins to manifest itself where complexity is too much for the innovatory modes of governance to handle. And then a hideous spectre materialises before capitalism: emergence cannot simply be switched off again, and if it can no longer be contained within pro-systemic forms, it will tend to manifest itself in contestatory ones. We will address this issue in detail in the final chapter, but a few conceptual issues should be introduced at this point.

Dissenting Networks and Why the Dominant Order Fears Them

'Polyarchy' is just one class of a problem which confronts a ruling system once it ventures beyond its comfort zone of industrial organisation and begins to experiment with the benefits of controlling society in a non-centralised and non-top down way.

In many respects, the key issue in the governance of complexity is the relationship between formal and informal sectors. In the real world, it has been observed that relations between the two sorts of system (for example systems of land-tenure (Durand-Lasserve and Mattingly, 2005)) tend to establish a modus vivendi of co-existence. Such an arrangement is an example of emergent spontaneous order in the sense that it happens by itself, and this would be good news for the dominant system: assuming it did not *itself* have to expend the energy on designing and maintaining control systems, it could just sit back and reap the benefits. This is the whole point of emergent governance, but although fine in theory it is not so easy in practice. The 'ideal type' of a subservient pluralistic system does not exist in reality, and many relationships which appear safe for a while may suddenly reveal subversive potential.

In order for capitalism to grab the value generated by informality (the great discovery of De Soto and postmodernism), the parallel sector must be given official recognition; but then, the more formalised it becomes the more it loses what makes it special. In the normal mode of operation, this problem can be regulated by exercising a repressive power over the informal sector, *just enough* for its clandestinity to keep it vulnerable, but not too much! A very similar argument can be made about immigration: the more vital immigration becomes to an economy, the more it must be repressed in order to ensure that it remains clandestine, therefore insecure and easily exploitable (Biel, 2003). This kind of regulation is susceptible of control by the global hegemon, which is exactly the point of the World Bank's interest in migrants, popular knowledge systems etc. But it is not an easy balance to maintain. The obvious solution is for the global hegemon to make some pact with the state *at a local level*, in order to constrain emergence within acceptable boundaries. But the informal structures will not necessarily take this lying down. If we adopt such a frame of reference, we can make interesting sense of some of the concrete research which has been done on formal-informal relations, for example John Cross' work on street vendors in Mexico: (Cross, 1998) complex structures (institutions) emerge both within the informal sector itself, and in its relations with the formal, enabling the informal sphere to make autonomous use of structures which are 'supposed' to co-opt it.

Emphasis on networks should not be seen as an alternative to class analysis, but the point is that networks contribute decisively to class mobilisation (hence the importance of neighbourhoods as a locus of interaction) (Stone, 1998). For this reason, they possess a latent radical potential, and circumstances could be envisaged where the mechanism of compromise-negotiation between local formal and informal structures begins to evade the control of the global centre. The notion of sovereignty is interesting in this context. If we define an attribute of sovereignty as something like "the capacity to arrive at autonomous compromises between grassroots and official (informal and formal) sectors, outside the control of the global hegemon," then the attack on the sovereignty of the Southern state in the current discourse immediately becomes easier to understand.

At the same time, networks unfold also in a non-state centric dimension. The most striking expression of this is the infosphere. Open Source Free Software draws upon a community which in this case is intrinsically global, within which development and creativity occurs, as Barma points out, "through a distribution, rather than a division, of labour", and is closely associated with "production close to use" (Barma, 2003). This looks very much like part of a blueprint for a new (old) social order. With respect to knowledge, the open/closed dichotomy can be seen in two different ways. From one angle, the return to specificity and 'boundedness' is a forward-looking (or, backward-looking to natural methods) riposte to globalised homogenisation. From another, closedness signifies a jealous guarding of the knowledge which guarantees power, and in this sense it is openness (as in open-source software) which is the more progressive. Both the openness and rootedness of knowledge therefore have potentially radical implications. Consistent with our thesis that capitalism has unleashed forces which will transcend it, these forces are not just actors (or agents) but *modes of interaction*. This is well expressed by Bauwens: "Within corporations P2P [peer-to-peer] processes can only partially thrive, because they have to protect the profit motive, but outside the corporation, this limit can be overcome, and those processes of 'production going outside the boundaries of the corporations' are increasingly showing that the profit imperative, and the private appropriation of the social-cooperative processes, is becoming counter-productive." (Bauwens, 2007) Some of the theories about emergence can be tested experimentally, the blogo-sphere and Wikipedia being interesting from this point of view. What is striking is the degree of accuracy of something which is not 'policed' in a conventional sense: an experiment of deliberately introducing errors into Wikipedia found that they were corrected within three hours.[10] Research suggests that under the right conditions crowds come up with answers that are at least as good as that of the most accurate member of the group; the main condition being that they be diverse in the sense of harbouring a great variety of kinds of knowledge (Aufderheide, 2007).

We will discuss in more detail later the key role of co-operation and reciprocity for future human social organisation. The point to empha-sise here is that on the one hand capitalism has been forced to open up these natural human modes of knowledge production in order to drive innovation; but on the other hand it finds these things terribly fright-ening. This line of argument adds a new dimension, which is neverthe-less fully consistent with the general argument of Marxism and of Lenin's imperialism theory, that the forces demonstrating the obsolete-ness of capitalism are produced by the development of capitalism itself. A battle then ensues when capitalism begins to emerge as the main thing holding back the developmental potential which it has itself unleashed. Thus, in the field of infosphere security, paradoxical though it seems, openness is actually more secure than closedness. By preserv-ing the secrecy of their code, the US software giants allow US secret services backdoor access to police information, which would be easily detectable in open-source code (Petreley, 2000). The internet is run by a body (Icann) under US state control, with the power, for example, to target a 'rogue state' by turning off its domain name; but this has pro-duced its opposite, an Open Root Server Network (ORSN) which mir-rors the internet, enabling it to continue if the US attempts to shut it down.[11] The centralism which vainly tries to control the system is chal-lenged by principles of redundancy emerging within it. This gives us fresh insights on the significance of the turn-of-millennium repressive shift: if network capitalism threatens to turn chaotic, the response is to repress the networks. The Bush clique's 'Rebuilding America's Defenses' report (2000) called for the US to take control over the 'international commons' of space and the infosphere, (Donnelly, 2000, pp. 50–1)

---

[10] This experiment seems to have been conducted a number of times, e.g. http://alex.halavais.net/index.php?p=794
[11] *Wall Street Journal*, January 19 2006

while at the end of 2002, Bush put forward a National Strategy to Secure Cyberspace,[12] envisaging draconian controls on the Web in the name of US national security interests and 'anti-terrorism'. But this course of action undermines the most creative development of capitalism ... and further demonstrates its obsoleteness!

The battle in the infosphere is very interesting for what it expresses about the contradictoriness of capitalism's efforts to access creativity, but of course we must emphasise that the fundamental force for change will be the social movement and its real social networks on the ground. But then, we could ask whether there is a possibility for the virtual and social networks to link up. If the marginalised elements begin to exchange information, something new and troubling might 'emerge' (in the systems-theory sense) from the sphere of unregulated (marginalised) social relations.

It was precisely this concern which began to worry the ruling order in the late 1990s, and this timing is extremely interesting because it is around this period that the repressive shift may have been instigated. It was the Zapatista uprising in Mexico, and its links with anti-globalisation protests, which made right-wing think-tanks sit up and take notice. Particularly influential in this climate of ideas was the publication in 1998 of a report by US military think-tank the RAND Corporation, exactly around the time when the East African embassy bombings were taken as an excuse to begin preparations for what was to become the 'war on terror'. This report identified a dangerous trend whereby "previously isolated groups can communicate, link up, and conduct coordinated joint actions as never before. This in turn is leading to a new mode of conflict – 'netwar'" (Ronfeldt et al., 1998). The report also introduced the notion of NGOs 'swarming', an image which highlights a sense of civil society operating in a chaotic way, making its own order through a process which outsiders can't influence. Although the Zapatista uprising had been launched on January 1 1994 (to coincide with the inauguration of NAFTA), what really made the rulers take notice was its role in stimulating a world-wide movement against globalisation. For example, in 1997 the network People's Global Action, meeting in Chiapas, had proposed a strategy of "co-ordinating decentralised actions" around major international conferences.[13] In an earlier era, life-and-death decisions about the world economy had been

---

[12] http://www.whitehouse.gov/pcipb/cyberspace_strategy.pdf
[13] Peoples' Global Action against 'Free' Trade and the World Trade Organisation, Chiapas, 29 November 1997, on www.hartford-hwp.com/archives/25a/024.html

taken in complete isolation from the real world, and suddenly, this was no longer possible. The dire predictions of the RAND Corporation seemed to be confirmed by mass protests at the Seattle WTO conference in 1999.

Repression is always present within network capitalism, as Foucault's work shows, but there is a key difference between the repression which works *through* networks, as in polyarchy, and that which seeks to shut them down because they are too chaotic. This is the fundamental issue. In the development from the end of the '90s, it began to look as though the latter kind was going to overtake the system, and thus *replace* indirect modes of rule. As I will argue in the final chapter, there are counter-attempts to restore an equilibrium between the two modes. However the repressive momentum, once initiated, will be hard to reverse.

Almost immediately, the system was able to rectify its aim at least to a certain extent. By lumping together the Zapatistas and anti-globalisation and naming them *explicitly* as the enemy, imperialism would have shot itself in the foot by encouraging an alliance between infosphere and the Left, weakening its potential for dividing the contestatory movement, and indeed for channelling the Web into 'safe' forms of information-exchange around commercial and lifestyle interests. This must be the reason why the ruling propaganda suddenly switched to downplaying the Zapatistas and invented Al Qaeda instead. Nevertheless, the underlying significance of this episode remains. As the *Communist Manifesto* so brilliantly observed, capitalism cannot avoid continuously revolutionising itself, and in pursuit of this goal, at some point it found itself obliged to access spheres of creativity which contradict its fundamental nature, and are desperately hard to tame. Networking and information can leak out beyond the safe regions of industrial management and civil society and it is precisely this that the Zapatistas picked up on and sought to emphasise.

The above problem can be considered a form of entropy internal to the institutional sphere, represented by the contradiction between growing complexity and the shrinking power to constrain it within exploitative forms. But this in turn unfolds against a background where inputs of physical energy into the system are no longer dependable. While this constraint confronts capitalism as an *external* limit, it should more accurately be seen as a signal of the physical environment's rejection of the social and institutional contradictions *internal* to capitalism, which have hitherto been exported into it. It is this dimension which we will now address.

CHAPTER FOUR

THE ERA OF FEEDBACK FROM ENTROPY

Information and the Possibility of a Change of Course

Our argument so far has shown that capitalism/imperialism is an adaptive system, but it has always been a high-cost adaptation, where each new phase seems to deplete some new physical resource. Historically, the system does not seem able to evolve into a low input/output mode. It could seem at times successfully to revolutionise itself and inaugurate eras of rapid growth, but only at the expense of an environmental depletion whose effects could merely be hidden, but would blow back later: thus, fossil fuels enabled capitalism to pretend it could abolish entropy by miraculously expanding value out of nothing, but eventually the payback is global warming, the drying-up of energy stocks, and the knock-on effects of both these factors on food. 2006–8 marked a watershed: in rapid succession, information on climate change, peak oil and food shortage became impossible to ignore.

The central question is, how does the system behave once this information is received? Can this at last force it into a previously impossible low-input mode? Our general answer in this chapter will be No, because the existing pattern of behaviour is too ingrained. But as we will see, what is interesting is precisely the detail: leanings in the direction of conservation (triggered for example by rising energy prices) do exist, but are neutralised by other factors; or indeed, 'green' ideas like biofuels are parasitised upon and perverted into tools to prolong the high-consumption regime. What is characteristic is not so much the impinging of *external* limits, but the combination of these with disorder manufactured within the system, which can no longer be dissipated as in the past. Social contradictions, partially buried in an illusory way by 'growth', then begin to rise to the surface and approach their own tipping points. As I argued elsewhere, (Biel, 2006) capitalist regulation has traditionally relied on manoeuvring between social and ecological dimensions, for example by 'funding' large-scale socio-political restructuring through intensified environmental depletion (as with the massive increase of energy-usage following 1945). But the downside is that, once the limits in both spheres begin to coincide, they reinforce each other.

Information that something is seriously wrong will initially be resisted. This explains why the crisis actually appears more sudden than it really is. The comforting assumptions of the past have been embedded in a kind of feedback process because, although at one level the ruling order is 'disinforming' the public, it is hard to do this without at the same time limiting its *own* access to the information needed for realistic decisions. Once a particular 'spin' establishes itself, it acts as a touchstone for the veracity of future information (Edwards and Cromwell, 2006). As recently as 2007 a mechanism of self-censorship was still observed on climate change: scholars who had evidence of the dangers of melting ice censored themselves, apparently for fear of losing funding (Hansen, 2007). Even the US-centred cult of positive thinking, with a turnover of $5.62 billion in 2005, (Ehrenreich, 2007) has been highlighted as a factor reinforcing denial.

Although information cannot be approached transparently, *it is nevertheless received*. But, as I will argue, it is processed in a distorted way, often with the result of intensifying the conduct which is causing the problem. The French term 'fuite en avant' captures this well. Or we can refer to an article in a patriotic American journal, which approvingly cites (as a model for contemporary policy) a classic story by Joseph Conrad: its hero, a ship's captain, saves his ship by steering straight into the heart of the storm, muttering as he does so, "Facing it — always facing it, that's the way to get through."(Kaplan, 2007) This is indeed the system's response ... but it won't lead to saving the ship!

Managing the Social Contradictions of Capitalism through Negative Energy Flows

Our argument throughout this book is that social contradictions are fundamental, and that the ecological crisis results from a battle to keep them at bay at the expense of accelerated environmental depletion. Most fundamentally, these contradictions are inherent to the system itself, have been there since the beginning and are still the same. But we must also acknowledge a path-dependency acquired *along the way*, from which it is difficult to depart. The detailed systemic features of capitalism were not predestined from the beginning, though we can construct their logic ex-post; an example, as we will see, is the world food system, another is the coupling of accumulation to consumerism, a trend which has driven capitalism into a peculiar cul-de-sac of its own making, known as globalisation. These path-dependencies crucially influence how the system behaves. It doesn't have a 'captain' in the strict sense, but it does have acquired reflexes upon which it will fall back in time of crisis.

Let's consider more closely the relationship between inherent and acquired characteristics. Among the fundamental issues of capitalism, two of the key ones are pauperisation (the manufacture of poverty as a concomitant to wealth) and the falling rate of profit. These have been intrinsic since the beginning, in a sense hard-wired into the system's rules. But *the manner of addressing* these issues has generated certain path-dependencies which were not initially predictable. Moreover, as I will now show, the responses to these two key issues have *co-evolved*, in such a manner as to make them now inextricably intertwined.

The rate of profit can be maintained by reducing the cost of living, making it possible to pay lower monetary wages; thus, the argument for repealing the protectionist Corn Laws in 19th century England was that cheap imported food would benefit the general rate of profit (the interest of landowners being therefore sacrificed for the sake of industrial capitalists). At the same time, according to Engel's law (formulated by mid-19th century economist Ernst Engel) the poorer a household the higher proportion of its income goes on food: if only the price of food could be reduced, poverty would seem to be reduced, while also leaving a larger slice of income to buy other goods and thus providing a market for new consumer industries. In this way, the interlinked responses to pauperisation and to the rate of profit issue resulted in a huge effort to drive down the cost of food.

And this in turn comes to be expressed in a more specialised form of path-dependency specific to the agricultural sector itself, which we will now begin to develop as a major focus of this chapter. Agriculture was tipped onto a course of reliance on chemicals, a course which, once embarked upon, is hard to reverse. The dangerous and unsustainable character of this was already clear to Marx. It began with a model of reducing all the conditions for agriculture to three chemical elements, a potentially fatal reductionism of which the model's originator, Justus von Liebig, became aware, and about which he warned in vain (Delwiche, 2006, p. 113). In the 20th century this approach gathered momentum with the introduction of pesticides and herbicides, before being even further intensified since World War II with the Green

Revolution, then with globalisation, the introduction of GMOs etc. If we call this line of development a path-dependency, what we mean is that every time a problem is encountered, it tends to be 'solved' by applying more of the methods which are causing it. It is difficult simply to move the rudder (to pursue the metaphor of the ship's captain) a few notches away from chemicals and towards organics, because the two are fundamentally incompatible: the organic approach builds the soil, the mainstream one depletes it through chemical inputs, which then need to be supplied in increasing quantities to *compensate* for the effects of that depletion. The only response which really makes sense would be a complete change of course, but this departs too much from learned modes of action. It is very difficult to deviate step-by-step from the established course. This interlinks with a social dimension: an alternative agriculture such as traditional no-till agroforestry cannot really develop in a top-down system (this is an issue which even pre-dates capitalism). It would require a high degree of grassroots capacity, innovation and above all *institutional* experimentation (for example, in the direction of popular regimes of resource-management) which are difficult to reconcile with exploiter-class societies. The result is that, for a mixture of reasons, once the radical alternative is closed off, the receipt of signals about impending food crisis will inevitably result in a more intensive application of the approaches causing the problem (for example, the wholesale introduction of GMOs): in other words, steering into the heart of the storm. The historic 'solution' to the base contradictions (falling rate of profit, pauperisation) has become so entwined with the food scenario as to make it difficult to change just *part* of the ensemble, lest the whole unravel.

One of the enduring myths of capitalist development is expressed in what is known as a Kuznets curve, i.e. an inverted 'U': however bad things may be during initial takeoff, it is believed that they will improve at a later, more sophisticated stage. This ties in with the concept of 'high mass consumption' referred to in Rostow's 'stages' theory of development, (Rostow, 1960) and of course with Engel's law. This reasoning was intially applied to poverty and inequality, which is dubious at many levels. Most obviously, poverty is exported to the global South. Even within the core, Townsend's analysis of the postwar decades suggests a picture of buying off certain strata or of expanding the middle range at the expense of the poorest (Townsend, 1979; Cole and Miles, 1984; Ginzberg et al., 1986). A consumer market is indeed created, but it needn't include everyone, even in the North (still less in the South);

the political imperative is simply that it create sufficient consensus among the relatively privileged in order to discipline the excluded and disaffected. In fact, the rise of consumer society never eroded the *relative* power of capital, as the research of Portes and Walton showed for the post-World War II USA (Portes and Walton, 1981). In a further projection of the Kuznets curve argument, it is asserted that environmental degradation similarly follows an inverted 'U', but this is even more questionable, since in order to build mass consumption while retaining (or increasing) the class divide, the only solution has been 'growth' at the expense of the environment: the figures for post-war energy demand which we gave in Figure 2 above bear no resemblance to an inverted 'U', on the contrary they show a steep rise, and it should come as no surprise that future projections continue on a very similar trajectory (Helm, 2007). But this trajectory cannot continue indefinitely: energy stocks are drying up, while at the same time the legacy of earlier depletion simultaneously bites back in the shape of climate change.

The notion of some sort of 'energy deficit' confronting capitalism is useful enough for a general grasp of the problem, but is not sufficiently precise to explain the detail of the crisis. It is therefore helpful to introduce here the notion of 'energy return on energy invested' (EROEI). Ideologically, as it happens, this is not a wholly satisfactory term because it sneakily implies that investment, really a category of capitalism, is a basic principle of existence! However, it does help us in representing inputs and outputs. This function is again well illustrated by the case of food. To begin with, we must note that EROEI does not encompass the whole of what is wrong with the food system: the depletion of the soil's *systemic* properties is an issue of complexity, which it would be wrong to reduce to a simplified energy input-output ratio. Nevertheless (while always guarding against reductionism), we can employ simplification as a tool in model-building. In this case, what is interesting is to explain how the poverty issue is embedded, in a disguised form, within the food question.

In a hunter-gatherer society, EROEI is completely transparent: if you expended more energy chasing a rabbit or searching a plant than you obtained by eating it, you would die. But modern agriculture pretends to escape this logic by inputting fossil fuels, for example into mechanisation and fertilisers (which in addition to their bad systemic impact on soil, are also energy-based), into transportation, refrigeration and distribution. Totting up these inputs, Glaeser and Phillips-Howard strikingly depict a system where at least 10 times as much energy goes into producing food as the food itself supplies, (Glaeser and Phillips-Howard, 1987) a calculation confirmed by many more recent studies. The British consumer is a hunter-gatherer whose energy inputs are conveniently ignored: s/he now travels an average of 898 miles per year by car to shop for food.[1] But even this statistic, interesting as it is, actually masks an even profounder problem: the key weakness lies *at the production phase* of food. Indeed, low-carbon campaigner Chris Goodall calculates that the environmental cost of walking to buy food is actually worse than driving.[2] The explanation is the quantity of energy used up (or entropy expelled in the form of CO_2 and methane, which in the systems perspective is simply another expression of the same thing) in the chain producing the food which we need to consume in order to replace the calories used in walking (this would not of course apply if you ate locally-produced fresh vegetables, but is true for a typical mainstream diet).

Such a highly energy-dependent food system has had dramatic results in *seeming* to improve poverty: whereas a British family as recently as the immediate post-World War II period spent a third of its income on food, a 21st century family spends only a tenth (Howden, 2007). This sends a comforting message of poverty reduction in the context of Engel's law, while at the same time opening up purchasing power for non-essential goods (assuming these are really purchased out of income, although as we will show later, the role of credit is in practice increasingly important). Thermodynamic logic has thus been totally sacrificed in favour of papering over the political and economic contradictions.

This gives us a really good basis for our analysis, but our model is still somewhat static. We must now improve it by looking at *flows*.

The natural world moves through circuits, or cycles: nutrients circulate through food chains, composting etc. An understanding of these was fundamental to traditional knowledge systems (Le Houérou, 1989). When capitalism came in, it subordinated everything to its *own* circuits, whose sole purpose is to expand the value of capital. Marx' political economy (for example as expressed in *Capital*) constantly makes reference to the notion of transformation. If we bear in mind that, as

---

[1] http://news.bbc.co.uk/2/hi/uk_news/4684693.stm
[2] The argument is extremely important, it is just a pity that tactically it could be twisted to exonerate motor travel, e.g. *The Times*, August 4 2007

Burkett and Bellamy Foster rightly point out, his thinking is fundamentally thermodynamic and metabolic, (Burkett and Bellamy Foster,
2006) each successive transformation in the circuits of expanded reproduction should also be representable in thermodynamic terms. Most
obviously, this takes the form of energy depletion. However, as we
showed in Chapter 2, a better representation is 'exergy', since this term
highlights a transformation of *quality*, whereby something concentrated
or ordered is degraded, the disorder 'released' in this process being an
expression of entropy. And it is precisely this qualitative issue which is
crucial in understanding flows, and more specifically nutrition.

Although in the capitalist cycles, as in nature, things circulate, the
process is not premised on *renewal* (except in the sense that there must
be sufficient extra capital to begin the next circuit at a higher level), or
on minimising input. There is a kind of metabolism, but not a natural
one; and it is highly dissipative in the degree of entropy it emits. There
is also a 'depletion' at the level of identity, a kind of alienation which
comes of trying to ignore and supplant nature. It should be noted
that socialism also needs to be aware of this issue, lest it seek to replace
the chaotic 'elemental force' of capitalism with a voluntaristic order-
ing which likewise ignores the real world – Bettelheim showed great
insight in remarking that China's 'retreat' from central planning would
be a good thing if it heralded a reintegration with natural cycles
(Bettelheim, 1965).

Therefore, we can say that the circuits or flows of energy/exergy have
become a kind of artery for the entropy of capitalism. They are both an
expression of the social contradictions which were transmuted (not
eliminated) through transposition into an energy-form; and a medium
through which value gives the illusory impression of self-expansion
through the sole operation of capital. Accumulation as a whole has thus
become co-dependent with transformation/depletion, and could not
exist separately from it. And, as we will see later in this chapter, the
form of capital itself has adapted to this relationship.

The more obvious flows are those of commodities. There is for example the energy cost of transportation. Shipping, which carries 90% of
world trade, is estimated to account for double the carbon emissions
generated even by air traffic.[3] It is interesting to note that so low is its
monetary cost, that one can gleefully transport not only commodities,

---

[3] *Guardian*, March 3 2007

but even garbage: in 2005 the BBC showed British domestic waste, ear-marked for recycling, being containerised and shipped to Indonesia for dumping as landfill.[4] The report presented this as a scandal because the public were hoodwinked, but of course even if this particular abuse were eliminated, the real scandal is that transport costs are so low as to make it *economical* to transport garbage halfway round the world. We are more used to thinking of the transportation of positive values than of waste, but in fact, in the systems perspective the 'useful' commodity already represents a reduction of quality in comparison to the exergy (energy, materials) which went into it, and in this sense is not dramatically dif-ferent from the garbage it will soon become (an assumption already present in the intentional expendability of today's commodities).

Globalisation as a whole is entirely premised on the fiction that the energy cost of such flows can be ignored indefinitely. Although textbooks would pretend that capitalist economics is all about scarcity, the true scarcity (of supply, of carrying capacity to absorb waste) consistently fails to be reflected in prices. It is strange that the period of peak oil was also that of incredibly cheap tourist air travel. Of course, at a more advanced stage of the crisis some price signals will indeed appear: in 2008 several airlines went bust.[5] Nevertheless, what interests us is the mechanisms which act *against* the recognition of signals, and will continue to do so as long as the flows which mediate depletion remain sacrosanct.

Our accumulation model in the previous chapter (see Figure 4 above) represents flows in a non-spatial way, essentially as a metabolic relation whereby capital assembles human resources and 'means of production' (i.e. exergy) and pumps out an unacknowledged high entropy (e.g. CO_2), together with an acknowledged product which then has to be sold in order to recommence the circuit. But these same flows can equally be represented spatially. Once we begin to do so, we directly confront the North-South relationship.

The Core-Periphery Dimension

It was dependency theory which showed that the circuits serving to reproduce capital also mediate relations between core and periphery (Amin, 1970). Most obviously, the core fuels itself *from* the periphery,

---

[4] BBC, Real Story: "Recyclers' rubbish dumped abroad", Dec. 5 2005, on http://news.bbc.co.uk/1/hi/programmes/real_story/4493728.stm. The programme reveals that about half of the 8m tonnes of domestic recycling material ends up abroad.
[5] *Guardian*, May 31 2008

but in another way, also exports its own social disorder *to* it. Such flows have been in place ever since the 'triangular trade' (investment in exporting slaves from Africa to the Caribbean, import of sugar to Europe to augment the capital used to capture more slaves etc.); they constitute feedback loops with which the very reproduction of capital is now bound up. Capitalism has thereby acquired a powerful path-dependency in the shape of depleting the South, a 'default mode', upon which it naturally falls back in any situation.

The ecological dimension in dependency theory was mostly weak, but in supplying it we can draw upon important analogies between the concepts of 'environment' (surrounding system) in systems theory and 'periphery' in dependency theory; (Biel, 2006) and upon the corre-spondences between *power* as a political, and as a thermodynamic cat-egory (Gale, 1998, pp. 131–138). At this stage of the argument, it will be most helpful to explore the contribution of Malcolm Caldwell. In what could be regarded as unfinished work,[6] Caldwell outlined some impor-tant insights; (Caldwell, 1970) it will be a major task of this book to push these further.

Of particular interest in our current context is Caldwell's notion of 'protein imperialism'. This highlights the fact that a *depletion of quality* is simultaneously a depletion of the South. In this respect, the meat industry supplies a particularly good case. If we focus only on the (non-spatial) depletion of quality, cattle consume 21 pounds of plant protein for each kilo of meat protein produced, a classic case of more being transformed into less. But if we now represent this spatially, it become clear that the North consumes most of the end-product, much of it directly at the expense of the South, for example in the conversion of fish (in the form of fish meal) into animal feed (Caldwell, 1977, p. 103). Therefore, the unsustainability of the cheap food system – which falsely makes it seem poverty is declining, while freeing enough purchasing power to create niche consumer markets – becomes itself embedded in North-South relations. Maps created by the Spatial Inequalities Research Group, University of Sheffield, strikingly show how the global distribution of wealth closely mirrors that of the distribution of a major fast-food outlet.[7] The North's 'obesity' here graphically expresses the

---

[6] Caldwell's politically-motivated murder in 1978 undoubtedly cut short a further development of his theory.

[7] Social and Spatial Inequalities Research Group, University of Sheffield, WorldMapper, on http://www.sasi.group.shef.ac.uk/worldmapper/index.html, maps nos. 169, 164, accessed March 2007

disease of over-accumulation and the general ill-health of an unevenly distributed IPE.

Today, criticism of the meat-production system often focuses on energy input and greenhouse gas emission. Emissions associated with US-style burger diets are more damaging than gas-guzzling cars;[8] while remarkably, producing a single cow uses as much oil as driving from New York to Los Angeles! (Leggett, 2006) But we should continue to learn from Caldwell the importance of emphasising also a decline in quality. If things are transformed (processed) too much, it is not difficult to understand why quality is degraded. There is an important issue for the nutritional value of the food, and its effect on human capacity. Here again, we can highlight the role of fish (consumed by the North as fertiliser and as animal feed) within the flows of protein imperialism. Since fish are the source of omega 3 fatty acids, essential to the functioning of the brain, questions are today being raised whether enough will be available to maintain human capacity; it has been discovered that even fish-farming consumes twice as much fish (in feed) as it produces! (Monbiot, 2006a) The poor and marginalised disproportionally suffer the ill-effects from over-processed, depleted junk food.

Payback for Earlier 'Export to the Future'

So far we have mapped a number of dimensions: the spatial, as well as the short time-scale whereby capital reproduces itself as quickly as possible and then begins another similar circuit at an expanded level. But there remains another critical dimension: the long time-scale. Entropy is exported not merely to the periphery, but to the future ... and at some point it will inevitably flood back. A powerful image is supplied by Oscar Wilde's story, The Picture of Dorian Gray (Wilde, 1891). It concerns a man who is able to live a dissolute life while appearing untainted because the physical signs of his degradation are exported to a portrait in his attic. This has many resonances: it is the ravages of capitalism's past excesses which now return to haunt, not just the mode of production itself (with the behavioural implications which we are addressing in this book), but in a broader sense the future of humanity.

---

[8] *Guardian*, Jan. 4th 2006

The clearest representation of this is climate change. China, despite being the world's most populous country and even with its recent extremely rapid recent industrialisation, has contributed less than 8% of the total emissions of carbon dioxide from energy use since 1850, compared with 29% for the United States (Revkin, 2007). According to a NASA specialist, Britain (followed by the United States) has the highest per capita responsibility for climate change based on the cumulative emissions of carbon dioxide since the start of the Industrial Revolution.[9] What this effectively means is that the South suffers twice: first, from the legacy of the destruction exported to it while colonisation and neo-colonialism were fuelling the North's industrial order; secondly through the payback on the entropy which was then being exported to the future, and now returns as climate change. It should be noted that projections suggest that the effect will be uneven in the opposite sense to the responsibility, i.e. the South which caused less of the problem will suffer more of it: the map of estimated mortality attributable to climate change exactly follows the North-South divide (Abbott, et al., 2006, p. 9).

The information reaching us today comes – like light from a distant star – as a legacy of *past* energy use; or, to use a more psychological metaphor, from a repressed past now erupting into the conscious realm. But a lot has been invested in repression. It is similar with the history of slavery, and indeed, the notion of reparations for climate change is surfacing in some quarters (Bolivian President Morales has called for 'reparations to the earth'[10]). Denial of the past inevitably makes it difficult to get to grips with the present. In an important sense, therefore, the system is psychologically as well as materially ill-equipped to assimilate the information now besieging it.

The Information from Social Degradation

At the same time as the past floods back, the issue which caused the problem in the first place – the losing battle to contain poverty while maintaining the expanded reproduction of capital – is continuing apace, and even accentuating. In this way, the mode of production now finds itself squeezed not just between its social foundations and ecological 'ceiling', but between its past and future.

---

[9] *The Independent*, December 17 2007
[10] c.f. www.youtube.com/watch?v=na3ZWOIus78

The 'fuite en avant' response is to greet any information on increased poverty by a fresh upsurge of growth, and then desperately try to magic up the energy needed to fuel it. Marx would reply to this with the one piece of information capitalism can never take on board, namely that the supposed solution – growth, i.e. accumulation – is what actually accentuates the poverty problem. The systems perspective would reinforce this with some complementary insights.

Most fundamental among these will be to view poverty as an expression of dissipation, of the export of disorder to a sink (or to put it the other way round, of the depletion of peripheral order as a reciprocal concomitant to the process whereby the core builds its own). It is true that a market is also required (this is the Keynesian argument to explain why it is in capitalism's interest to address poverty), but a fairly restricted stratum of the global population suffices. The basic spectre of entropy is not so much the restricted purchasing capacity of the segment which *does* consume, but rather how on earth to manage the marginalised, without their social disorder spilling back to subvert the system's functioning.

Against this background, social decay is expressed most acutely in widening differentials or polarisation.

As we saw in Chapter 1, the key to understanding pauperisation is to grasp the dialectical tension between 'relative' and 'absolute' aspects. Most obviously, the former emphasises the class differential, the latter the entropy. But it is clear that a trend towards increasing relative disparities would also signal the system's growing entropy, and this is where polarisation becomes important because its increase is not merely quantitative, but would encounter qualitative tipping points. According to UN statistics, whereas at the beginning of the 20th century the difference in per capita wealth between rich and poor countries stood at about 9:1, by the beginning of the 21st century this had widened to 100:1; with much larger differences of over 10,000:1 between the top decile of the rich countries and the bottom decile of the poor ones.[11] The tipping point would have two interdependent aspects, neither of which is a sufficient explanation on its own: a qualitative degeneration of livelihoods and nutrition, and loss of identification with a system which preaches consumerism while denying to the majority the possibility *to* consume.

[11] United Nations University, World Institute for Development Economics Research (WIDER), *Wider Angle*, 2, 2005, p. 1

As long as growth persisted, the problem could be kept under wraps, so the question is, how would the system behave if growth were to become constrained? It is the undying merit of the *Limits to Growth* report of 1972 that it already anticipated this question, committing the cardinal sin, from capitalism's perspective, of saying that if growth were excluded, poverty could only be addressed by a change in distribution (Meadows, 1972). This dangerous truth was subsequently buried beneath a mountain of 'sustainable development' verbiage, while in practice capitalism found a way, through globalisation, to carry on growing even more frantically for a further generation. This does not of course mean that the globalisation era did – even in the heyday of its apparent success – really overcome the limits, but rather that a way was found to 'sequester' the entropy in a kind of leaky cavern. What we witness today is the problem of today's capitalist development *added to* the payback for the phoney solution to the 1970s crisis. How will this play itself out in practice?

The *Limits* made its argument, albeit correct in the abstract, in the technocentric spirit of getting the ear of the prince, but this is not how social change really happens. Instead, Marx was absolutely right in saying that the key instrument of change is struggle: irrespective of whatever objective limits may exist, the working class can, through struggle, improve its status relative to capital (Marx, 1969 c). What will happen in a crisis situation is that at some point struggles to defend livelihoods will qualitatively increase. And this process of struggle, while of course immediately a *relative* defence of 'slices' of a cake (and in this sense seemingly reformist), in substance exposes capitalism in a political way by shrinking its effective room to manoeuvre and bringing its underlying entropy to the surface; it therefore inevitably has revolutionary implications.

A ruling order wishing to defend itself should at least possess accurate information about its own social contradictions. For example, Victorian capitalism gathered information that it was totally destroying its social base, and was able to take corrective action (by limiting child labour, improving urban sanitation etc.). It didn't steer into the heart of the storm, but instead adjusted its course. Superficially the World Bank poverty discourse and Millennium Development Goals (MDGs) look like a contemporary version of this warning faculty (notably in the rehashed attempt at a Victorian-style quantification of absolute poverty), but the parallel is misleading. In the 19th and through much of the 20th centuries, there was still leeway, not of course to solve the problem, but to export it (from core to periphery, from the human social system onto the environment, and most importantly from present to future). This has now disappeared: the core is too sick internally, the lack of absorptive capacity in the periphery too starkly apparent ... and on top of all this, the ecological limits are coming into focus. If there is no solution to a problem, this makes it quite hard to acknowledge its existence. In seeking – through the appointment of Paul Wolfowitz as its head in 2005 – to turn the World Bank into a frank appendage of the White House, the Bush clique was merely acknowledging the system's need to shut its eyes to the amplitude of a problem it had no way of solving.

Although Wolfowitz was ousted by the Bank itself two years later, this could not address the fundamental problem: the poverty industry has become, not a true information-giving faculty, but a mechanism of spin and denial. Tellingly, for all today's obsession with poverty, accurate information is strangely difficult to find (Biel, 2010). Of course, in order to prove that globalisation is associated (as cause and effect) with a fall in poverty, some figures must be cooked up, and this happens in the following way. First the Bank hands Southern states a responsibility, via Poverty Reduction Strategy Papers (PRSPs) to demonstrate 'pro-poor' growth. But since the statistical issues in poverty-measurement are sufficiently opaque, (Macarov, 2003) governments retain plenty of scope to massage the figures to show a favourable trend at a single-country level; then all the Bank has to do is to add up these cooked country-level statistics to show that poverty is shrinking at a global level! Even then, the spin is only possible through a blatant misinterpretation of the Chinese data. China's earlier Maoist policies, while creating the basis of economic development, also ensured that many services were provided by the collective (or in the case of food in rural areas, directly consumed by producers). Statistically, people therefore appeared poorer than they really were, because they had relatively little need for money. Now that China has moved beyond basic needs, in real terms the destruction of the collective may often render living conditions more difficult; however the influx of wealth creates the appearance of a phenomenal reduction of poverty in comparison to the earlier artificial baseline. If one adds these Chinese statistics into the global ones, then because of the weight of China's population it seems that both global poverty and the North-South differential have improved! And because this is allegedly a result of globalisation, countries who want further to reduce poverty are forced to hitch themselves closer to the very process which is causing it.

Distribution is mostly a taboo area, which explains why the MDGs are firmly rooted in the sphere of absolute poverty and basic needs. Nevertheless, provided that the relative class power of the core capitalists is never called into question, the World Bank permits itself a sanitised version of relative poverty, (Ravallion, 2003) through which the ruling order hypocritically slams Southern elites for not sharing *their* wealth. The point of this – besides providing an excuse for social engineering – is to create the illusion that globalisation has indeed provided the fund to alleviate poverty … if only Southern elites didn't obstinately refuse to share it; by a devious logic, the South thus finds itself blamed for its own exploitation.

The systemic side of poverty is similarly a somewhat dangerous area for the establishment. Nevertheless, here too a tame and exploitative usage of certain systems concepts can be borrowed from the new management-speak. This is notably the case with the concepts of tipping points and networks, central to the 'sustainable livelihoods' framework espoused by Britain's Department for International Development (DfID). The basic proposition, in itself correct, is that the qualitative dimension in poverty is experienced once shocks disrupt the support networks, making it very difficult to claw one's way back even to the poverty line. Let us take a typical example of this argument, (Meikle, Ramasut and Walker, 1999) and translate it into diagrammatic form.

We can interpret this in the sense that the day-to-day struggle entraps people in a place where they oscillate around the poverty line. If the oscillations become too wild, that line would lose its hold as an attractor. The situation would then become chaotic, which might result in unpredictable forms of emergence dangerous to the ruling order. The 'soft' face of the dominant discourse is a targetted social

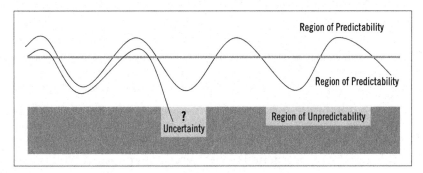

Figure 6: Visual representation of sustainable livelihoods

engineering to prevent this happening; the hard face is the policing of the excluded. But in either case, intervention is confined to the area at, or around, the tipping point, and completely abdicates any appreciation of the wider societal-environmental factors which make that tipping point exist in the first place.

Energy and Identity

Through polarisation, an increasing proportion of the world's population finds itself marginalised. Since they might become disaffected, the whole point of the 'stakeholder' discourse is – analysed through Freire's critical lens (Freire, 1972) – to make them *think* they have a stake. But the existence of the marginal segment plays a very important economic role: while they are not needed themselves as consumers, their very existence motivates everyone else continually to demonstrate that they are *not* among these unfortunates; and the best way of doing this is ... to consume! This imparts a strange dynamic: the worse poverty/inequality becomes, the more consumption increases. Analysed in this way, we can suddenly understand why these two trends have run in parallel in recent years.

The big question for us in this book is always the energy demands underpinning social processes. Usually, energy is consumed for the purpose of making something else happen, and in this sense is an *effect* of consumerism. But what if energy were consumed for its own sake? In this case, it would be the very act of consuming *energy itself* which demonstrates that you are not one of the poor. This is the proposition which we will now consider.

According to the 'environmental Kuznets curve' (EKC) model, energy degradation should decline with more advanced levels of development (in a similar way to social inequality in the classic Kuznets curve). The most straightforward way of critiquing this argument is to say that, if it is true that the North becomes 'cleaner' by becoming partially de-industrialised, this is only possible because it imports industrial goods from Asia. This distortion can be redressed by factoring in the wider responsibility generated by relations with the global economy, whereupon, for instance in Britain's case, it becomes apparent that an official reduction in emissions has been faked through false accounting, and that in the 15-year period to 2005, emissions for which Britain can be considered, in a wider sense, *responsible*, had actually increased by

THE ERA OF FEEDBACK FROM ENTROPY   133

19% (Helm, Smale and Phillips, 2007). If the core economies become more 'virtual', this merely reflects an evolution to appropriate the profits from globalised industry through their control of banking, intellectual property, brand identities, futures trading etc.

But this level of critique, though interesting, is inadequate. It still takes at face value the EKC assumption that current depletion mainly occurs in the South (albeit, not their 'fault'). But in reality, research surprisingly reveals that a significantly de-industrialised North still uses the same proportion of global energy as at the time when it monopolised industry (Podobnik, 2002). How are we to interpret this? Here, we again may be witnessing an ingrained acquired characteristic, one which the mode of production seems unable to shed, *however much its component economies are restructured* (i.e. industrialised, de-industrialised, 'virtualised' etc. etc.). It is as if the pattern of energy consumption is a constant, a 'character in search of an author' which must, if no longer coupled to manufacturing, find something else to couple itself to. To interpret this surprising finding, we may need a deeper understanding of consumption itself.

Consumption is not just buying a product; it is an act of liquidation. Thermodynamically, as we have seen, it signifies a liquidation of the quality represented by exergy. But, if growth is 'the problem' (McKibben, 2008), we should also consider the psychological dimensions of consumption, and here the Marxian notion of alienation may help. Consumption in any society is, as Robert Meister shows, an act of creative destruction: a human trait of desire is liquidated in the consuming act; (Meister, 1994) societies from the earliest times devoted a significant proportion of their capacities to cultural products and articles of beauty. Now, this human trait could be seized upon by capitalism and developed in a perverse way to become consumer*ism*. An alternative future society could develop in a different way, enabling it to 'autolimit' itself – André Gorz's term (Gorz, 1992) – without being tied to a narrow definition of basic needs. But under capitalist conditions, consumption may now be impossible to disentangle from consumer*ism*. Perhaps as a result, energy use has become somehow *coupled to the consumption phase rather than to the production one*. Most obviously, consumer goods have often been defined by the fact that they consume energy, the car playing a pivotal role in postwar capitalism: ten per cent of the world's oil is burnt on US roads, and half a million dollars spent every minute on importing it (Williams, H., 2007). But more broadly, since the largest growth sector for energy consumption is classified as 'residential',[12] it looks as though energy demand may have re-focussed itself on lifestyle. It is hard to think of any future development of capitalism changing this.

It is clear from dialectics that identity is in an important sense what one is *not*. We see this in Spinoza's principle "every determination is negation", or, in the form developed by Hegel, "What something is, ... it is wholly in its externality" (Hegel, 1969, p. 528). Systems theory confirms this: the identity of any system is dependent on the area from which its boundary separates it and which determines it negatively (Zwick, 1983). The very identity of the core is therefore wrapped up in proving that it is *not* the underdeveloped past (its own history) or the underdeveloped present (the South) ... and this is demonstrated through the act of consumption. If we take this together with Meister's point that desire is associated with liquidation, an interesting hypothesis suggests itself. In a high-throughput society, the identity of the system itself (the only thing its adaptation aims to preserve) has become fused with the main mechanism of reproduction (consumerism); and this fusion operates around the consumption (in the sense of liquidation) of energy. It was Richard Nixon who said, "There are only seven per cent of the people in the world living in the United States, and we use thirty per cent of all the energy. That isn't bad; that is good. That means we are the richest, strongest people in the world, and that we have the highest standards [of] living in the world. That is why we need so much energy, and may it always be that way"(Kegley and Wittkopf, 1979, p. 169); more recently, the George W. Bush administration seconded this: "The American way of life is a blessed one ... The President also believes that the American people's use of energy is a reflection of the strength of our economy, of the way of life that the American people have come to enjoy."(Hamilton, 2007) Particularly telling is the image of Texans raising the level of their airconditioning in order to enjoy log fires (Hamilton, 2007). There is a surreal logic in this, if we understand that resource-consumption and identity have become locked in a feedback loop. Precisely to demonstrate that there is still vitality in the system and that it is not doomed, its participants must keep ritually performing the very act which in fact dooms it.

---

[12] c.f. World Resources Institute, *Earth Trends Data Tables, Energy Consumption by Economic Sector*, Washington DC 2003, on http://earthtrends.wri.org/pdf_library/data_tables/ene5_2003.pdf

It is difficult to acknowledge any information which challenges these assumptions.

It is against this background that we suddenly enter an era where simultaneously those social contradictions which have traditionally been defused through high energy consumption are on the increase, and the actual energy available shrinks. Although, as we have seen, the system heavily distorts its information with respect to the first part of this proposition (i.e., poverty), it is relatively more open to information on the second part: the notion of peak oil has rapidly achieved acceptance. However, because of the link with identity, peak oil information cannot be translated into strategies of reducing consumption. Instead it is processed in a distorted way to justify some weird forms of conduct, which we will now consider.

The Peak Oil Debate

Just as climate change is information from the 'suppressed past', peak oil is in a way information from the future, in the sense that it forecloses options. For a while, isolated establishment figures warned that it was coming, while the mainstream shut its eyes; however, the official US government Hirsch report of 2005 can be considered a watershed: peak oil has *become* the mainstream.

Let's consider exactly what it means. In the simplest form, demand is predicted to increase, while production falls (Kanter, 2007). But the issue can be further concretised in an interesting way, which Hirsch explains well: "Peaking is a reservoir's maximum oil production rate, which typically occurs after roughly half of the recoverable oil in a reservoir has been produced. In many ways, what is likely to happen on a world scale is similar to what happens to individual reservoirs, because world production is the sum total of production from many different reservoirs."(Hirsch, 2005, p. 11) Since oil reserves come in discrete packages, and each of these individually reaches its peak, the only way to meet increasing demand is to add new reserves. For a long time reserve additions outpaced increases in consumption, but this was dramatically reversed around 1985 (Hirsch, 2005, p. 15). Since then, there has been an increasing shortfall of new reserves added.

But now we must enter another, deeper layer of explanation, where the official response begins to lose its bearings: the relationship between peak oil and EROEI. We can explain this in the following way. Peak oil does not mean no oil: there is still plenty, but it is increasingly difficult to access. Now, if this is the case, how would the information present itself? Most obviously in terms of the main form of information recognised by capitalist economics, namely price. But if the price goes up, previously uneconomical oilfields or residues of oilfields would suddenly become viable, so in this sense scarcity would tend to regulate itself. This is partly what has been happening recently because whenever prices rise, effectively available oil also increases. But here we come to the crux of the matter: this is true *only up to a point.* That point would occur *not* when oil is really exhausted, but rather much earlier: when the real, thermodynamic rationale begins to overwhelm the artificial monetary one, in other words if more energy (or by extension, exergy or scarce resources like water) must be invested to extract and process the oil than it eventually supplies; at this point the economic price would become irrelevant. Capitalism has thrived up to now by ignoring thermodynamic rationale, but we might expect that once this irrationality begins to invade the energy sector itself it would find nowhere to hide. This would provide a very important objective determinant of limits. But of course (a recurrent theme of this chapter), what is often the most interesting is when crisis drives capitalism into a mode where it *departs from* logical rationale.

In order to understand this better, let's first consider another, crucial level of analysis in the peak oil issue: the relationship with complexity and unpredictability. This dimension is nicely described by another leading establishment contributor to the peak oil debate, former senior advisor to the National Iranian Oil Company, Ali Bakhtiari. Explicitly referring to the qualitative shifts of systems theory, Bakhtiari outlines four transitional phases between 2006 and 2020. But the important point, he rightly emphasises, is that *his own projection can only be based on the mindset of the present,* i.e. pre-peak logic. Post-peak logic when it comes about

> "will bring about explosive disruptions we know little about, and which are extremely difficult to foresee. And the shock waves from these explosions rippling throughout the financial and industrial infrastructure could have myriad unintended consequences for which we have no precedent and little experience". (Bakhtiari, 2006)

As we will explain in a moment, such shock waves are themselves only part of a wider pattern of unpredictable and extreme events. Our argument will show that the system does indeed adapt, in its own way, to complexity ... but mainly in the sense of giving up on the attempt to understand it, and instead, somehow adopting a behaviour which we could describe as 'parasitism upon chaos'.

Finally, we must just re-emphasise a truth which both mainstream market economics and Malthusianism tend to ignore, but which both Marxists and imperialists (in different ways) understand quite well: *effective scarcity is heavily influenced by politics*. I will develop this point later, but it is clearly essential if we are to to make sense of the processes to be unleashed by the coming phase transitions.

We have now established an overview of the peak oil issue. How is the system responding at present?

It is first worth remarking that the very notion of oil 'reserves' is a case of spin: one might expect the term to mean something 'in the bank', but in the case of oil, 'reserves' avowedly means only a hypothetical prediction of what future production is *likely* to be (Newmann and Burk, 2005). There is nevertheless a trade-off between the need to manufacture confidence and the need for sufficient realism. In the mid 2000s, the establishment therefore became uneasy about excessive distortion: in 2004 Shell was forced significantly to downgrade its oil and gas reserves, while leading finance consultants Deloitte Touche proposed a uniform, centrally-defined and expert-policed set of criteria (Newmann and Burk, 2005). This is different from poverty statistics where spin is primary; with oil, it must be tempered by an element of realism.

Assuming that it has acquired some rough information about limits, two lines of defence now present themselves to the ruling order. The first is, while partially taking on board peak oil information, to maintain the pretence that there is some way of salvaging an oil-based economy. Thus, leading Edinburgh-based energy consultancy Wood Mackenzie opines: "It becomes unclear beyond 2020 that conventional oil will be able to meet any of the demand growth";[13] but on this assumption, something called 'unconventional oil' presumably exists. What exactly is this? There is a strong suspicion that it means abandoning EROEI in order to get it. The current spin takes the form of arguing that, through a technological fix, more oil than expected can be extracted from existing oilfields; (Mouawad, 2007) and also, more specifically, that a huge bonanza awaits in Canada. At one stroke, 'reserves'

---

[13] *Financial Times*, February 19 2007

would be increased, but it would mean accessing heavy low-quality oil. Not only will this increase the feedback from climate change, (Lydersen, 2007) but the fixes needed to access it, for example the injection of water and natural gas, would consume other scarce resources. This is why some more realistic establishment figures try to puncture the false optimism. US investment banker Matthew Simmons describes such methods as "like turning gold into lead"; (Lydersen, 2007) or, in the case of the Canadian Tarsands (where in effect energy from clean oil is used to process exceptionally dirty oil to make it somewhat less dirty), a specialist speaks of "using lobster to make imitation crabmeat" (Mackovich, 2007). These images well depict the dilemma of a mode of production vainly trying to magic away entropy.

Despite these objections, the system continues stubbornly to cling to its first line of defence. But it needs to be supplemented by a second. This hinges on a simple proposition: the current trajectory of energy *demand* is sacrosanct, and, if oil cannot fully supply it, it must (and can) be met from alternative sources. This line of argument is extremely important for us to analyse, because, unlike the first, it can pretend to respond to the climate change issue as well as to peak oil, and therefore provides a basis for imperialism to 'capture' certain parts of the green agenda.

In general terms, this issue is more complicated than the oil-reserves spin, because if workable technological fixes exist they should be supported. But first, we must recognise that they could never keep up with energy demand along the current trajectory. Wind power is clean but one has to stop somewhere well short of a point where the entire surface of Germany is covered with turbines. The discourse which uses green tech as an excuse to maintain consumption is therefore in the last analysis mere illusion. Creative accounting typically serves to inflate *current* emissions reduction resulting from 'green' fixes; (Monbiot, 2007) and even more interestingly, a supposed solution is somehow borrowed from the *future*, in the shape of offsetting (planting trees supposedly equivalent to the emissions generated through air travel, or paying other countries not to pollute). It has correctly been observed that the offsetting notion either suffers the same flaw as that of oil reserves in the sense of counting hypothetical future benefit as current benefit, (Smith, K., 2007) or, like indulgences in the medieval church, deculpabilises current conduct.[14] When the US published a high-profile catalogue of hypothetical future techno-fixes (injecting chemicals into the

---

[14] An excellent parody of the offsetting idea is the Cheatneutral website http://www .cheatneutral.com/ and video on http://www.youtube.com/watch?v=f3_CYdYDDpk

upper atmosphere, mirrors in space etc.), (Dean, 2007) the timing was clearly designed to make it seem the situation was not irreparable after all ... and so consumption could continue unabated.

In fact, reliance on technological schemes for meeting existing energy demands are usually vulnerable to hidden costs: it often turns out that what is supposed to be the solution is really part of the problem. Besides the general fallacies of offsetting, current agendas of using GM tree plantations as carbon sinks would be ecologically disastrous if genes (for example those which reduce lignin or kill insects) were to spread to natural forests, something which experts agree is impossible to prevent (Petermann, 2005). Another remarkable case is the sudden discovery that large dams make a serious contribution to global warming. One would tend to think that dams' main problem is a trade-off with the damage they do to *local* ecosystems and the populations which have co-evolved with them, but it now transpires that the rotting of surface organic material is a major global sources of the emission of methane, a far more dangerous greenhouse gas than the CO_2 whose emission dams are supposed to reduce (Lima et al., 2007). And the research which conveys this important finding is itself an unconscious illustration of the problem: being stuck in the mindset of refusing to question consumption, the authors merely look to a *further* technological fix, in this case capturing the methane.

Much of the green tech agenda can be considered progressive in itself – e.g. solar panels – and the reactionary aspect only comes in where it serves as an excuse not to question accumulation and growth. But there are certain areas where imperialism has actively captured parts of green tech and created something *intrinsically* reactionary. This is above all the case with biofuels. Here we are entering into one of the weirdest manifestations of the crisis, which fully shows the distorted way in which the information is processed, and then translated into action.

Bush's State of the Union address 2007 took the lead in proposing the production of 35 billion gallons of alternative and renewable fuels by 2017. However, it is important to stress that this was not a mad dream of Bush alone: the whole capitalist world joined in and indeed the supposedly 'greener' countries like Germany used their green credentials to lend ecological credibility to a programme which Bush himself was honest enough to promote essentially on national security grounds. The simple question of how, with a growing world population, one can justify withdrawing land from food production was somehow ignored.

This heralds a new era of grabbing land to grow biofuel crops, which somehow seems to turn the clock back to the age of colonial plunder: according to one study, the life expectancy of Brazilian cane-cutters in the ethanol chain is lower than that of colonial slaves (Zibechi, 2007). The entropy is therefore offloaded not just onto nature, but onto society; and, because the land is withdrawn from food production, food security of the most vulnerable is undermined. Nor is the issue merely quantitative: as with protein imperialism, there is a net reduction of nutritional quality, hence of capacity. Mexico has already witnessed mass protests triggered by the rising price of tortillas, attributed to the diversion of corn to ethanol production. (Ronneburger, 2007) The qualitative dimension is that tortillas, a recipe directly derived from the Mayas, have traditionally provides Mexicans with 40% of their protein and helped maintain sound levels of health (reflected for example in a very low incidence of rickets); people are now forced by rising prices onto a less nutritious diet (Roig-Franzia, 2007).

Even if biofuels were genuinely a free energy source, they could never keep up with demand. But it is important to note that an EROEI problem exists here too. Increasingly, we learn that biofuels themselves suffer a net energy shortfall (Anslow, 2007). It has been shown that "To produce a liter of ethanol requires 29% more fossil energy than is produced as ethanol….. The corn feedstock alone requires nearly 50% of the energy input."(Pimentel and Patzek, 2005, p. 66) Of course inputs in systems terms are not the same as *imports* in international economic terms: the whole point is to make the USA less dependent on oil producers. But even this is questionable. The high inputs of nitrogen fertiliser needed to nourish the corn feedstock are themselves derived from natural gas, and US stocks of this are also beginning to dry up (Morrison, 2007). So addicted is the system to energy that it seems impervious to any rationality in its last-ditch defence of consumption.

A New Regime of Nature

Bakhtiari's prediction of "explosive disruptions we know little about" is of far wider relevance than merely to peak oil. An era of great complexity is beginning.

We have spoken so far in this chapter about a metabolic political economy which treats the environment as an external condition. Under traditional society, it hadn't entered into people's minds to see nature as external. It was only with capitalism that this separation was brought in. This brought a *potential* for the individual to grasp her/his destiny with a greater sense of freedom, an issue which we will address in the following chapter. But the latent progressive potential remains unrealised and unrealisable while capitalism holds sway. Instead, identity is merely coupled to an impossible dream of controlling or mastering the natural world.

Once this illusion begins to fall apart, the sense of self is lost, and this very fact is *itself* a shock. Consumption, linked to identity, is called into question, while the learned response of mastering nature no longer seems to work. And this now-unmasterable nature manifests itself in the shape of more specific shocks which, moreover, interact with human processes in unexpected ways. For example, a polarised political economy creates strong pressures for migration to those areas where work is available, a trend which already preoccupies the ruling order; what if climate catastrophe were to superimpose itself, triggering an *additional* exodus?

Certain data suggest a shift to a situation where the abnormal becomes normal; or, extreme events occur more frequently. For example, with respect to hurricanes, there is a non-linear pattern, witnessing sharp shifts between so-called 'regimes'. A feature of the most recent period beginning in the late '90s is a sharp increase in *major* hurricanes (Holland and Webster, 2007).

The point is that it is not just the individual hurricanes themselves which are violent: the abruptness of the phase transition to the current regime *itself* represents the real shock. There is an interaction between degradation of the large-scale earth system, and of local ecosystems. Thus, when Hurricane Katrina struck New Orleans in 2005, there was both a large-scale cause resulting from climate change – extremely high water temperatures in the Gulf Coast contributing to transforming it suddenly from Category 1 to Category 5 as it passed from the Atlantic Ocean to the Gulf of Mexico – and a more immediate one, springing from the destruction of local wetlands which heightened vulnerability (Gelbspan, 2005; Worldwatch Institute, 2005). 2007 was a year of 'chaos' for Britain's ecosystems, plants and animals being thrown into disarray by a succession of extreme conditions making it impossible for them to decide what season it was.[15] Even nature is struggling to adapt, so how about humanity?

---

[15] *Guardian*, Dec. 27 2007

Crisis can of course mean opportunity. The immediate context of the Mao quote we used to introduce this book – about an era of "great struggles which will have many features different in form from those of the past" – was obviously political; but in a deeper sense, the politics of imperialism is itself a reflection of the attempt to grab nature, and of the revelation by the nature in question is both more fragile, and at the same time more intractable in its resistance, than was supposed. The challenge now is to our capacity at a socio-political level to *respond* to such a powerful shift in the humanity-nature relationship.

It must be emphasised that complexity is not, per se, an excuse for abandoning the possibility of policy and vision. For example, climate change is undeniably complex, but, as recent methodologies show, uncertainty in no way rules out building useful models of its future development, addressing both mitigation and adaptation (Collins, 2007). It is therefore indeed possible to turn crisis into opportunity. If both natural and human systems, in parallel, enter an era of great change and major shock-waves, in a strange way the historic separation between the two systems may thereby be resolved. This may bring hope for a future where, faced with extreme challenges, we are forced to reunite the social and ecological realms.

But in the context of the current mode of production, interlocking between the two systems may occur in a highly damaging form. Although it is true that capitalism cannot continue as before in *ignoring* ecological events, the problem is that distorted information may be translated into policies or modes of action which actually make things worse. This is where the relationship with complexity becomes interesting: the elements of an already complex crisis begin to *interact with the effects of the system's behaviour in response to it*. Multiple feedback processes can result. Before considering these interactions in more detail, let's first attempt a composite picture of a mixed ecological and economic-institutional crisis by considering the case which has been our particular focus in this chapter: food.

The Approaching Food Crisis

As we have shown, cheap food is needed to stop people making revolution, to maintain the rate of profit and to maintain the proportion of income devoted to the non-essential consumer goods which propel accumulation. However, its continued availability is now under serious threat. Food will probably be the most serious aspect of the crisis into which we now enter, both because of its impact on livelihoods, and because it underpins the all the rest of the capitalist IPE. Our particular interest here is complexity. In appreciating this, it may be helpful to conceive of the following nine aspects. The key issue is always their interrelatedness, and how several of them relate in a mutually reinforcing way.

Firstly, we must understand that the crisis has origins independent of peak oil. *Capitalist agriculture has long been set on a course which depletes the soil.* The soil is different from exergy because the key thing being depleted is complexity itself, i.e. the interaction of different organisms, and its replacement by simplification and reductionism. The essential characteristic of non-organic agriculture is that diminishing returns caused by soil degradation are met by further artificial inputs, in other words a positive feedback loop undermines the possibility that information from the approaching crisis will initiate some healthy negative-feedback response. The failure of one technical fix stimulates the search for the next (e.g. GMOs). This is one of the best illustrations of why the ruling order steers into the heart of the storm.

Secondly, peak oil now comes into the picture. This itself has three main aspects. To begin with the chemical inputs are themselves often derived from fossil fuels. Second, there is the effect of mechanisation: as accumulation in industry becomes insufficient, agriculture, no longer just an external support to maintain the industrial rate of profit (by reducing subsistence costs), becomes itself a major sphere of accumulation, and thus subject to the law whereby increasing mechanisation (serving to augment the productivity of labour) is necessary if one is to remain competitive. Finally, a third demand arises from the hitherto-suppressed energetic costs associated with the international division of labour: the growth of food miles, transport, refrigeration and marketing have all added vastly to the energy profile, falsely counted as a free resource. This has been further qualitatively increased with globalisation and the dominance of supermarket-led buyer-driven chains sourcing 'non-traditional' agricultural cash crops from the South (out-of-season beans from East Africa etc. etc.).

The accumulation process even to some extent captures what which *should* be the solution, namely organic agriculture. There are indeed leanings towards negative feedback in that organic food has recently become popular in the North, and, although only a niche market which arguably widens the inequality between rich and poor, this does at least reflect a correct understanding of the lack of safety and shrinking nutritional value of mainstream produce. But a high-throughput organics could well be worse in many environmental indicators than non-organic, (Trewavas, 2001) and since it is a niche market, it is not surprising that 70% of organic food currently consumed in the UK is imported, as against only 30% of non-organic (UK Government, 2005). This is why it is not enough to say 'organic', we have to insist on low-throughput agriculture.

These factors are made worse by a *third* issue which now comes into play: the quest for *biofuels, competing with food production* for the available land. The ill-effects on the South have recently been high-lighted, but less well known is the fact that even in Britain, rapeseed, mostly exported for biofuel to Germany, has escalated dramatically ... to constitute 11% of all crops![16] And this in turn contributes to the movement *opposite to* organics: rapeseed requires massive doses of nitrogen-rich fertilisers (with attendant risks of leaching nitrates into aquifers), as well as an average of three herbicides, two fungicides and two insecticides during its growing season.[17] An FAO report published even before Bush's State of the Union Address 2007 showed that indus-trial demands, particularly for ethanol, were *already* pushing up coarse grain prices; (United Nations Food and Agriculture Organisation, 2006) similarly, corn-based animal feed would be sacrificed in favour of ethanol with a knock-on effect in pushing up meat prices (Morrison, 2007). Price increases constitute a kind of signal, but their effect, far from redressing this disastrous course, is mainly to export the problem, as far as possible, to the South. Thus the effect of rising corn prices in the US, triggered by the ethanol boom, stimulates US agribusiness to switch from soybean to corn cultivation, while in compensation, an increased input from sugarcane, as opposed to corn, is sought for etha-nol production; both these trends combine to have disastrous knock-on results in Brazil, which now supplies both sugarcane-based ethanol and soybeans to the US economy, (Valle, 2007) with devastating effects on the local environment. Thus, the entropy, is shuffled around with increasingly unpredictable results. Rising demand for palm and soya oil to satisfy EU regulations for an increased proportion of biofuels in energy consumption becomes an incentive for deforestation (Pearce, 2005) .... leading to a worsening of the climatic situation that the

---

[16] *Guardian*, April 19 2007
[17] *Guardian*, ibid.

biofuels claim to alleviate! These absurdities are currently managed by transmuting part of their effects into a kind of social entropy exported to the poor. Amazingly, the amount of grain to produce a tank load for a 4x4 vehicle would feed a family for a year.[18] It has always been the case that livelihoods of the poor and marginalised form a kind of sink where 'lost information' unpalatable to the system is dissipated.

This is not to deny that some information can filter through to sections of the elite, if not in terms of their life experience then at least in business terms. Executives of agro-multinational Cargill (usually the villain and target of grassroots protests), who probably have plenty to eat themselves, nevertheless opposed the ethanol agenda on the grounds that it pushes up corn prices and competes with livestock and processed foods.[19] But the whole point of our argument is that, while such information *does* exist, the capitalist system *overall* operates in such a way as to neutralise those signals which might incite to a change of course.

And this is where we come to the *fourth* aspect of our model of the food crisis. There are two forces to which everything else must pay homage: *finance capital and the militarised state.* As we will see in more detail later in this chapter, the interplay between these two agents works to neutralise the price signals which, in an imaginary capitalism composed only of productive capital and market relations, might warn society of impending disaster. Locked in an embrace, these imperialist agents promote a course where food (and everything else) is wholly subordinated to a logic of so-called security (needless to say, defined in a manner diametrically opposed to a meaningful livelihoods definition of security). Thus, in supposedly ultra-liberal America, $2 billion of state subsidies to ethanol production come *on top of* an already heavily-subsidised corn-producing agroindustry.

Against a background where these four factors are beginning to interact, a *fifth, climate change*, now enters in as detonator of the crisis. A study, which analysed data since 1981 in order to estimate what global production in 2002 *would have been* in the absence of climate change, concluded that "The wheat and maize production lost to climate change is roughly equivalent to the total wheat and maize production of Argentina." (Lobell and Field, 2007). The research shows that, as one might expect, climate change can favourably affect yields, up to a point, but then tips over and begins to diminish them.

---

[18] *Independent*, March 5 2007
[19] *New York Times*, June 25 2006

It is remarkable that such results were already visible during that time-period, since it is probably *after* 2002 that things began to get really bad. Thus, in 2006, Australia was suddenly gripped by a climate-induced agricutural disaster. Like Argentina, Australia has played a major role in supplying the world food market (typically supplying 14 per cent of wheat traded worldwide), and then at one stroke its production was cut by half.

We can now add a *sixth* factor: *water.* Of course, this can be seen as a sub-category of climate change – what occurred in Australia was drought – but we must recognise its independent causes. The traditional approach uses composting, mulches, green manures, intercropping etc. to conserve moisture; indeed it is possible to have a viable agriculture which focuses *mainly* on the harvesting and flow of water, as in the celebrated case study of Zimbabwean farmer Zephania Phiri Maseko (Lancaster, 1996). In contrast, it was very characteristic of the Green Revolution to compensate for neglecting the management of a healthy soil by treating water as a free resource. Remarkably, under today's system, each person's daily food consumption involves the conversion of 2000 to 5000 litres of liquid water to vapor each day, one kilo of wheat, for example, requiring the evapotranspiration of 1,790 litres (Molden and de Fraiture, 2004). This cannot be met by rain fed agriculture, and if met by irrigation, the ecological impact will be considerable. Again, we can say that this problem, though a product of capitalism, would be inherited by any social system. But the point is that capitalism cannot solve it, because the issue is not just an agro-technical one, but rather essentially institutional, i.e. one of resource management. A viable solution, available under a different social system, could be co-management of water resources for multiple uses (Molden and de Fraiture, 2004). But this response cannot develop within the current mode of production, except in a contestatory sense.

In considering the issue of diminishing crop yields, another *seventh* factor enters in alongside climate change – the *loss of diversity*: a feature of 'modernised' agriculture has been its increasing homogenisation around just a few crops, and just a few *strains* of these crops. This is an extremely important manifestation of capitalism's failure, its lack of preparedness to respond to shocks arising from the complex crisis, and therefore its inability to take humanity forward. Surely the decline of yields would not be so great if many different strains of crops had been cultivated in parallel, as was always the case under traditional systems.

This takes us to an *eighth* issue: *capacity*. The ability to respond to shocks is not just an issue of genetic diversity, but ultimately of human capacity, in this case expressed as widely-diffused agricultural knowledge. Factory farming reduces the empathy with animals, which the traditional farmer needed to have (Johnson, N., 2006). And Richard Heinberg interestingly describes a crisis in skill, where the average age of American farmers is approaching 60, and the proportion of principal farm operators younger than 35 dropped from 15.9 percent in 1982 to 5.8 percent in 2002 (Heinberg, 2006). This is of crucial importance because in the coming period, skill will be at a premium, if we are to improvise solutions to unexpected events. Over millennia of human development, capacity was intrinsically associated with diversity: as Goonatilake shows, the relationship between cultural diversity and development is somehow analogous to that between biodiversity and evolution; (Goonatilake, 1982) a widely *distributed* capacity, a plurality of possible responses – redundancy in the systems vocabulary – is always the basis for solving new and complex problems. And we can add to this the issue raised by ecofeminism, that traditional cultures were themselves focused on the preservation of diversity of genetic resources (Shiva, 1988). All this will have to be rediscovered.

A *ninth* factor now enters in, whose impact is only just beginning to materialise, but which may eventually turn into the most important single feature of the crisis: *massive hazard* arising from within the food system itself. Massive hazard is a classic instance of export to the future. Its most obvious current manifestation is disease among factory-farmed animals: chickens are cheap because the risk associated with disease is ignored in terms of economic decisions until it actually materialises – the phrase about 'chickens coming home to roost' is all too literally true! But in general, in a framework where heterogeneity and diffuse capacity are lost, the response to worrying information is always to go further down the path-dependent road of pushing technical fixes in defiance of the precautionary principle, and thus actually to intensify the crisis which is supposedly being solved. The major current expression of this is undoubtedly GMOs: as the crisis develops, increasing risk stimulates the system to ever more risky modes of conduct.

We have thus identified nine interdependent factors, and taking them all together, it is not surprising that a global food crisis is now upon us. In 2007, it became clear that "In the past 12 months the global corn price has doubled. The constant aim of agriculture is to produce enough food to carry us over to the next harvest. In six of the past seven years, we have used more grain worldwide than we have produced. As a result world grain reserves – or carryover stocks – have dwindled to 57 days, the lowest level of grain reserves in 34 years."(Howden, 2007) As we will see later, scarcity is not the only factor determining price, because the effect is amplified by speculative finance capital. Nevertheless, the underlying unsustainability of the food system will increasingly manifest itself in price. The era of artificially cheap food is over. A high-profile 2009 UN report on drugs interestingly revealed that a recent fall in opium production reflects not the success of repression but the fact that it is now more profitable to cultivate wheat![20] The era of artificially cheap fuel is, at the time of writing, not yet over but when it comes, it is certain to impact still further. What we have seen so far is only the beginning. The likelihood of food crisis detonating a major social revolt is very real.

The Era of Complexity and Capitalism's Failure

It should be noted that the issue of adaptation is independent of whether or not environmental regime shifts are anthropogenic. In any case, we still have to respond, and this requires a social order which unleashes, and doesn't stifle, variety and capacity. This is just where capitalism fails. Just when humanity most *needs* a resilient system, it happens to be ruled by a mode of production which is inherently disempowering and homogenising ... and is moreover introspectively consumed with its *own* crisis.

The latter crisis would, even in the absence of ecological constraints, be of unprecedented scope. Somehow, the institutional capacity to solve major structural problems seems to have exhausted itself.

In the previous global crisis – that of the 1970s – there were still new ideas capitalism could try; indeed, when that crisis was at its height in 1974, Amin and Frank conducted an interesting exercise in futurology, exploring such possibilities (Amin and Frank, 1981). But although capitalism escaped intact on that occasion, it achieved this at the expense in an internal shrinkage of governance options, in a sense, an entropy of the institutional sphere. Perhaps we can say that there is a finite vocabulary of 'cards' which can be played, and at the end of the '70s, the

---

[20] *Guardian*, "Price of wheat, not war on drugs, has biggest effect on production", June 29 2009, p.4

whole hand was laid down at one go: the creative destruction of modernism, delocation of industrial production to Asia, the dissolution of state property, the furious commodification of all areas of life. This leaves the system with no fresh 'get-out-of-gaol' card when a new crisis comes along, with the result that today, when the mode of production unwillingly finds itself 'in charge' of humanity's response to the ecological crisis, it is at the same time submerged in an intractable problem of salvaging *itself*, through the search for a new regime of capital accumulation which obstinately refuses to materialise.

In fact, the problem is a qualitative one. It is not just that salvation from the '70s crisis required the playing of too many cards, but that it required a unique and irreplaceable wild-card: the experiment with complexity (something Amin and Frank didn't foresee). Having traversed this and grown disillusioned, the system is effectively despairing of complexity just at a time when a response to rapidly-growing complexity is most needed (one cannot in any case aspire to dominate a complex situation, but can work *with* it). The origins of this surrender lie in the social sphere. The experiment in complexity-governance conserves managerial energy by unfolding capacity and emergence within safe parameters, but it is reasonable to hypothesise a tipping point when the managerial energy expended in *containing* the emergence exceeds that which is realised. It is a bit like an institutional form of the EROEI problem: an analogy suggests itself with nuclear fusion, where the energy required by the powerful magnets that confine it always seems to outstrip the energy it supplies (hence the well-known quip that at any point over the past 40 years, viable fusion power has always been 40 years away![21]).

As a result, within the social sphere, an increasingly unmanageable complexity begins to shift into a disordered state – maybe chaotic, but maybe also (which would be even worse from the ruling interests' point of view) favourable to countersystemic creativity and innovation. The response is to impose – through the 'war on terror' – a dictatorial regime of homogenisation and thought-policing which stifles exactly the thing humanity most needs in the face of its current challenges, i.e. a multiplicity of creative responses. What I am calling the 'lords of chaos' scenario is, as we will see in the next chapter, the diametrical

---

[21] This is not to negate the importance of current fusion research, but its contribution can only be to a future society, not to saving the present one: if the present setup continued for 40 years it would be too late to save anything.

opposite of a governance of complexity. And a ruling order in the throes of despair about *social* complexity is surely ill-equipped to handle it in the environmental sphere.

Complexity is indeed a major distinguishing factor separating this crisis from those which capitalism surmounted previously. Cause-effect relationships are unpredictable: you can for example employ sanctions to create a kind of consolidated semi-chaotic 'low' order as a repulsion effect, as in Iraq after the first Gulf War or more recently in Zimbabwe, and this is quite functional in using the spectre of chaos to frighten people off from social experimentation; but in Cuba sanctions had the less desired effect of promoting creative emergence and self-reliance. Core and periphery are more intertwined, for example through migration, a natural response-mechanism when the periphery is depleted too much; migration in turn generates huge capital flows which threaten partially to escape the accumulation circuits, and which it is tempting to assimilate to 'terrorist' funding. The periphery will not absorb as much disorder as it used to: partly because there is too much chaos for the entire system to contain, but partly also, as in Latin America, the social movement is rebelling against its sink status, by unfolding creative forms of emergence. The ruling order seeks to 'bag the mess' in those regions it no longer understands, but has lost its accustomed bearings in defining these. Failing to see which regions should be policed by 'hard' or 'soft' power, it allows a generalised repressive reflex to overtake it.

The fact that capitalism is in crisis does not mean it will roll to a point of collapse. It is 'stuck', but could remain stuck for a long time in a degenerate form. There is something profoundly correct in the way original imperialism theory (for all its secondary weaknesses in appreciating the adaptive options *then* still available to capitalism) understood the nature of this era as both a decayed phase, and one where the ruling order readies to defend itself to the death – and drag humanity to the grave with it. The conclusion therefore remains: "if you don't hit it, it won't fall" (Mao, 1969, p. 19).

The system's recent development thus suggests the evolution of what may be called a consolidated decayed form. This possesses two complementary opposite sides: an 'escape to the past', i.e. a reversion to simple top-down control; and an 'escape to the future', i.e. parasitism upon chaos. Neither is in fact viable, but the system could for some time remain oscillating between these two non-viable options.

In the next chapter I will illustrate this duality in more detail in relation to militarism, which holds within it both commandist and the chaotic features. But militarism interacts closely with the other key imperialist feature, namely finance capital. It will be helpful briefly to consider finance capital at this point in our argument, because its new modes of operation throw important light on the crucial question posed at the beginning of this chapter: why are the signals of impending exhaustion (which under capitalism are supposed to be conveyed by price) triggering the 'wrong' responses? The degenerate state is not a static state, because the whole socio-economic system, however devoid of internal dynamism, is, *as an ensemble,* in motion, drifting towards the vortex of ecological crisis with humanity as its passenger.

A mixture of an objective shift to an epoch of complexity and unpredictability, and a diminishing of society's ability to *respond* to such a challenge, have created a backdrop of insecurity. A reflection of this has been widespread mainstream interest in the notion of risk, which was beginning to take shape in the early 1990s; and it was Ulrich Beck who played a major role in highlighting its importance conceptually (Beck, 1992).

Beck was right that this development is extremely significant, but there are major flaws in his interpretation. Effectively, he assumes that material threat to livelihoods is a thing of the past, a characteristic of early industrial society now replaced by a new set of anxieties suffered by post-industrial citizens whose material wants have largely been satisfied. This suggests he was isolated from the living conditions of the masses in any part of the world, and most notably in the majority world, the global South. In reality, material threat to livelihoods is on a global scale getting worse, not better.

A non-Eurocentric perspective on risk would place this in historic context. Conventionally, the obvious way of 'mapping' capitalism is to trace the transfer of value, as something *positive,* as in Amin's accumulation on a world scale (Amin, 1970). But in systems theory, the global metabolism can equally (and often more interestingly) be viewed as a handling of *negative* values: the core system improves its own predictability through the dissipation of insecurity. This notion dovetails perfectly with the Black Marxist approach. Precolonial African systems had created a strong framework of order, reflected in the extent to which people could live their life under conditions of security – far higher than was the case, for example, in England at the time of its initial foray into the slave trade (Du Bois, 1965). But with colonialism, as Rodney brilliantly shows, we find an export of social disorder which parallels – and in some respects is more significant than – the more obvious *import* of physical resources (Rodney, 1972). Nor is the psychological dimension of insecurity a new issue, as Fanon's work shows; (Fanon, 1968) we can legitimately regard *disturbance* in the psychological sense as a manifestation of a destroyed equilibrium. This perspective is still fully up-to-date, revealing not just the *historical* roots of today's 'conflicts' and 'state failures' which preoccupy the dominant discourse, but equally a continuing mechanism for the displacement of insecurity to the periphery.

Beck was right, however, that some sort of qualitative change was occurring in the 1990s, and if we arm ourself with the systems perspective, class analysis and non-Eurocentrism, we are in a good position to understand what this really was. The point is that risk has itself become an explicit category in mediating the exchanges or transformations which constitute the mode of operation of the capitalist IPE, as we will now see.

The Role of Finance Capital in Profiting from, and Accentuating, Disorder

Finance capital doesn't ignore the new era of uncertainty (where the abnormal becomes normal), quite the opposite. Thus, in risk insurance, the phenomenon known as 'fat tails' describes a situation where events at the outlying reaches (tails) of the bell curve[22] of probability are 'fattened' by unpredictabilities. But the risk is *embraced*, and effectively welcomed. This can happen because, parallel to the shift towards abnormality in physical systems, finance capital has undergone its own, complementary shift to abnormality, and the two become interlocked.

If we speak of a malignant form of capitalism, as imperialism theory rightly does, this does not mean we are counterposing it to an OK, 'natural' form. The reason that the reformist, 'natural capitalism' discourse (for example, that of Lovins (Hawken, Lovins and Lovins, 1999)) fails to stand up is that capitalism is *inherently* unnatural; this is exactly why Marx based his theory on the contradiction between capitalism and nature, implanted since the beginning of its story, and gradually playing itself out ever since. Capitalism nevertheless had a 'nature' of its own, for example the competitive market and the production of real commodities. With the advent of imperialism, the change was that it became

---

[22] The normal curve is like a bell because probability in the middle range is far higher than at either edge, where it tends to flatten out.

'unnatural', as compared not just to its physical environment (because it always was, so there is no change), but to its *own* 'normal' mode of operation. It was indeed the logical development of that very 'normal' mode which had led to its own eventual self-negation. Marx already perceived such incipient trends. Thus, in arguing that reproduction "can be understood only as motion, not as a thing at rest", (Marx, 1971 p. 108) he clearly takes a systems perspective, showing that large components of a given capital must take the form of money capital, in order to keep productive capital functioning; (Marx, 1971 p. 357) and the more this happens, the more it begins to assume an 'abnormal form'. The course remains normal "so long as the disturbances during the repetitions of the circuit balance one another"; but when this is not the case, a larger volume of money capital is needed as a shield against disruption (Marx, 1971, p. 110). And with the increasing repetition and scope of such disturbances, "the more does the automatic movement of the now independent value operate with the elemental force of a natural process, against the foresight and calculation of the individual capitalist, the more does the course of normal production become subservient to abnormal speculation… (Marx, 1971, p. 109)." This passage is full of insights which can be developed in interesting ways. Capitalism initially introduced an alienation whereby the constructive relation with nature was abolished, leaving only a destructive elemental force, supposedly 'tamed', but which in fact eventually reveals itself merely transposed into the shape of a brutal operation of capital itself, a creature of human social development which now consumes those who created it.

The above process was characteristic of the capitalism-imperialism transition at the end of the 19th century, and inaugurated a basic feature of imperialism which has remained in force ever since – the dominance of an increasingly uncontrollable finance capital. But what interests us here is to understand how this speculative capital begins to behave under the impact of a new set of circumstances, namely the complex crisis triggered by ecological blowback. The natural forces from which capitalism had temporarily shielded itself through transposition, are suddenly re-asserting themselves in *direct* form. Abnormal capital thus encounters abnormal ecology! Let's consider how it reacts.

Capital is itself over-produced.[23] It then floats around the world economy in many forms. There are for example $4 trillion in foreign

---

[23] Anon, "The Current Crisis, a Crisis for Over-Production of Capital", *Social Relations* (Milan) March 1992

exchange reserves, $11.6 trillion in assets held outside the US, plus collateralised debt obligations etc (Bowring, 2006). But it cannot merely hover around in a static way: it is its nature that it must try to grow. It must moreover do so on the basis of the possibilities presented by the IPE at any given time. It is under these conditions that it encounters the incipient crisis ... and responds by embracing it as a means to make money!

The concrete forms taken by finance capital in its embrace of external environmental risk can only be understood against the background of new developments in its *internal* mode of operation, i.e. its preying upon society. We must first briefly analyse these.

Imperialism created not just finance capital but concentration, i.e. the giant corporations. By the time of the counter-attack against modernism, these had become top-heavy. Finance capital then assumed a predatory role, hence the 'raiding' activity of the 1980s. The latter has more recently been paralleled by what seems to be its 21st century equivalent, 'leveraged buyouts' conducted by so-called private equity. Often, the same (corporate or individual) personalities involved 20 years earlier are still active today, for example, Kohlberg Kravis Roberts (KKR), author of perhaps the most famous of the older generation of raids, the 1988 hostile takeover of the giant R.J. Reynolds-Nabisco; and some recent raids, notably the $7.4 billion takeover of the Chrysler motor corporation by Cerberus Capital Management in 2007, look on the surface exactly like the earlier forms.

However, the similarity may be deceptive. In the '80s, as I argued in a previous study, the top-down corporations and conglomerates were dinosaurs in a new world of downsizing and outsourcing, and it is not surprising that predators evolved to pick them off (Biel, 2000). The regime of accumulation, then in its ascendancy, is now in decline. So perhaps beneath the apparent continuity lies a difference in substance. In fact what happens today is that the notion of a 'public company' (public to the capitalist class), apparently one of the great institutional creations of the entire capitalist epoch, is suddenly overturned, and companies are taken back into private hands. Even an apparently merely quantitative narrowing of the group which controls and benefits from the system could have qualitative significance, and we will consider in more detail later the social significance of such an increasing concentration of wealth and power *at the top*. But the key qualitative issue to highlight for our discussion in this chapter is that there is no longer any accountability to the capitalist class in a wider sense, and this in turn relates to the crucial question of information: it becomes easier to suppress signals which might trigger negative feedback and hence avert disaster.

This may provide a clue about the special features of today's raiding. Lenin described imperialism as parasitic, and there is an essential difference between a predator and a parasite! The raiders of the '80s were predators because they went for the quick kill; perhaps today's are truer parasites. When the abuses of raiding attract critics even within the establishment – who call for regulation of the capital which funds leveraged private-equity buyouts (Mackintosh and Arnold, 2007) – the raiders defend themselves by saying that they are in it for the long haul and not merely planning to cut and run. Maybe we can pay them the compliment of acknowledging that this is partly true! Typically, the debt incurred through the buyout is shifted onto the company while the raiders continue paying themselves large fees, (Guerrera, 2007) while increasingly, finance houses are not merely *investing in* the major corporations, but starting to own them directly.[24] This may be the conduct of the true parasite, clamping itself to the body of the host to suck its blood on a long-term basis.

Having established this framework, let's now consider how the new modes of finance capital approach risk.

In a certain sense, capitalism has always been upfront about welcoming risk: the standard argument is that, in investment, return is higher if risk is higher (McDonald, 2007). Now, there is a strong element of deception here, inasmuch as profit is made to appear as a *reward* for taking risk, conveniently glossing over the fact it actually derives from the exploitation of labour, and that the person whose livelihood will be most at risk if the enterprise goes bust is the worker, not the capitalist. Nevertheless, in an old-fashioned industrial-capitalist situation where the entrepreneur stakes his accumulated wealth on a hunch, the argument is not entirely false. But today's situation is quite different because the main arena of risk (encompassing all aspects of the structural crisis, economic and environmental) is severed from the real economy and from any particular productive decision. Instead, the reference-point is the general climate of insecurity in which we live,

---

[24] In fact the boundary between finance and industrial capital was already blurred: industrial capital was beginning to operate as though it were finance capital by making more of its profits out of speculation (for example on currency) rather than on manufacture; now this is simply happening the other way round.

and investment in *this* risk could only be parasitic, not productive. We saw this when, with Zimbabwe locked in crisis, the Zimbabwean stock market emerged as one of the best performing in the world! An economist explains this: "Where some see crisis others see opportunity"[25] (this of course signifies not opportunity to build a new world, but merely to parasitise upon the decay of the old).

With insecurity thus becoming profitable, the flows of capital accumulation begin to draw on this parasitic definition of risk and treat it as one of their key operating principles.

The main mechanism for this is hedging. In the first years of the 21st century, the floating-around (overproduced) capital increasingly moved into hedge funds: between 2002 and 2007, the value of assets managed by these nearly tripled, from $592 billion to about $1,500 billion; in the latter year, 93 out of the 100 wealthiest traders in the world were hedge fund managers (Teather, 2007). Since there is always too much capital, it must desperately seek the talisman which at a given time seems to multiply it, and suddenly, that has become risk. The objective basis for this is surely the crisis itself: the more unstable the mode of production, the more investment latches onto the symptoms of its own instability. And since hedge funds are, like private equity, not open to ordinary investors, and thus excluded from normal scrutiny (even of the capitalist class, as would be the case with a 'public' company), decisions are insulated from any feedback from their consequences. Now we are getting closer to an understanding of why capitalism steers into the heart of the storm.

What hedging supposedly means is that you insure yourself against one eventuality by betting on the alternative eventuality. From a logical point of view it is hard to see that this can achieve anything, because the aggregate of all such operations would merely cancel each other out. Establishment management theories (translating this proposition into the terminology of market economics by saying that investment decisions should already incorporate the response to risk) do indeed admit this logical problem (Crouchy, Galai and Mark, 2006). From the practitioners' point of view, never mind the logic, if it works in terms of making money it can't be too bad: profits do indeed accrue at every point in the hedging chain. But in our attempt at a critical model, we

---

[25] quoted in *Guardian*, April 25 2006

cannot be entirely satisfied with this explanation; we have to look for a deeper reality underlying it.

To answer this, let's again consider regulation. As I proposed elsewhere, (Biel, 2006) there is a strong argument (insufficiently understood in mainstream regulation theory) that what really underlies regulation is a shifting around of insecurities between different regions of the socio-ecological map (between core and periphery, between social and physical entropy). Now, hedging could play a significant role here. Given that, as Mao observed, it is difficult to catch ten fleas with ten fingers, (Mao, 1985, p.499) the available resources would need to be concentrated in such a way as to neutralise the most pressing issue at a particular time. Objectively, regulation has always done this, for example amid the ruins left by World War II the social risk confronted by capitalism was extraordinarily high, and this was effectively offloaded onto the physical environment by the pursuit of ecologically-costly growth strategies. But what is different today is the degree of complexity. Surely regulation itself must adapt to these conditions by operating in a new way, one where it mimics the emergent behaviour of the complex systems it confronts. Our general argument is that this is very difficult for capitalism to achieve, but it may be possible in pockets. On this reasoning, perhaps hedging constitutes an evolved mechanism to search, in a spontaneous manner, the most appropriate sink for insecurities at a particular time. Of course, to say it is 'evolved' does not mean, as in Hayek's right-wing notion of spontaneous order, that it is 'the best of all possible worlds'. It has merely evolved to facilitate a process which is itself in a larger sense unsustainable, i.e. the maintenance of a mode of production which *as an ensemble* drifts into the vortex. Such a system may appear internally regulated (like the table-tennis players used to illustrate the Theory of Relativity, whose rules within their own reference-frame remain consistent) until one takes account of the movement of the whole.

In this context, the psychological dimension may well become key. After all, regulation is itself in the last analysis an exercise in denial: by shifting entropy around, you can pretend (including to yourself) that it doesn't exist. Today it is more than ever necessary to create an illusion that dangers can be guarded against, and hedging may well fulfil this function. At least as important as physical dissipation is to dissipate the anxiety associated with the risks it generates. Perhaps also a separation of anxiety from its true object (how capitalism is messing up the environment and society) then facilitates the 'capture' of this ambient anxiety by reactionary 'security' discourses.

This brings some way towards an understanding of the speculative economy, but not yet to the heart of the matter. Regulation theory as a whole still suffers a deficit in coming to terms with entropy because, however important the institutional conditions for multiplying capital, we are still left with the question that such multiplication cannot come out of nothing: in any development, some form of destruction must act as its counterpart. In a past/future, ecologically sound system, this condition is supplied by the exhaustion of the sun's fuel during its 'main sequence'; but under capitalism, it is supplied by a non-sustainable form of destruction, i.e. that of the ecosystem and its resources, as well as by the self-consumption of society. This brings us back to the distinction we posited in Chapter 1, between fictional and *dematerialised* values. Hedging is indisputably fictional, but nevertheless, must be associated with a real entropy. In order to verify this, some specific links should be identified.

If we consider the dimension of the destruction of society, we can highlight the risk to livelihoods. For example, currency speculation claims to respond (reactively) to *existing* vulnerabilities, but in fact its prophecies are self-fulfilling: a *supposed* vulnerability of a country's economy may have no objective basis, but by speculating on it you create it. The resultant increase of suffering on the part of poor countries and peoples, the reduction of the quality of their social order, becomes the destructive counterpart of the augmentation of speculative capital. In a recent and more sophisticated form, the rules of the game function so that the oppressed become agents in their own exploitation: as insecurity rises, Southern countries wishing to insure themselves against speculation on their perceived vulnerability do so by accumulating reserves which by definition must be safe, so they have typically taken the form of low-income-yielding US Treasury bills. Thus, as Tina Rosenberg shows, the US has been financing itself at the expense of the South: from a break-even point in 1997, capital-flows shifted increasingly in a South-North direction: in 2006 the negative balance from the South had reached $784 billion, up from $229 billion in 2002 (Rosenberg, 2007). In its 21st-century form, imperialism thus effectively neutralises the flows of investment *to* the South which had been more characteristic of the 1990s. This actually looks like an ingenious way of transferring to the core the benefits of the shift of industry to the periphery! As our earlier discussion of industrial management systems implied, the export of risk down the chain simultaneously drives value *up* it.

On this basis, we can better understand how speculation *creates* the vulnerability to which it claims to 'respond'. If we now apply this to hedging, we can see how, by investing in leveraged buyouts, hedge funds may generate a social entropy in the form of either job losses or healthcare and pension cuts: there is a reciprocal motion, livelihoods shrinking as profit swells. Although profit is here no longer dependent on the volume of real commodities as in Victorian-style entrepreneurial risk, it still finds a real entropy to act as its counterpart. The next step is then to drill down further into the detail, and at this point we again encounter the consumption issue with which we began this chapter; this raises issues which at last bring us close to the peculiar distinguishing features of the contemporary political economy.

As I have argued, we should avoid an underconsumptionist reading of the crisis (in the narrow sense of failing to find a market), and the systems perspective helps us here because it views consumption in a deeper sense, as an expression of the movement from order to disorder. Both the liquidation of physical resources (exergy into waste) and the creation of social entropy are spinoffs of an accumulation process which requires a destructive counterpart, and the more specific problem of finding someone to buy the product is simply a subcategory of this. The 'sink' which absorbs disorder (the poor, the marginalised) is at least as functional to a dissipative system as is the stratum which pays for the product. Nevertheless, as I will now argue, in the most recent phase the two facets have become intertwined in new ways, the social entropy reflected in the degradation of livelihoods becoming coupled, as its destructive counterpart, to the creation of a market.

In the 20th century model, as we showed earlier, consumerism already rested upon a fiction, insofar as the thermodynamic cost of food was suppressed, making it appear, in terms of Engel's law, that a larger proportion of income is available for non-essentials. Nevertheless, at that time the slice of income liberated by the phoney cheapness of food really existed. But in the 21st-century form, it seems that this single fiction is not enough. Instead, a second fiction must be added, whereby *purchasing power itself becomes imaginary*. Hence the immense escalation of consumer debt, surely one of the most significant of all recent developments. The figures are far in excess of what one might intuitively guess: consumer debt in Britain alone crossed the £1 trillion

(£1,000 billion) threshold in 2004,[26] and had climbed to £1,300 billion in 2006.[27] This must be one of the weakest points of the system, because it would be hard to identify any location within the capitalist IPE where there is the value to pay this off, even at the very summit of the pyramid where most of the wealth is concentrated. You would need to expropriate forty Bill Gateses[28] to pay off the consumer debt of Britain, a single OECD country! And under this heading, a more specific aspect of debt-fuelled consumption, upon which the economy increasingly relies in order to stay afloat, is real estate: the US mortgage security market has been estimated at $6,300 billion (Morgenson, 2007).

Consumer debt illustrates perfectly how fictional-ness and real entropy, far from being contradictory, are intimately linked. The purchasing power doesn't, in any real sense, exist, but the social degradation caused by debt certainly does: British consumers pay £93 billion in annual interest on their loans[29] ... for the privilege of fulfilling an essential service for capitalism, at the expense of an increasing insecurity of their livelihoods, which in this case is very real. The more oppressed you are, the more you pay: home-loans cost more for black people and other minorities in the USA (Knight, 2007). The hypocrisy is that the system punishes them for supplying the very thing (risk) which it welcomes as its prime lubricant. But conceptually, the important point is that the scale of deprivation within the sink population is clearly increasing as a reciprocal counterpart to the creation of a market.

Of course, the potential insolvency of borrowers exposes the lenders to risk, but as might be expected, this too can be parasitised upon, giving rise to positive-feedback loops. Thus studies reveal the suppression of information which would normally have prohibited granting mortgages; (Rucker, 2007) and risk to lenders can itself be hedged, generating profits at another point in the chain. Debt is collateralised, i.e. pooled, in the form of funds in which shares (tranches, carrying different levels of risk) can be taken. High-risk collateralised debt then becomes a major area of investment, and even 'respectable' investors like pension funds increasingly buy into it (Tett, 2007b). In this way, capitalism further 'auto-parasitises', not just upon the phoney solution

---

[26] BBC News Thursday, 29 July, 2004, on http://news.bbc.co.uk/1/hi/business/3935671.stm

[27] *The Independent*, 28 Sept. 2006

[28] Gates' estimated wealth was $58.8 billion in 2008, according to *Guardian* March 6 2008

[29] "One in four face unmanageable debt" *Guardian*, January 3 2008

to its consumption problem, but even to the unravelling of the phoney solution!

Elements within the establishment are aware that the funds themselves will in turn necessarily become vulnerable to the very risk from which they profit, (Tett, 2007a) and it was precisely exposure to collateralised debt obligations which hit hedge fund manager Bear Stearns, when it could find no-one to sell them on to. As a specialist in restructuring insolvent hedge funds (one of several professions apparently evolving to parasitise upon parasitism!) notes, "There seems to be too much cash chasing too few opportunities..."[30] The IMF nervously warns that "Financial markets have failed to price in the risk that any one of a host of threats to economic stability could materialise and deliver a massive shock to the world economy"(Thornton, 2006) But this misses the point. It is precisely such risks which draw finance capital like moths to a flame. With this level of auto-parasitism, the system looks to have become locked into a self-consuming spiral with no escape route.

Of course, since the human social system is not a closed but an open system, i.e. it is inserted within a physical environment, capitalism has traditionally found an escape route: when the social sphere gets too unmanageable: it simply increases ecological degradation to compensate. But crucially, this escape route is today much less open than at any time in the past. Feedback – including that arising from the delayed effect of the post-1945 surge of environmental depletion which underlay capitalism's most audacious restructurings – is now asserting itself.

What is the impact of these changes? There is still transposition from the social to the ecological domain, but it takes a new form. It is no longer possible to ignore risk ... but it can be embraced. The methodologies evolved for parasitising/creating social risk (consumer debt, leveraged buyouts etc.) increasingly serve as paradigm as the system now embraces the fragility of its *physical* environment. Signals of impending crisis thus becomes an invitation to supplement the exploitation of social risk by developing the comparatively unexplored territory of environmental risk. An interesting case will help explain how this works: energy hedging.

In an ideal liberal market, a reduction in energy supply would cause price rises and hence provide an incentive to reduce consumption (negative feedback). But if you have hedged against this risk, the price

---

[30] quoted in *Financial Times*, August 14 2006

rise would be neutralised by profit from the hedging operation which would increase in value. The negative feedback thus disappears. On this basis, the energy sector becomes the most exciting one for hedging. Already, according to its acolytes, "there is almost unlimited risk .... There is operational risk, geopolitical risk, event risk, regulatory risk, weather risk, tax risk, and other risks that add multiple dimensions to the more linear and traditional thinking of hedge fund land." But this is not the end of the bonanza: there is something even better on the horizon: "These externalities are also about to be overwhelmed by 'environmental risk' which is the wave beyond the current energy hedge fund euphoria" (Fusaro and Vasey, 2005a). In an interesting (presumably subconscious) choice of phrase – bearing in mind that climate change is one of the main manifestations of the risk – the 'euphoric' advocates of energy hedging enthuse: "We continue to expect the green space to really heat up further..."[!] (Fusaro and Vasey, 2005b: 3). One senses the same quasi-extatic bliss as when US military-political figures discuss terrorism: a new frontier of opportunity.

In the first place, hedging tends to cancel out the healthy negative feedback which would result if scarcity pushed up prices. But the effects may even go one step further, into the realm of *positive* feedback which actively encourages depletion. We can understand this in the sense that hedging profits from insecurity, and therefore actually likes it. The 'green space' referred to encompasses all the opportunities to cash in on impending catastrophe, and is only accentuated by the neo-liberal response to climate change, which creates new markets related to emissions. A *Financial Times* survey highlights a 'green gold rush', the regulated market for carbon credits being expected to reach $68.2bn by 2010. Here, huge profits can be made from marketing credits, supposedly to offset emissions, but which typically deliver little real effect.[31] In this way, even 'green' economics is subsumed into the expanded reproduction of capital, thereby intensifying the mode of production which causes the crisis to which it claims to respond.

The feedback loops we have just discussed assume that speculative finance capital operates merely within its own fictional sphere. However, there is worse. Just as hedge funds create real *social* entropy – by financing leveraged corporate buyouts which may then destroy livelihoods – so they also interfere directly within the energy sector. The precursor of this was the Enron Corporation: although it went bust

---

[31] *Financial Times*, "Industry caught in carbon 'smokescreen'", April 25 2007

in December 2001 (in the biggest corporate bankruptcy in US history), Enron nevertheless anticipated an important mutation of imperialism. Part of what it did was hedging: the sales pitch on its website revealed how a power company, worried that global warming would reduce its profits (because people would need less power for heating), could pay a premium to Enron to insure against this result;[32] as Henry Liu points out, such options are inherently easy to offer, since the more catastrophic the outcome, the less likely the insurance-seller will be around to pay: "For $10, I will guarantee you live to 150. If you don't, come to my office and I will pay you $1 million."(Liu, 2007) But the other aspect is that Enron was also operating in the real world, and could thus materially influence the trends which were being speculated upon. It bought heavily into the power and water sectors of developing countries, which neo-liberalism and Structural Adjustment were forcing them to sell off (and because Structural Adjustment packages included compulsory devaluation – allegedly to improve the competitiveness of exports – these resources were dirt cheap). Hedge funds today buy heavily into the supposed energy sectors of the future, particularly the Canadian Tarsands,[33] a scenario which, as we have seen, is inherently absurd because of its negative EROEI, but where there is no informational reality check. Particularly notable has been the involvement of speculative capital in rising food insecurity. A study of the Australian agricultural crisis of 2006 reveals food price rises to be increasingly determined not by supply and demand, but by the futures market, the grain market being "changed by the sheer amount of speculative capital being invested by hedge funds and other investors who are enjoying easier access to the commodities market thanks to advances in electronic trading."[34] The final piece in the jigsaw is that investors hedging against peak oil invest heavily in biofuels on the assumption that this will become a growth sector, thus turning the 'ethanol boom' into a self-fulfilling prophecy, and (by withdrawing land from food crops) further intensifying the global food problem. In fact the collapse of Enron may actually itself be part of this evolutionary history: as a public company it was slightly vulnerable to informational reality checks,

---

[32] http://www.enron.com/wholesale/weather/two.html, accessed 6.10.02
[33] c.f. a conference organised by the Strategic Research Institute, on http://www .srinstitute.com/conf_page.cfm?instance_id=30&web_id=948&pid=555   accessed March 2007
[34] *Financial Times*, October 16 2006

so private equity has risen to the surface as a 'fitter' institutional solution whereby capital can be better insulated from reality.

In the above analysis, we have viewed finance capital as an out-of-control, elemental force, dragging humanity towards disaster by picking up the signals of crisis and distorting them into positive feedback. This is consistent with the theory of alienation, and has the advantage of countering any excessively instrumental or conspiratorial reading of imperialism. Although this perspective emphasises the *objective*, its highlighting of information hopefully prevents it from degenerating into structural determinism.

However, having said this, it must be recognised that our model is so far incomplete, simply because imperialism cannot be *reduced* to finance capital. The real essence of imperialism is finance capital's interaction with the militarised state, with which it develops symbiotically. Once we bring this dimension into play, the process appears rather more deliberate and less spontaneous. Nevertheless, the conspiratorial element clearly present in the clique around George W. Bush, can be analysed objectively as a response – albeit not an inevitable one – of a system assailed by troubling information and imprisoned by narrowing choices. This issue will form the focus of the next chapter. As an introduction, I will draw our current discussion to a close by highlighting those aspects of the information from entropy which lead us directly into the political sphere.

The Political Dimension and the Plunge into Militarism

The fact that the foreign policy of the big powers (USA, Britain, France, Japan etc.) promotes the interest of their *manufacturing* corporations is obvious so we needn't expand on it; it is however worth emphasising how active they are in promoting also finance capital. Enron's predatory activities received huge government support. While that corporation's links to the Bush family and their cronies are well known, it is important to signal the key role played by Clinton in backing perhaps the most decisive Enron project – the takeover of the power sector in the Indian state of Maharashtra.[35]

Once again, we are confronted by the truth of Marx' words that under conditions where "man from the beginning behaves towards

---

[35] c.f. for example http://www.ei.enron.com/presence/projects/india_main.html

nature, the primary source of all instruments and subjects of labour, as an owner, treats her as belonging to him ... the man who possesses no other property than his labour power must, in all conditions of society and culture, be the slave of other men who have made themselves the owners of the material conditions of labour."(Marx, 1970, p.13) This is fully in accord with the systems theory perspective, for as Gale shows, power has both social and thermodynamic dimensions, and the key issue is how the two interact (Gale, 1998). In backing the corporate takeover of the power and water sectors in the South, the imperialist state pursues exactly the agenda of controlling resources in order to control people. We cannot therefore hope to understand the socio-ecological crisis, under conditions of imperialism, without grasping the interaction between finance capital and the military state.

And this takes us to a still more important issue: struggle. The reason Enron collapsed was, to a significant extent, that it overreached itself in Maharashtra by directly taking on the mass movement. Defeat in India weakened the whole corporate edifice, precipitating its demise.

Struggle is absolutely fundamental to our model, and we must understand how it connects with the objective constraints defined by the Second Law of thermodynamics and EROEI. Such constraints manifest themselves in the real world not directly, but only mediated through socio-political processes. Marx' anti-Malthusian argument to the effect that workers' income is determined as much by struggle as by objective laws, (Marx, 1969 c) can legitimately be extended to the sphere of exergy: the *effective* availability of resources – their 'scarcity', and even its reflection in price – is politically determined. The Malthusian position is reactionary precisely because it pretends to be apolitical but is in reality eminently political in the way it uses so-called objective scarcity to undermine struggle.

This argument is equally relevant to the peak oil issue. The 1970s 'energy crisis' occurred when, as Hirsch's graph shows, oil had not yet peaked, and this made it more obvious that scarcity was political (c.f. the 1973 Middle East war and OPEC boycott). The work of Nore and Turner, appropriately entitled *Oil and the Class Struggle*, (Nore and Turner, 1980) well reflects the spirit of that time. But I believe its fundamental argument is still true today, and the new-found objectivity of the peak oil situation should not be allowed to obscure it. Actually, we should speak not just of class, but of national struggle, and the relationship between the two is an interesting problem, (Massarat, 1987) an issue which we will address in later chapters; indigenous struggles are also central to the issue. But in any case, the key notion is struggle.

Even in the today's situation where peak oil is a reality, the expression of scarcity is mediated through a complex mix of class, national and indigenous movements (as, for example, in Bolivia), rather than asserting itself as an abstract objective limit.

The way that this impacts on the core is extremely interesting. The entropy of a closed system increases with time, and up to now, the core could behave as though it is *not* closed, because contradictions shaped by poverty and the rate of profit could be dissipated into the physical and social periphery. But today, the core finds itself squeezed in a pincers movement, as both environments (physical and social) reject its attempted dissipations. The two rejections are linked in a feedback relationship, inasmuch as peak oil gives bargaining power to radical movements in producer countries (e.g. Venezuela), thus helping them to fight back against their status as a social sink for capitalism's contradictions. This narrows the core's room to manoeuvre. How would it respond?

In fact, however self-deluding it may be about the objective limits facing it, capitalism is fairly realistic about the challenge posed by struggle. It is amusing to observe a leading defender of energy hedging strongly affirming the existence of an energy crisis, while denying the reality of peak oil (Vasey, 2005); his vested interest is to deculpabilise finance capital by showing that the crisis is caused by politics rather than by economic factors, but he is nevertheless partly right. And the state/military wing of imperialism is similarly not fooled. Matthew Simmons was invited to present his radical peak-oil model to the Pentagon.[36] The point is that, whereas the ruling interests will not process this information into a decision to reverse their disastrous course towards the abyss, they *will* process it … into repressive political options.

Let us consider in more detail what these options are. One facet is to look for a strategy to *defeat* the popular/nationalist struggles, for example to destroy the experiment initiated by Venezuela's Hugo Chávez of using oil revenues to develop a new kind of 'direct democracy' (Manwarring, 2007). But assuming this counter-attack fails, the North would need a fallback option: somehow to make themselves more independent, both from oil itself and therefore from its Southern producers.

---

[36] see the presentation on http://www.simmonsco-intl.com/files/Energy%20 Conversation.pdf

The notion of independence from oil (always assuming, of course, that current trends of consumption are maintained, which is capitalism's basic premise) is centrally focused around the ethanol programme. The delusoriness of this beggars belief. Given that the current annual consumption of fossil energy represents 400 years of plant and animal deposits, (Dukes, 2005) the notion that one could possibly replace current consumption by biological resources on a one-to-one basis is nonsensical. But our point is precisely that economic logic alone cannot explain the system's direction: it is only when a security consideration is brought into play that almost anything can be made to appear justified – even 'turning gold into lead'..

Complementary to this is the other side of the fallback strategy, independence from the South. An interesting example is a high-level brainstorming exercise called North American Future 2025 Project, initiated under the auspices of the Washington-based Center for Strategic and International Studies. (Peschard-Sverdrup and Armand, n.d.) It looks very like a recipe for the US to re-focus its accumulation on Canadian resources and Mexican cheap labour. The interesting point is what this tells us about the particular form of path-dependency called globalisation. To ditch globalisation would be an admission of failure, for then capitalism must abandon any pretence of continuing to *develop*, and admit that it is a mere decadent rump of a mode of production, viciously guarding the scattered enclaves where its writ still runs. This could only be a last resort. Nevertheless, things have come to a point where such a scenario cannot be ruled out, at least as a contingency plan. Although North American Future is still couched in globalisation-speak (i.e. maintaining the region's global competitiveness), between the lines we sense a preparation for regional autarky. Should the revolution in South America prove uncrushable, that continent will be cut adrift. Preparations began at a NAFTA summit in 2005 for the establishment of a North American Union, along the lines of the EU, by 2010, and the Council on Foreign Relations' explanation of this project emphasised strengthening *external* borders, with the establishment of a 'security perimeter'. (Council on Foreign Relations, 2005) Energy-wise, the centrepiece was Canadian oil; the US Department of Energy pressured Canada for a massive increase in its production,[37] talking up its resources to investors as "believed to hold more than all reserves of

---

[37] *CBC News*, January 18 2007

the OPEC countries combined". (Strategic Research Institute, 2007) Although the NAU scheme has so far come to nothing, its existence is indicative of a certain mindset. In a narrow sense it is of course true that, if US policy causes sufficient chaos in the Middle East, oil prices will rise enough to make it 'viable' to exploit Canadian resources and thus increase regional autarky. But when the EROEI becomes negative, only a distorted security logic could justify this.

The above facts suggest something interesting about the relationship between finance capital and the state in generating such absurdities.

In mainstream economic thinking, the assumption is that public policy steps in to correct the bad environmental externalities generated by the market. This is most obviously true in the pre-neoliberal branch of economics developed by Arthur Pigou, (Pigou, 1932) but even neoliberalism would theoretically accept some action in the form of establishing legal rights, quotas etc. But the real world of contemporary imperialism looks very different. Here, the state may actually act as accomplice to the most regressive activities of finance capital; or even, and this is important, perhaps goad it into worse excesses than it would spontaneously generate. In the nuclear industry, for instance, risk has always been suppressed through state intervention (in Britain's Dounreay reactor, samples for monitoring being allegedly collected with an old wellington boot on a piece of string (Monbiot, 2006b)). But although finance capital welcomes risk up to a point, it is unlikely that this degree of risk could be insured ... or hedged. This is where the state comes into play, encouraging the export of risk to the future by simply denying massive hazard. In the USA, where no new nuclear plants had been proposed since the 1970s, nuclear suddenly became *seemingly* an attractive option again: but only because the 2005 Energy Policy Act provided 20 years insurance cover in case of a reactor accident, as well as loan guarantees for up to 80% of construction cost and state guarantees to absorb the full cost of any holdup due to litigation (Holzer, 2006). By distorting economic information, the state (as guardian of the militarised definition of 'security') thus pushes even further in the direction of potential massive hazard than does a finance capital itself addicted to risk.

Bush (to his credit perhaps, in contrast to the hypocrisy of other imperialist leaders) never bothered pretending to be green: his major 2007 speech introducing the ethanol strategy, despite a passing reference to climate change, overwhelmingly emphasised security. (United States Government, 2007) But in principle there is no reason why a similar policy – which in *substance* is about continuing to consume energy at all costs while trying to insulate oneself against the political leverage of the Southern producers – could not be presented under a green guise. This is in fact increasingly likely in the future. The British government, for example, has found a much more cunning way of backing nuclear power: its competitor, energy from conventional power stations, is taxed for being environmentally unsound![38] This creates an illusion of economic viability without the existence of any apparent subsidies, and with a side-effect of confusing the environmental issue by presenting itself as 'green' ... a brilliant achievement, which imperialist policy will surely increasingly imitate. But this of course is only spin – it doesn't solve the real problem.

The 'Colonisation' of Security

The issue of hazard leads us to a paradox in the notion of security which we should now explore. What the ruling discourse calls 'security' (i.e. militarism) actually makes the world less secure, while at the same time the signals from real insecurity, in particular environmental hazard, are neglected. Surely, the two tendencies are connected: *it is the militarised security discourse which in some sense pumps dry the debate on the danger to the ecology and to society.*

The ruling order builds its credentials on combating insecurity on behalf of society, on rebuilding the structure which the era of unpredictability dissolves. To do so, it claims exceptional (extraordinary) repressive powers. The notion of 'terrorism' is convenient in conjuring up everyone's nameless fears of some threatening or chaotic force. In the United States, you have more *real* risk of being killed by a law-enforcement officer than by a terrorist, (Singel, 2006) but the discourse turns this reality upside down, such that capitalism's own failure becomes the justification for an entrenchment of its dominance. As a result, the whole debate which should be about a solution to crisis becomes siphoned into building the repressive apparatus.

To understand better such instances of 'capture' or appropriation, it is conceptually useful to consider them as cases of 'enclosure'.

The historical reference for 'enclosure' is the time when, during the breakdown of mediaeval England, public spaces and commons were

---

[38] *Guardian*, January 12 2008

appropriated as private property. In an extended sense, we can develop this usage in several ways. At a discourse level, the *definition* of a useful good like security is appropriated: rather than signifying something of common benefit – such as the conditions enabling people to look forward to a safe future where they can lead their lives in a mutually enriching way – it is twisted to mean militarism. But underlying the discourse, something also changes materially, and this is what we need to understand.

Capitalist development spreads spatially by breaking down spheres of non-monetary reciprocal exchange, but in so doing, in some strange way, *encloses also itself*, by limiting its future developmental scope. It is this latter aspect which explains the entropy. Inspired by Luxemburg, (Luxemburg, 1913) we can picture capitalism moving along its time axis by expanding into more and more of the finite area which has not yet been commodified … and thereby exhausting the terrain which rests. The institutional condition may often be primary, because to appropriate a physical resource one must first break up the ideological and social systems which evolved to protect it. Here, we can consider the 'enclosure' of knowledge, (Marglin, F. and Marglin, S., 1990; Zelem, 1991) or the attack on women's ascribed role as nurturer of the natural world, (Merchant, 1990) within the gender division which underpins traditional formations.

In an important sense, this is a battle over 'regimes'. The type of organisational regime which capitalism hates is one which manages resources as a 'commons'. To attack these is a consistent theme from earliest capitalism till the present day. Even when the mode of production has ceased going anywhere, its learned response is that, in order to progress, it must consume regimes. This must be why the Bush project so explicitly asserted itself as an attack on the surviving commons (Donnelly, 2000, pp. 50–1). But in the degenerate phase, the liquidation of commons is insufficient to nourish the beast, so alongside it, the system begins to gobble up even its own creations. This applies particularly to what is known as public goods.

The public sphere is different from commons because it is not intrinsically subversive, quite the contrary: it served to prop up the exploitative system. Nevertheless, popular struggles to defend livelihoods could make claims on the public sphere, and this too could be prevented by subsuming it into the region of accumulation.

Something changes qualitatively within the enclosed space: we could say that the future is shrunk through a depletion of diversity.

Commodification cancels out concrete, diverse specificity (for example, use value), reducing everything to a generalised and abstract measure of value. In fact, loss of differentiation is often considered a key representation of entropy: in some theories of astrophysics, black holes have an exceptionally high entropy because they cancel out all specificities of the things they draw in (Luminet, 1992, p. 193). We could experiment with a 3-D model similar to the light-cones of astrophysics where the arrow of time goes in one direction and geographic space and institution-space make up the other two dimensions; at some point space-time curves sufficiently to entrap (enclose) everything within a horizon wherein differentiation is lost.

Of course, the metaphor is not exact and this is precisely our point: the assumption of irreversibility does not hold because, although the loss of cultures and bodies of knowledge from the past is perhaps irreversible, what is retained is an inherently human faculty for networking which can reconstitute differentiation and serve to rebuild society from the base. The entropy of capitalism is therefore not an irreversible decay of human history as a whole. But mainstream institutional theory offers only a weak defence against further encroachment (enclosure) on regimes and on the public sphere. Elinor Ostrom, for example, exhibits a certain naivety when she seeks, by classifying institutions according to certain general rules, to compare their performance in relation to different problems or resources and uphold the continued relevance of regimes or public goods *for what they do best* (Ostrom, 2005). The obvious fallacy is that the dynamic of capitalism is *not* determined by what works best, but by what serves accumulation. The fact that commons regimes or public goods are good ways of administering resources has not stopped capitalism destroying them, quite the contrary, *capitalism breaks them up precisely because they are effective*, and therefore hinder appropriation.

This is true of neo-liberal privatisations in general, but what interests us particularly is the application to security. It is consistent with the institutional perspective to consider security as falling somewhere within the sphere of commons or public goods (Walls, 2007). In the abstract, security might be seen as a public good, inasmuch as one person's enjoyment does not diminish another's (quite the contrary, it would seem), and it is both difficult and pointless to exclude others from its benefits. But this assumption never holds up against the reality of class society. By analogy, clean air seems to be a good wherein one person's enjoyment does not diminish another's, yet in practice environmental hazard has always been exported to poorer districts. Similarly, 'public order' is always in practice a way of protecting the 'haves' against real or imagined threats. Nevertheless, it is hard to escape a sense that the most recent period has seen the enclosure of public goods getting qualitatively worse. Instead of having beneficial spill-over effects to the rest of society, security goods are increasingly fragmented, 'gated', and defined in a frankly exclusionary sense, while chaos is left to take over outside these enclaves. Against this background, those like Bollier, (Bollier, 2001) who emphasise the need to *defend* commons regimes (albeit initially within the restricted sphere of what they are 'best at'), are objectively progressive. The dominant mode of production cannot actually concede to an alternative institutional mode the right to occupy a certain space, even a restricted one: for example, the regime-based solution to the problem of water management (Molden and de Fraiture, 2004) clearly contradicts Enron-type logic and anticipates a future beyond capitalism.

If we take security in a 'normal' sense, i.e. as a desirable good for humanity (freedom to lead one's life, to fulfil one's potential free from disruptive uncertainty), then it is inherent in all goods; for example, agriculture is not just about regimes protecting land and knowledge, but ultimately about food security; or, in the ecofeminist literature, traditional institutional arrangements preserved the genetic variety shielding humanity against environmental shocks (Shiva, 1988). For this reason, the intrinsic subversiveness of commons regimes is that they uphold popular, non-militarist approaches to security.

This comes to the fore at a time like this when society is faced with immense and destabilising challenges and capitalism fails to respond. Simultaneously, during the 2000s, capitalism on the one hand abdicated leadership in the face of shocks to livelihoods, on the other hand, plunged headlong into repressive 9/11-style security discourses. It is hard to escape feeling that the two are reciprocally related. In France in 2003, 11,000 people were killed by a heatwave; New Orleans in 2005 witnessed unprecedented scenes of devastation and suffering. The system exhibits total contempt for the victims – Black people, the elderly and the poor – who far outnumber, and will continue to outnumber, even the most inflated assessments of the victims of so-called terrorism. But who has proposed a 'war on the administrative neglect of the causes and effects of climate change', or the incarceration of French ministers and FEMA officials on Guantánamo? A clear expression of this reciprocal relationship (the suppression of real danger, the elevation of phoney danger) can be found in the Bush administration's so-called 'one percent doctrine', promulgated by Vice-President Dick Cheyney: if there is the merest possibility of some 'terrorist' danger, it should be treated as though it was a certainty (Suskind, 2006, p. 62). This looks very like a parody of the precautionary principle in ecology, precisely the thing which is being squashed down as the military agenda rises: imagined threats are treated as certainties, while real ones, including biological and nuclear hazard constantly manufactured by the system, are denied.

Indeed, the Hurricane Katrina disaster of 2005 may serve as a microcosm of the whole international political economy. Because repressive 'security' definitions have sucked in the whole territory of crisis-response, the reaction could only be to implement contingency plans designed to respond to 'terrorism'. At one New Orleans bridge, people were permitted to evacuate by car while those trying to leave on foot were turned back by armed police.[39] In a counter-response, the struggle for environmental justice *becomes* the social conflict in the sense of acting as a vehicle for the information from entropy which the system ignores, upholding a socially meaningful definition of security and thus necessarily challenging the abusive definitions of the dominant order.

---

[39] *North County Times*, October 31 2007 on http://nctimes.com/articles/2007/11/01/news/nation/15_32_9510_31_07.txt

MILITARISM AND STATE TERRORISM
AS A RESPONSE TO CRISIS

Introduction: Chaos and Order

Our aim in this chapter is to interpret the repressive and militarist phase which began around the turn of the millennium. By understanding its place within the history of capitalism, we will have an idea of where it may be going next. Let's begin by considering the system's own discourse: that which focused everything around notions of 'terrorism'.

This took as its excuse the events of 9/11 2001, but in reality was clearly in place well before that date. Britain's Terrorism Act 2000, with its sweeping attack on civil liberties, predated 9/11, as did the publication, also in 2000, of what can be considered a manifesto for Bush's project, a think-tank report from the 'Project for the New American Century'; the latter includes a section entitled "Creating Tomorrow's Dominant Force" which anticipates "some catastrophic and catalyzing event – like a new Pearl Harbor."(Donnelly, 2000, pp. 50–1) We can therefore be categorical that the policy shift anticipated 9/11, rather than responding to it. In fact, preparations went back at least two or three years earlier: the 'Project for the New American Century' was founded by Bush's inner clique in 1997, and the idea of using 'terrorism' as an excuse to launch this project can be dated to around 1998 (Perl, 1998).

Most obviously, the notion of a terrorist enemy here functions as a smokescreen, under which the system can prepare its own terroristic clampdown on dissent in the face of approaching crisis. But it would be a mistake to see the 'terrorism' discourse only as cynical propaganda. It also represents a horrifying vision which *really* plagues the ruling order: the tip-over into a regime of unpredictability, of challenges which render its existing tools totally useless, of information whose meaning it can't decipher. The destructive reflex is a pathological response to such a failure of comprehension.

Our focus is contemporary, but for this very reason we must go back to history. The ingredients of the Bush madness were present in a shadowy way, or as secondary currents, within earlier imperialism. Through a qualitative change, they suddenly rose to the surface to become the main current. Something flipped.

What triggered such a flip was a mixture of internal and external causes. Externally, as we have seen, available energy is drying up. But something changes internally too: a sense that complexity has become too much to manage. From this perspective, 'counter-terrorism' really signifies a frantic striving to 'outlaw' complexity. The internal and external attacks are linked by feedback relationships: up to a point you can extract energy from a complex system because it permits a high degree of spontaneously emergent order, but once the unpredictability of that emergence becomes too threatening, you switch back to a control reflex.

In a simplistic Malthusian reading, the tipping point is some absolute number, but by now it should be clear that we can more usefully represent 'limit' as a degree of complexity. For Michel Baranger, complexity grows and becomes chaos when you have to admit defeat in seeking to comprehend it; you then draw a line around the region of chaos, an action which he calls 'bagging the mess' (Barranger, n.d.). He adds a further metaphor: the boundary of disorder becomes stretched and folded like the dough used to make flaky pastry, until it is impossible to separate from the area of order which it wraps itself around; eventually you just have to 'bag' this whole area, because you can no longer comprehend the relationship between points within the supposed sphere of certainty.[1] "Bagging the mess" is a great analogy for the 'war on terror', a category into which you can stuff every inconvenient actor or situation. The notion also again suggests enclosure. Typically in capitalist history, enclosure has meant extracting some region from an inchoate 'state of nature' and bringing it into the sphere of predictability, where it could be assimilated into the circuits of capital reproduction. Today, this has perhaps gone into reverse. Alongside a fallback strategy on the gated enclaves which are still manageable, the puzzling regions of society must be quarantined in some Guantánamo of the mind. In a linked process, the *physical* nature, which was thought to

---

[1] Another way of expressing this is that the area of chaos has become fractalised (Baranger n.d.)

have been tamed and shackled, now wreaks an increasingly extreme and unpredictable revenge.

In general systems theory, chaos means non-linear development, the possibility of bifurcation, the amplification of small changes. It is therefore creative, particularly in the phase transitions between periods of order. It is true that any system must develop, at different periods, stable patterns or 'regimes' where the parts fit together into definite roles, avoiding *constant* flux by absorbing challenges to the stability of its day-to-day relations. But it must also be ready to abandon a particular regime if the system's wider integrity requires this. Chaos is therefore functional, and need not be scary. But the repressive facet of class society has always justified itself by playing on fear of chaos, manipulating insecurities (both real threats to livelihood, and anxieties about imagined ones) to justify repression, depicting the ruling class as the last bastion of order. The phrase "l'ordre règne à Paris" employed after the violent suppression of the Paris Commune of 1871, expresses this association: order = repression. In political theory, the argument goes back to Hobbes, in practical politics the manipulation is as old as class society, with the 'terrorism' discourse merely its latest form.

What is special about capitalism – this was surely one of the great insights of the *Communist Manifesto* – is that it has needed to revolutionise itself *so often*. For this reason, there has always been a massive gulf between its 'real order', and the simplistic Hobbesian 'security' argument from which it derives legitimacy. If we make a systems reading of Schumpeter's notion of creative destruction, it is clear that the mode of production actually works *with* chaos to ensure the transition between accumulation regimes (AR). It thereby monopolises for itself the *creative* fruits of chaos, while the destructive ones are exported downwards, or outwards to the periphery or margins. What it gains is a phase of stability (order) in the shape of a new regime to ensure profits for the next long cycle; what is sacrificed is the kind of stability or predictability to which ordinary people might aspire – employment, access to land, food security.

But this brings us to a major paradox. To achieve the selective distribution of risk and benefit, the aspirations of the masses must be suppressed. A high degree of militarism and repression are therefore needed, and these tend to work in the direction of an intensification of centralised and top-down control. But systems theory shows that such methods are precisely the wrong way to run a system. This suggests an interesting reading of imperialism: the fusion of the militarist state with giant, centralised and hierarchical industrial corporations would create the risk of a self-destructive dynamic: by centralising too much, the system would lose its ability creatively to access the chaotic function.

Interpreted in this way, imperialism must constantly be at war with its own nature. But it was Gramsci's insight, the more remarkable because he was actually in a fascist gaol while writing his major work, (Gramsci, 1971) that the top-down aspect of imperialism was always counterbalanced by something else, a diffused power which operates in a different kind of way. Making a systems reading of his argument, we could call this the attractor, the thing which gives the system its overall flavour. And crucially, *the attractor in systems theory is not a centralising force*; it resides in the relations of the system itself, not at the centre/top. Control over society thus operates through a diffused force of habit which could be exploited, during crisis, to counterbalance the popular creativity which also arises at such a time. At the end of the 1960s there was a huge creative upsurge, but capitalism was nevertheless able to pump it dry and channel everything in the direction of a new capitalist AR, imposing its logic upon what might otherwise have been an open-ended process of human renewal.

Today's situation is however different from all previous structural crises. Firstly, today's ecological challenges are ones to which *no* capitalist regime has ever responded, or could respond. Secondly, it is no longer clear that capitalism has the institutional vocabulary to invent something new, even within its internal socio-economic frame of reference.

If society were left to itself, this situation would trigger a post-capitalist survival response in which humanity would operate in a decentralised way; in Africa's Sahel, when top-down interference was removed, people began to reconstitute the ecology.[2] This is because the co-operative faculty, suppressed by the dominant mode of production, will re-assert itself. In general evolutionary theory, development (however open-ended) operates within a bounded set of possibilities (Reason and Goodwin, 1999). And although society's post-capitalist development will be extremely open-ended, it is likely to channel itself into something recognisable as commons regimes, an issue we will

---

[2] c.f. "Can't see the desert for the trees", *New Scientist* Vol. 197 No. 2649, March 29 2008, pp. 42 ff.

explore further in the final chapter. In this case, the creative fruits of transition are pulled into the direction of the kind of order conducive to popular livelihoods: predictability is improved, for example in the sense of food security.

But of course, capitalism will not meekly fade away and allow the people to take over. The problem, however, is that whereas in the past it could propose an alternative mode of social organisation *under its own leadership*, as with the neo-liberal attractor in the late 1970s, today this is not so easy. In contrast to the open-endedness of overall human development, the bounded set of developmental possibilities under capitalism has always been restricted and may now have run out. We could then read the 'war on terror' as a repressive reflex of a degenerate state of capitalism no longer capable of operating with chaos in a creative way. If the mode of production can no longer be embodied in a viable AR, the whole mode itself is called into question. The Bush project was not predetermined, but it does fit the logic of the entropy of capitalism, in the sense of offering one response to a difficult question: systems must relate to chaos somehow, and what happens if they lose the faculty to relate to it creatively?

Networks, and a 'Diffused' Form of Chaotic Repression

It might seem that the response to this question would be a reassertion of top-down and centralised control. Indeed, the repressiveness of the early 2000s looks partly looks like this.

But what if there is also a *diffused* repressive force within the system? Such a perspective is anticipated in Foucault's work: while addressing issues similar to those discussed by Gramsci, he sees the diffused, networked power not *only* as a 'soft' form of mental slavery through force of habit (repressive primarily in the psychological sense), but also as something physically, violently repressive.

We can add that, whereas 'soft' power functions best in the context of the stable attractor of a viable capitalist AR, the diffuse violent force would be the opposite: it would come into its own precisely *in the absence of* such stability. The result could be a 'strange' attractor, a degenerate state (condition) of capitalism, highly repressive but with its repression partially decentralised. Such a system would once again be capable of working with chaos, but now in a uniquely destructive way.

This has always been a latent feature within imperialism and although political economy did not pick up on it very well, we can catch its reflection in art. Here, I will refer to a remarkable poem by W.B. Yeats:

> "Turning and turning in the widening gyre,
> The falcon cannot hear the falconer.
> Things fall apart, the centre cannot hold."

It seems that Yeats is talking about a collapse of Hobbesian central control, but it is really the attractor collapsing. As a result, something new, but bad, may emerge:

> "And what rough beast, its hour come round at last
> Slouches towards Bethlehem to be born?"
> (Yeats, 1963 pp. 211)

The beast is an emergent property of the system itself, but the ruling order can try to channel its destructiveness towards those it wants to get rid of. The Black and Tans sent by Britain to terrorise Irish republicans were irregulars, not really centralised, and the effect is to feed upon, and intensify, a more general societal decay. This is precisely the paradigm which we want to investigate more closely in this chapter: the hidden face of capitalist rule, the non-Hobbesian governance-through-chaos. The fact that the ruling order seeks to *use* this chaotic faculty does not mean that ultimately it is *really* under control: it could end up destroying the system which created it, along with much of humanity, in a kind of high-entropy 'hum' where information and diversity are lost, but which continues until its energy source runs out (there is enough to fuel it for a while and beyond that it doesn't care). When it is no longer possible to use stable new ARs to squeeze out popular creativity, badly-emergent 'beasts' will be used for this purpose. This is the developmental trend which humanity should oppose, and for this reason we need to understand it.

The images we have employed suggest an evolutionary metaphor. In Schumpeter's words, "The essential point to grasp is that in dealing with capitalism we are dealing with an evolutionary process" (Schumpeter, 1942, pp. 82). But he had in mind a 'normal' form where chaos can still just about be tamed by viable ARs. In the evolutionary literature, the notion of "deformed fitness landscapes" is particularly interesting (Kauffman and Johnsen, 1991). It maybe suggests the explanatory power of topology, or an analogy with space-time curvature in Einstein's model. The attractor would *normally* operate by distorting the selection-by-fitness of emergence forms. But evolution also includes catastrophic events. Some subsidiary forms could become dominant under these conditions. The chaos-governance trend has always existed as an undercurrent but was restrained from becoming the main course while the attempt to 'govern complexity' still prevailed. Bush represented the beginning of a loss of confidence that the ungovernable *could* be governed, and as such it looks, Janus-like, to both past and future. It was indeed a *retreat* to something primitive, a petulant, violent rejection of emergent properties just too difficult to grapple with; the rejection of evolutionary theory is highly significant in this regard, since true evolution is dangerously unpredictable and could well portend the mass extinction of capitalism! Evolutionary theory is also inseparable from environmental constraints, so the two aspects of Bush's denial are logically linked. But the Bush dérive also looked *forward* to one possible outcome of the bifurcation of the course of human development: a degenerate, high-entropy condition of capitalism. Despite its cultivation of repression, it did not wholly try to turn the clock back to centralism in the modernist sense. The arrow of time makes this difficult, and will continue to do so, for all the apparent neo-Keynesianism of certain post-Bush policies. This is a legacy from which any future capitalist governance regime will find it hard to escape. The beast is difficult to cage.

Rhizomes have been used as a metaphor for non-hierarchical emergent forms because, requiring no central trunk, they can propagate from anywhere. This has inspired some approaches to popular resistance, a thesis which we will consider critically in the final chapter. But in keeping with our focus on repression in the present chapter, it is interesting to note that Deleuze and Guattari, who introduced the metaphor, are explicit that rhizomes include "the best and the worst: potato and couchgrass" (Deleuze and Guattari, 1987 pp. 7). The 'worst', like couchgrass (a perennial weed spreading through self-propagating pointed roots capable of piercing barriers) is a chaotic form which propagates through evolutionary space. It can constitute a coherent emergent 'beast' without needing to be centrally controlled.

In the deformed landscapes, the adaptation to chaos will be localised. The establishment grasped 'terrorism' as its lifeline because it seems to provide some distinction between those regions which remain comprehensible, and others which sink into chaos. This sense of manageability is however illusory and, since terrorism can encompass anything and everything, it potentially means that the whole system is incomprehensible.

In its attempt to fill evolutionary space, the 'terror' discourse requires an enemy. One solution was the 'netwar' theory about the Zapatistas (Ronfeldt et al., 1998) which as we have seen developed side by side with the gestation of the Bush project. Nevertheless, this approach was risky because Zapatista-inspired networks (or rhizomes) *do* represent something threatening to the ruling order, and it was unwise to give them gratuitous publicity, much as McCarthy had done with Communism. The myth of the al-Qaeda network was safer because, *even if it did turn into a self-fulfilling prophecy*, it would simply feedback into the repressive form of poly-nodal self-propagating development and give flesh to the badly-emergent 'beast'.

We will now make the argument concrete by considering the 'terrorism' issue within postwar imperialist history.

Justifying Real Terrorism from Above by Manufactured 'Terrorism' from Below: Historical Antecedents and Contemporary Forms

As we will see, the notion of 'state of exception' is central to our topic. In a coup d'état, the state of exception overtakes the system from its summit. This is always a possibility which the system has up its sleeve. In Britain in 1968, establishment figures seriously debated a coup,[3] and although it sounds like treason, no-one was ever prosecuted for it. This is simply because a system like capitalism built on persuading some people to work hard for others' profit is inherently vulnerable to people wising up, particularly in times of structural crisis. But the post-9/11 repressive shift, although similar to a coup in its dismantling of law, developed in a more subtle and oblique way, spreading from somewhere within the system rather than just from the top.

Where exactly did it spread from? To answer this, we must disaggregate core and periphery and employ a non-Eurocentric standpoint. In the colonial context, the use of 'dirty' and extra-judicial methods was never a measure of exception, but rather the normal mode of

---

[3] see for example a number of details mentioned under parliamentary privilege in a debate in 1996 on http://www.parliament.the-stationery-office.co.uk/pa/cm199596/cmhansrd/vo950110/debtext/60110-43.htm; also *Time Magazine* "Sedition in the Establishment?" 13, 1981

control. Even during the Cold War, British counter-insurgency justified itself at least as much – for example in Malaya or Kenya – by brand-
ing the enemy as terrorists, as it did by the Cold War discourse of
anti-Communism. By employing terror tactics (e.g. strategic hamlets)
against the liberation movement and the population as a whole, it provided a paradigm for the whole NATO repressive apparatus. Latin
American security forces were schooled by the US in repressive techniques in its infamous School of the Americas, and the continuity with
today's 'war on terror' is direct: in 2004 Congress voted to continue
running the School – cosmetically renamed Western Hemispheric
Institute for Security Cooperation (WHINSEC) in 2000 – even while
the Abu Ghraib atrocities directly inspired by it were being exposed.

Radical critics of the contemporary discourse often argue that any
discussion of 'terrorism' must include *state* terrorism. If by 'state' we
mean 'employed by the ruling order', this is fine. It is problematical,
though, if 'state' implies top-down, because we must also take account
of chaotic forms. The Venezuelan peasant movement coined a term,
'paraimperialism',[4] which suggests something profound about the system. Because the sphere of pro-capitalist terrorism is extra-judicial, it
naturally connects with criminality. If Foucault is right that the profound realities of the system are revealed at its extremities, this may be
Colombia where at least one US company has been forced to admit to
paying money to right-wing death-squads (Forero, 2007).

An important issue arises here. The reference system in systems theory is the one which maintains its order by shifting entropy to its environment. In a future non-stratified human society, the reference system
will be inclusive and the benefits derived from solar degradation
shared; but under capitalism, divisions between classes, between core
and periphery, between the privileged and the excluded, permeate everything. All capitalism cares about is 'its own', and the various definitions of margins and periphery are useful only to fuel the core order, or
act as sink for the disorder it constantly strives to expel. From this follows a highly contradictory reality: on the one hand, imperialism
obsessively devastates its periphery so as to demonstrate that disorder
is effectively being exported; on the other, it is obsessed with policing a
fragile order *within*. This explains the duality of today's repressive

---

[4] National Peasant Front Ezequeil Zamora (Venezuela) *We will defeat the paramilitaries with the people organized*, June 2006 on http://a-manila.org/newswire/dis-
play/391/index.php

phase, on the one hand obsessively *exporting* violence, on the other actually highly introspective, in its dismantling of human rights within the core itself. The unprecedented increase of internal surveillance, for example in Britain, is surely significant: it typifies a system frantically clinging to the illusion that its own world is under control, remains comprehensible, can be differentiated from those ambient chaotic regions where information is so overwhelmed by noise that surveillance would have little point.

This duality must be reflected within our analytical model. On the one hand, we must remain true to the non-Eurocentric standpoint and never lose sight of the colonial origins of repression. On the other, as we will now see, it is also the history of *introspective* repression which crucially helps us understand the antecedents for recent trends.

Our key concern is the rhizomes: the *self propagating* facet of the repression which presents itself as counter-terrorism. Ideally you would create a self-maintaining enemy – which is, or is supposed to be, terrorist – to justify the use of diffused extra-judicial methods in repressing society as a whole. Here we must again clarify our attitude to 'conspiracy' theory. In this book, we centrally recognise the role of agency in human affairs, but the agency is mainly that of social forces. If the current era is one of heightened uncertainty, it is understandable that the creative potential is initially swamped by feelings of alienation and disorientation. The plethora of conspiracy theories is one manifestation of this: it suits the ruling order to nurture this tendency, so that understanding about real conspiracies can be swamped and discredited amid a welter of lunatic theories, some of them (such as the notion of gold-filled vaults beneath the World Trade Centre) perhaps deliberately propagated for this purpose. In this book, we are generally sceptical about conspiracy theory, but at the same time, we do need to acknowledge real conspiracies where they are present. By sticking to well-attested facts and strong circumstantial evidence we can avoid the pitfalls.

Terrorism from below really exists as a historical trend; in fact it has been consistently criticised by the Left on the grounds that it takes the 'propaganda of the deed' (assassinations etc.) as an excuse not to conduct mass work. On this basis, the ruling order, to supply itself with an enemy, need only create propitious conditions for such a terrorist response to 'self-engineer', whereupon repression would stimulate it further, and the feedback begin. To this we must add that it's not only the 'enemy' which should be self-propagating, but also the repressive power which claims to oppose that enemy. The true dynamic would thus require the the interlocking of *two* such self-propagating forces. This would be an eminently systemic governance-by-chaos.

Before considering this proposition in practice, we should mention a second definition of terrorism, which has likewise been seized upon and moulded by the ruling order: resistance against an occupying armed force through sabotage, killing of collaborators etc. This approach, terrorist in a strict sense because it prevents the occupiers enjoying any security, was considered fully justified when employed by the World War II anti-nazi Resistance.

When Britain was threatened with invasion, Churchill wisely decided proactively to create a secret underground resistance movement, the Auxiliary Units,[5] equipped with buried caches of advanced weapons and explosives. The whole point is that these are 'cells' in a biological sense, they are not centralised, and are therefore difficult to 'take out' by controlling a 'centre' or 'top', which doesn't exist (allegedly, the first act of the AU following invasion would be to kill their own controller, the only person who understood the network as a whole). But this tradition became an excuse to create something which rapidly took on a sinister dimension (so much so that the history of Britain's intelligence operations, even against Hitler, is largely off-limits to this day[6]): following World War II, proactive resistance movements on the AU model were established against the eventuality of Soviet or left-wing 'takeover' (in fact, these two things should be considered qualitatively different, but they were strongly assimilated by Cold War discourses). The US and Britain thus collaborated to establish clandestine armies throughout Europe. Effectively, a parallel power came to be diffused within the system. The clandestine forces, staffed by right-wingers and sometimes known as 'stay-behinds', were supposedly sleeper cells but rapidly constituted an active military and indeed political force, bypassing the official institutions. The secrecy remained total, the public and even most official politicians remaining completely

---

[5] The fact that these forces existed was kept secret after the War. A few details emerged in a book by Lampe, David *The Last Ditch: Britain's Resistance Plans against the Nazis* (Cassell) 1968, but it was only in the early 2000s that this history became widely known.

[6] The family of anti-nazi German hero Paul Rosbaud, who infiltrated Hitler's nuclear programme, confront a wall of silence in attempting to get MI6 to recognise that these events ever occurred: see Bowcott, Owen "Spy left out in the cold: how MI6 buried heroic exploits of agent 'Griffin'" *Guardian*, September 22 2007

unaware of their existence until some information about the Italian branch (codenamed Gladio) surfaced in 1990. Swiss scholar Daniele Ganser has usefully assembled the scanty details about this history (Ganser, 2005).

The principle is clearly a mixture of an element of central control alongside an emergent and self-propagating network. The centralised element is that the system, initially run by a 'Clandestine Committee of the Western Union', was secretly integrated into NATO on the latter's formation in 1949 and then, since 1957, placed under the command of an Allied Clandestine Committee chaired by the head of NATO, the Supreme Allied Commander in Europe (SACEUR, always an American). But we can only fully appreciate the emergent aspect of the stay-behinds by introducing a notion which will be important to our subsequent enquiry: the 'strategy of tension'. In an interview, Ganser defined the strategy in this way: "It is a tactic that involves carrying out criminal acts and attributing them to someone else. By the term tension, we mean emotional tension, all that which creates a feeling of tension. By strategy we make reference to that which increases people's fear in regard to a determined group."(Cattori 2007) To what extent the stay-behinds still exist today is obscure, but the important point is that this approach – creating fear to justify repression – has now become generalised in a much wider sense. Britain's Director of Public Prosecutions warns that a "fear-driven and inappropriate" response to 'terrorism' could lead Britain to abandon respect for fair trials and the due process of law.[7] But this is presumably exactly the point.

Considered in this way, the strategy of tension acted to 'turn on' the symptoms of chaos in order to justify repression, and from this angle it remains partly centralised. In understanding this 'centrally-planned' dimension we can look to one of the most remarkable incidents of the Cold War: Operation Northwoods, a secret plan drawn up in 1962 for conducting terrorist actions and blaming them on Cuba to provide an excuse for an invasion.[8] What is so fascinating about Northwoods is its duality: on the one hand rooted in the Cold War, on the other so

---

[7] *Guardian*, Jan 24 2007
[8] United States of America, Department of Defense, Joint Chiefs of Staff, Memoramdum to the Secretary of Defense "Justification for US Military Intervention in Cuba", March 13 1962. The photocopy of the original document can be downloaded on the National Security Archive of George Washington University, on http://www.gwu.edu/~nsarchiv/news/20010430/northwoods.pdf

contemporary from today's viewpoint. The project thus envisaged "a logical build-up of incidents to be combined with other seemingly unrelated events to camouflage the ultimate objective..."; this would "place the United States in the apparent position of suffering defensible grievances ...". An appendix provides a sample list of manufactured incidents which could form part of "a single integrated time-phased plan". These include bombarding their own base at Guantánamo to make it seem to have been attacked by Cubans and the conducting of a phoney Cuban terror campaign, involving bombs and hijacks. Although the US conspirators were prepared to kill real people – for example by sinking a boatload of refugees en route to Miami – the programme also envisaged a simulated sinking, funerals of mock-victims, and most remarkably an elaborate scheme whereby the passengers of a civilian chartered aircraft would disembark at a secret location where the aircraft would be switched for an identical unmanned drone, which would then be shot down over Cuba.[9] US Chairman of the Joint Chiefs of Staff General Lemnitzer, the main planner behind Northwoods, was also centrally responsible for co-ordinating the stay-behinds in Europe, so we can reasonably consider the two projects to be part of a single strategy. The similarity to more recent events is uncanny: it has been remarked that the putative leader of 9/11, Mohammed Atta – a hard-drinking, cocaine-snorting playboy/'fundamentalist' – was based in Florida, the home of CIA-inspired terror networks, as well as the activities such as drug-smuggling which help finance them (Zarembka, 2006).

While much of this looks contemporary, Northwoods had a crucial weakness (could this be why it was never implemented?): its approach to launching self-propagating cycles of terror seems very unpromising. The Soviet bloc, despite adventurism on the Cuba missiles issue, was fundamentally cautious, and sufficiently centralised to prevent any unmanageable terrorist cycles developing. Under these circumstances, the US would have to expend all the energy itself in continually stoking the violence, which totally contradicts the principles we have outlined, about self-propagating emergent 'beasts'. The ideal would be merely to *kick-start* a cycle which would subsequently be self-maintaining. We can for example refer to details beginning to emerge about British policy in Ireland involving the use of Unionist terrorism; particularly

---

[9] ibid.

interesting is the revelation that military intelligence would impose an Out Of Bounds (OOB) order, effectively withdrawing all police and military activity while the operation was taking place, (Mackay, 2007) so that the 'normal' sphere of law and order is temporarily suspended. In contrast, in Iraq in September 2005, when two men dressed as Arabs and equipped with explosives were caught and revealed to be British secret service personnel, they were accidentally (presumably because there was no OOB) detained by official Iraqi security forces, where-upon Britain (in defiance of the Iraqi state it claimed to uphold) sent tanks to smash down the prison where they were held.[10]

In these examples, the process is now systemic in the sense of being self-propagating, but it still appears to be 'turned on' from above. It is not yet a true rhizome. But there are cases where the dynamic has appeared much more to take on a life of its own. Here what we find is a fusion with a murky layer of criminality and corruption rather than some sanitised top-down conspiracy.

The most striking historic case was in Italy. It seems clear that the secret parallel power was not only directly promoting right-wing ter-rorism, as in the 1980 Bologna station bombing, but also in some way encouraging the development of contestatory, supposedly left-wing terrorism such as the Red Brigades, who kidnapped and assassinated Aldo Moro in 1978. The establishment wanted rid of Moro because he was negotiating the entry of the Communist Party of Italy into the rul-ing coalition, and it is most likely that they master-minded the opera-tion from above while it was conducted by people who were sincere militants at the base. Although Gladio's existence was secret at the time, these events closely follow the approach characteristic of it. Conspiracy theories abound with respect to the Moro killing, and if the truth even-tually came to light, it might be even wilder than what can be imagined (for example, we know that journalist Mino Picorelli, who obliquely alluded to the hidden logic for killing Moro when it happened, was himself murdered soon afterwards; (Willan, 2003) later he was shown to have strong links with the Masonic lodge 'P2' which helped to run the secret power structure[11]). But something much less spectacular but

---

[10] see for example http://www.guardian.co.uk/world/2005/sep/19/iraq; http://www.washingtonpost.com/wp-dyn/content/article/2005/09/19/AR2005091900572.html?nav=rss_world#

[11] It is therefore perhaps reasonable to assume that he was liquidated for breaking the omertà whereby insiders of the parallel power were supposed never to reveal its

possibly even more telling occurred in the history of Belgium: the 'Brabant massacres', random and motiveless killings of working class people carried out between 1982 and 1985 by masked gangs in public places; these are widely attributed to right-wing elements linked to the stay-behinds, and given official unwillingness to investigate the atrocities, this remains the most plausible explanation.

This short survey has indicated something festering within the heart of imperialism which provides all the ingredients for a system-slippage into chaotic repression. It would naturally come to the fore when imperialism has 'given up' on order in a conventional sense, and falls back on promoting 'bad attractors' for their own sake, thereby supplying the West with the oxygen of terrorism it requires.

This is particularly interesting when we come to Islamic fundamentalism. We know that fundamentalism was propagated deliberately by the US (together with allies Saudi Arabia and Pakistan), both to pump out the space for left-wing creativity in the Middle East and to create an Afghan Vietnam for the Soviets. The former head of the US visa bureau in Jeddah, interviewed by the BBC, testified that at that time he "was repeatedly ordered by high level State Dept officials to issue visas to unqualified applicants ... What I was protesting was, in reality, an effort to bring recruits, rounded up by Osama Bin Laden, to the U.S. for terrorist training by the CIA" (Ahmed, 2002, p. 178). On the surface, this all appears very controlled. Indeed a U.S. consultant optimistically told the *New Yorker* that their Saudi allies had assured the White House that "they will keep a very close eye on the religious fundamentalists. Their message to us was '*We've created this movement, and we can control it* [our emphasis].' It's not that we don't want the Salafis to throw bombs; it's who they throw them at—Hezbollah, Moqtada al-Sadr, Iran, and at the Syrians, if they continue to work with Hezbollah and Iran."(Hersh, 2007) But it is far from clear that such control was either possible or, from the system's point of view, desirable.

As in the Italian case, the fusion with criminality is key. It is really a mixture of underworld crime and upper-class crime (an important feature of imperialism), the two being often hard to distinguish. It is at this point that the Bush family link becomes quite interesting. For example,

---

existence; later, Prime Minister Guilia Andreotti was found guilty of Picorelli's murder; but because it was Andreotti who albeit unwillingly revealed the existence of Gladio in 1990, one has to wonder whether he was not himself being punished for breaking the omertà.

all generations of the Bush dynasty, together with many other segments of the US political class, have belonged to an elite Yale University secret society, Skull and Bones; although literature critical of this connection tends to come from the paranoid conspiracy wing, (Sutton, 2002) what interests us is that it does seem to espouse a doctrine of 'creative chaos'. According to this reading, when Prescott Bush built strong economic ties with the Nazis, he was not only after *immediate* profit, but also pursuing the systemic goal of stirring up international strife, from which future profit could be derived. Such an approach could easily be adapted to a situation where violence is less centralised than under the Nazis. It is important to note that much of alleged Al Qaeda funding continues to transit through Saudi Arabia,[12] and it should no surprise that terrorism is simultaneously financed and combatted from the same direction. The relationship is cosy in the realm of upper-class criminality, and the right-wing governments of Islamic states fall in with this. Whatever the truth of the existence of a network called Al Qaeda, there is no disputing that the Bin Laden family is part of another network, namely that of international finance capital, nor that another part of that network is the Bush family. A good case is the Carlyle Group, an investment firm focused in the defence sector which special-ises in cultivating influential political figures, one of its leading execu-tives being George Bush sr. and one of its major investors the Bin Laden family (Lazarus, 2001).

The Destructive Impulse Takes Over

The above analysis suggests somehow a rational manipulation of chaos. Nevertheless, it represents in a sense imperialism's pessimistic strand, where it gives up hope of maintaining order by 'normal' means. As such, there is always the risk of its acquiring a life of its own and losing contact with any rationale. Then it is no longer a deliberate exploitation of chaos, but becomes *itself* chaotic.

Of course the notion of risk as opportunity is firmly situated at the heart of the respectable capitalist economics, and in this sense the Bush clique's 'creative chaos' appears no different from what capitalism in general has always done. Nevertheless, from its origins within the mainstream, it is possible that this trend has spun off in a mad direc-tion by losing contact with potential negative feedback from reality,

---

[12] "U.S. Tracks Saudi Bank Favored by Extremists" *Wall Street Journal*, July 26 2007

and beginning instead to parasitise upon the symptoms of its own out-of-controlness.

This is not to say that the descent of society into disorder is unstoppable, but rather that the line which *promotes* this has become embedded within the imperialist system. It is both propagated *from* the centre/ top, and at the same time tries to make itself independent *of* the centre/ top, in order to undermine the chances of future imperialist leaders reversing it – this was the Bush 'mission'.

We are in no way implying that this is the only line of development. In contrast to the *ecological* momentum to 'steer into the heart of the storm' considered in Chapter 4, the politico-military momentum is less firmly established. Indeed at some levels, the chaotic trend may indeed seem weakly embedded, and (encouragingly) obstinate in refusing to become self-propagating. Why, we may ask, was it necessary to launch *so many* gratuitous provocations against Muslims and Arabs, the crudeness of which often beggars belief? When US Deputy Undersecretary of Defence for Intelligence Lt. Gen. William G. Boykin, who doubled as a Christian fundamentalist lay preacher, repeatedly preached sermons upholding the 'war on terror' as a Christian war against (Islamic) Satan, Donald Rumsfeld pointedly refused to criticise him.[13] We could add the appointment of a Christian fundamentalist British army commander, the fact that out of all the atrocities in the world, the only one which is criticised by the mainstream is Darfur, and even more notably, the US-backed war conducted by Christian Ethiopia against Moslem Somalia: when the Ethiopian invaders identified certain Somali clans as troublemakers and punished them collectively, a specialist commentated: "When the Sudan government bombs villages in Darfur, it's called genocide. But when the Ethiopians bomb civilian areas...nothing is said. Is it because this is perceived to be part of the war on terror?"[14] Israel has the green light to dream up increasingly outrageous measures against Palestinians. Just like industrial clustering which sometimes obstinately refuses to respond to policies seeking to trigger it, a huge energy is expended in stimulating supposedly emergent properties!

But we must also be aware of a possibility that the chaotic trend is more deeply embedded than this might imply. More than just the

---

[13] BBC, Friday 17 October 2003, "US is 'battling Satan' says general", on http://news.bbc.co.uk/1/hi/world/americas/3199212.stm

[14] *Guardian*, April 7 2007

messianic illuminism of Bush-Blair, it represents something about a system which has exhausted its 'normal' line of development.

Following our earlier discussion of entropy, we might expect the destructiveness of imperialism to be genuinely correlated with the order it tries to build: capitalism is an immense edifice (think of the built environment, infrastructure etc.), so logically – even while we might condemn not just the cost, but the edifice itself – it seems we should recognise some correspondence between the amount of destruction and the amount of order being built. But what if the system, having 'learned' that destruction is a necessary concomitant of order, then begins to pursue destruction as an end in itself?

State terrorism and massacres usually have *at their origin* some rational calculus leading to a building of order. In the case of collective punishments, the massacre at Oradour-sur-Glane in occupied France aimed to terrorise people into accepting the order the Nazis wished to build. Or, in the case of terror-bombing, the Spanish fascists' bombing of Guernica in 1937 set a precedent for, for example, the nuclear bombing of Japan which had as its explicit rationale to impose a diktat on the development of *world* order. A mixture of terror-bombing with collective punishment has been fully evident in the more recent phase of imperialism, as we clearly see in the notorious statement of NATO commander of the air war against Yugoslavia, Lt. Gen Michael C. Short in 1999: "If you wake up in the morning and you have no power to your house and no gas to your stove and the bridge you take to work is down and will be lying in Danube for the next 20 years, I think you begin to ask, 'Hey, Slobo, what's this all about? How much more of this do we have to withstand?' And at some point, you make the transition from applauding Serb machismo against the world to *thinking what your country is going to look like if this continues* [our itals.]."(Drozdiak, 1999) US 'shock and awe' tactics were designed to browbeat not only Iraq, but by extension any people standing up to the diktat. Israel's policy of collective punishments serves very explicitly as a model and laboratory for the whole of Western power: the USA directly trained Israeli forces in the techniques which were tried out in the well-known attack on Jenin in the Spring of 2003, particularly the use of armoured bulldozers, and then sent observers to study the experiment on the spot.[15]

---

[15] *Guardian*, April 2 2003

Supposedly, all this serves a strategic objective. But already, such conduct is on the way to becoming 'unhinged' and pathological. At this point it will be important to introduce the notion of 'exterminism'.

The 'fundamental point of the notion of exterminism is to suggest a unifying principle between the ecological issues addressed elsewhere in this book, and the military-repressive apparatus: exergy is destroyed, and so are people. The connection we will propose should still be considered intuitive and not fully developed; nevertheless, it makes sense in terms of the way systems behave.

The term 'exterminism' probably originated in E.P. Thompson's attempt to explain nuclear politics, at a time which in retrospect can be seen as the closing phase of the Cold War (Thompson, 1980). The cold warriors pretended their logic to be 'strategic' in the sense of serving some rational military or political objective; but it had actually, Thompson said, spun off in a direction where destruction became its own justification. Note that 'terror' (one of our main subjects in this chapter) was a central point of reference in nuclear 'strategic' terminology.

Actually, the arms race around 1980 was a bad example to choose because it was much more deliberate than Thompson thought: the West was deliberately pushing it to force the Soviets to divert expenditure from social projects, and thus to break down the Soviet system. Nevertheless, we can accept a core of truth in the notion of an irrational and out-of-control 'system-slippage' (the French term *dérive* expresses this well). As we will see in a moment, there is indeed a specific application to the nuclear issue, but let's first consider it in a wider sense. Mark Jones, in a number of discussion-group postings in the early 2000s, began to develop the concept of 'exterminism' to suggest a link with Malcom Caldwell's incipient thermodynamic imperialism theory (Jones, 2001). Although not yet clearly formulated at the time of Jones' death in 2003, I believe this direction is exactly the right one. I will now build on these insights to address exterminism as a phase transition of the imperialist adaptive system which occurs when, faced with unmanageable complexity, a petulant destructive attractor begins to overwhelm it.

Such a tendency has always lurked within the entrails of the ruling order. In pathological mode, the system, having 'learned' that order-building is associated with destruction, begins to focus on destruction per se, with only a vague sense that order will somehow emerge in the process. At capitalism's origins we find, in the desire to 'break' the

194 CHAPTER FIVE

environment to man's will, a passion which goes beyond rationality. In traditional society, mining was considered an act of violence, and once this taboo was broken down, society swung to the opposite extreme, flaunting its violence and making a virtue of it, as we see in Carolyn Merchant's brilliant discussion of the scientific work of Bacon (Merchant, 1990). Or, at times of crisis the system is desperate for transition to a new stable form. Modernist urbanism exhibited a passion for demolishing what went before which is not fully explicable simply by wanting to get one's hands on the empty land. Griffin convincingly analyses World War I as a ritual mass suicide, a rite of passage: (Griffin, n.d.) there is no rational sense of the destination to which this 'passage' leads, merely a faith that one will emerge.

The colonial sphere was always a strong repository of exterminism. Here, we confront the weakness of Thompson's analysis which we may attribute to his Eurocentrism: in focusing on the East-West arms race, he explicitly rejects the concept of imperialism. I would, on the contrary, see imperialism as the central factor pulling together the threads of exterminism in its contemporary form.

The quest for resources, which supposedly underpins imperialist rationality, is itself to a significant extent an 'unhinged' destructive impulse. With the recent system-slippage, as we saw in Chapter 4, unhinging has become more general: when Texans crank up the air-conditioning in order to enjoy their log fires, there is a sense of ensuring that capitalism truly is 'the end of history'! If it is doomed anyway, it might as well burn up everything while it still exists: "après moi, le déluge". On this basis, it would not be surprising if the calculus of militaristic destruction were similarly unhinged. Native American scholar Ward Churchill pointed out in the aftermath to 9/11 (Churchill, 2005), that the US is prepared to regard virtually any number of innocent deaths as acceptable collateral damage (Churchill has been persecuted ever since for having stated this straightforward fact). But even this argument assumes some rational war aim which the deaths are collateral *to*. Instead, if a cornered capitalist mode of production has itself acquired the mindset of a 'suicide-bomber', bringing humanity and the natural world to the grave with it, we can suddenly understand a bit better why the 'terrorism' discourse is psychologically so important to it: it transposes onto the 'other' a derangement which has overtaken the system itself.

Let's now apply this framework to the Iraq war.

As an exercise, it is again quite possible to reconstruct rational goals for the Iraq war. We should first, in difference to the conventional Left explanation, argue that the West's intention was not simplistically to augment its own stocks of energy: regime change was a genuine goal in its own right, and if the experiment in tame, non-nationalist institutional order could be brought to fruition in Iraq, the blueprint could simply be adapted for Brazil, or wherever the next target is. Of course such an institutional experiment would require high energy inputs, but this condition could be met in Iraq, making it the ideal guinea pig. Some data would confirm this interpretation: Paul Wolfowitz boasted in March 2003 that "We're dealing with a country that can really finance its own reconstruction relatively soon", while Office of Management and Budget Director Mitchell Daniels Jr. explained in more detail how oil and gas revenue plus confiscated Iraqi assets could fund 'reconstruction'.[16] The experiment would therefore have zero cost for the occupier! This is probably what a rational imperialism would have done. It would imply breaking with the colonial precedent of grabbing and depleting all the resources, but it would be logical to do this, since the larger institutional gain outweighs the *immediate* thermodynamic sacrifice.

We can then construct a reasonable argument showing how these goals broke down. To begin with, the energy crisis makes it difficult to abstain from plundering *any* available litre of oil: in fact, as we will see later, the energy cost of military operations is now so high that it would be pointless having a perfect institutional blueprint for occupation if one did not have the energetic conditions for implementing it. It is therefore easy to fall back on the atavistic response, inherited from colonialism, of plundering everything, but then the governance experiment would lose all credibility with the local population. At the same time, you can't go back to a totally commandist rule, as in the postwar occupation of Japan, because today's reality is too complex. These contradictions imprisoned the Iraq occupation from the beginning. For example, the shutting down of state-owned factories (which used to employ half a million people) reinforced disorder because dismissed workers were forced to look for alternative strategies, which often meant joining militias in order to acquire the main entitlement which

---

[16] *Los Angeles Times*, April 4 2003

chaotic systems recognise: weapons. In response, when Deputy Undersecretary of Defense Paul Brinkley attempted to reopen the factories and browbeat patriotic US retailers like Wal-Mart to import the products, the State Department attacked him as a Stalinist, and reportedly enlisted the CIA to rubbish the policy (Chandrasekaran, 2007). These contradictions will remain fundamental to any search for a new imperialist governance, and if they effectively undermine any stable solution, the likely alternative is for the violent, anomic form of chaos to become itself a mode of governance; the advantage would be to squeeze out Latin America-style creative emergent properties, such as participatory resource governance.

The above thought-experiment looks on the surface very convincing. Nevertheless, it omits certain facts which are arguably the really important ones. There is, instead, a strong case that the Iraq war, rather than being a rational social engineering experiment which 'went wrong', was exterminist from the beginning.

The starting point is in many ways the sanctions policy imposed on Iraq in 1990, as a result of which "at least several hundred thousand children who could reasonably have been expected to live died before their fifth birthdays,"(Reiff, 2003) together with the unopposed massacre of tens of thousands of fleeing Iraqis (the infamous 'turkey shoot') at the end of the first Gulf War in 1991. Then we come to the 2003 invasion itself. We can begin by noting apparently gratuitous acts like the plundering the cultural heritage of one of the most important civilisations in history and the destruction of infrastructure. Then we face a further drastic increase in mortality. The very significant *Lancet* report of 2006 revealed that pre-invasion mortality rates of 5.5 per 1000 people per year (already high because of sanctions) rose to 13.3 per 1000 per year. The research estimated that as of July, 2006, there had been 654 965 excess Iraqi deaths as a consequence of the war, corresponding to 2.5% of the population in the study area, 601 027 of which were due to violence (Burnham et al 2006). This base figure is regularly updated by several observers using appropriate methodologies, and reached the one million mark in mid 2007.[17] Columbia University professor Les Roberts, co-author of the Lancet report, later accused Britain and the US of 'triggering' a catastrophe worse than the Rwanda

---

[17] see http://www.justforeignpolicy.org/iraq/counterexplanation.html for an explanation of the methodology

genocide. He pointed out that the last health minister of the Iraqi 'government' to have attempted an honest assessment was sacked after his ministry produced reports suggesting that most casualties were caused by coalition forces (Roberts, L., 2007). 'Triggering' may be the operative word. Genocides are chain reactions and those who foment them may not be *directly* involved in all their ramifications – the massacres in Algeria spring to mind, where security forces (perhaps disguised as their enemies) directly intervened only at certain points in the chain, but still bear responsibility for the what happened over-all: those who initiate such processes must be aware of what they are triggering.

In developing the notion of exterminism, we have tried to broaden it from the specific form in which it was originally proposed in relation to the context of the nuclear arms race. However we must now note that exterminism does indeed have a specifically nuclear dimension. In fact, in some strange way, the nuclear dimension of exterminism has actually got worse *since* the end of the Cold War. While the system was still bipolar, although it encouraged the build-up of nuclear arsenals, it inhibited their actual use, even against third parties. Now that the West, in its overweening ambition for *undivided* power, has removed the bal-ancing factor of the Soviet bloc, this constraint has disappeared.

The nuclear threshold in a classic sense applies to the use of explo-sive weapons, and in this sense, we cannot be certain whether it has been breached. It is widely believed that the neutron bomb – a Cold-War thermonuclear weapon with reduced blast but enhanced radiation – was employed by the US when they were unable to win the battle of Baghdad Airport in April 2003, (Smith, L., 2007) but this can-not at the moment be proved. However, what we must realise is that there is something much worse about which we *can* be certain, namely the employment of so-called depleted uranium (DU) which is effec-tively a weapon of radiation. While the ruling forces scare-monger about the possible use of a 'dirty bomb' by Al Qaeda, they have been doing exactly this on a massive scale in Iraq. Let's consider DU as a case of exterminism. The crucial thing about exterminism is that, while it isn't wholly planned and can't even necessarily be said to follow a rational purpose, it nevertheless emerges from mechanisms within the system. In this case, it happens in the following way.

Entropy is released in the destruction of exergy. In the case of fossil fuels this takes the form of peak oil and climate change. The civilian nuclear industry is fallaciously supposed to be 'clean' because there is no greenhouse gas emission, but actually the entropy is measured in the problem of decommissioning plants, and in dangerous waste. This is where DU enters the picture: somehow, the notion evolved of turning the waste from the nuclear industry into a product. Of course, it is always logical to find a use for waste, but it doesn't bother capitalism in general to do this. But in this case, the use is munitions. This is only possible against a background of an existing exterminism, since the the subject-peoples against whom the weapon is to be employed are not considered fully human. DU munitions create true nuclear fallout, and as such are qualitatively little different from Hiroshima, where most of the suffering resulted from fallout, not from the actual blast. Long-term health effects for the entire population are potentially devastating. Even now, the information is largely stifled, and only here and there campaigners have painstakingly fought to bring certain details to light. These are remarkable enough. Overcoming considerable obstruction, researchers obtained data from monitoring stations in England which clearly show a significant increase in levels of uranium in the air exactly coinciding with the US bombing of Iraq in 2003, and at a time when predominant air currents were blowing from the Middle East towards Britain (Busby and Morgan, 2006). This was sufficiently high to give rise to health concerns in Britain, so one can only imagine the implications where the weapons were actually used. In another case, religious groups in South Korea forced the US to declassify a 2003 document detailing the number of its DU weapons stockpiled in that country: the number was 2,700,000 (Jung, 2005). There is no rational purpose, but nevertheless a kind of logic embedded in the system itself: destruction pursued for its own sake, somehow venerated as the 'price' for a futile attempt to rebuild a collapsing order. It is not just collateral damage, Iraq is the ritual sacrificial victim.

There are clear analogies with the Vietnam War, when capitalism was similarly locked in a structural crisis and a new accumulation regime was hard to find. Though there was a certain rationale (the quest for exergy in the shape of the Asian 'raw materials' which, as the Pentagon Papers make clear, (Sheehan, 1971) the US aspired to control), there was also always a ritualistic element in exporting the destructive chaotic forces onto an 'other', for whom civilised rules did not apply. The obsession with 'body counts' was one expression, seeming to demonstrate a positive 'balance' (in the accountancy sense, *solde* in French) whereby more destruction was being pumped out of the core than it was manufacturing, so that its own net order could improve.

But this was a losing battle: the violence kept blowing back into the core, culture becoming obsessed by destruction,[18] while the disorders suffered by veterans forced medicine to discover post-traumatic stress disorder.

The continuity is clear, but today's crisis is even worse, both because of ecological feedback and because the failed experiment at complexity-governance closes off the main avenue of innovation which eventually rescued capitalism from the 70s crisis. The response is if anything even more pathological. What has changed in comparison to Vietnam is that denial has reached even more extreme levels.

In the case of Vietnam, although the body count had to be positive, it was somewhat like a conventional imperialist war with a significant sacrifice of one's own troops. This aspect has not been eliminated: it is interesting that a senior British airforce officer raised with new recruits the possibility of their being ordered to conduct kamikaze missions, (Glendinning, 2007) while bodies of US soldiers were routinely (until family protests ended this practice) flown home from Iraq as commercial freight,[19] making it look a bit like the 'trade balance'. Nevertheless, there is possibly an encouraging form of the entropy of capitalism, in the shrinking power of its discourses to inspire sacrifice: people found it symbolic when the US military cemetery in Fort Riley, Kansas ran out of space,[20] as though some limit had been reached, of the number of US citizens who might tolerably be sacrificed.

But the system has responded by generating an extraordinary myth of denial, never approached by any previous generation of capitalist warfare, the notion of a war with zero cost: the philosopher's stone of war, the imagined escape from entropy.

One form of this response would be to increase the scope of proxy war. In certain cases, the whole armies of third-world states are treated as mercenaries for the US, through arrangements which look quite like the subcontracting and outsourcing characteristic of current economic management. The Indian press noted that Pakistan receives $100 million per month effectively for hiring part of its armed forces to the

---

[18] It would be extremely interesting to explore the reflection of this in fiction; the work of J.G. Ballard seems to have made a remarkable contribution in this respect.

[19] *Seattle Times*, April 7 2007

[20] *Reuters* "U.S. military cemetery running out of space", September 20 2007 on http://uk.reuters.com/article/latestCrisis/idUKN2039677420070920

US;[21] on the other hand, India itself, along with several other countries, has negotiated an Acquisition and Cross Servicing Agreement (ACSA), formerly an administrative tool of NATO but extended to non-NATO countries, which permits the US to 'borrow' its military facilities and settle up at the end of the year.[22] Ethiopia's proxy war against Somalia in early 2007 forced more than a third of Mogadishu's population to flee as refugees.[23]

But this approach of course doesn't address the ritual side. War is an enactment of something, a message which cannot adequately be delivered by proxies. How then to square this with the avoidance of casualties? The response has been a new discourse of war, the myth of a war so high-tech as to be risk-free for those perpetrating it. On this premise, body counts would no longer be functional because there is no longer a 'balance' to monitor.

Perhaps the most obvious form this takes is the notion of a war which can be won wholly from the air, without having to send in ground troops, sustained by the mythical 'pinpoint accuracy' of new weaponry. The latter myth was exposed by leading historian of warfare Gabriel Kolko in an analysis of Israel's attack on Lebanon in 2007, an attack which failed in its avowed aim of destroying enemy combatants and instead had to fall back on the indiscriminate destruction of civilian areas (Kolko, 2007). But of course, we could just as well argue that the point of terror-bombing has *always* been to target civilian populations. It is important to note that the US was bombing Baghdad not only when attacking it, but also when it (theoretically) controlled it;[24] and, as Edward Herman points out, there is a significant parallel with Vietnam, where the area which suffered most from US destruction was the South, which was supposed to be friendly (Herman, 2007). One is again reminded of the phrase from the Vietnam War, "It became necessary to destroy the town in order to save it";[25] interestingly, the man

---

[21] *Times of India*, July 14 2007, on http://timesofindia.indiatimes.com/US_renting _Pak_army_for__100_million_a_month/articleshow/2202810.cms
[22] *Hindustan Times*, "India, US close to inking military sharing pact", July 14 2007 on http://www.hindustantimes.com/storypage/storypage.aspx?id=2081b12a-9584-4d49 -968e-1a2262950c22&&Headline=India%2c+US+close+to+inking+military+sharing +pact
[23] *Guardian*, April 27 2007
[24] AFP despatch, "US bombing 'terror targets'", on http://www.news24.com/ News24/World/Iraq/0,,2-10-1460_2074616,00.html accessed 26.2.07
[25] The phrase, attributed to a US commander, appeared in an Associated Press report from the scene by Peter Arnett, dated February 7 1968

who first reported this famous phrase in 1968, Peter Arnett, was fired by NBC in 2003 for his critical reporting in Iraq![26] In Afghanistan – where the main zones of combat have been much more difficult of access for observers than Iraq – the situation is possibly worse: the occupation forces, mandated by a servile UN, are perceived by the local population as acting arbitrarily, totally above or outside any sort of law (Chipaux, 2007). As in Vietnam, the fact that the 'enemy' is indistinguishable from the population serves as an excuse to massacre people indiscriminately, and since they are an out-group, an 'other', they are legitimate sacrificial victims for a destruction mystically relied upon to generate order. At worst, you would have to pay compensation in a few instances (the going rate in Afghanistan is $2000 per victim (Chipaux, 2007)). It is more than just Guernica-style terror-bombing, it is a bit like 'bagging the mess': in a fractalised chaos situation, things have just become too embroiled to make sense of which regions are loyal.

But the high-tech myth goes much further, and it is these further ramifications which become really important. Currently a significant proportion of military R&D aims to robotise war. Indeed, a widely-discussed article in the US opinion-forming magazine *Harper's* in early 2007, proposed a totally robotised war to replace ground forces (Luttwack, 2007). A major feature of this is to make slaughter increasingly like a computer game, and this is where the denial takes on a pathological dimension unattained by earlier imperialism. Indeed, recently developed US military robots are controlled by troops using actual Nintendo handheld devices borrowed from computer games.[27] Taking this a stage further, pilotless drones, one named the 'Reaper' as a symbol of its destructiveness,[28] fly physically in Iraq and Afghanistan but are controlled from a base in Nevada where the pilots are psychologically distanced from the destruction they carry out.

The entropy from which this claims to escape is of course still there, only it occurs in a more concealed form: psychiatric disorder, suicide or radiation poisoning. For this very reason, veterans tend to get shunted aside because they are an uncomfortable reminder. British

---

[26] see *BBC News 24*, Tuesday, 1 April 2003, "US network sacks top journalist" on http://news.bbc.co.uk/1/hi/world/americas/2903503.stm

[27] *New Scientist*, March 29 2008, p. 26

[28] c.f. Associated Press, "Bomb-laden 'Reaper' drones bound for Iraq", *USA Today* July 15 2007, on http://www.usatoday.com/news/world/iraq/2007-07-15-reaper_N .htm

Iraq war veterans suffering mental disorder have encountered 18-month waiting lists for treatment, and the charity Combat Stress discerns "a trend which suggests there will be 'significant' demand on the NHS [National Health Service] in years to come to treat mental health disorders associated with fighting a war."(Slack, 2007) The US military is preoccupied with desertion rates: a Navy psychiatrist, explaining that "They are scraping to get people to go back, and people are worn out", cited the case of a soldier who chopped off his trigger finger with an axe to avoid redeployment.[29] An official survey of the mental health of troops found that anger at extended or multiple deployments made them more likely to mistreat Iraqi civilians.[30] As with Vietnam, the first accounts by disillusioned and disturbed US Iraq veterans very much confirmed this to be true (Hedges and al-Arian, 2007). But while the invaded country bears the immediate brunt of this anger, some of it again blows back into the core itself. It would not seem far-fetched to suggest that a rise in psychological trauma somehow reciprocates the reduction in physical casualties.

Even these examples do not yet touch on the true essence. Beyond even the robotisation of weapons or troops lies the vision of a robotic total machine, entirely replacing the human will. Decisively breaking with the world of Clausewitz and the old imperialist generals, a self-managed adaptive system would surf over the world of chaos beneath. It is this dimension, the ultimate embodiment of exterminism, which we must now consider.

The Self-Propagating Chaotic Machine

Once again, what is interesting is both the continuity with earlier trends, and the tipping-points whereby these unmoor themselves from rationality.

Perhaps the most obvious manifestation is the decentralisation and privatisation of the repressive sphere, a tremendous departure from the Hobbesian monopoly of violence. Of course, at first sight this development presents itself as merely another form of 'complexity-capitalism', with its self-forming networks and chains. Just like

---

[29] *New York Times*, April 9 2007
[30] *Guardian*, May 5 2007

industrial production and everything else, 'security' becomes a chain of sub-contracted tasks.

But this argument is not wholly convincing, because there is no reason for capitalism to be so honest as to follow its own precepts. The New Public Management was successful, not in *really* being more efficient, but in handing over lucrative sectors to the sphere of private accumulation through the breakup of the 'public' sphere. However, in the military sphere it would be more surprising if inefficiency were considered irrelevant.

But this rational calculation surprisingly doesn't seem to hold. For example, the strategy of tension has always worked through disinformation, and an example of the rip-off companies emerging to parasitise on war is the Lincoln Group, which targets the niche of providing this 'service'. It specialised in planting pro-US stories, written by the US military, in the Iraqi media, a fee of $2000 being payable for each such story.[31] But the plausibility of the Lincoln Group's stories was found to be extremely poor.[32] There is no reason to suppose that the quality of other contracted functions is any better. So perhaps the repressive sphere, rather than rationally manipulating chaos, has itself been overtaken by chaos.

One reason is that the repressive function, instead of being just a distinct, external support to accumulation, has become directly part of it. The privatisation of any repressive service – for example parking wardens or prisons – creates an incentive to multiply the offenses which their work is theoretically meant to discourage. But what makes this worse is the interaction between state and capital, who, as with the nuclear industry, ethanol etc., seem to have entered into a dance of death wherein each goads on the other towards a level of chaos which neither individually could attain. As we noted in Chapter 4, finance capital is for its own reasons also chaotic, so the two can coalesce, forging a common currency notably out of risk. To typify the corporatisation of the military, we could cite the mercenary army known as Blackwater USA (Scahill, 2007), subsequently renamed Blackwater Worldwide and more recently 'Xe'. Its operatives in Iraq claimed the military's immunity from civil law, while at the same time also being immune from military law (and, it should be noted, they do not appear

---

[31] *The Independent*, 30 March 2006
[32] ibid.

CHAPTER FIVE

in military casualty statistics). They are subject to greater risks than normal soldiers, with contracts being further 'subbed' down a chain which is difficult to follow (Scahill, 2007). It is significant that it was the killing of some Blackwater soldiers in Fallujah which sparked off a wholesale US destruction of the town, and, besides Iraq, this company was heavily involved in post-Katrina New Orleans and looked to be deployed in Southern Sudan too. In Latin America, the 'war on drugs' (the regional equivalent to the 'war on terror') is largely privatised, an example being DynCorp, effectively a private airforce operating both helicopters and fixed-wing aircraft over Colombia, Bolivia and Peru.[33] Alongside corporate interests directly engaged in 'security', a new generation of rip-off companies has evolved in a Darwinian sense to thrive off an endemic climate of war. An example is US corporation BearingPoint, which assumed a leading role in planning the economic 'reconstruction' of Iraq; a Republican party donor, the corporation acted as contractor to USAID in drawing up the contract for the Iraq reconstruction, which was then awarded to itself![34] It then drafted the Iraqi hydrocarbons law which bestows unprecedented powers on foreign oil majors through 'production-sharing agreements' and the right to repatriate profits. Although at one level this all looks very much like the economic management chains, there is something qualitative in the degree of insecurity created once the violent repressive sphere itself begins to lurch out of control.

In a development foreshadowed by the Black and Tans and the stay-behinds, the repressive sphere fuses with criminality. As Foucault says, "Delinquency, controlled illegality, is an agent for the illegality of the dominant groups."(Foucault, 1975 pp. 279) The issue addressed in Brecht's Threepenny Opera is that the official world's relationship with its 'margins' is ambiguous. On the one hand, it repulses those who can't or don't want to conform, savagely repressing them through aggressive doctrines of social inclusion; on the other, it establishes a close symbiotic relationship with certain of the criminalised elements which emerge in this 'margin'. These trends were always present within imperialism but have qualitatively increased to become predominant.

A significant aspect of paraimperialism is the deliberate evasion of responsibility, which is of course central to the issue of 'renditions'

---

[33] *The Nation*, June 4 2001 on http://www.thenation.com/doc/20010604/vest20010523
[34] c.f. *Independent on Sunday*, 18 January 2007

(i.e. the torture of suspects). Former chief of the CIA's Europe division, Tyler Drumheller was quite upfront about this when he approvingly remarked that "whenever someone was overzealous in some dark interrogation cell, President Bush and his entourage could blame someone else. ... If they [the rendition teams] didn't do paramilitary actions for a living, they would probably be robbing banks."[35] But the fusion with criminality operates from both directions: not only is the private sphere a conduit to the criminal underworld, but the official sector itself becomes more irregularised. As a member of US recruitment personnel recognised, "We're enlisting more dropouts, people with more law violations, lower test scores, more moral issues ... We're really scraping the bottom of the barrel trying to get people to join."[36]

An important element of the dissipation of responsibility is to hook up with criminal elements in the periphery. For example, the leader of one Pakistan-based Baluchi group backed by the US has been described (by a 'senior fellow on counterterrorism' at the Nixon Center) as "part drug smuggler, part Taliban, part Sunni activist".[37] But perhaps the best illustration of this theme is the tale of the Kosovo Liberation Army (KLA). This was a largely criminal group at the centre of a huge international crime network, a fact detailed in amazing testimony by Interpol Assistant Director Ralf Mutschke to the US Congress in December 2000; (United States Government, 2000) Mutschke also mentions the likelihood of links with Osama bin Laden's organisation and the presence of bin Laden himself in Albania, a theory which has surfaced in many press reports over the years (Chossudovsky, 2001). The KLA suddenly found itself – with the complicity of a tame UN – transmuted into a force of order: the UN Interim Administration Mission in Kosovo (UNMIK) simply held a ceremony where, in their own words, they "transformed the former Kosovo Liberation Army (KLA) into a civilian agency charged with providing emergency response and reconstruction services" (United Nations, 2000) under the name of Kosovo Protection Corps (KPC). General Agim Ceku, former KLA military Chief of Staff (a Croatian military leader trained by US private paramilitary firm Military Professional Resources Inc. under contract from the US administration, and widely suspected of

---

[35] *Der Spiegel*, January 29 2007
[36] quoted in *New York Times*, April 9 2007
[37] ABC News Exclusive: The Secret War Against Iran, April 03 2007 on http://blogs.abcnews.com/theblotter/2007/04/abc_news_exclus.html

anti-Serb atrocities (Scahill, 2006)), simply became the new organisation's head. The KPC is not supposed to be a military force, but this is pure fiction: already within the first month of its existence, a secret report compiled for UN Secretary-General Annan showed that it was responsible for murders and many other abuses;[38] eventually, by June 2006 Annan was obliged formally to admit that violent attacks by Kosovo Albanians against Serbs and other minorities "appear to be part of an orchestrated campaign."

Again, the analogy with economic management systems suggests itself. While the latter do partly access a genuine faculty for spontaneous order, they also very much serve as a convenient excuse for the core firm's avoidance of responsibility for the social devastation upon which it profits. Rolando Elizondo has spoken of an 'entropy of responsibility' (Elizondo, 2001). Below a certain level of the subcontracting chain, the realm of management no longer seems to apply, and this is very much true of the military sphere as well. DynCorp, for example, "highlights how the whole phenomenon of privatizing military functions has enabled the government to evade oversight to a shocking degree."[39] Viewed from this angle, in cases like the KLA and the renditions, it is merely *convenient* to create the *appearance* of something chaotic which can't be controlled from the centre/top. In the case of the Iraq occupation, there is similarly a strong dose of this. Perhaps the clearest example is the Facility Protection Service, a security force introduced by the US occupation administration in 2003. Three years later, Iraq puppet government minister Bayan Jabr, estimating the number of this force at 150,000 plus 30,000 civilian security guards, blamed them for the violence and described them as "out of order, not under our control";[40] at the same time, US sources critical of Paul Bremer's Coalition Provisional Authority blamed Jabr himself for recruiting the Facility Protection Service and filling it with Shiite militias (Silverstein, 2006). If these mutual accusations between supposed allies seem strange, what unites them is a commitment to the entropy of responsibility: if no-one controls the situation, no-one is responsible for it.

Nevertheless, this cannot be a full explanation. We again confront the issue of quantity and quality. Subcontracting has always existed but

[38] *Atlanta Journal-Constitution* March 14th 2000
[39] quoted in *The Nation*, June 4 2001 op. cit.
[40] BBC 12 April 2006: "Iraqi death squads 'not police'" on http://news.bbc.co.uk/1/hi/world/middle_east/4901786.stm

the way it was used in the '80s management systems was so extensive as to unleash a genuinely emergent phenomenon, one characteristic of a still-dynamic capitalism which could use self-organisation creatively for its own purposes (i.e. in the form of industrial clusters and value chains). Similarly, paraimperialism has always existed, but in its recent expression has unleashed something characteristic of a no-longer-creative capitalism able only to parasitise upon the destructive symptoms of its own decadence. It is the number and variety of private or irregular forces somehow linked to 'security' operations which makes the phenomenon qualitatively different to anything seen before. In Iraq, there were several layers, reaching from the US occupation forces, through the subservient Iraqi institutions, privatised armed forces guarding civilian occupation activities, and various militias, and crucially the relations between all these elements were *themselves* chaotic. US central command conducted a census of contractors performing functions which would formerly have been considered military, concluding that in 2006 their number was 100,000[41] (military specialist Stan Goff estimates that 25,000 of these could be considered direct military operatives, the remainder being involved in support operations[42]). Yet another study showed an incomplete (because it fails fully to encompass private security personnel) tally of 180,000 people currently employed by the US occupation forces, outnumbering the actual troops (then 160,000). This reveals a complex picture of many different roles, including cheap third-world labourers hired to carry out menial tasks at US bases ... because it would be too dangerous to employ Iraqis who might be disguised insurgents!(Miller, 2007) Britain was shown to have spent £165 million on hiring private security companies in Iraq over the four years to 2007, plus another £43 million in Afghanistan, while about one third of US expenditure on the 'reconstruction' of Iraq was diverted to security.[43] When the sphere of violence expands to such a degree, it would tend to overwhelm the whole of society, the supposedly 'normal', 'judicial' sphere (in Foucault's sense) losing any distinct identity. Value and entitlements accrue to those who control the gun, and guns are not in short supply: they have become a commodity like any other, available on the market; and in case this was not enough, the

---

[41] *Washington Post*, December 5 2006
[42] http://stangoff.com/?p=444#comment-49018
[43] *Guardian*, April 2 2007

US managed to 'lose' 190,000 of its own weapons in Iraq![44] How different from the Hobbesian monopoly of top-down violence, something which still prevailed during the Cold War when the superpowers could largely restrain their proxies.

This looks very like a qualitative tipping point where it is no longer simply *convenient* to depict the system as chaotic (in order to evade responsibility), it genuinely *is* chaotic. Deprived of negative feedback, the war momentum would be unstoppable.

In what senses can we speak of this dynamic as a 'machine'?

There is a certain sense, in the Bush project, of designing the 'rules' of something which would then operate autonomously. The *pre-emptive* nature of Bush doctrines is thus analogous to a kind of adaptive programming: the machine receives initial instructions about what to recognise, and you then sit back to watch it take its own decisions. Already in 2002, Defense Secretary Rumsfeld laid down that "defending the United States requires prevention and sometimes preemption" (Rumsfeld, 2002). Action thus becomes automatic against any state (or by extension, we might say any individual) deemed 'likely to' offend (the only proviso being that full-scale occupation and regime change could only be carried out in one country at a time (Rumsfeld, 2002)).

A further qualitative development was the concept of Total Force promulgated by the Pentagon's 2006 Quadrennial Review. Here, the military is explicitly fused with private capital. The previous chapter revealed how finance capital has learned to parasitise upon, and thus amplify, chaotic features in the physical environment, so it should be no surprise that capital enters a similar pact with the military sphere, where each goads the other to propagate disorder, the rules of their interaction operating to neutralise negative feedback. Even where financial signals might urge caution, this is neutralised by the political sphere: thus, in 2007, Halliburtons, the notorious US corporation linked with the Bush clique which profited enormously from Iraq 'reconstruction', was actually cool on attacking Iran because it had a profitable relationship with the existing government ... only to find itself savagely attacked by Democrat senators for being unpatriotic and aiding 'terrorism'![45]

---

[44] *Guardian*, August 7 2007
[45] *New York Times*, May 1 2007

The result is an adaptive and autonomous repressive machine – instinctively identifying its targets by their presumed behaviour – which now becomes inter-meshed with a finance capital itself parasitising on chaotic symptoms. There is a strong sense of a deliberate rejection of the strategic decision-making central to the traditional notion of warfare and diplomacy. Interestingly, under Bush, the President's Intelligence Oversight Board (an independent, though not publicly accountable body conducting secret reviews of CIA practice) was permitted to atrophy (Solomon, 2007). Although partly this would serve the goal of 'plausible deniability', one has to suspect a deeper reason: the system needs to insulate itself from any feedback from reality, if it is to pursue its chaotic, millenarian course.

The chaotic 'machine', although in an immediate sense a legacy of the Bush clique, is surely the product of a certain line of development (albeit not pre-ordained – we must again avoid determinism) of the imperialist *system*. Its mode of operation is on the one hand more systemic than ever before insofar as it rejects strategy and allows things to follow their emergent course; and at the same time less systemic insofar as it signals the failure of indirect, Gramscian forms of hegemony over a genuinely complex system, in favour a simplified vocabulary of control which privileges violence.

The fact that Iraq was the theatre of an experiment for a future era of *endemic* war is explicit. The experience was for example used as the basis for formulating a new strategy known as the 'Capstone Concept for Joint Operations', wherein, as the Chairman of the Joint Chiefs of Staff gleefully remarks, "we incorporate the lessons gleaned from those conflicts while looking to the future to examine the capabilities we will need to fight tomorrow's wars. We are transforming in stride – conducting operations while preparing for the future fight." (United States Department of Defense, 2005 b) He seems intoxicated by such an environment where war feeds off itself. As with all such feedback processes, while the *momentum* is generated internally (from its own systemic rules), the energy has to be supplied from outside. And since the Capstone Concept specifically relates to the period 2012–2025; we can tie this in with peak oil predictions, giving a fairly concordant time frame. While the energy which supplies the militarist machine is drying up, this only intensifies the incentive to militarise further in order to grab what remains. But the interesting point is how the Concept proposes to do this. It is explicit in regarding all military responses as complex adaptive systems. A situation of "interaction with any number of private, nongovernmental, regional and international organizations," (United States Department of Defense, 2005 b, p. 9) can therefore be presented as a new, complex and pluralistic governance mode appropriate to the era of complexity, and suited to adaptive planning.

The above strategies are couched in systems jargon, but how systemic are they in reality?

If the US merely destroyed the top-down system of Saddam, a more diffuse social order might reconstitute itself, but if this were genuinely emergent it might go in inconvenient directions. The advantage of an ersatz pluralism, where all the 'actors' are merely emanations of the ruling order, would be to squeeze out any unpredictable grassroots initiative. But to call this a complex adaptive system is pure nonsense: the level of information and diversity is very low. Far from constituting the governance equivalent of the systemic turn, this actually signifies the bankruptcy of any such attempt. We could either say that military functions have been privatised, or turn the argument around and say that all functions have become militarised. There is 'creep' in both directions: a report by Republican staff of the Senate Foreign Relations Committee revealed that US embassies were increasingly becoming militarised, some now functioning effectively as command posts with military personnel having all but supplanted ambassadors;[46] on the other hand, British military circles lament that, precisely because all tasks are now militarised, the specifically military culture is diluted, with decisions no longer taken on intrinsically military grounds (Norton-Taylor, 2007).

But, if it is true that this is not systemic in a creative sense, it is indeed systemic in the sense of generating cycles of repression and disorder, feeding off one another. The robot has become Yeats' 'beast'. This hybrid creature stumbles in a direction no-one seems quite to understand.

Once in place, it hardly seems sufficient for the war machine to remain as a purely latent threat, it must demonstrate itself in action against a succession of fresh targets. Perhaps this is the reason for the drumming-up of what looked like a real war fever against Iran in the late Bush period. At the time of writing, this has abated, perhaps through a combination of popular opposition and 'Realist' tendencies in the establishment which we will consider in the next chapter.[47]

---

[46] *New York Times*, December 20 2006
[47] As we will see later, Realism tries to inhibit the development of a positive feedback relationship between ideology (including one's own propaganda!) and policy.

Nevertheless, a danger remains which is not confined to invasion plans against particular countries but is rather embedded within the chaotic-exterminist tendencies of the system itself. Even if a frontal attack on Iran failed to materialise in 2007, the pursuit of chaos in the region continued unabated. There is nothing new about divide and rule, or about the use of a 'bloodbath' myth to justify colonial occupation, but what may be new is the qualitative intensity of a seemingly deliberate chaotic momentum. There is a strong argument that the fomenting of civil war was integral to US policy in Iraq, (Catalinotto, 2006) and this has wider implications for the whole region. By initially backing Sunnis against Shiites it was possible to initiate a wider series of repris-als, (Davis, 2007) and reports of CIA backing for ethnic minority ter-rorist groups in Iran conform to a similar pattern (Lowther and Freeman, 2007). The US Marines hired a subsidiary of a private consul-tancy firm, Science Applications International Corp., to advise on the ethnic composition of Iran, and although the project allegedly served "a better understanding of and respect for the various aspects of culture in those countries", a *Financial Times* study found it more likely that the aim was to see whether "Iran would be prone to a violent fragmenta-tion along the same kind of fault lines that are splitting Iraq (Dimmore, 2006)." If we picture an imperialism no longer able to work 'with' civil society, how might it rule a chaotic world? The answer could not be better symbolised than by the new 104-acre US 'embassy' in Iraq, the largest in the world, costing $592 million:[48] completely fenced off from local society and including, significantly, its own energy supply, it is not 'plugged' in any way into the local reality, certainly not for legitimacy, not even for any of the public utilities. Amid a sea of disorder, a net-work of such bastions could criss-cross the globe.

The Auto-cannibalism of Capitalist Democracy

The above can be seen as an external projection of disorder, but its source is also a decay of the system from within. Imperialism used to claim a higher level of civilisation which bestowed the right to rule the world, and after World War II there was a subsidiary argument

---

[48] *North County Times*, May 19 2007, on http://www.nctimes.com/articles/2007/05/20/news/nation/13_75_945_19_07.txt

contrasting Western democracy and human rights with the Soviet bloc system, as in the creation of the postwar Council of Europe. But with the 'war on terror' this whole edifice falls apart, as the core begins somehow flaunting its own degeneration. Why is this?

The answer is connected with an intrinsic link between the order-chaos issue in systems theory and the issue of human rights, which we can begin to understand by considering its historical context.

Ever since stratified systems arose, the benefits of social order have been the preserve of a privileged group, who justify their monopoly by holding some group of humanity beyond the sphere of normal rights and law, stigmatising them as 'disordered', treating them as both the negative determinant of their own identity, and as sinks for the absorption of real disorder: as in the caste system, for example. How does capitalism fit into this history? We could make out an argument that it had a progressive facet in its origins because it needed to overturn the *hereditary* determinants of status that rigidified earlier stratified societies and restricted their development, and then further extend this line of reasoning to say that by the time of imperialism, in the early 20th century, this progressive role was exhausted. This would be roughly the position of the Popular Front in the 1930s, which we might paraphrase as follows: "Capitalism, in overthrowing feudalism needed to introduce the rule of law and this, although largely a mere disguise for the rule of the bourgeoisie, could be taken up by oppressed classes and nations in fighting against arbitrary rule. In its imperialist phase, capitalism has exhausted its progressive aspect and therefore, in fascism, turns the clock back to something even worse than the worst medieval tyranny which the capitalist Enlightenment had sought to escape from. In resisting this trend, a broad unity can be built, which – since reverting to pre-imperialist capitalism is not really an option – would objectively have a revolutionary character."

But this argument, however plausible, is linear and fundamentally flawed. We cannot understand today's problem by looking only to a later, degenerate form of capitalism; instead, we must look to contradictions embedded in the system from its very beginning. We can start by considering the insights of Erich Fromm. It is particularly significant that, writing at the time of fascism, Fromm sought his explanation not in the degenerate form which fascism seems to present, but in capitalism's origins: in his striking analysis of the Reformation, he shows how the overthrow of feudal obscurantism and tyranny created, alongside the possibility of freedom, a difficulty in taking this on board:

a rootlessness and desire for security which implied the acceptance of, *or even craving for*, new forms of authoritarianism (Fromm, 1942).

Let's consider the implications from a systems perspective. *The responsibility of emergent spontaneous order is scary.* In this sense, the 'fear of freedom' argument links very well with the issues addressed by Paulo Freire. We could further develop this in an ecological context, because the capitalist revolution offered not just to free humanity from the personal determinants of servitude, but also from the constraints which made us subservient to nature, a promise with a certain progressive potential but carrying a terrible potential cost. The fear of freedom then appears as *fear of the responsibility for embracing the creative facet of chaos.* This gives capitalism the opening it needs: it can offer to relieve the people of this responsibility, and assert its own forms of rule. The *specific* form of that rule evident in Fromm's day was the top-down, authoritarian form, but what was not so obvious at the time was that, in its fullest development, the authoritarian strand within capitalism is actually a mechanism for maintaining its own complementary opposite, a sphere of contained 'freedom' in which the creative principle of emergent order is channelled into directions uniquely conducive to capital accumulation.

This latter development only came to fruition with neo-liberalism. The neo-liberal take on freedom, however distorted, was successful in playing upon an intrinsic human perception that emergent order is better than commandism. It was the most *emergent* accumulation regime (AR), and also the first which tried to work with complexity. Its strength was to operate genuinely as an attractor, building upon people's instinctive realisation that centralism was not the right way to work. Actually, it was capitalism's own centralising form – modernism – which was being overturned, but this was conveniently used as a tactic to blame socialists. This is why, I would argue, neo-liberalism could be presented as, in Boltanski and Chiapello's words, a 'second liberation.'(Boltanski and Chiapello, 1999 p. 509) The ideal would be a self-regulating exploitative system which didn't need to be run from the top: Friedrich von Hayek, the godfather of neo-liberalism, essentially proposed a systemic reading of laissez-faire (Hayek, 1978). Since the emergent order, in this definition, was derived from the untrammelled pursuit of individual interests, neo-liberalism could also pose as an upholder of individual *rights*. Conventionally, we might see market fundamentalism as the characteristic feature of the 1980 AR, but in reality this was never its strongest suit: the self-regulating system in the form of laissez-faire economics was a myth anyway, but what is not a myth is the real substance of the co-optation of a corrupted form of the natural instinct to relate through co-operation, reciprocity and trust, as expressed for example in industrial clusters.

Against this background, freedom was now freedom to self-exploit oneself in the interests of the bigger accumulation dynamic, while authoritarianism, as with Pinochet, slotted into place in defining the rigid parameters within which development would be tolerated. Neo-liberalism was therefore a much more efficient mode of rule than the Nazism of Fromm's day, because the authoritarian facet was held in some equilibrium with (contained) emergent order. It could exploit people's fears but for a certain period in the late '80s it could also make political capital out of upholding human rights (as we will see in a moment) as a concomitant to the collapse of the Soviet system. The 'end of history' discourse was therefore not only a way of fooling the masses: it reflected also capitalism's *own* delusion: that it had finally attained the grail of a self-equilibrating system, and succeeded, where Hitler failed, in building a 1000-year Reich.

Today this delusion stands exposed. This brings us to an important point, crucial to the *specificity* of the current crisis. The 'end of history' discourse was partly correct, but not in the way its proponents thought! It was capitalism's last card, as though the system had finally attained the nirvana of a *controlled complex system*, only to find this immediately snatched from it. The crisis therefore, although in form a structural crisis of the neo-liberal AR, is in substance a 'general' one, i.e. that of the capitalist mode of production as such – it was the mistake of the old Comintern 'general crisis' theory to pronounce the existence of such a crisis prematurely, but today it really *is* upon us. Repression then becomes unmoored from its role in facilitating a functioning AR, and becomes instead a *substitute* for one. Freedom, emergence, even complexity itself, can no longer reliably be contained, and must therefore be suppressed.

So far, we can re-interpret Fromm in an interesting way using systems theory, but the weakness is his Eurocentrism. Although serfdom was abolished within the core itself, there was always an excluded 'other', who constantly pays the price for the building of core order. Again, while it is absolutely correct to look back to the origins of capitalism, this must above all be to its *colonial* origins, which from the beginning marked capitalism with features more repressive and genocidal than anything in European feudalism or the Roman slave system.

The US Constitution was written by a slaveowner (Thomas Jefferson), and even the French Revolution, as C.L.R. James shows, compromised with slavery (James, 1982). This in no way belittles the value of defending the US Constitution against authoritarian administrations, but this can only be meaningful if we appreciate the deep truth that capitalist order could never have been maintained without the degradation of its periphery. This is true at all levels, most basically that of the political economy, but what concerns us specially in this chapter is democratic and human rights. These were always selective. The core's own (limited) democracy was used perversely to justify its superiority, and hence its 'right', indeed even its *duty*, to conduct atrocities in the colonial sphere in the name of progress.

In a sense, we can represent the periphery as *all* the excluded, irrespective of where they find themselves. Within the geographical boundaries of the core, only the ruling class is the true core which benefits from the global energy flows. Nevertheless, the majority core population is relatively privileged in comparison to the South, but only *provided that it observes the norms.* 'Inclusion' is equivalent to the acceptance of these norms, the excluded being those who for whatever reasons either reject or fail to conform to an intrusive regime of surveillance. As Foucault shows, the marginalised (prisoners, mental patients) experience something intrinsic to the system, but which is hidden from the majority; David Sibley's research among Gypsies explains this in an interesting way (Sibley, 1995). While repressing the excluded, the system also *needs* them in order to frighten the majority about the dire consequences which will befall them if they depart from their cosy acceptance. We are again reminded of Hegel's words that identity *is* the thing which that identity excludes. With globalisation, these internal boundaries begin to inter-penetrate with the geographical (North-South) core-periphery relationship: just one of the troubling manifestations of complexity which haunt the ruling order. An underclass of migrants is more and more savagely policed, often in the name of counter-'terrorism', ghetto-ising them into a highly insecure status where they can easily be exploited. This helps us place the 'fear of freedom' in its wider context. It may play an essential function in keeping the majority onboard, but it can't rule the whole system: those beyond the pale have always been kept in their place through naked terrorism, and don't really have any freedom to fear.

Racism, and whatever other determinations identify groups as outcasts, serve to enlist the majority's desire not to be part of the 'mess'.

Immediately after World War I, savage racist riots broke out against the colonial peoples who had been transported to the metropolis to help the war effort; (Jenkinson, 2007) we might interpret this as a bid by the majority, only recently herded to their deaths in the trenches in a sub-human way, to restore the old lines of demarcation where only the excluded were treated as cattle, that the majority may remain cocooned in a masked form of exploitation. Eventually, the blurring of boundaries could also promote solidarities. But this will only happen through struggles to transform truncated and selective notions of human rights into genuinely universal ones.

The rulers, too, want to maintain categories: if the mess is conveniently 'bagged', one knows what to repress. Yet this very act of enforcing the boundary also subverts it: to maintain the non-bagged region free from contamination, more and more repression is paradoxically focused inwards, into the heart of the system itself. This is precisely why much of the democratic and human rights developed during capitalist history have recently been dismantled.

In this context, we can introduce Giorgio Agamben's important analysis of the notion of 'exception', within the sphere of law (Agamben, 2005). As he shows, once the possibility of a state of exception is accepted there are no limits to those to whom it can be applied, so in this sense it is self-contradictory: it is no longer the exception, but the norm! The repression of terrorism is extra-judicial, but by this very act the judicial sphere which claims to define the exception is itself implicitly abolished. If rights can be denied to *some* people, they can potentially be denied to *all*. The boundaries delimiting the person or act to whom/which extra-judicial measures can be applied do not exist, because the state which claims the power to act arbitrarily can itself determine those boundaries arbitrarily. This is the beast, which has always lurked within the entrails of the system, and at a particular tipping-point overtakes the system as a whole, nourishing itself by consuming the entire institutional edifice from Magna Carta onwards. The exception is always *potentially* the norm, what has changed today is that this potentiality has been actualised. The stay-behinds were supposed to be activated in extreme circumstances: a Soviet invasion, the collapse of the constitutional order, a situation where only raison d'état remained. But post 9/11 such a situation has become endemic. Foucault's work indeed implied such a tipping point when he spoke of an undercover "silent war" as preparation for a "last battle" which would put an end to politics (Foucault, 1975).

The Hollowed-Out Core and the 'Great Reversal'

As the core auto-cannibalises its own democracy and human rights, an opposite motion occurs in the periphery, with the rise of democratic movements there. This is what I will call the 'great reversal'. However difficult it is for imperialism to find any fresh ideas, this restriction doesn't apply to the mass movement because there is no shortage of ideas about an alternative *to capitalism*. The spiral to disaster can be halted and social order rebuilt through a struggle which takes many dimensions; the aspect of that struggle which mainly concerns us in this chapter is democratic and human rights.

Let's consider the historical background to the great reversal.

The oppressed and marginalised have always fought to *universalise* law and rights. For example, Orphism was a belief system espoused by the downtrodden in the ancient world, (Thompson, G., 1941) whose hymn addresses Nomos, the spirit of law "Ever observant of the upright mind, and of just actions the companion kind. Foe to the lawless, with avenging ire, their steps involving in destruction dire. Come, blest, abundant power, whom all revere, by all desired, with favouring mind draw near; give me through life on thee to fix my sight, and never forsake the equal paths of right."[49] This expresses the eternal conviction that there will be some justice out there somewhere.

Early capitalism picked up from feudalism as the obstacle and target of this struggle, as we see from the Diggers of 1649 through to the 19th-century Chartists. What enabled the core just about to control it was the existence of the periphery. Unruly working class people were once physically shipped to the colonies. But with early imperialism, a more structured solution was found: all you have to do is engineer national solidarity behind the imperial endeavour, while the super-exploitation of the periphery enables core capitalists to maintain or improve their class power *relative to* their own labour, even while making political concessions in the direction of democracy and thus facilitating the co-optation of working class political parties. And eventually a self-regulating system could emerge: tripartite bargaining between the state, employers and labour unions.

Paradoxically, the main way for the core to assert its own higher degree of democratic and human rights is precisely to act externally in

---

[49] c.f. http://www.theoi.com/Daimon/Nomos.html

contravention of those rights. Again, this is about asserting a *boundary*, a line of demarcation, or as Hegel puts it, "What something is, ... it is wholly in its externality": (Hegel, 1969) by constantly rehearsing the non-nomos in your external dealings, you obtain confirmation that the internal sphere is somehow different, superior. This again suggests the issues addressed by Agamben, but Agamben's Eurocentrism lies in his failure to perceive that the real repository of the repressive exceptional power has always been the North-South relationship, and it is partly from this source that the evil spreads.

If we add to this Stephen Bunker's theory, (Bunker, 1985) we can see how the core's institutional 'superiority' is embedded within *material* core-periphery relations: the exploitation of the South's physical resources (exergy) is also a depletion of, in a sense, its social and institutional vitality and diversity. Peripheral governance systems are therefore likely, because of their institutional depletion, to be more simplified (reductionist, top-down, repressive) than those of the core. This in turn confirms the notion that the core has the right to rule the world because of its superior institutions! It is not surprising, then, that even after colonialism ended, the Cold War saw most of the periphery ruled by dictatorships. This looks like a neatly self-regulating system, but as we have described it, it is too determinist and unilinear. What Bunker's theory misses is precisely the crucial thing: struggle. In a human system bifurcation is influenced by 'information about the future' (or in fact, about alternative futures, and hence by choice). The larger struggle is built from *particular* struggles, but if these are to target alternative futures there must be concepts linking them. We earlier suggested the battle over the definition of 'security' as a unifying theme, and in the previous chapter concluded with the case of environmental justice, which asserts a meaningful definition of security applicable to livelihoods. In the present chapter, since our focus is political, we will particularly discuss *rights*.

However depleted certain groups may be through exploitation, there is always a counter-tendency for the more oppressed to take the lead in struggle, as in the tradition of the Orphics. In fact the reason the Cold War dictatorships were there was not that they just 'happened' as a deterministic expression of the depletion of their country's resources, but that they were needed to suppress democratic struggle (Anyang' Nyong'o, 1987). If we take into account the degree of *mobilisation* around rights, the periphery was perhaps always more advanced on the human rights front, in comparison to the relatively cosy and non-confrontational class relations in the core.

The great reversal was thus always implicit as a possibility. The core deeply feared it, and strove to resist it. What was feared above all was that the South would become the standard bearer of humanity, thus reinstating the line of human development as the dominant current, in place of the capitalist line which has side-tracked development over several centuries.

The mode of production has always been vulnerable at times of structural crisis, and one of the main forms this took was slippage of the North's dominance. In the next chapter we will address more broadly, in a political economy framework, the hypothesis of a slippage of the Eurocentric (Atlantocentric) character of the system whereby creativity would shift to the periphery, a notion which the ruling order on the one hand propagates to create the illusion that capitalism still has vitality, and on the other bitterly resists where it might imply a *real* redistribution of power. But it is actually in the human rights field that this slippage may be most marked. Once again, what counts is the level of struggle and mobilisation. The substantive situation in the periphery remains repressive, but the degree of mobilisation is strong, whereas in the core the ruling order demolishes constitutions with barely a squeak of protest.

While colonialism still existed, the necessary contingent form of the struggle for democracy was the fight for national self-determination. The core's response was above all one of *fear*: a fear clearly articulated in the original formulation of the term 'third world' by Alfred Sauvy: (Sauvy, 1952) the masses of the South were the sans-culottes, the great unwashed who menace the natural order of privilege. A doctrine was needed which could twist the notion of the rule of law in such a way as to justify special repressive measures against them. This was supplied by the theorist of 'power politics' Georg Schwarzenberger, who sought a rationale for freezing out the newly-independent states from the South, while simultaneously using the menace of their assertiveness to cement unity among the North: the more 'advanced', civilised stage of international politics would be reserved for internal relations within the North itself, who constitute a 'community' within which the rule of law would apply; whereas the South (referred to contemptuously as 'bamboo states') must be dealt with by naked force (Schwarzenberger 1964).

There is a direct line of descent to Tony Blair: what many Left critics of Blair miss – in depicting him as a mere *follower* of Bush, and in presenting the Iraq war as narrowly about oil – was that his fundamental motivation was surely to demonstrate against any upstart (and therefore, to bolster one's own confidence) that the order still holds, that the hereditary rulers still rule. This is clear in the writings of Blair's special foreign policy advisor, Robert Cooper: "The postmodern world has to start to get used to double standards. Among ourselves, we operate on the basis of laws and open cooperative security. But, when dealing with old-fashioned states outside the postmodern continent of Europe, we need to revert to the rougher methods of an earlier era – force, pre-emptive attack, deception, whatever is necessary to deal with those who still live in the nineteenth century world of every state for itself. Among ourselves, we keep the law but when we are operating in the jungle, we must also use the laws of the jungle."(Cooper, 2002)

Cooper's quotation is revealing to the extent that it confirms important truths: what is being defended is hereditary privilege – racist in the sense that 'jungle' and bamboo derive from the same discourse – and more specifically that the real enemy which incites the hereditary rulers to close ranks against the South is national self-assertion, not 'terrorism'. Despite some minimal lip-service to traditional notions of superior civilisation – by imposing on the periphery the 'law of the jungle', the hope is that they will behave as beasts and thus confirm the supremacist premise – the real determinant of civilisation has been reduced merely to a way of treating not people, but *states*. What matters is not human and democratic rights, but a gentlemanly conduct of inter-state relations. This is an extraordinarily important admission. The great achievement of imperialism after World War II was to realise Hobson's dream of an interdependent West, wherein their collective supremacy is managed as a common property regime of the 'haves', and this must be preserved at all costs. If in the coming crisis, the elite sees the safeguarding of collaboration among the imperialist powers as the last line of defence, the whole content of the definition of 'civilisation' will be sucked into this one area. And, reciprocally, *it is depleted in other areas*, notably in the sphere of human and democratic rights within the core itself. That the cementing of inter-imperialist collaboration and the destruction of the rule of law are intrinsically linked, becomes clear if we consider that it is precisely *through* their macabre dance of death – the 'war on terror', the occupation of Afghanistan – that the great powers ritually seal their blood-pact.

Let's consider more closely the historical dialectic of the great reversal.

As in socio-economic relations so in politics, the early neo-liberal AR imparted a false sense of permanence. Popular movements against

Cold War dictatorships were cunningly hijacked, as a battering ram to break down the old forms of simplified top-down rule which were inefficient from a systems perspective and restricted the development of capitalism itself, a change which would facilitate a controlling form of governance more appropriate to complexity. Struggles against excessively centralised Soviet-bloc political systems could also be brought on board. Although there is always a fundamental essence in the popular democratic struggle (c.f. the Orphics) which can't be corrupted, capitalism gained significant success in channelling it into safe confines. With freedom to enter the economic market-place the central reference point, it seemed perfectly reasonable to permit a development of the international law on human rights, secure in the assumption that it would facilitate a self-regulating peripheral 'low order' (i.e. 'polyarchy') under the banner of 'civil society'. It is important to understand this background of the *early* neo-liberal AR, because the Bush-Blair era, marking the onset of the *declining* phase of that AR when everything came unstuck, witnessed a panicked attempt to reverse these trends. We can then see Bush-Blair not only as a reversal of the whole democratic/human rights tradition since Magna Carta and habeus corpus, but also, more specifically, as the auto-destruction of the more recent human rights legacy of the neo-liberal AR itself.

I would see the 1980s human rights legislation as being in some sense impelled by the mass democratic movements (and therefore progressive in essence), but *apparently* safely constrained within parameters where it could not be turned against capitalism. It is very interesting to examine institutionally how this was achieved. The key legal issue was that states have often claimed a sovereign right to exclude any outside intervention in how they treat their own people, whereas the human rights movement says no, this should not be permitted. A major form of imperialist browbeating had always been to diminish the South's sovereignty, forcing states to amend their internal laws in conformity with 'international' norms (in fact dictated by the ruling interests). This was the basis of the Roosevelt Corollary, countries being forced to use their politico-legal system to protect US investments. The Uruguay Round of GATT and the whole process leading up to the WTO (likewise initiated in the '80s) were doing exactly the same thing in forcing countries to protect the 'intellectual property' of transnationals. Attacking sovereignty is therefore actually a good idea for the *global* rulers. The sentiment is transposed directly into 21st-century discourse: for Richard Haass, Colin Powell's director of policy planning, "Sovereignty entails obligations ... If a government fails to meet these obligations, then it forfeits some of the normal advantages of sovereignty ..."[50] This argument focuses on *economic* 'obligations', but by extension, it must have seemed perfectly safe to intervene in Southern states also on a human rights front. A certain overlap between imperialism and the NGO world also helped in this respect: as *Le Monde diplomatique* far-sightedly pointed out, the notion of a sovereignty-ignoring 'humanitarian intervention' could play into the hands of imperialism (Gresh, 1988). Concretely, the creation of international tribunals to try crimes of genocide could dispense a 'justice of the victors'.

It all appears neatly sewn up. But despite this manipulability, I would argue, there was something fundamentally progressive in the fact that the Zeitgeist was shifting to a critical examination of repressive structures, and eventually imperialism would consider this too threatening.

Although we surmised that the restriction on sovereignty might be considered 'safe' for the dominant power, in reality the US had never been entirely happy with any law or institution which might restrict its *own* sovereign 'right' to act arbitrarily in the international arena. In the next chapter, we will analyse this in detail with respect to one of the key issues of humanitarian law, the International Criminal Court (ICC). At this point, let's consider the case of the UN Convention Against Torture (adopted 1984, entered into force 1987). Significantly, the US felt itself obliged to provide a get-out clause by stipulating that "... nothing in this Convention requires or authorizes legislation, or other action, by the United States of America prohibited by the Constitution of the United States as interpreted by the United States".[51] As we will see later, "interpreted by the United States" establishes an arbitrary Presidential power to ignore *any* law. The imperialists were therefore already worried about the implications.

Eventually, an establishment counter-attack against human rights law would come. It is significant that in 1998 former Chilean dictator Pinochet was arrested in Britain and a historic picket began, stretching over a year and a half, which fully explored the progressive potential of the new human rights law. This is exactly the period to which,

---

[50] quoted in *Guardian*, Tuesday April 2 2002
[51] http://www.unhchr.ch/html/menu3/b/h_cat39.htm

our wider analysis suggests, we can date the beginnings of the repressive shift, something which we can now see as a way of clamping down on the uncontrollability of human rights.

We can see this in relation to what may be considered a logical development of the Convention Against Torture, namely international legislation against Disappearances (government-sponsored secret detention), which constitute one of the most significant forms of human rights violation. Disappearances were once mainly an internal tactic of governments, the classic case being the former Argentinian dictatorship during 1976–83 (although even worse than Pinochet, this dictatorship was shielded at the time through a certain complicity between the Soviet Union and the West). But today, with Guantánamo and the renditions, the issue of Disappearances has now been internationalised ... and more important, it is mainly the imperialists themselves who are orchestrating these directly. Thus, whereas Thatcher had no problem signing the Convention Against Torture, by the time the International Convention for the Protection of All Persons from Enforced Disappearances was established in February 2007,[52] the US and Britain refused to endorse it. This marks a kind of backlash, not only against the progressive use of human rights law by the anti-Pinochet picket, but in fact all progressive developments since the Nuremberg Trials. As Dietrich Muswiek says, it is not just Iraq which is "being reduced to debris and ashes" but also the whole "international legal system as we have known it since the end of the Second World War."(Murswiek, 2003 p. 1)

At this point that we can really begin to appreciate the implications for the international system, because it is the grassroots democratic struggles in the periphery which now openly become, what they always were implicitly, the main force in defence of democratic and human rights. Just at the time when the imperialists were trampling on these rights, in Pakistan mass popular demonstrations engulfed the entire country when Chief Justice of the Supreme Court Iftikhar Mohammad Chaudhry was sacked by the Musharraf regime for his attempts to investigate Pakistan's own Disappearances; (Masood, 2007) history will probably confirm the great significance of this movement. Although, with the subsequent ditching of Musharraf, Pakistan

---

[52] for full text, see Office of the United Nations High Commissioner for Human Rights on http://www2.ohchr.org/english/law/disappearance-convention.htm

remains repressive, what counts above all is the *mobilisation*. It is precisely in response to this threat that interventionism against the South is being stepped up. Bush's speechwriters frantically sought new concepts to justify this, such as 'islamofascism' and totalitarianism.[53] With the mass movement in the periphery increasingly taking over the battle for democratic rights, this could go in directions highly threatening to the dominant interests (it might for example include things of value to working people like rights to a job!). The core needs to pre-empt this by asserting its own definitions ... notably of a strange conception of democracy which seems to be counterposed to human rights, as in Iraq.

The great reversal means that core and periphery now move in opposite directions. From its side, the periphery takes up the banner of humanity (in relation to the theme of this chapter, on the human rights issue, but in the final two chapters I will broaden this to encompass the whole socio-economic line of development). The natural trait of equitability and democratic decision-making is rediscovered, while capitalism's counterattack against its own human rights discourse is resisted. The struggle exposes the sickness of the core's supposition that it can demonstrate its supposedly higher civilisation by acting with total inhumanity *externally*. The motion from the opposite direction is also that the core becomes hollowed out *internally*: by seeking frantically to demonstrate that it is *not* the area of chaos, it enacts an introspective repression and surveillance so intense as to destroy the nomos which supposedly imparts its credentials to rule.

It is always a myth to assume you can practice evil externally while remaining pure within: this again takes us to Aimé Césaire's view of fascism as an internal projection of the genocides wrought by colonialism. (Césaire, 1972) But earlier forms of capitalism had managed to preserve, not so much an effectively higher content of democracy and human rights, but rather a stable balance between open and concealed repression. The underlying repressive networked power discussed by Foucault should remain unnoticed by the majority, or as Brecht expressed it in his ballad of Mack the Knife: the violence is normally kept under wraps.[54] But this balance is somewhat fragile. 'Order', in an

---

[53] according to some bloggers, his subsequent use of these concepts was limited only by his difficulty in pronouncing words of more than three syllables

[54] "Mackie Messer trägt 'nen Handschuh, drauf man keine Untat liest", Brecht, the Threepenny Opera.

efficient exploitative system, should not entirely equate to repression (as in 'l'ordre règne à Paris'), but should have partly the character of a predictability supported by the rule of law. If the latter disappears, only the repression remains.

If poverty and social entropy are manufactured *by capitalism*, we would actually expect the main 'factory' producing them to be situated in the core. This realisation may turn out to be extremely important.

Traditionally the core would export its disorder to the periphery, but what if the latter no longer accepted it? In a mechanical, Malthusian reading, this would happen when the periphery was incapable of absorbing any more (a thermodynamic and political reading of 'under-consumptionism'?), and of course there is an element of truth in this, why else would the ruling discourse be preoccupied with maintaining peripheral 'sustainable livelihoods' in defiance of a systemic collapse which might undermine the periphery's capacity to function as a sink. But more profoundly – and such an interpretation is surely in the true spirit of Marxism – the people no longer *tolerate* being treated as a sink. The element of agency, of struggle, is key. This is exactly how the great reversal operates: as the periphery rebels against its sink status, this forces the core to find a way to manage its disorder internally.

In pursuit of this goal, the system has apparently acquired an interesting characteristic, scarcely predictable a priori from the origins of capitalism, but which seems to have acquired a path-dependency: a significant proportion of the disorder is allowed (encouraged?) to fester within the core of the core, i.e. the USA. In the next two chapters I will develop this argument in more detail.

For the purposes of our current argument, the US prison system provides a good example. The USA has for long periods ruled its Black population through naked terror, and even today maintains a large proportion of that population in what, if the Soviets had done it, would be called a gulag. With 13.5 million people imprisoned annually, the USA can plausibly lay claim to being the world's most repressive society. The female prison population increased from 5,600 in 1970 to 161,200 in 2001!(Sudbury, 2005) As Julia Sudbury points out, the internal and the external are linked in the sense that the changes are part of policing an international political economy which brands increasing numbers as outlaws for questioning globalisation (Sudbury, 2005). Nevertheless, the fact is that this repression is managed internally. With the incarcerated population increasing by nearly 50% between the early

'90s and 2004 (calculated as a proportion of total population),[55] it would not be surprising if there was a point where quantity passed into quality.

We can gain insight into how this relates to the 'war on terror' from a profound observation by Christian Parenti: "Even though most people are not arrested on terror-related charges, *the war on terror has shut down that developing mainstream critique of the whole repressive project* [our emphasis]"(Lidal, 2005) This exactly confirms the evidence we cited earlier: the 1980s and early '90s witnessed a risky development of progressive debate on human rights, which the ruling order desperately had to shut down. In turn, with the pretension of a higher level of rights within the core beginning to collapse, you might experience a chain reaction: the more voided of substance internally the core becomes, the more frantically it projects externally a pseudo-normative interventionism. There was a time when there was some real content in the claim of a rule of law in the North/West: the Enlightenment notion of human rights, the Anglo-Saxon legal system – with its concept of habeas corpus – which can be viewed as a genuine emergent system evolved over centuries of customary and case-law, the Grotian approach to international law with its attempt to extrapolate a notion of natural law on the basis of *jus gentium*. In a space of a few years since the end of the 1990s, most of this has been scrapped.

It may not appear immediately obvious why core capitalism is dismantling a legal system which has served it well in the past. The simplest explanation is that there is a plan to prepare proactively an apparatus to suppress the struggles which are sure to occur when the crisis begins to bite. This is no doubt partly true. There is very much a sense that the system is pre-emptively manufacturing a situation where ecological protests, for example, can be assimilated to terrorism. At a major conference, a Congressman, citing the authority of the FBI, openly compared eco-activists to Al Qaeda: "This is a weed that has come into the lawn and if you don't cut it out, it will spread"(McInnis, 2002) (an interesting metaphor in relation to our earlier discussion of institutional 'gardening'!); and a remarkable *Guardian* investigation revealed how a US arson campaign attributed to green activists may

---

[55] Kings College London, International Centre for Prison Studies, *Prison Brief for the United States of America* on www.kcl.ac.uk/depsta/rel/icps/worldbrief/north _america_records.php?code=190

well be deliberately orchestrated in order to justify repressive measures (Vidal, 2008).

Nevertheless, we shouldn't make excessive assumptions about the degree of strategic intentionality. Fundamentally, it is the system itself which has veered onto this course: if you abandon the experiment with complexity-governance and can't remount the arrow of time to centralism, the result is likely to be a destructive tantrum whereby the rulers begin to function as 'lords of chaos'. Although Bush represented this tendency at its most pathological, it is surely more widely embedded within the turn taken by imperialism as a whole. The approach is exterminist in the sense of being carried away by its own mad logic and, as in the collective ritual slaughter of World War I, mistakes the enactment for the result: the entire human rights edifice since Magna Carta is *gleefully* dismantled with a messianic fervour. Tony Blair's passion for dismantling a thousand years of the legal system somehow suggests the passion of 1960's modernism for destroying the earlier capitalist built environment (interestingly, a Blair government completely out of ideas rediscovered the purely destructive facet of modernism, shorn of its progressive side, as in the 'Pathfinder' programme for the demolition of a quarter of a million homes[56]). In sum, a ritual enactment mystically believed to herald a rebirth of order. Definition-creep with respect to the 'terrorist' label perfectly reflects the entropy expressed in the narrowing of the sphere of what can be controlled 'normally', hence the fallback on generalised destructiveness. British local authorities routinely employ the supposedly anti-terrorist Regulation of Investigatory Powers Act to conduct surveillance of people suspected of a vast array of crimes stretching to rogue trading, benefit fraud, antisocial behaviour, illegal shellfish-gathering, and even to check whether a family has been living within the correct school catchment area (Morris, 2008 a). Or to put this argument a different way, the repressive side of the system's mode of rule, always present as Foucault showed at its margins, has grown outwards from there to engulf, *and to become*, the 'normal' sphere.

Let's briefly try to get a sense of the repressive shift within the core.

In one respect, manipulation of the political machine increases. Even the US establishment expressed disquiet when Bush began to

---

[56] c.f. http://www.fightforourhomes.com/

introduce apparently riggable voting machines,[57] one of the main man-
ufacturers of which was a strong Bush supporter![58] The political class
has done well out of the electoral circus, so is unwilling to see it shut
down. The Military Commissions Act of 2006 authorised the President
to declare anyone, including a US citizen, an 'enemy combattant' ...
and even to define what this term means. The John Warner Defense
Authorization Act of 2007 effectively overturned the law (posse comi-
tatus) which prevented the federal government for using the military
for domestic law enforcement; now the President is authorised to use
troops with respect to a natural disaster, or any other condition. Bush
was the first modern president never to veto laws ... he didn't need to,
because he generalised a methodology, initiated under Reagan, for
issuing 'signing statements' allowing him to ignore any provision of any
law which is in conflict with the constitutional duties of the president,
as defined by himself. This amounts to rule by decree (Savage, 2006).
The most important aspect of these new powers were drawn from
Bush's interpretation of his role as commander in chief of the armed
forces. Thus, in the case of several Congressional laws prohibiting the
use of US troops in Colombia, he simply filed signing statements signalling his intention to ignore them. In the wake of the Abu Ghraib
scandal in 2004, Congress found itself obliged to introduce a range of
new provisions, for example to retrain military prison guards on the
requirements for humane treatment of detainees under the Geneva
Conventions, to perform background checks on civilian contractors in
Iraq, and to ban such contractors from performing "security, intelligence, law enforcement, and criminal justice functions;" these again,
Bush decided to ignore. Although some of these cases directly relate to
external repression, the challenge is to the internal rule of law.

There is indeed some sense of an internalisation of repressive methods previously deployed against the periphery. Although to devastate
the USA in the same way as Iraq (for example, with DU) is unlikely,
weapons which could be focused on the poor and spare the rich
would be OK. US Air Force Secretary Michael Wynne even said that
new 'non-lethal' weaponry would be tried out in US crowd-control

---

[57] see for example http://www.usatoday.com/news/washington/2006-06-26-e
-voting_x.htm; http://www.cnn.com/2006/US/09/19/Dobbs.Sept20/index.html;
http://www.guardian.co.uk/world/2007/aug/01/usa.uselections2008
[58] http://www.cbsnews.com/stories/2004/07/28/sunday/main632436.shtml

situations before being employed abroad.[59] A secret operation in 2005 named Granite Shadow involved the deployment of special forces in the USA under the excuse of contingency plans to deal with 'weapons of mass destruction'.[60] There is a strong sense of an agenda for imposing martial law in the US. Effectively, this draws on the same approach as the stay-behinds, mediated through Reagan-era plans for 'continuity of government' (COG), (Scott, 2006) in building a parallel military-political power which completely escapes constitutional constraints. Early in 2006 a subsidiary of Bush-croney corporation Halliburtons was awarded a contract to build "temporary detention and processing capabilities," and a further aspect of creeping militarisation would see the Federal Emergency Management Agency (FEMA) increasingly replaced by the military. Once again, New Orleans is highly symbolic: the 'emergencies' could be ecological or political, they are just part of a wider mish-mash of unpredictability, to which the rulers respond with fear and a repressive reflex. If special powers have *become* the norm, it is logical for anyone who opposes them to be considered a terrorist. Thus, constitutional scholar Walter F. Murphy, emeritus Professor at Princeton University, discovered by accident (when refused a boarding pass for a plane) that he had been placed on the 'Terrorist Watch list', apparently for having written an article drawing attention to Bush's constitutional violations (Wolf, 2007). Parallels have often been drawn between Hitler's exploitation of the Reichstag fire of 1933 to destroy democratic rights, and Bush's Patriot Act. A 2007 Senate Bill "To pro-vide greater transparency in the legislative process" would severely restrict the right of anybody to address more than 500 people in drum-ming up opposition to any legislation. An amendment to the Patriot Act allowed the president to make "interim" appointments of attorneys that last indefinitely, and this was reflected in a wave of sackings of in-post attorneys and their replacement by people close to the govern-ment. The Bush administration's Immigration Bill was used in an attempt to smuggle in a database of *all* US residents. The list could go on and on.

But the complementary opposite of this apparent top-downness is that the things which are escaping constitutional control, and hence control as such, are precisely the privatised, shadowy world of

---

[59] CNN report on http://www.cnn.com/2006/US/09/12/usaf.weapons.ap/index.html, now removed from site

[60] http://www.defensetech.org/archives/001818.html

'informal' repression which embody the chaotic and decentralised modes of operation which we have been studying. Since one of the major aspects of the 'signing statement' tactic involves refusal to disclose the *information* stipulated by Congressional legislation (for example, on the use of wiretaps), this deprives the capitalist state of any internal mechanism for an independent reality check. What was being weakened, then, was not just limitations on the power of the centralised (Hobbesian) executive, but also anything which might check the growth of *chaotic* forces.

There was a very explicit recognition of a historic shift into a new era. As Naomi Wolf points out, previous situations where democratic rights were suspended had a clear time-frame, (Wolf, 2007) as indeed we might expect from a state of exception, but this time the abolition of constitutionality was open-ended. The 'war on terror' was always officially promoted as a 'long haul',[61] and Brigadier Gen. Mark O. Schissler, Defense Department deputy director for the 'war on terror', in a highly Islamphobic interview with the extreme right-wing paper Washington Times (owned by the Moon sect), describes a "generational war" set to last 50 to 100 years, the problem being to sustain the "American will" over that period when the country was used to wars of only three or four years.[62] Since the 'American will' was already turning against the war at that time, this could only be read as a recipe for the suppression of dissent.

This clearly exhibits a sense of stepping into a qualitatively new repressive phase, with no expectation of ever restoring normality. Although the momentum for dismantling law and human rights was at its most frantic in the Bush-Blair era, and has slowed subsequently, one cannot say it has been reversed. The inability to rule in the old way is thus surely an admission of failure, which fully confirms our sense of a new era of struggle. With its core increasingly hollowed-out, capitalism reveals its inability to run society. It is up to the mass movement to take up the challenge, and to unleash a rich variety of experimentation, providing democracy and human rights with a new content.

---

[61] see for example http://www.globalsecurity.org/military/library/news/2002/03/mil-020324-dod01.htm

[62] "General foresees 'generational war' against terrorism" *The Washington Times*, December 13 2006 on http://www.washtimes.com/national/20061213-010657-5560r.htm

CHAPTER SIX

ORGANISATION OF THE TWENTY-FIRST CENTURY INTERNATIONAL SYSTEM

The Scope and Limitations of a Non-Eurocentric Capitalist Mode of Production

We have remarked that a mode of production could retain its dynamism only if it could be embedded in a viable accumulation regime (AR) – otherwise, it could only exist in a degenerate state (while the analogy is not strict, our usage of this term is influenced by the idea, in astrophysics, of 'degenerate matter' whose entropy is high and where normal structure is lost). This is precisely the expression of entropy which peeps through the Bush project.

To characterise the tendency which leads to this degenerate state, we use the French term dérive to represent a kind of 'slippage', where feedback loops accentuate a trend once initiated, a bit like braking when you skid, and where signals which might theoretically act to correct the slippage are processed by finance capital (through hedging etc.) in such a way as to make it worse. This slippage may not have been inevitable (we are not in the realm of teleology or determinism) but it acquired a strong momentum; it was indeed probably the subjective intention of the Bush clique to make it irreversible. The preferred solution for capitalism would still be to escape this destructive and pessimistic course, and instead discover a new AR. But this is easier said than done. The entropy of capitalism, while fundamentally thermodynamic, is manifested more immediately as an exhaustion of ideas.

In a human system no issue of system-development can be separated from agency, and in this chapter we increasingly emphasise the importance of information about the future. But first, as an exercise let us imagine the mode of production in a more structural sense, purely as an entity 'programmed' to seek its survival and reproduction. The only absolute rule we prescribe is that it maintain the expanded reproduction of capital; as long as this is fulfilled, everything else could be sacrificed.

This line of argument suggests an interesting possibility. Out of all the imaginable 'new ideas', surely by far the most radical and exciting would be that capitalism salvage itself by adopting a non-Eurocentric (or, non-Atlantocentric) form. What currently prevents this is the dominance of the traditional core, but in our thought-experiment it could be sacrificed: an era of rapid evolution could then follow its extinction.

I will argue that this scenario cannot be realised, but that in certain respects it exists as a 'blocked' tendency, and much of the reality of today's political economy follows from this. In fact, it is precisely against the background of an abortive transition to non-Eurocentric *capitalism* that development of an *anti*-capitalist transition will occur. Before proceeding, let's briefly summarise the reasons why it is blocked.

Firstly, the ecological conditions are lacking. Any 'displacement' scenario would presumably be a prolongation of globalisation, but our earlier arguments surely call into question the validity of *any* prolongation of this model (Eurocentric or otherwise). Indeed, the desperate search for energy plunges the system into a militarism totally at odds with the kind of governance needed for a complex system like globalisation; the addition of extra, competing power-centres could only make this worse.

Secondly, it has never been shown that capitalism can exist without some social periphery to exploit, or into which it can export its disorder. If the existing periphery became the core, it would need to find its own periphery, at a time when even now there is no more room, globally, to absorb all the ill-effects of current social and economic disorder.

Thirdly, capitalism has always been Eurocentric. Although it is perfectly possible to imagine an alternative fictional scenario with a different geographical centre, the real historical process has created feedback loops whereby, through the exploitation of thermodynamic power, the core keeps control over the military and political levers which in turn helps it gain more resources. It is hard to imagine this being voluntarily sacrificed, or the capitalist mode of production conducting the most radical restructuring of its history under conditions of extreme vulnerability.

Fourthly, assuming that the historic core would not *concede* power, the periphery would have to grab it. The only basis for doing so would be powerful national movements. But local social contradictions make it inconceivable that, in a given country, a coalition strong enough to achieve this could be constructed under the auspices of an exploitative system such as capitalism. Although coalitions of a new type are in fact perfectly possible, this can only take place in pursuit of an alternative social order, as I will argue later.

The drive towards an overthrow of Eurocentrism is nevertheless real. This would make sense in terms of the negation of the negation because Europe has been fairly peripheral in the wider compass of pre-capitalist human history. The notions we have just introduced, of the hollowed-out core and great reversal, would suggest that this unnatural dominance is ripe for being overthrown. Such a scenario suggests optimistic long-term possibilities for a future non-capitalist human development. But what are the *immediate* implications? Where its own creativity dries up, capitalism has learned to parasitise upon almost anything it can find. If history has introduced the theme of displacement to the periphery, could not the historic core find a way to 'tame' and exploit this, at least temporarily, to prolong its own existence?

In addressing the political economy implications of this question, we should just bear in mind that no form of the mode of production is viable unless these is a corresponding form of international relations (IR). Although IR is a projection of political economy into the superstructure, it is also an essential condition for political economy itself to function.

We can begin with an early argument by Marx. Here, he proposes the idea that the bourgeoisie was at the time of writing (mid 19th century) experiencing its 16th century (the period of its initial flowering) *for a second time*. The task of this second 16th century was to create a world market. The deductions from this premise are twofold: one (optimistic for the radical forces, pessimistic for capital) is that, once this mission was accomplished, the second 16th century would "sound its [capitalism's] death knell just as the first ushered it into the world"; the second is that, probably as an initial effect in this process, the revolution would be "crushed in this little corner of the earth [the West, the historic core], since the movement of bourgeois society is still in the ascendant over a far greater area" (Marx, 1965). Although it has never been a Marxist position that capitalism must 'exhaust' itself *before* it can be overthrown (which would be a determinist distortion of entropy), it is right to recognise that it is more difficult to overthrow a mode of production which is still dynamic.

Let's now consider what changed with imperialism.

Insofar as it was ever true that capitalism could renew itself from the periphery, this of course meant renewing itself as an *exploitative* system. And imperialism did indeed allow capitalism to prolong itself for a century and more through colonial and neo-colonial exploitation, of this there would be no dispute. This in turn raises the possibility of a global anti-imperialist movement, which could in principle save the radical movements from being 'crushed'. The duality of imperialism is that, whereas on the one hand its critics were quite correct to see it as a *decadent* form of capitalism, on the other, the 'second 16th century' took longer than Marx expected, and in some respects did not get underway in earnest till the 1980s. Consequently, the system retained some vitality at least until the last years of the 20th century.

Today's discourse of the rise of Asia serves to create the impression that the mode of production is dynamic even now. But in fact, this discourse is nothing new: notions of an 'Asia displacement' go back to early imperialism. It is interesting to revisit these, because in fact what they say is far from encouraging from a capitalist standpoint.

The spirit of that period was well captured by Spengler's notion of the "decline of the West", (Spengler, 1928) enormously influential in its day. Although suffering from a linearity and determinism character-istic of grand cultural theory,[1] Spengler's work captures the decadence in an interesting way. There is no sense whatever of capitalism *regenerating* itself from the East, quite the contrary, capitalism simply *is* the expression of the decadence of occidental society, and its (unlamented) decline will, indissociably, be also that of the West. He paints a strik-ing picture of a decaying order with shrinking possibilities, thus genu-inely contributing to our imaging of entropy. We have to be wary of parts of the argument, because Frank presents a strong case that capitalism *could* have developed elsewhere, consigning Europe itself to peripheral status (Frank, 1978). But this is fully compatible with a view that the feedback loops of *actual* capitalist development have embedded a Eurocentric path-dependency. In this case, Spengler would be right that capitalism itself would fall with the fall of its his-toric core.

Today's simplistic 'rise of Asia' discourse employs a subterfuge to avoid taking a stance on these great questions of principle. Thanks to the 'end of history' idea, there is allegedly no possibility of future human development being anything *other* than capitalist, and by this sleight of

---

[1] although Spengler was a strong opponent of Hitler, his ideas to some extent fed into Nazism's manipulation of popular disillusionment with capitalism. The Nazis sought to salvage capitalism by disguising it under a national-cultural form.

hand, capitalism itself disappears as a category. Therefore the question of whether displacement is *towards or away from* capitalism is swept aside. In its place, inconsistent *volkisch* notions (for example simplistic discourses about Confucianism) are typically thrown into an eclectic mish-mash. This confusion infected even progressive circles, perhaps the most unfortunate example being Frank's last book *Re-Orient*, (Frank, 1998) where capitalism similarly disappears as a category, leaving only some amorphous Eastern-centred 'movement of history'. In critiquing all these distortions, we must emphasise that it has never been possible to divorce either Eurocentrism itself, *or its hypothetical demise*, from capitalism. In the real world, any supposed anti-Eurocentric re-focusing of the world system could not be neutral with respect to capitalism. It could only take two forms: a displacement of capitalism itself, or a movement against it.

Hobson well understood, in relation to the development of Asia, a profound truth which has in fact a wider relevance to all cases of co-optation (for example, the 'Polanyi factor' of knowledge-based networking, or the 'sustainable communities' idea which we will consider more fully in the final chapter): *in order to survive, the system must parasitise upon sources of vitality wherever it can find them.* The key problem then becomes how to *control* them while doing so. But if we translate this general truth into the specifics of IR at a given time, we can appreciate also the limitations of what Hobson could grasp at the time he wrote. In his day, the relationship with trade liberalisation was obscure because it seemed that imperialism had made capitalism irrevocably top-down and nationalistic; it was therefore hard to see how Marx' notion of the world market could possibly be factored in. But in retrospect it is clear that the 'second 16th century' was simply placed on hold, to be reactivated later, first in post-World War II multilateralism, then with a further massive impetus under globalisation. The realisation of this potential in turn opened up two contradictory features: firstly, the possibility for much more subtle control mechanisms reaching beyond the hierarchical and state-centric methods of early imperialism, and into the realms of complexity; second, the new limitations which begin to appear once complexity becomes just too ... complex.

Hobson was one of the first to conduct an exercise in futurology, and his predictions about the rise of Asia appear stunningly prophetic. But before we marvel at his genius, we should recognise a degree of self-fulfillment: a racial stereotyping of industrious and 'cunning' Chinese was deeply embedded since the 19th century origins of imperialism;[2] Africans for example suffer a different stereotyping and so would have little chance of being anointed the 'chosen people' of capitalist futurology. In this sense, the non-Eurocentric paradigm of capitalism is actually itself an embodiment of Eurocentrism! As we have seen, capitalism's adaptation was such that, increasingly, it could not rest content with accessing merely cheap labour from the periphery, but must parasitise also upon the creative tools of innovation and entrepreneurship, and these are exactly the racially ascribed qualities of Chinese. Of course, the real China has exploited the imaginary China, so this is actually a multi-layered power-struggle. What we are witnessing is in some respects a subordination of Asia which has begun to 'go wrong'.

The four limiting factors we mentioned earlier, now confront the displacement tendencies in a complex and uneven way: for instance, the ecological constraints might lead to a re-surfacing of early imperialist notions of competitive scarcity, and in this case the South would – on a zero-sum premise – be viewed as a rival to be squashed down. On the other hand, the system might, in exterminist mode, burn up the remaining resources in a blaze of glory by pushing win-win (positive sum) scenarios premised on eternal growth. These different combinations provide plenty of scope for alternative informations about the future (which may be expressed in alternative scenario-building) among sections of the elite. What interests us particularly is the more adventurous end of the spectrum: does there exist a constituency which – in its strategic vision, its information about the future – loves capitalism so much that it is prepared to sacrifice the leadership of the historic core?

Here, the key motive would be a need to remove some *blockage* on capitalist development. As we might expect, such a perspective may be found among the extreme globalising faction, that which wants to sweep away not only ecological constraints, but also obstructive vested interests in the industrial powers. Typically, it would see the injection of fresh ideas – even of leadership – from Asia as the only possible driver of change. The most obvious location of this perspective is in business/finance circles; the chief economist of Morgan Stanley, for example, said: "Thank you, China, for showing us the way" (quoted in Harris, 2005). But more surprisingly, we also encounter it in the

---

[2] see for example http://www.njedge.net/~knapp/scholarl.htm

intelligence community. Thus, December 2004 saw the publication of the US National Intelligence Council's '2020 Project' (a revision of its earlier 'Global Trends 2015'), which argues that by 2020 globalisation "is likely to take on much more of a non-Western face", and "Asia looks set to displace Western countries as the focus for international economic dynamism". The argument is concretised by a politics-fiction scenario, in the form of a letter from the head of the World Economic Forum to a former US Federal Reserve chairman on the eve of the annual Davos meeting in 2020: "At the turn of the century, we equated globalization with Americanization. America was the model. Now globalization has more of an Asian face and, to be frank, America is no longer quite the engine it used to be. Instead the markets are now oriented eastwards …Ten or 15 years ago we did not realize the extent to which the Asian giants were ready to take up the slack. The Chinese and Indians have really maintained the momentum behind globalization". (United States Government, 2004)

We can easily argue that this is just propaganda to bolster the confidence of a failing capitalism. Nonetheless, we must be open to the possibility that the discourse is partly genuine. It draws somewhat upon Hobson's strategy of embracing the inevitable Asian development, the better to master it, but what Hobson couldn't foresee was that a heightened international division of labour (IDL) would have to be emergent, i.e. (partly at least) self-organising. Would the historic core have the courage to allow this emergence to run its course? This seems unlikely. While pushing trade liberalisation, the US has always demanded in return many concessions under the excuse that these were needed to buy off its own protectionist and isolationist interests, with the paradoxical result that the champion of free trade is itself economically nationalist. America's own more conservative futurologies try to scare the world that if the US is not sated by still more concessions, it will turn to autarky. In opposition to this, it is not illogical for the radicals to argue that removing such blockages requires some exogenous 'shove', to be administered by Asia. The inducement for the US political class to accept this shove is that, if it persisted in its obstructionism, the second 16th century would go ahead anyway, in spite of and *against* it. This is quite a powerful argument.

Provided one is prepared to accept some measure of qualitative system-change, the Hobson scenario – of accepting the inevitable and 'riding' it – may be still viable. A good case is the issue of South-South technical co-operation. Although conventionally this would be seen as a threat because it would create an alternative knowledge centre, an opposite approach could be envisaged where the core would *promote* this development in order 'ride' it from the outset and thus prevent it assuming an independent and more threatening form. Thus, the World Bank, British Council and OECD jointly organised a Brazil-China-India meeting on sharing knowledge strategies in 2001, known as the Wilton Park initiative.[3] The core powers might also compete for influence within this trend. It is not impossible to foresee a 'selfish' scenario where the US, instead of retreating into autarkic 'North American futures', tries to salvage itself from the shipwreck by casting the old world adrift and instead hitching itself to the rising powers (the more so since Russia threatens to promote a 'Brazil, Russia, India, China' caucus in an attempt to rediscover the geopolitical role lost with the fall of the Soviet system).

What processes would drive such a new international order? Free-marketeers might look to market-propelled emergent processes, but that dogma is unconvinving in practice. Instead, elites would look more to the kind of emergent order arising from new configurations of inter-*state* relations. An interesting case is the proliferation of 'Gs', those groupings of states into which IR decision-making is increasingly organised.

Until recently, no dilution of the North's undivided decision-making power was entertained. When, in the '70s, the South had launched its own pressure-group, G77, the historic core resisted with all its might, creating G7 to ensure it retained control. *Economically*, some demands of G77 were co-opted as part of the neo-liberal AR, notably the industrialisation of parts of the periphery (before the South realised it was pushing at an open door in demanding industrial development, the door swung open and they collapsed head-first into a new subordinate role). But politically, the core rejected any dilution of its dominance: through structural adjustment it treated Southern statehood in an openly vindictive and disdainful way. This is actually surprising because there is no reason in principle why political demands should not be as co-optable as economic ones, on condition that the mass movement remains marginalised: indeed it might be the best way of maintaining such marginalisation. The suffocating non-innovation of the 1980s

---

[3] see OECD, Accueil : Science et innovation: "Brazil, China and India Share Knowledge Strategies, Wilton Park (UK), 17 April 2001" on http://www.oecd.org/document/9/0,2340,fr_2649_37417_2373065_1_1_1_37417,00.html

therefore bequeathed unfinished business: both a demand, and scope, to broaden governance. A good case of this has been the establishment in 1999 – significantly at the initiative of G7[4] – of the G20. Interestingly, this had the effect of squeezing out another grouping of the same name established by the developing countries themselves (originally on a specific agenda of agricultural trade, but whose scope was subsequently enlarged to address wider structural issues of the global economy). The point about the G7-defined G20 is to create the illusion of a broadening of decision-making, while keeping it under tight control. The message is that there is no longer a need for interest-groups or caucuses pushing specific agendas, because the major countries are all in it together.

We could say this is merely a way of buying off states which might otherwise lead a challenge to the historic core, in the spirit of Lyndon Johnson's dictum that some people are better to have "inside the tent pissing out, than outside the tent pissing in". Not that the Southern elite has access to what really happens in the tent, but they are made to feel wanted. Thus the London economic summit of April 2009 which could just as well have been G7 in terms of effective decision-making, was cosmetically conducted in the form of G20.

But the problem is that if change is confined to a merely cosmetic level, this would rule out the really big structural changes necessary to salvage capitalism. There are therefore also strong arguments to create a much less cosmetic form of enlarged governance.

The starting point is a recognition of the important role of agency in economic restructuring. While official pronouncements still affirm the free-trade dogma, elite future-systems brainstorming exercises have dared to question this in an unexpectedly frank way: thus, admitting that the function of economic systems is to channel resources in the direction of capital, it is questioned whether liberalism is really an efficient tool to achieve this (Rynn, 2003). The National Intelligence Council scenario quoted earlier, though not quite so frank, is equally unimpressed by laissez-faire; it says – repeating the point twice for added emphasis – that "It is unlikely that the system would be self-regulating." (United States Government, 2004) This admission is very telling, and helps us appreciate the governance dimension of the elite Southern 'shove'. According to this argument, the point is not so much to sweep away hindrances to free trade (as the more simplistic pro-Asia

---

[4] Yet another confusion: this grouping subsumes earlier attempts known as G22 and G33.

discourses would suggest), but rather to generate a partly *designed* scenario which could be emergent only at the level of North-South elite
dialogue, not at the level of laissez-faire market transactions. For some
time, a certain constituency has argued that G20 should gradually "succeed" (in effect *replace*), as the arbiter of the world economy, a G7
increasingly unable to fulfill this role (Bergsten, 2004).

An obvious basis for dialogue would be a common commitment to
state-centricity. Traditionally, the Southern challenge had, since the
Bandung Conference of 1955, taken the form of a conventional assertion of sovereignty. This suggests grounds for a convergence between
Northern and Southern elites in marginalising the masses and excluding any direct input from them. But this could not be a complete
answer: on the one hand, Southern sovereignty is also dangerous to the
North in diluting the latter's hereditary rule and limiting resource-
plunder; on the other, a situation of complexity cannot wholly be run
in a top-down way. For a combination of these two reasons, conventional state-centricity would need to be supplemented by some injection of pluralism. Ideally, this would involve non-state actors *which are
not mass movements*, and this is where NGOs come in. Because these
tend, for reasons we have addressed, to dislike sovereignty, they could
be employed to counterbalance any threat from the Southern states.
We could call it an international form of 'polyarchy'. But if this were
merely a disguise for divide and rule, and for stablising the existing
status quo, the criterion of system-change would again be lost.

Following this logic, the most radical pro-capitalist scenario would
even go so far as to enlist the mass movement itself, alone capable of
really shoving the system into a new alignment. The analogy would be
the French Revolution where the mass movement demolished the old
structures, and capitalism waited in the wings to occupy the deserted
battlefield. Most striking perhaps is the recognition that the Seattle
anti-WTO protests of 1999 were a *good thing* for capitalism: (Rode and
Deese, 2004) they helped break up archaic governance structures and
clear the way for something new.

Authoritarian versus Systemic Power in International Relations

Let's consider the implications of this scenario-building in terms of
international relations theory. From a systems perspective, state power
and systemic emergence are opposites because top-down or centralised

systems restrict spontaneous order, but capitalism has found ways to reconciling them temporarily in stabilising a given AR. This used to mean a self-regulating 'balance of power' *between* centralised states: not a true balance, since (at least since the beginnings of imperialism in the 1870s) it failed to prevent massive conflicts, but it did maintain a familiarity of structure, a certain predictability. The problem is that divisions between competing powers stood in the way of the collective governance Hobson advocated, while at the same time the dirigiste economic model influenced by Friedrich List (List, 1983) was scarcely compatible with a world market. This problem was addressed in post-World War II IR by using Cold War bipolarity to maintain some structure, under cover of which the capitalist powers could reduce the economic and political nationalism directed against each other. But then with Reagan, the agenda was to get rid of the USSR, and hence of bipolarity. This would potentially leave an integrated capitalist world with delusions of omnipotent power over the world system.

Such dangers are best understood by comparison to the tradition in capitalist IR known as Realism. Making a systems reading of Realism, we can recognise that it is about information. The reactionary side of Realism is that it rejects any feed-*forward*, in the shape of normative information about alternative futures; it recognises only the cynical and fatalist fixation of power politics with conflict and war and does not embrace a transition to co-operation. However, the more useful aspect of Realism is its understanding of the need to maintain feed-*back*, in the sense of information from reality: this would guard against hubris, millenarianism, believing your own propaganda and getting carried away by power or ideology (i.e. against all the things which came to be personified by Bush). Above all, what counts is not a subjective decision to foreswear hubris, but a balancing force which objectively *obliges* you to do so. The Cold War had this: serious scholarship in no way supports the simplistic vision that the US was 'containing' an aggressive Soviet Union, (Jervis and Snyder, 1991) on the contrary, systemic constraints rendered the latter quite circumspect; thus, the US was spared the burden of omnipotent delusions. At the end of the 1970s the school of mainstream IR theory known as neo-realism explored the self-regulating systemic features of the balance of power, (Waltz, 1979) and more specifically the analogy with liberal economics and its 'hidden hand' emerging through free competition. Superficially this looks like an IR for the neo-liberal era, but the argument was flawed because balance was actually on the decline. Against this background, we can see why the end of the Cold War shifted international politics into uncharted territory. It can be argued that the system never really found a post-Cold War form, and indeed *the ability of the Bush-Blair madness to seize control of it is not unrelated to the absence, within that system, of balancing mechanisms*, of negative feedback to curtail a runaway dérive.

It is not difficult to see what the post-Cold War balancing factor 'could' have been: an independent role for the Southern states which would replace that of the Soviet bloc in counterbalancing the North's omnipotent fantasies, and at a theoretical level, this would be very much in the spirit of Realism. At a practical level, however, it would go completely counter to the whole tradition of supremacism embedded not just in Realism but in every other aspect of capitalist IR: a power balance *within* the white world was one thing, but a balance incorporating the South would be quite another. In one of Blair's major speeches, he asserted the need to bring the politics of globalisation into line with the economics (Blair, 2006). He is absolutely right that the IR system has never 'fitted' the current era of political economy very well, but in fact his own contribution went in exactly the wrong direction. Not only did he reinforce the mad positive feedback of Bush, but his reign in many ways contradicted the only meaningful sort of balance which could have been introduced, an opening-out to the South. Capitalism, in its real development, therefore sabotages the creative possibilities of a new capitalist IR, by reinforcing a claim to sole power by the 'old' centre.

Rejection of a Rules-Based System

If we move outside the sphere of conventional notions of balance based purely on power, there is another way we could imagine solving the problem of structure in IR. Suppose that after the fall of bipolarity, a rules-based order arose in its place. This would not simply be a rehash of balancing attempts, but would take a different route.

But there is a very powerful habitus acting against this solution, embedded since the origins of imperialism, and which it has proved unable to shed. This takes us to the key issue of multilateralism. The kind of multilateralism which the powers enjoy is the one we can call (borrowing a term from Nabudere (1977)) multilateral *imperialism*. This is a club, in effect a regime whose participants voluntarily observe the discipline of *not pushing their competition to a point where it might undermine the premises of their joint dominance.* The kind of multilateralism they hate is anything where – either in economic or in military affairs – they might be subject to the discipline of either an international institution, or some embodiment of the international 'community' (incorporating, horror of horrors, small states of the South). They demand a punitive power where the sole legislator, judge, jury and executioner is themselves, untrammelled by any nicities of evidence or procedure. Today's domestic anti-'terrorism' legislation establishes merely putative 'offenses' where no actual act needs to have been committed, and where the standard of proof is lower than for a traffic contravention. But the international situation has always been like this. US policy in particular traditionally rejects any multilateralism which might restrict its individual right to take action.[5]

This is the established pattern, but surely now it should change. And indeed, it did appear in the '80s that things were moving in the direction of change. Whatever the reticence in broadening out to some 'Gs' of the South, the same restriction did not seem to apply to rules-based institutions. Two examples seem to run in parallel: the international law of human rights, and the WTO.

On the surface the rise of such rules-based structures looks like an excellent development from imperialism's point of view. The moment the Cold War came to an end in the late 80s (and the coincidence of timing is surely not accidental), it appeared that the crude structure of bipolarity was being replaced by a far more sophisticated one appropriate to complexity, and at first sight it is impossible to find anything threatening to the dominant interests. After all, rules-based institutions look like an ideal vehicle for indirect forms of power ... provided you can manipulate the rules, which is surely the case. For example, key provisions of the WTO serve in effect to internationalise US domestic trade laws, notably the famous Section 301 of the US Trade Act; WTO decisions are governed by its own version of 'consensus', which aims "certainly to give weight to the views of countries that have power in the trading system. This is not likely to change." (Jackson, 1998 p. 45) And we could say something very similar about the new

---

[5] This is why the US resisted joining the inter-war League of Nations – which it had nevertheless sponsored – and why the International Trade Organisation, proposed as a complement to the World Bank and IMF at the Bretton Woods conference of 1944, never took off.

normative approach to human rights, which we discussed in the previous chapter. One of its spinoffs was the advent of a new kind of institution, the International Criminal Court (ICC). Similarly to the WTO, it seems totally 'tamed'. Indeed, as a US professor approvingly remarked, "The United States bullied its way into getting the US stamp on almost every single provision in the International Criminal Court statute. It really is a US statute with just a couple of exceptions." (quoted in Guyatt, 2000 p. 70) This actually looks like a big improvement on old-style imperialism, and elements in the post-Bush US leadership did indeed for a time express interest in revisiting a rules-based scenario. But the whole weight of history goes against this, and we have to understand why.

The Clinton administration, despite misgivings, eventually signed the Rome treaty establishing the ICC, but that was in 1998, just before the watershed which we have identified as the tipping point of the new repressive phase. Bush then took the unprecedented step of repudiating America's signature. A key ingredient in the anti-ICC campaign was to browbeat individual countries to sign 'bilateral impunity agreements' (BIAs), to the effect that a government will not surrender or transfer US nationals accused of genocide, crimes against humanity or war crimes to the ICC, if requested by the Court (if the USA did not intend to conduct genocide, crimes against humanity and war crimes, would it be necessary to do this?). The American Servicemembers' Protection Act (2002) even authorises the President to use "any means necessary" to free US citizens and allies from ICC custody (presumably this implies making war on the ICC itself?). In 2002 the USA further forced through a Security Council Resolution (1422) granting perpetual immunity from prosecution for such crimes for its forces engaged in UN operations; although eventually, following the Abu Ghraib revelations, it was unable to get support to renew this resolution, it then simply fell back on intensifying the pressure for BIAs. The Nethercutt Amendment (2004) further cut all economic aid from any country which ratified the ICC treaty but refused to sign a BIA.[6] The pressure seems to be essentially placed on weak developing countries, about 100 of which had been forced to sign them (NATO/OECD members being apparently exempt, presumably on the grounds that as members

---

[6] see Coalition for the International Criminal Court, *Overview of the United States' opposition to the International Criminal Court* on http://www.iccnow.org/documents/ CICCFS_US_Opposition_to_ICC_11Dec06_final.pdf

of the ruling coalition they are sufficiently hand-in-glove with the USA anyway).[7]

What is truly amazing is the extent to which *any* degree of subservience by the institutions seemed insufficient. A tame UN defined 'threat' in such an all-encompassing way that it need not be imminent, making pre-emptive military action fully justified, "whether the threat is occurring now, in the imminent future or more distant future; whether it involves the State's own actions or those of non-State actors it harbours or supports; or whether it takes the form of an act or omission, an actual or potential act of violence or simply a challenge to the [Security] Council's authority." (United Nations, 2004 a) In this way, imperialism receives a blank cheque to attack any country where the notion of threat is purely speculative. But even this was not enough: the UN had had the effrontery to smuggle into the package an insistence that the action be *multilateral*, (ibid.) and this is what cannot be tolerated. While it is OK to tolerate – or even encourage – a broadening of the 'Gs' involved in *economic* decision-making, the power of the core over the repressive apparatus – law, military intervention – not only cannot be diluted, but must actually be *strengthened*, to compensate. It is therefore no accident that the rise of globalisation has been accompanied by, and *counterbalanced* by, new approaches to organised collective military dominance. It is this military power which underlies everything and ultimately is designed to ensure that economics and politics don't develop in a way threatening to the established interests. This does not abolish the drive to a non-Eurocentric capitalist mode of production, but it 'blocks' it, resulting in a powerful contradiction fundamental to much of the contemporary IPE.

Dominating Information about the Future

This involves outlawing any information about the future which may conflict with the dominant one.

The control of information however carries two risks: firstly, that the oppressed will realise they are being brainwashed and switch off;

---

[7] see Amnesty International, *States that have entered into an impunity agreement with the USA*, updated September 2006, on http://web.amnesty.org/pages/int_jus_icc _imp_agrees. In many cases these agreements, signed by governments, would still need to be ratified by national assemblies, and campaigns were underway to stop this happening.

secondly, that the ruling actors will receive distorted feedback from reality. The whole art of capitalist information-management is to make the manipulation subtle enough to avoid the former danger, while ensuring (this is a key tenet of Realism) that elites' *own* perception is not distorted: for example, McCarthy had to be ditched when his anti-Communist propaganda threatened to degenerate into the feedback loops of true paranoia. Nevertheless, in 'dominating knowledge', it is never entirely possible to maintain a cynical distance. The manipulation of information is effective precisely because it operates through feedback loops whereby expectations are confirmed; but it is the nature of loops that they can get out of control.

When working normally, the loops operate in the sense that a story which confirms the dominant image is will be believed uncritically, which in turn bolsters that image, which in turn makes it more likely that the next such story will be believed. This systemic process is embedded in various ways, for example in a use of terminology which legitimises the actions of repressive forces and de-legitimises resistance, a key example being reporting on Israel: (Edwards and Cromwell, 2005) if Israel grabs someone this is 'arresting', if Palestinians or Lebanese grab an Israeli it is kidnapping. The 'massacre of Timisoara' story at the time of the collapse of the eastern bloc is a notorious example of a completely fabricated story which attained global impact simply because it conformed to, and was therefore in a sense validated by, the expectations created by the dominant paradigm (faked photos of a non-existent massacre by Ceaucescu in Romania were never questioned because they confirmed what everyone expected to hear). If one is hearing what one is predisposed to believe, normal standards of evidence no longer apply: Robert Mugabe served the ruling discourse well in discrediting the more serious third world rulers who may attempt to assert sovereignty in the face of Western diktats and even the wildest allegations about him could be published as true without a shred of evidence (Vidal, 2005). Such systemic loops have always existed, but the approach has been further refined for an era of pluralism (not of course pluralism of ideas, but of institutions!): instead of the state *directly* massaging the media, this happens through the medium of private consultancies and NGOs. An interesting case is the 'dead babies' scam during the first Gulf War in 1990: Amnesty International published a story that Iraqi soldiers had stolen incubators from a Kuwaiti hospital, leaving babies to die on the floor. This report was since shown to be a fabrication by a PR firm hired by Kuwait;

but there is, in addition, widespread suspicion that British intelligence had infiltrated Amnesty UK in order to use them as a respectable 'front' (Wokusch, 2002). At times the projection of disinformation comes unstuck, as with the story of Private Jessica Lynch ('rescued' in a stage-managed media coup from the hospital where she was being treated by Iraqis), who later bitterly attacked the Bush administration for manu-facturing her 'heroism';[8] or the case of Iraq war soldier Pat Tillman, really killed by friendly fire, who was faked as a heroic victim of Iraqi 'terrorists'. By and large, however, the whole apparatus has not yet been called into question. Besides these particular cases of disinformation, we find a more generalised ideological clampdown. Thus, whereas the '80s and '90s had witnessed debates in the US about the history of slav-ery and genocide, a backlash occurred in the 2000s. Florida Governor (and brother of the then President) Jeb Bush signed in June 2006 a new law on the teaching of history which says: "American history shall be viewed as factual, not constructed, shall be viewed as knowable, teach-able, and testable, and shall be defined as the creation of a new nation based largely on the universal principles stated in the Declaration of Independence." It includes new emphasis on "flag education, including proper flag display and flag salute", as well as on the need to teach "the nature and importance of free enterprise to the United States economy."(George Mason University, 2006) The rise of Islamophobia similarly challenges even the limited and manipulative multicultural-ism which had been developing in capitalist society. Needing to dis-cover self-assurance, the system reverts to its default setting, where its sense of mission, of right to rule, is strongly Atlantocentric. At this point, this is no longer mere cynical manipulation, but rather a kind of self-brainwashing by the system itself. It would destroy even the cli-mate of debate within the ruling elite necessary to offset the system's sclerosis; a return to the dark ages of uniformity and dogma would shut off future development. The despot doesn't wish to be bothered by facts or evidence: he wants to imprison people at will on mere suspicion, to invent new crimes and reserve the prerogative of defining them, to invade countries on a whim not because they constitute a present threat but might at some time in the future do so. At a particular point in this chain, reality becomes irrelevant, the rulers themselves becom-ing imprisoned in the trap supposedly reserved for their subjects.

---

[8] *The Times*, April 25 2007

Leading journalist Ron Suskind reveals that Bush was with his own connivance fed a distorted information-set, so as to render his actions more single-minded, and his pronouncements more credible (Suskind, 2006 pp. 99, 175). The 'one percent doctrine' (which treats any supposed risk, however minute, as a certainty) was effectively a blank cheque to treat any fantasy as real. Bush's dislike of science, with its standards of proof, is symptomatic.

The abuses we have just mentioned may be among the aspects of slippage most easy to correct in the post-Bush phase. Nevertheless, there remains the uncomfortable fact that Bushism was a mad response to a genuine issue: previous generations of capitalist elites could afford to be Realist because they were not receiving such dire information about the future of the mode of production, notably in an ecological sense. Bush's denial is only too eloquent, its very extremism marking him as the first statesman of the new ecological age. The system is indeed at a loss as to where it is going. Whereas developmentalism claimed to be going *somewhere*, the 'end of history' discourse made the fatal error of claiming that neo-liberalism has no beyond. Once it becomes clear that capitalism *must* discover something beyond neo-liberalism, it is disoriented. This is the problem capitalism urgently needs to answer: how to generate some new information about the future.

Reinventing the Federation of the Western States

But the core would not admit any information about a future which it itself no longer rules. The *methodology* of visioning might be innovative, drawing upon the brainstorming and visioning techniques of the new management systems, but the content will necessarily be conservative. Indeed, what is supposed to be information about the future may really emerge from the past, from a reawakening of imperialism's murky demons. It is precisely in this way that the sense of mission ('mission statements' are after all an indispensible part of any self-respecting new management-speak) is formed. In the last analysis, the fundamental issue is not about how to open out to the South, but about how to restructure the North in such a way that multilateral imperialism can continue to control the future.

First and foremost, this means re-conceptualising the US leading role. The US vocation has historically been to uphold 'free trade'. Now, unlike 'free market' (a notion wich the rise of oligopoly and finance capital has rendered completely empty), free trade in the sense of an abolition of tariffs, quotas etc. does represent something of real substance: exactly the substance of the world market predicted by Marx. If the great powers reverted to competitive nationalism (which is a *possible* form of the entropy of capitalism), the mode of production would be doomed. So the stakes are very high. The special position of the US is premised on an assumption that disaster would follow were it to become isolationist (meaning that it would either stop actively promoting global free trade, or even become nationalist itself), leading to a feedback process of protectionism and reprisals, an assumption which was for decades shamelessly exploited by the USA to gain privileges. Indeed, the autarkic 'North American futures' scenario seems destined tactically to make isolationism look more viable and realistic, thereby warning other capitalists that they are playing a dangerous game should they attempt to cultivate more independence. But despite the abusive elements in this argument, it is partly true: global capitalism does really need the USA.

There is a strange duality in this relationship: the US is not only privileged but also (as we saw in discussing its prison regime in Chapter 5) a kind of repository for the entropy of the entire mode of production. From this standpoint, the old debate about whether the US is 'in decline' or not is a false dichotomy. As fountain-head of global capitalism, that country necessarily incorporates its contradictions in particularly acute form. It is therefore both 'in decline', and for the very same reason also 'dominant' in the sense that shoring up the United States economy and society becomes the system's main (dominant) goal, to be achieved by any means necessary. J.G. Frazer wrote his anthropological classic *The Golden Bough* out of fascination with the duality within traditional society, whereby the same man is at once priest-king and sacrificial victim (Frazer, 1998). The USA possesses a similar duality, but with this difference: unlike the sacrificial priest-king it cannot be hunted and slain, because there is no successor. It is therefore preserved, bleeding but venerated. The then WTO head Supachai Panitchpakdi was right, on this reasoning, in arguing that "the fiction that there is an alternative to the WTO — or to US leadership — is both naïve and dangerous" (Panitchpakdi, 2004). If the US is not handed the lead of the globalisation project, and indeed rewarded for leading it, the mode of production is finished.

But the carrying to fruition of this project, i.e. the world market predicted by Marx, creates a new terrain of contradictions. The institutional structure of globalisation harbours the twin dangers of a rules-based system and an arena where Southern elites might contest hegemony. This provides an added incentive to strengthen the core's autocratic rule. An important dimension of this task is to refurbish the Anglo-Saxon core within the core. Here we again see the paradox that, as the system most wants to vision its future, its reference points are in the past.

In this book we talk a lot about British imperialism not only because it was written in Britain but because there seems to be an intrinsic importance to the US-British nexus. But we need to understand its true function. Mark Curtis' approach is, for example, not very helpful: (Curtis, 1998) he merely lists various examples of US-British collusion on reactionary projects. It is true that, with the world's second highest level of government spending on military R&D and the largest military corporation outside the USA (BAE Systems), (Langley, 2005) Britain's role in the militaristic project is central. But we need to push the analysis towards understanding *systemic* roles. It seems that Eurocentrism could more accurately be called Atlantocentrism: a refurbishment of the hegemony of the white world around a core of Anglo-Saxon nationalism.

The most obvious aspect has been collaboration in the kind of terrorism which presents itself as counter-terrorism. We saw how the parallel politico-military power throughout the capitalist world was historically run collaboratively by the US and Britain, and in the last analysis remained loyal to them. In the more recent context, we can refer to the discipline which, disguised as *study* of terrorism, really serves to manufacture arguments for condemning popular struggles as terrorist and justifying real terrorism against them. Toolis aptly describes this school as "a sullied sub-academic doctrine fused from cold war hatreds and the last counter-insurgency struggles of empire in Malaya, Kenya, Cyprus and Ireland"(Toolis, 2004) A good example of this level of networking is the Centre for Studies in Terrorism and Political Violence (CSTPV) at the University of St Andrews, set up in close collaboration with US military think-tank the RAND Corporation.[9]

Alongside collaboration in practical repression, equally important is the ideological dimension. At its most embarrasingly crude, author Andrew Roberts typifies the apologist for empire who is also an advocate of joint hegemony of the USA and Britain, two countries which "in

---

[9] see http://www.st-andrews.ac.uk/intrel/research/cstpv/

the majestic sweep of history ... had so much in common – and enough that separated them from everyone else – that they ought to be regarded as a single historical entity;" and "remain the last, best hope for Mankind"; (Roberts, 2006) Roberts was still being feted at a literary luncheon in the White House in February 2007.[10] Nevertheless, this washed-out conservatism is somewhat discredited (one of its leading proponents, Conrad Black – who feverishly advocated a notion of 'Anglosphere' derived from classical Europhobia – was even ditched by the establishment itself). Instead, far more typical is a seemingly forward-looking approach which builds strongly on networks, thus giving the impression of an Atlantocentrism appropriate to the systemic turn. Brainstorming is a technique to stimulate emergent properties, and if this faculty can be enclosed within the core, peripheral information-building will, by a reciprocal motion, be depleted, thereby undercutting the possibility of informations about alternative futures, even of a (non-Eurocentric) capitalist kind.

Since an era of complexity could not be satisfied with the old-style diplomatic level of relations, a networking which cross-cuts state boundaries was therefore initiated. In its initial, 1970s, form – represented by the Trilateral Commission which inspired the creation of G7 – this spanned the North as a whole, but in its more recent form it has been more specifically Anglo-Saxon. In an important sense, the British-US axis underpinning the Iraq war was created in the mid-1980s in a project which on the surface appeared to have nothing to do with militarism. Its most visible form was the 'British-American Project for the Successor Generation', whose founder, Nick Butler, described it in explicitly systemic terms as a network, part of civil society (Beckett, 2004). The distinguishing feature is that, in contrast to the clapped-out conservative Atlantophiles, it consciously encouraged dissenting and unconventional voices and fresh, creative thinking as the only way to generate the off-the-wall thinking and unpredictable interactions needed to give birth to an imperialism for the 21st century. One invitee was, for example, radical Black poet Benjamin Zephaniah, who can reasonably be considered a genuine critic of the dominant order. The system needed fresh ideas, and the white, male world of upper-class clubs was a luxury it could no longer afford. This is however an inclusiveness in the interests of exclusion, in the sense that it was hoped that

---

[10] *Guardian*, March 23 2007

P2P networking among the elite would unleash genuine innovation in better controlling and exploiting the masses. Hence, the networking strand of Atlantocentrism, in appearance so different from the 'sullied doctrine' of counter-terrorism, actually provides the latter with a fresh rationale for intervention. However trendy and innovative the form, the actual content drags the system backwards, into its most archaic and militarist realms.

This will be clearer if we understand the actual content of the 'new' ideas yielded by the North-North networking process. Essentially, it includes a strong tendency to reinvent notions of empire, and thus reverse the verdict on the colonial era. Its point of reference lies in the more normative trend which had grown within imperialism around the turn of the 19th–20th centuries, claiming to spread social benefits rather than simply exploit colonies for their raw materials.

The fact that democracy-promotion is potentially the most aggressive form of imperialism is confirmed by its rising influence during the course of the Bush adminstration. Neocon columnist Robert Kagan thus remarked that in Bush's second term, policy was increasingly 'unmoored' from the terrorism issue (Kagan, 2005): rather than merely being *against* something, it claimed a right and duty to 'normalise' political systems worldwide. For the old-style Realists among Bush's critics, (Ryn, 2003 p. 383) this was precisely the problem: by pursuing what they contemptuously called 'democratism', all restraint would be lost.

But despite the openly right-wing usage of democracy-promotion by Bush, the more typical line would be a pseudo-Left rehabilitation of empire on the grounds of social responsibility. This is the trend which may well lurk within the apparent corrective to Bush's reactionary politics in the most recent period, whereby it is claimed that Bush, by keeping too much of the war on terror's frank power politics (as in the coalition with repressive Southern states), undermined the true potential of democracy-promotion.

Tony Blair was fond of saying that left-right lines of demarcation are no longer relevant, (Blair, 2006) and while this is in a general sense untrue, it does raise a real issue, albeit one which we should interpret in a sense opposite to that of Blair: the real line of demarcation is pro- or anti-imperialist. The progressive camp is focused round the anti-imperialist Left but could reach out to alliances with various forces opposed to authoritarianism, war and surveillance, which might include old-style Realists, 'paleocons' and right-wing libertarians. Similarly, the pro-imperialist camp can embrace some elements reminiscent of 1900s social- and liberal imperialism, as well as various NGO arguments in favour of intervention under a humanitarian guise. It is mainly from the latter direction that a refurbished interventionism arrives. This draws inspiration from early 20th-century 'enlightened' arguments for empire as a civilising force which typically attacked the establishment on the ground that it would be morally wrong to abandon the colonies until the civilising 'job' was complete.[11] Its more recent incarnation could be seen, in the British context, in the Euston Manifesto,[12] issued by a grouping of intellectuals many of whom may be thought of as on the 'left' of the conventional political spectrum; their distinctive position (bolstered, for example, by a Serbophobe reading of the breakup of Yugoslavia) is to attack the rest of the left for insufficient enthusiasm in backing, or indeed inciting, US 'humanitarian' interventions.

While presenting itself as a correction to the mad hubris of Bush, a shift in the direction of liberal imperialism might in reality push it further. After all, the classic imperialist position did retain some sense of restraint. The Roosevelt Corollary described intervention as 'reluctant', and, while this is deceptive if it implies that countries *not* actually being invaded are free (at any level of capitalist society, domestic or international, when you are not actively being policed it is precisely that you have internalised society's norms and self-censor your ideas and actions), the Corollary is at least moderate in that the criterion of correct order is somewhat narrowly defined. Civilisation effectively means respect for US economic interests. Even Robert Cooper's form of pro-Empire argument retains a legacy of Realism because there is no sense of intervening to 'civilise' the South (who are virtually considered uncivilisable), you merely act to smash them before they smash you. But now we witness a social engineering whose result (if recent experience is anything to go by) is likely to be the very 'collapse of society' it is supposed to prevent.

Let us consider the practical implications of democratism. It would serve to redress the potentially dangerous loss of control which in Chapter 5 we called the 'great reversal', the shift in the focus of democracy to the South (by this we mean not democracy as something static, but above all the experimentation to generate information about the future of what democracy might *become*, its possible new content

---

[11] for a good example of this liberal imperialist argument see Campbell, 1945

[12] Euston Manifesto, statement of March 29 2006, on http://eustonmanifesto.org/joomla/index.php?option=com_content&task=view&id=12&Itemid=38

and forms). The purpose of the core 'promoting' its own version of democracy would be to stifle such innovation.

During the Cold War, as Amin showed, the advanced industrial states could have the luxury of inclusive, Keynesian politics and economics because their pauperisation tendency had been exported to the periphery (Amin, 1977). The result was that peripheral states were typically top-down dictatorships, and the core could congratulate itself on being more democratic. But then anti-dictatorship movements swept Africa and Latin America, and precisely because democracy is not static, the focus of dynamism threatened to escape the core's control. This takes us back to the issue of what follows the dismantling of any top-down system. The post-1945 order was a very controlled one, whether we look at industrial management through the state and TNCs, or at the Cold War. When this is removed, there are several possibilities: a contained emergent order, a situation of creative emergence which escapes the hold of the historic core, or 'bad' forms of chaos. From the standpoint of the hereditary rulers, the first is preferable, the second must be avoided at all costs, and the third is a fallback mechanism to avoid the worst case.

In the early phase of the 1980 accumulation regime, a manipulated system could be maintained, essentially by 'unmooring' democracy from sovereignty. Multiple political parties could 'debate' ad infinitum and ad nauseam provided they agreed with IMF-World Bank dogmas of the moment (initially market fundamentalism, subsequently a cosmetic commitment to poverty-reduction whereby Southern countries are made responsible for the earlier wrong policies which the IMF forced them to follow). At the same time, popular discontent with Soviet commandism in the Eastern bloc provided imperialism with cheap credentials for promoting its brand of democracy. But more recent events have reawakened the spectre of the centre losing its hold. As we have seen, both in Robert Cooper's ideas and also more generally in the 'war on terror's' claims to face an 'inhuman' – effectively subhuman – enemy, the ruling order illogically claimed on the one hand the mission to impose its will on the rest of the world because it is more civilised, and on the other, the right (indeed, the duty) to do so by the most violent, dictatorial and immoral means. Here, democracy has become 'unmoored' not just from sovereignty, but from human rights. In the face of this moral vacuum, it is not surprising that novel alignments have arisen, for example in Latin America, aiming to introduce new content to democracy. In response, the core must above all leave no space for institutional *experimentation*. It's a bit like the control of the seed multinationals over experimentation in farming: the system cannot tolerate diffuse innovation, or any autonomous emergence which might go in creative directions. The free creativity of brainstorming must therefore either be ring-fenced within the elite – as in the 'British-American Project for the Successor Generation' – or pre-defined with a stultifying rigidity, as in the decision-making model for changing defective lightbulbs taught to workers under the Japanese management system. Control over innovation is recentralised.

The most immediate threat is that radical Southern elites will claw civil society away from the influence of the core. Chávez argues, drawing upon Gramsci, that in situations where the state becomes radicalised under the influence of grassroots movements, it will no longer operate in harmony with civil society in a repressive sense, leaving civil society as the preferred medium of intervention by the core (Wilpert, 2007). In response, peripheral elites could develop a mixed institutional strategy. Although a state which openly shunned civil society would be extremely vulnerable, (Gowans, 2007) a wiser strategy may be to pretend to accept the civil society discourse and try to mould it. The global core attempts to push notions like decentralisation and subsidiarity in a safe and sanitised form, channelling them in such a way that they serve merely to atomise society and undermine any coalescence around progressive nationalism; but Southern countries too could play at this game. Khanh Tran-thanh explains how the 'transition' system of Vietnam created its own manipulated civil society to counterbalance that 'promoted' by the West (Tran-Thanh, 2003). In turn, US establishment sources are wise to such a danger: "In addition to impeding democracy assistance efforts, regimes are adopting pro-active approaches, channelling funds to anti-democratic forces and using ersatz NGOs to frustrate genuine democratization."(Lugar, 2006) This makes it only too clear that genuine democracy is simply what the US says it is: US-approved ersatz NGOs are OK, locally manipulated ones are not.

It might seem that core and peripheral elites have an interest in negotiated solutions to this arm-wrestling match, on a basis of mutual distrust of grassroots unpredictability, but this would not be viable in the long, strategic term: we keep returning to the same issue fundamental to our discussion in this chapter: any shift of power to the periphery must make up its mind whether it is capitalist or not. In the former case, it comes up against all the contradictions of a capitalist mode of production, which as an ensemble is in crisis: the accumulation of one particular country or region could no longer possibly be separated from the global accumulation circuits. In the latter case, the new alignments do indeed have a future but must then sever themselves from imperialism.

In the short term, it is in principle perfectly possible for the core to negotiate a new pact with peripheral elites, but what eventually undermines this in practice is that the core remains viscerally hostile to any definition of sovereignty which would dilute the rule of the Euro-American world. The characteristic proposition is that: "the decision to intervene promptly to keep small threats from turning into big ones must lie with those who take seriously the notion of sovereignty as responsibility: the world's democracies (including in particular the United States and its major democratic partners in Europe and Asia). Democracies know—in a way that nondemocracies do not—that real sovereignty, like real legitimacy, resides with the people rather than with the states."(Daalder and Kagan, 2007) Alongside the strange assumption that being voted in by your own people gives you the right to overthrow the state power in any *other* country, there is a supplementary argument against multilateralism: the international community is made up of nondemocracies, therefore it should be ignored. Of course, it is true that a strongly normative commitment to human rights should continue to limit sovereignty in the sense that law is not merely the positive emanation of the sovereign. The Grotian position of a universal *jus naturale* underlying positive law remains necessary as an antidote to the bad side of Realism, its espousal of 'might is right'. But the whole question is where we seek the agents of change. The assumption in some academic debates on international civil society, (Chandler, 2004) that the rise of Gorbachev and international NGOs in the post-Cold War context brought about a lasting change away from the bad side of Realism, is far too naive. In fact imperialism, while opposing all the positive aspects of sovereignty, has itself led the counter-attack against the one thing which really should limit sovereignty, namely human rights.

One basis for the imperialist counter-attack against human rights was the loss of the other side of Realism, its sense of restraint. The millenarian frenzy of Bush and Blair cannot be understood outside the context, both of a delusive post-Cold War unipolarity, and of the seemingly unlimited power of intervention made possible by the weakening of the sovereignty of the South via structural adjustment. Even if neoliberalism somewhat weakened the state within the core itself it did so to a lesser degree, with the result that the core's *relative* international power increased vis-à-vis the South. In one of the more pernicious developments of the normative, anti-Realist argument, this growing core-periphery disparity of power is explicitly welcomed because it increases the capacity of the former's politico-military apparatus to be enlisted by NGOs for 'humanitarian' intervention (Keck and Sikkink, 1998).

The spectre of chaos has always been used to justify the imposition of order, and in the old Hobbesian argument this came from the top or from the centre. But the manipulation can also appeal to the more correct perception that order is an emergent property, and hence more akin to pluralism and decentralisation. Today's discourse attempts to play on both registers at once. The Roosevelt Corollary in its time had referred to a "general loosening of the ties of civilized society", (Roosevelt, 1904) and today's unipolarity plays on the same theme, permitting the West to present itself as the last bastion against chaos. A certain NGO argument inserts itself within this reasoning: thus Bernard Kouchner, whose organisation Médecins Sans Frontières actively promoted 'humanitarian' intervention by the great powers (Gresh, 1988) has described himself as a "specialist in the collapse of society";[13] and on this basis was chosen to head the 'international' (actually NATO-controlled) regime in Kosovo. While the military side of humanitarian intervention comes 'from the top', the NGO role also permits imperialism to explore pluralism in a safe form, counteracting the aspect of local civil society which might define its relationship with nationalism and the grassroots movement on a radical basis. But the inconvenient thing is that the core has little credibility for conducting humanitarian intervention, and if it desperately seeks to manufacture one, as in Darfur, (Mahmood, 2007) it is a bit too obvious that Southern Sudan is rich in oil which needs to be prized away from Chinese.

But if the humanitarian intervention argument remains somewhat weak the new development discourses offer a kind of hybrid, which supplies some humanitarian veneer to the regime of surveillance and intrusion. Already a country's 'obligations' (in the terminology of the Roosevelt Corollary) have been extended to liberalising internal markets, 'enabling' foreign investment, enforcing TNCs' intellectual property rights etc. This is now pushed further by an imposed obligation

---

[13] c.f. http://www.theconnection.org/shows/2003/03/20030310_b_main.asp

to reduce poverty and corruption, thereby creating some kind of synthesis between economic conditionality and humanitarian intervention. Britain's official pronouncement that "the market fundamentalism of the 1980s and early 1990s has been thoroughly discredited", (UK Government, 2000, p. 23) looked like a climbdown over the failures of neo-liberalism, but could, sneakily, be employed to smuggle in something worse, an even broader intrusive programme going beyond market issues into ones of governance. For example, as in the World Bank interpretation of relative poverty by Ravallion, (Ravallion, 2003) the global rulers (while themselves mercilessly exploiting Southern human and natural resources) preach to local elites that they must fund the reduction of social entropy out of their own income. This could in turn be linked with other systemic forms of social engineering, such as the 'sustainable livelihoods' tool promoted through British aid, which effectively tries to contain poverty within a certain boundary, where it will not quite tip over into disorder. Where the old imperialism used the notion of 'loosening ties' in a purely rhetorical way, today's has given itself the justification for a pervasive intervention to neutralise unpredictable emergence. The social engineering programme can then move freely between 'humanitarianism', the enabling of globalisation or anti-poverty, mixing them in various combinations. For example, campaigner Bob Geldof urges an extreme market fundamentalism, according to which poverty would be redressed if all institutional restrictions were removed on the 'freedom' of African economies to restructure themselves around the production of cheap export goods.

In this way, although the end of Cold War rigidity could stimulate a more emergent exploitative system, the unpredictability of emergence is so threatening that the process has to be tightly controlled. In some respects we could even say that, with democracy promotion, still more power is clawed back by the core. The notion of 'guided democracy', once a fig leaf for the authoritarianism of *local* elites,[14] today seems apposite to what happens at an international level. Vice-President Cheney even flew to Iraq in 2007 to tell parliament to end its two-month summer recess in order to pass more quickly the law effectively handing over oil resources to the multinationals.[15]

---

[14] The term probably originated with President Sukarno of Indonesia in the early postwar period, but has been widely imitated.

[15] *Le Monde*, May 11 2007

Democracy is a bit like emergence: it ought to be unpredictable. In the deeper sense, the content and institutional forms of democracy should be free to develop in unexpected directions, something which is of course totally unacceptable to the ruling order; but even if we take the narrowest definition of merely *electoral* democracy, even here the core cannot tolerate unpredictability: the result of elections must conform to expectations. Thus, in Latin America, if a coming election threatens to produce an undesired result, a frequent tactic is to sponsor polls showing what the "real" result should be, and then declare the eventual election rigged (Carlson, 2007). Or, if we take the case of the former Soviet republics, when Georgia's Mikheil Saakashvili – the most loyal lackey of the World Bank, NATO and the White House – polled 97% in the 2004 presidential elections, such a high figure was considered perfectly plausible. But when the more pro-sovereignty Alexander Lukashenko polled 83% in Belarus in 2006, the size of the vote was taken as evidence of fraud (Clark, 2006). This is the contradiction at the heart of assimilation, already familiar from the colonial context: assimilation offers the promise of becoming 'like' the oppressor (and therefore seemingly losing your subordinate status), but the very act of accepting that promise – sealed as it must be by fealty to the ruler's discourse – becomes an acknowledgement of servitude. Sometimes a dictatorship is better treated than a democracy where people vote the 'wrong' way. The whole Palestinian people suffer a special collective punishment (in addition to the endemic collective punishment they routinely suffer anyway) for having held an election which happened to produce the wrong result; Israel controls the tax revenues and refused to pay them to the Hamas government, [16] while the US openly armed warlord factions of Fatah. But by refusing to recognise elected regimes, imperialism also insulates itself from reality. The declaration of bankruptcy of the systemic phase of capitalism therefore occurs where the outcome of emergence becomes totally predictable, and no contradictory information is admitted at all.

Not just in intra-country systems, but also in the world system, post-Cold War emergence appears dangerous and incites to ever greater efforts of control. Earlier threats to the core's decision-making monopoly came at a state-centric level, as with the 'democratisation of international relations' proposed by the Third World movement of the 1970s,

---

[16] *New York Times*, Jan 19 2007

where the definition of democracy was very limited, uniquely state-centric and top-down. Even so it was desperately resisted: in fact the main reason for fearing multilateralism was that, with developing states now in a majority, the oppressors could be outvoted. But at least that threat moved within familiar statist categories. Today's form of 'democratisation of international relations' would come from somewhere beyond the scope of conventional practices, premised more on social movements.

It might seem that this would actually be in some ways more amenable than conventional state sovereignty, and could be co-opted in order to neutralise the latter. But what limits this possibility is the unpredictable nature of what these social movements might become. Once again, the information about the future is hard for imperialism to recognise. What really explains the apocalyptic, viral imagery employed by the influential RAND report of 1999 about the Zapatistas and their anti-globalisation role (the 'swarming' thesis) is the dilemma of a ruling system squeezed between an increased difficulty of maintaining centralised order, and a tendency for *de*centralised order – civil society etc. – also to slip, to become unmanageable. This danger could be met by a form of intervention to 'select' (by analogy with a manipulated social Darwinism) the acceptable institutions. Typifying this, *The Economist* (quoting the RAND study) responded to the Seattle protests of 1999 by recognising the anti-globalisation movement as a serious enemy, "a model of everything the trade negotiators were not", and urged the WTO to learn from the experience of then World Bank head James Wolfensohn in co-optation and divide-and-rule tactics: "His efforts have diluted the strength of 'mobilisation networks' and increased the relative power of technical NGOs (for it is mostly these that the Bank has co-opted)".[17] This shows how a new, systems-based power might theoretically operate, but it is far from obvious that it will work in practice. Another British establishment source, published by the Royal Institute of International Affairs at around the same time, urged a far more indiscriminate and brutal attitude to civil society: "The whole notion of a 'civil society' which has claims of its own to represent and speak for the people of a country is misguided when that country has a democratically-elected and responsible government: persons who are not elected, and not accountable to a duly elected

---

[17] *The Economist*, 11th–17th December 1999

and generally representative legislature, can have no such status. (Even more, the notion that there exists an 'international civil society', and that the NGOs speak for it, is doubly misleading)" (Henderson, 1999 p. 58).

This clearly foreshadows the repressive option, and we must be aware of a real sense in which the War on Terror was a direct response to the challenge posed by the Zapatistas and Seattle, a response – in a peculiarly infantile and petulant form – to a complex system just too difficult to understand. The more obvious reaction would be to centralise again and rule from the top, but this is not going to work. The alternative, clearly revealed under Bush, was for imperialism to begin to rule, *even at an international level*, through chaos. The antithesis of political order becomes the principle of politics itself. Beneath the mask of millenarian self-assurance, this was in fact a pessimistic response, an admission of incomprehension. The capitalism of the 2010s will seek to redress this, and restore a more stable controlled complex order. But this will not be easy, as we will now see.

CHAPTER SEVEN

CONTRADICTIONS IN THE CONTEMPORARY PHASE OF IMPERIALIST GOVERNANCE, AND THE FORCES FOR CHANGE WITHIN IT

Maintaining a System's Core Features through Adaptation

In this chapter, I will argue that the social system has entered a partially chaotic phase where rival attractors dispute the way forward. On the one hand capitalism seeks a viable 'regime' to embody it (and within this, there are competing possibilities); on the other, humanity seeks an issue to the crisis, which would have radical long-term implications: a new mode of production. The future will be played out between these different possibilities, and through the interplay (for instance, partial co-optation) between them. Of course, the struggle unfolds at many levels, of which a crucial one will be culture and the realm of ideas. Since our focus in this book is international political economy, we will only be covering part of the terrain; we will however at times allude to the ideological and psychological dimensions. A measure of the entropy of capitalism is the weakening of *all* its different attractors.

A system's drive to self-preservation is not necessarily a conservative response. It can imply acceptance of drastic change as the necessary *condition* for that self-preservation.

In general systems theory, as Atlan points out, what characterises a complex adaptive system is the "property to react to noise in two opposed ways without ceasing to function" (quoted in Taylor, 2001 p. 137). We can interpret this to mean that, while you embrace information as a form of order which keeps chaos at bay, you must also be prepared to embrace chaos as a creative force. We further learn from systems theory that "chaotic or complex dynamics may appear in cycles alternating with linear dynamics."(Eve, 1997) Systems cultivate stability, but chaotic episode are the raw material of the phase transitions which prevent them stagnating.

These statements could apply equally well to the human social system, or to the capitalist mode of production: each has a drive to preserve itself, the two being fundamentally incompatible. In this book, our loyalty is, in a normative sense, to the human form of adaptation (while this may sound anthropocentric, it is really a creative application of ecocentrism because only if the human adaptation defeats that of capitalism can the environment be saved). But our immediate task is to analyse the adaptations of capitalism, since this defines the context in which the struggle unfolds. In this chapter we will suggest a few pointers to understanding capitalism's current adaptations, our main theme being the desperate difficulty for it to maintain its own definitions of order ... and the opportunities for change this opens up.

An ordered system is, in Ilya Prigogine's words, 'far from equilibrium', in the sense of being strongly differentiated from its environment. Now, Prigogine's readiness to transplant this concept from physical to human systems is questionable,[1] and this critique is interesting: were we to state the goal of a future sustainable society in terms of its being far from equilibrium, this would sit uneasily with its need to cultivate steady-state features and closeness to ecological forms of order (as in the mirroring of rain-forest characteristics in the inter-cropping patterns of sustainable agriculture). But there are in fact different ways in which we could understand the 'far from equilibrium' idea. The form which we should cultivate is one where a high degree of information in society is radically distanced from a purely random distribution, one where there would be nothing but noise. The problem with capitalism is that, during the period when it has taken control over the direction of human development, it has pushed the 'far from equilibrium' notion into a malignant form: the accumulation imperative drives society incessantly to run in order to stand still. It is surely a great achievement of the *Communist Manifesto* to give such a flavour of a mode of production which can never be at rest with itself. The culmination of this is globalisation, with its strong tendency to homogenise, to sacrifice the diversity which alone permits information to exist.

Development is open-ended. In a complex system, even if we call it purely objective, we can't predict how it will develop. But added to this, is the scope for agency. This is why, if we speak of a survival *reflex*, this should not be understood as an automatic 'knee-jerk' reaction: against the background of objective tendencies, agency plays a strong normative role.

Like equilibrium, chaos can also be approached in a multi-faceted way. There are non-linear ecological phenomena, such as weather, and

---

[1] c.f. for example the discussion in *Encylopedia of Human Thermodynamics*, http://www.eoht.info/page/Far-from-equilibrium

there are also manifestations of chaos within society. In one respect chaos is a creative force, and in this sense, the crisis acts as a trigger for humanity to reactivate its non-centralised creative emergent properties, diffuse initiative and redundancy: by 'reverting to type', it can re-learn how to operate in a natural way and free itself from the bad experience of its capitalist episode. But the advanced decay of the mode of production also triggers unhealthy and damaging chaotic tendencies, for example, diffuse forms of militarism. One of the main lessons of our earlier analysis has been the system's adaptation to parasitise upon the symptoms of its decay, to develop symbiotically with its own chaos: as in the informalisation of the military and so many other features.

We have also shown how, although capitalism is basically opposed to the natural, diffuse forms of human innovation, it can evolve to parasitise upon these too, for example with industrial clustering. Now a further possibility presents itself. Although the human survival reflex is basically incompatible with the survival of capitalism – if capitalism retains control, humanity is doomed – it is not impossible that capitalism could itself parasitise upon certain aspects of that survival mode, for example by encouraging 'sustainable communities' sponsoring islands of low-input order, and thus limiting the kind of chaos which rips apart the social infrastructure. The regions fully controlled by capitalism are restricted, so it needs all the help it can get.

An observer from Mars might ask why humanity doesn't just embrace the chaos since it is there anyway, and treat it as an opportunity to kick out capitalism. But for the reasons addressed by Fromm and by Freire, in times of uncertainty one tends to cling to the system one knows, and which seems capable of delivering some sort of order, even though objectively it is precisely this order which is the problem. Capitalism's trump card is that it can enlist the very chaos it causes as an argument for keeping people loyal.

At least this works for the moment, but it will not work forever. There is a possibility for society to run itself in a different way, and is important to understand that this does not involve a complete initial rejection of all existing organisational forms. When a system moves to a new equilibrium, what counts is its *ensemble* dynamics, not its particular components. There may be some continuity and familiarity with respect to the latter, which will help people retain a sense of security during the transition. The new order may thus *initially* arise partly through a re-assemblage of 'found objects'. However those which are to become significant in the new structure may only occur as a minority trend within the old one, their important function in the new structure 'selecting' them for further development: worker co-operatives or community supported agriculture can survive under capitalism without really being *of* it.

In fact, we can say that today's sustainability crisis has triggered 'special' forms of chaos, to which capitalism would have to try (and probably fail) to adapt in a new way. This can be contrasted with the 'normal' way of working with chaos to which it has been used up to now, namely as a transition to a new accumulation regime (AR). The AR is what embodies the fundamental conditions of the mode of production in a concrete form where they can retain a certain stability during a definite epoch (which can be called a long cycle for example); the 'normal' form of chaos is the necessary process of transition between two such regimes. We can define regime in this sense as a way of organising society, and in a future non-capitalist society this might take the form of something like a 'regime of regimes', i.e. a social order made up of local systems of resource management. For capitalism, the regime it pursues is conservative in the deepest sense in that its purpose is to preserve the existing mode of production, but is revolutionary with respect to earlier embodiments of capitalism, for example in making a bonfire of its own sacred cows as it did when it ditched Keynesianism and modernism in favour of neo-liberalism. This is really the meaning of Schumpeter's notion of creative destruction. The new problem faced by capitalism today can be understood under two interlinked aspects: a replacement to the neo-liberal AR can't be found; and new chaotic features – such as extreme ecological events and their effect on food supply – are beginning to impact. Even historically, the transition to the next AR has never been easy: crises in the 1930s and 1970s appeared insoluble at the time. But today capitalism comes face to face with the energy problem: previous AR solutions were contingent on huge energy boosts (mass production under Keynesianism, accelerated long-distance trade under globalisation), which are no longer available.

If it is true that the 'normal' development of capitalism would require it to be embedded an in AR, the question logically arises, were it to *fail* in finding such a regime, would this be a good or bad thing for humanity? In principle, we can say it is good. Despite the subjective preference people might have to pin their hopes on capitalism getting out of jail one more time, objectively a new consolidation would only delay – fatally delay in fact, given the ecological issue – the crunch time when humanity finds itself forced to take up the baton and, through a much more far-reaching creative destruction, find its eventual equilibrium in the shape of a new mode of production. But these are not the only two possibilities. A third also suggests itself: what happens if capitalism fails to generate an AR but persists in sticking around? It is this latter problem which we will now consider.

The Spectre of 'Cold' Imperialism, and the Ruling Order's Attempt to Conjure It

Since the last years of the 20th century, the system began to relate to chaos in an abnormal and malignant way (i.e. that associated with George W. Bush), *which is difficult to reconcile to the creative generation of a new AR.* The reason for this can be understood as follows. Wherever systemic order is deficient, two possibilities open up: imperialism may either revert to centralist, top-down rule; or it may begin to rule in a diffuse chaotic way. The two are not incompatible and the first decade of the 21st century witnessed a certain interpenetration between them. But the second aspect is the less obvious, and has been particularly important to our enquiry so far; it is therefore important to consider how it may develop in the coming period.

Borrowing some imagery from astrophysics, in the initial phase of its decay the mode of production would flare up like a dying star in a blaze of glory, burning much of its remaining fuel in a massive burst. This is one facet of exterminism, and although Bush took it to extremes it is perhaps implicit within the whole epoch of neo-liberalism. We can see this burnup most obviously in physical energy terms (Thatcherism's fuelling by North-Sea oil, or more generally globalisation with its huge energy demands); more broadly, we could see the 'blaze' also in institutional terms, with so much innovation being consumed so quickly, leaving nothing to explore for the future. The 'end of history' notion was supposed to have optimistic connotations for capitalism, but from today's standpoint it has an ominous ring! It could be the end of human history; and, from capitalism's standpoint, it could signify the 'end of' its normal phase of development and the transition to a peculiar, degenerate form.

Pursuing our image, once the energy burst exhausts itself, we may hypothesise, imperialism would settle into a 'cold' or 'dark' form. There is a sneaking sense that cold/dark imperialism is indeed the logical successor to neo-liberalism, a horrible thought which today's capitalism desperately hopes it can conjure away. Entropy would continue to be high, but in this case manifested primarily as loss of information.

To think in this way is not such a leap for capitalism as one might imagine. We could be misled by the ecological literature, particularly that critical of capitalism in a post-modern sense (and therefore focusing on 'discourse'), into thinking that unlimited growth is what *really* guides the system. In truth, imperialism more typically retained an acute sense of scarcity, derived from its roots in social-Darwinism. This is not to say that consciousness of scarcity *moderates* capitalism's tendency to depletion; on the contrary, the war machine doesn't only feed industry, but feeds *itself*, as it captures and consumes energy sources. The great battles of World War II (El Alamein, Stalingrad) followed this logic. War is itself a high entropy activity. Amazingly, a Pentagon study reveals today's military to be consuming 16 times as much fuel per soldier as it did in World War II, the Defense Department itself being the USA's largest single energy consumer (Bender, 2007). The recommendation that the Pentagon 'green' itself by switching to alternative/renewable energies is surely nonsense, because this can never happen with *regular* warfare. But if we start thinking in irregular terms, this is where the 'cold' imperialism scenario could become superficially plausible. It is often remarked that wartime scarcity gave Britain a foretaste of today's ecological crisis, triggering responses ranging from urban agriculture through large-scale recycling. But it also triggered low-intensity *warfare*. Thus, the stay-behinds constitute a paradigm for an alternative, parallel mode of organisation, with units sustaining themselves indefinitely with minimum external input. 'Low-intensity warfare' could mean 'low-input', since self-organisation tends to be energy-efficient. This could come into its own in the current circumstances.

Perhaps it is at the fringes of the ruling order where such scenario-building is most explicit. A representative case is John Robb, who claims to be a former mission commander for a "black" counterterrorism unit. His theory is interesting in expressing in a relatively thorough way a logic which pehaps implicitly underpinned the Bush project, but which the official sphere dare not spell out in full (Robb, 2006). The argument is roughly as follows: in 'terrorism', the US faces a new kind of enemy which is networked and self-modifying [again, we are reminded of the 'swarming' thesis from the RAND study discussed earlier]; it should be noted that Robb here conjures an enemy in some sense patterned on neoliberal capitalism: 'open source' war, employing people who are essentially subcontractors, who could be doing election-fixing or any other activity the rest of the time [c.f. our earlier discussion of rendition teams].[2] In response, the corporations and the rich will 'opt out' of the official security system, much as the wealthy do from the health system, depending instead on private security companies to protect them, and guard their corridors of access (networks) to other elites. Centralised provision will wither and in its place, communities take care of services themselves, leaving the poor to survive or not as best they can. At some point (Robb is very precise: 2016!), these developments will be revealed as something positive: the reference system [capitalism] will itself, through confronting a networked enemy, have evolved into a networked form while also becoming more self-reliant in energy. If Bush, in his apocalyptic frenzy, was seeking to facilitate this degenerative sequence, we might hail him as a great ecological thinker within the earlier imperialist tradition, for example that analysed in the Sprouts' excellent book (Sprout and Sprout, 1965). Certainly, there was no illusion about capitalism being able to prolong its *normal* growth phase in a 'green' way: it must instead jump into an abnormal trajectory.

But any assumption that 'cold imperialism' could be a valid form of the mode of production is actually spurious, and this is why the mainstream will seek desperately to banish the nightmare: it simply does not offer any true solution to system survival. Most obviously, the system cannot just go into 'sleep mode' in an attempt to hibernate by reducing its metabolic rate: it could not for a moment suspend the reproduction of capital, which would be equivalent to the death of the capitalist organism. Expressing this slightly differently, *it is absolutely impossible to reproduce capital purely within the gated enclaves*: some 'exchange' with a periphery has always been needed. This does not just mean the accustomed forms of exchange such as North-South relations, but more broadly (a dimension particularly relevant to today's situation where the human survival reflex cannot simply be ignored) some relationship with the 'lifeworld', the sphere of genuine human existence. By unmooring its *own* networks from the lifeworld, the 'cold' scenario would repudiate exactly what is most important, the implantation of the core within a wider society which 'hosts' it, in the sense that a parasite is hosted.

---

[2] see Robb's blog, http://globalguerrillas.typepad.com/globalguerrillas/2007/04/nigerias_open_s.html

Superficially, it might seem, if the system sought survival by 'losing' itself within the networks, this would constitute an adaptation to an era which is not just one of scarcity, *but of complexity*. This is exactly how its apologists might seek to present it. But such an argument, similar to the propaganda we analysed in Chapter 5 about the Iraq occupation being a complex adaptive system, would be total nonsense. In fact, as with the Bush project as a whole, this line is actually a *retreat* from complexity, an admission of defeat before it. The notion of power residing in the networks, foreshadowed with extraordinary prescience by Gramsci and Foucault, is an advanced stage of *governance*; whereas the 'cold imperialism' scenario is the negation of governance. Expressed in the language of core-periphery relations: as the islands of predictability shrink, the lifeworld of emergence becomes alien and hostile viewed from the core, whose tools for parasitising on its social creativity begin to decay and atrophy. The *only* forays from the gated enclaves are repressive. Oh for the certainty of the 1980s, when micro-credit appeared a foolproof recipe for transmuting initiative into entrepreneurship and imprisoning it in a capitalist framework! The Bush era symbolised above all a capitalism which became *tired*: tired of the bothersome responsibility for analysing things. Analysis is hard work, how tempting to sweep away this endless nitpicking which hampers the system's bold, messianic advance. By depicting Al Qaeda as a diffuse network, imperialism seeks to justify its own chaotic features. The end point of such an argument would be to break free from the dimension of conventional international and domestic politics altogether, and indeed a certain constituency of systems-oriented hawks would say that, with conventional politics completely useless in controlling the new dispensation, the upside is that politics can joyfully be abandoned as a *constraint*. In a situation where "Our adversary sidesteps with abandon through networking and innovation", "We must out-terrorize the terrorists, out-think/out-network the insurgent, cheat the enemy, hobble him, and own the shadows."; "We must become comfortable with chaos, think like the Chinese, and accept chaos as opportunity." (Grange, 2007) This looks very like a realisation of Foucault's prediction of a "last battle" which will put an end to politics (Foucault, 1975). In this scenario, the systems approach becomes a totally repressive, as opposed to co-optive, tool.

Under the 'cold imperialism' premise, how would the ruling order conduct its repressive forays beyond the enclaves? The philosophy of the stay-behinds is logically similar to the cybernetics of artificial intelligence in the sense that you are creating a self-propagating and adaptive agent derived from an initial set of rules. With the advent of military robotics, discussed in Chapter 5, the human contingent form can be eliminated. Particularly striking is the Energetically Autonomous Tactical Robot (Eatr), a project strongly promoted since 2003 by the US Defence Advanced Research Projects Agency (Darpa):[3] it forages for biomass to provide its own energy source. Though its promoters were recently forced to deny that it would eat the corpses of the humans it killed, (Johnson, B., 2009) it remains incontrovertible that this represents a self-sufficient machine which could continue to propagate destruction in an extremely low-energy environment. Although 'Eatr' allegedly recognises whether it is consuming human or vegetable biomass, we may safely assume it has not been burdened with circuitry distinguishing the 'good' nose-to-the-grindstone citizenry who exploit themselves according to the gospel of De Soto, from those rebellious elements who deserve to be eliminated. Repression could only be indiscriminate.

Precisely because this nightmare scenario is not an aberration but proceeds from the innermost being of imperialism, it will continue to have a certain existence. Were it to overtake the system as a whole and become its *main* mode of organisation, this would spell doom for capitalism, so the latter will (in its more sane and un-Bushlike moments) resist this outcome. But what alternative can it offer? The obvious answer would be a stable new accumulation regime, but can capitalism really create one? I would have to answer no, because of the following factors: firstly the internal contradictions (pauperisation, difficulty of reproducing capital other than in a purely fictitious way), secondly the ecological condition which makes it impossible to continue managing the internal contradictions at the expense of the physical environment (i.e. through 'growth'), as was done in the past; thirdly, the exhaustion of institutional vocabulary: the complexity solution was the last major card, and this has been tried and failed.

In a way, capitalism now inherits the problem of 'blocked development' which could in earlier times – as beautifully expressed in dependency theory or in Jimmy Cliff's song 'Sitting in Limbo' – be exported to the periphery. Today, the neo-liberal faith is shaken, as we can see in the awarding of a succession of Nobel economics prizes to heterodox

[3] Self-forming networks and machine learning are two key areas of DARPA focus. (United States Government, 2009)

thinkers like Amartya Sen (1998), Joseph E. Stiglitz (2001), Paul Krugman (2008) and Elinor Ostrom (2009); although the Swedish Academy's citations are typically phrased so as to make their contributions seem purely technical,[4] this fails to hide the fact that the system is desperately seeking inspiration from those who have rightly criticised not just the abuses, but the *substance*, of neo-liberalism. But the system cannot in reality separate itself from neo-liberalism because it is no nearer to finding something to put in its place: this is precisely the limbo where it sits. To quote Eliot, "last year's words belong to last year's language and next year's words await another voice"(Eliot, 1943) ... but that voice is never going to come from *within* the system, not even from its heterodox reaches. The 'old world' of continental Europe languishes under dark clouds of racism and xenophobia which inhibit the discovery of anything new. The USA might give the illusion of creativity by deconstructing some of the terrible abuses which accumulated under Bush (though there is little sign of this happening in practice), and perhaps *pretend* to be creating an AR. But this illusion cannot hold up forever.

If the 'new voices' won't come from within, the most extreme reform scenario would be to borrow them from the regions of the human life-world, notably ones where the survival reflex is strong. Initially at least, it Obama seemed to represent a certain tendency to seek that renewal from the only area of creativity: the margins, where denial about social entropy is least possible, and where creative edges still exist. It's a bit like the permaculture principle of seeking renewal at the margins and edges where the field meets forest. But although there is some mileage in this approach, as we will see later, the fundamental problem is that the grassroots is precisely the area which pauperisation has either depleted or radicalised too much for it to be easily co-optable.

Accumulation means not just the growth of wealth, but its concentration: the two are inseparable. It should not therefore surprise us that as the economy 'grows', poverty gets worse. If we consider divisions at a global level, UN statistics show that, whereas at the beginning of the 20th century the difference in per capita wealth between rich and poor countries stood at about 9:1, by the beginning of the 21st century this had widened to 100:1; with much larger differences of over 10,000:1 between the top decile of the rich countries and the bottom decile of

---

[4] c.f. http://nobelprize.org/nobel_prizes/economics/laureates/

CONTEMPORARY PHASE OF IMPERIALIST GOVERNANCE   273

the poor ones. (United Nations University, 2005 p.1) Polarisation has thus become an escalating trend, and not only is there no obvious mechanism to mitigate or regulate it, but if the supposed cure (growth, accumulation) is actually its cause, the resultant loop can only lead to disaster. Both accumulation and pauperisation express uncontrollable forms of disequilibrium. In Asia, the supposed success story, half a billion remain unemployed or underemployed;[5] more specifically, in India, the country supposed to restore vitality to capitalism, during seven years of immense 'growth', the percentage of malnourished (i.e. clinically underweight) under-3 children dropped by only one percentage point, from 47% to 46%.[6] The point is that, with the core consuming the periphery, the periphery has nothing left to consume but itself, an argument graphically put by Arundhati Roy: "We have a growing middle class, reared on a diet of radical consumerism and aggressive greed. Unlike industrializing Western countries, which had colonies from which to plunder resources and generate slave labor to feed this process, we have to colonize ourselves, our own nether parts. We've begun to eat our own limbs. The greed that is being generated (and marketed as a value interchangeable with nationalism) can only be sated by grabbing land, water and resources from the vulnerable."(Roy, 2007) The marginalised do indeed harbour that creativity which arises at the edge of chaos, but not in a form which one could imagine being accessed by the ruling order. In India, the 'outsiders' are the radicals, sometimes called Naxalites. If a huge proportion of the population is alienated to such a degree, this gravely limits the possibilities for interchange across the core-periphery boundary.

Spheres of Exergy, Spheres of Predictability

Thus, although real 'new voices' abound within human society and carry a lot of information about the future, they remain largely unintelligible to capitalism, which could not distinguish them from mere noise. In the search for something of which it *can* make sense, the mode of production stands in the role of the central character in Beckett's *Krapp's Last Tape*: it can only replay its past, as we will now see.

---

[5] *Financial Times*, April 28 2006
[6] *New York Times*, Feb. 10 2007

In systems theory, chaos and order are not uniform within a system. If we make a complexity reading of the notion of uneven development (a major teaching of dependency theory, Amin, 1973), we could say that order is a matter of defining the boundaries of what can be comprehended. Imperialism's current task is thus to clarify those regions and enclaves in which its writ does still run, the condition being that, in the aggregate, they supply it with enough energy. More specifically, it must connect up the areas it controls (or – which is the same thing expressed in information terms – *understands*, where there is an institutional language comprehensible to it), assembling them to form a meaningful text, which ideally (though we are sceptical for the reasons just given) would convey the sense of a viable AR.

Historically, the paradigm for the quest to impose/maintain order is colonialism, which in its time encompassed both the demand for physical energy, and the psychological drive to claw out areas where the rules are respected and hierarchies hold. This is in fact the very 'tape' which today's system keeps replaying.

We could approach this problem from two angles. On the one hand, referring to our earlier discussion of Baranger's 'bagging the mess', (Baranger, n.d.) we might focus on delimiting the regions of *dis*order, and quarantine them from an ambient system which can still be considered stable; on the other, we could, from the opposite stance, regard the ambient environment as chaotic, and carve out enclaves where predictability still survives. Both perspectives exist today, but perhaps as the overall system becomes increasingly recalcitrant to the ruling definition of order, the dominant trend is towards the latter, i.e. the 'gated communities' paradigm, which could be expanded into a metaphor for the entire IPE. This also suggests a fresh perspective on the notion of 'enclosure', central to the ecological debate, an issue to which we will return in a moment. Enclosure has a strong psychological dimension, which runs right through the relationship between colonialism and identities; and at the same time it is rooted in physical energy, since a dissipative system like core capitalism must, to maintain itself physically in a condition far from equilibrium, access supplies of exergy (which is itself matter held far from equilibrium in a highly concentrated and pure form, strongly differentiated from its environment (Dincer, 2002)). The need to delimit the territories upon which order can be imposed is therefore at the same time a need to ensure predictability of the access to resources.

Each imperialist power initially delimited such 'spheres of influence' from its rivals, which is the introspective aspect of enclosure. But in substance, they were collaborating to secure a collective dominance. The Conference of Berlin (1884–5) which regulated the scramble for Africa was essentially collaborative, while the 'Open Door' policy on China foreshadowed the solution which materialised after 1945, essentially an open access regime for resource plunder. What ultimately mattered, and was ruthlessly pursued under the guise of the Cold War, was predictability of access, and it was better for the Powers to pursue this collectively, rather than in opposition to one another.

In an important sense the problem is institutional, and at first sight we might expect the core to invest heavily in local institutions which could guarantee such access. But in practice, resource hunger is such that any experimentation in governance in the periphery is limited by the core's unwillingness to fund it by subtracting from the value available to its own accumulation.

The colonialist typically claims to be fighting chaos, but what he really fears is any order-creation faculty which escapes his control. In a context of crisis, he more specifically fears the creativity at the edge of chaos, the raw material of change, which could become subversive. Although much of our argument has stressed the very new features (peak oil, climate change) which trigger today's survival reflex, we must also recognise, by adopting a non-Eurocentric perspective, that from the beginnings of colonialism and neo-colonialism, life for the oppressed was *never* sustainable. The maroons (escaped slaves) in Jamaica established self-contained, low-input 'spaces', which from the oppressor's standpoint would presumably be considered chaotic, and many profound arguments about self-reliance, both economic and moral/spiritual, have emerged in the context of liberation movements. Thus in an important sense the human survival reflex actually predates the ecological crisis, and today's ecological movement will commit grave errors if it fails to reconnect with this history.

Updating this to the present, let us now consider how Latin America and Africa reflect different facets of the abiding problematic around chaos versus predictability.

The ambiguities, contradictions and tipping-points inherent in the quest for spheres of predictability are well expressed in Latin America. With Cuba, where interesting experiments link self-reliance to reduction of input, imperialism's approach is to quarantine manifestations of unpredictable creativity to prevent them infecting the rest of the system. But clearly, this is now failing: the whole region now witnesses a more generalised experimentation, which in some respects looks towards a post-capitalist institutional endeavour. Much of this is only confusedly *anti*-capitalist, but crucially it is difficult to encompass within a viable mode of regulation of core-periphery relations. The interesting point is now the ease with which a sphere of predictability (where tame institutions guarantee stable access to resources) can tip over into a one of dangerous experimentation. Latin America was supposed to be the laboratory for De Soto's attempt to convert human creativity – via debt-slavery – into a subservient parody of capitalist entrepreneurship, and if the system had continued along the old trajectory this approach could hypothetically have been adapted to co-opt amenable forms of the human survival reflex. But this possibility is undermined by the new features: unmanageable complexity, and the radical power of agency from below.

Alongside the creative aspect of chaos, there is also the 'bad' kind to which we have referred often in this book, and this too is on the increase. Anomie in the sense of decayed social order is partly manufactured within the core itself and as far as possible exported to the periphery: for example, the drugs-based economy which in turn spawns its own form of militarism, both of which are exported in the form of social entropy into the peripheral supply chains. Up to a point, the bad form of chaos can be used as an instrument for militaristic control, as in the 'war on drugs', Latin America's equivalent of the war on terror. But this is no basis for stable (exploitative) order. Therefore, from a combination of these two forms of chaos (creative and destructive), Latin America is becoming too hot to handle. For a while, the US had invested in plans to expand NAFTA into the Free Trade Area of the Americas (FTAA), which we could see as a kind of 'co-prosperity sphere' (borrowing this term from the wartime Japanese empire) embodying its regional hegemony; but now this scheme looks dead in the water.[7]

NAFTA itself still appears to remain as the 'citadel', the last bastion, and temporarily at least, by sowing chaos in the Middle East, the US did itself a favour by pushing up oil prices to a point where, by 2004, Canada had overtaken Saudi Arabia for oil exports to the US, (Klein, 2007) providing for the moment a predictable energy source. But manifestations of social disorder are surfacing in a big way in Mexico, so NAFTA cannot be considered fully reliable either.

It is therefore not surprising that the US has tended to hedge its bets by developing Africa as an alternative backyard: 2006 saw the US for

---

[7] Accessed on July 1 2009, the official FTAA website, under What's New, listed only a communiqué of February 2005! See http://www.ftaa-alca.org/alca_e.asp

the first time importing more crude oil from Africa than from the whole Middle East (Galland, 2007).

In fact it is Africa which most strongly revives all the colonial demons, those which condemn imperialism to replay its past, just when it most needs innovation. Thus, 'state failure' doctrines look back to fairly atavistic colonial attitudes to governability. An interesting expression was the doctrine, enunciated by Bush's Deputy Assistant Secretary of Defense for African Affairs Theresa Whelan, of 'ungoverned spaces', this term being defined as a "physical or non-physical area where there is an absence of state capacity or political will to exercise control". (quoted in Piombo, 2007) This clearly leans towards the reading of chaos which can mean either a geographical space or a category of complexity (for example, one overwhelmed by noise).

The obvious way to confirm that you *do* still control a space is to have a military base there, but this is a high-cost option (not just financially, but because it makes 'soft' power less convincing). For this reason, 1980s military doctrines began to favour rapid deployment as the lower cost option. But the traumatic failure of the 1992 Somalia intervention led to a rethink. As an alternative to both bases and rapid deployment the US came up with something which seems at first sight a comparatively innovative and forward looking re-invention of imperialism, i.e. one which is governance-based: the US would build a web of new-style political systems presented as, modern, non-corrupt and progressive, the Ugandan government of Museveni being its archetype. By aligning itself with alleged dynamism on the margins, the core could, it seems, enlist some of this dynamism in the service of its institutional solutions. Since 'good' governance means on the one hand imposing order and on the other wholeheartedly embracing globalisation, this argument achieves the difficult feat of being at the same time Hobbesian, and anti-sovereignty insofar as it facilitates globalism's open-access regime. The US even played the anti-colonial card, vaunting to its African audiences the liberatory potential of global free trade as against the chasses gardées of the clapped-out European powers. The Africa Growth and Opportunity Act (AGOA) of 2000 was this policy's flagship.

Although this strategic shift was quite good as a propaganda coup, there was actually very little substance in any claim that it represented a new beginning. The mode of rule by the new leaders remained simplified and militaristic, and crucially, they were seemingly authorised to spread their 'benefits' by invading others. This was formalised in the

Africa Crisis Reaction Initiative (ACRI) launched in 1992 whereby Africa conducted its own peacekeeping ... with US support. Interesting in this context is a government in Ethiopia which, issuing from a supposedly Left-wing struggle against the pro-Soviet junta (differentiating it from, for example, the *conservative* forces which fought the Soviets in Afghanistan), provided some progressive credentials to a new wave of imperialism to which it quickly became subordinate, its allotted role being to invade Somalia at the behest of the US. It should also be noted that the new militarism finds supplementary justification by claiming to keep the lid on bad-chaotic forms of emergent militarism, such as, in the Ugandan case, the Lord's Resistance Army.

Many of the issues of chaos and its supposed alternative seem to refer to one central reference point, Rwanda. The genocide there in 1994, involving the massacre of at least a million people, indeed poses profound questions, central to our understanding of the future of humanity. But what presented itself as an intervention against chaotic violence has turned into a recipe for militarism. The argument we often find in radical critiques of US Rwanda policy, namely that the *principal* US motive was old-style inter-imperialist rivalry against France and Belgium, is surely wrong: the point was rather to experiment the imposition of a new mode of imperial *governance* by proxy. The classic justification for the supposed new order is to impose a nomos in place of chaos (anomie), the propaganda coup being that US-trained Kagame's Rwanda Patriotic Front (RPF), which had launched the war during which the killing occurred, could re-invent itself as agent of the nomos which ended it. US security collaboration under the auspices of ACRI served as a cover for US Special Forces to train the Ugandan army, part of this task being subcontracted to one of the shadowy private security forces, Military Professional Resources Inc (MPRI) which similarly trained the Kosovo Liberation Army (KLA), Croatian Armed Forces and the Colombian Military (Chossudovsky, 2003). The RPF was actually part of this Ugandan army until it renamed itself. Effectively, then, the RPF takeover was a US-proxy imposition of nomos in a partially-engineered (and of course partially emergent, in the sense referred to in Yeats' poem) chaos. No sooner had this been secured than the RPF was able to use the spillover of the Rwanda refugee problem as an excuse to invade Congo, the real strategic target. With Congo under control, imperialism could acquire the resources which help it artificially to keep at bay its own disorder: for example, consumerism and social control in the core are kept ticking over if there can be a constant turnover of new generations of mobile phones using Congolese materials. This was achieved at the expense of an increase of the bad features of chaos in Congo itself: decentralised violence and insecurity.

This mode of operation provided something of a paradigm, because a brief period of 1997–8 saw the US expanding its partially-privatised military training programme to 21 African countries.[8] At the same time, with rapid deployment now becoming too costly in energy terms, this was supplemented by a resurgence of old-style military bases: by 2005 the number of such 'installations' run by the Department of Defense outside US territory was revealed, in a Pentagon financial report, to number 737; (United States, Department of Defense, 2005a, p. 15) this approach was particularly in evidence in Africa, where a "Trans-Sahara Counter Terrorism Initiative" (TSCTI), apparently geared particularly towards oil-rich states, (Lubeck et al, 2007) was paralleled by the establishment in 2007 of a specific Africa Command (AFRICOM) in place of the mixture of other Cold War regional commands which had previously operated in that continent.

All these regionalisms (NAFTA, AGOA etc. and their military equivalents) are in the last analysis ways of defining spheres of predictability sufficiently comprehensible for capitalism to secure, at least for a time, a basis for its mode of production. The genuinely new feature is that the bad forms of chaos are qualitatively worse than at the time of the Cold War, when the superpowers had generally kept control over arms supplies to their proxies, and mainstream armies were still directly run by the core states, rather than subcontracted. We could say that imperialism stands with one foot firmly in the colonial past, the other in a murky terrain where finance capital unmoored from the real economy fuses with a deliberately uncontrollable militarism.

The Futile Quest to Rebuild 'Soft' Power

This just shows how deeply embedded militarism is within imperialism: it raises its head even when the claim is to pursue good governance.

---

[8]   They were: Benin, Botswana, Cameroon, Congo, Equatorial Guinea, Ghana, Guinea-Bissau, Ivory Coast, Kenya, Malawi, Mali, Mauritania, Mozambique, Namibia, Rwanda, Senegal, Sierra Leone, Togo, Uganda, Zambia and Zimbabwe. See Duke, Lynne "US faces surprise, dilemma in Africa", *Washington Post*, Tuesday, July 14, 1998 on http://www.washingtonpost.com/wp-srv/national/longterm/overseas/overseas3a.htm

In relation to the Hobbesian premise (that centralism is needed to banish chaos) contemporary militarism stands with a foot on each side of the divide: itself chaotic (both in its mode of operation and its results) while also treating the chaos it causes as an excuse to for top-down, repressive responses. To put it mildly, this is no basis for a genuine adaptation towards complexity. The big question is whether the militarist dérive could be reined in somewhat, in the interest of shifting the system away from its tendency merely to parasitise upon chaos, into something more like genuine governance appropriate to a complex system ... a solution which might form part of a hypothetical new AR. In an effort to rectify the repressive excesses of the 'war on terror', it would be logical to re-emphasise 'soft' power, and it is no coincidence that, in Britain, Tony Blair's successor immediately began speaking of soft power.[9]

In the US, it was already apparent to Bush's critics that the US must regain the high ground, refurbishing its democratic credentials in order to squeeze out the radical redefinition from below. The Great Reversal, whereby the core itself stands exposed as the main enemy of democracy and human rights, must be resisted at all costs. Zbigniew Brzezinski, the architect of Carter's policy in Afghanistan, testified before the Senate Foreign Relations Committee in February 2007 with a bitter attack on the Iraq policy: "Its collateral civilian casualties as well as some abuses are tarnishing America's moral credentials"; similarly, according to former UN ambassador Madeleine Albright, "We have lost the element of goodness in American power, and we have lost our moral authority".[10] The basis of this critique is the assertion that the war on terror's 'coalition of the willing' had pushed a crude line of 'might is right', hooking up with some dodgy governments in the process.

In reality, this critique is deceptive: if we take former Pakistani dictator Pervaiz Musharraf to typify such 'wrong' regimes, it was far from the case that he was *embraced* into the coalition, on the contrary, Pakistan was browbeaten into it. Musharraf's statement that he was simply told (by US Assistant Secretary of State Richard Armitage) that either "you are with us" or you should "be prepared to be bombed. Be prepared to

---

[9] *Guardian*, July 13 2007

[10] Associated Press, "Albright says next president must 'restore goodness of American power'" on http://www.examiner.com/a-580724~Albright_says_next_president _must__restore_goodness_of_American_power_.html

go back to the Stone Age"[11], is not disputed for the essentials, merely over the exact wording. But the real basis of the establishment backlash against Bush's coalition is that the Pakistani opposition, wrongly presented as fundamentalist, is really focused on national independence and democracy. This is dangerous for the West, and Bush's crude bullying only made it worse. Rather than going out of its way to be identified as the enemy of democracy movements, a creative imperialism should have the flexibility to intervene on the democracy side as well, promoting its own manipulated notions to squeeze out unpredictable emergence. Such an adjustment is logical, and in the short term may enjoy some success: recent democracy movements in Tunisia, Egypt etc. may be unwelcome to the global rulers, but at least it's safer if they focus on attacking domestic tyrants rather than the imperialist system those tyrants served.

Nevertheless, at a strategic level imperialism still fundamentally remains in the role of Krapp sifting through his tape collection, perhaps a different box, but old ones nevertheless. What surfaces is a response from within the entrails of an imperialism traditionally condemned to oscillate between unsatisfactory alternatives: sometimes viewing the 'natives' as mere inconveniences in its quest to grab their natural resources, sometimes as human resources to be exploited; sometimes frankly dragooning them, sometimes claiming to 'assimilate' them into an imitative parody of its own institutions. Whatever the pretence of breaking the mould, it will in reality merely be re-treading the stale pathways between these complementary opposites. This is notably the case if one were to pin hope on democracy promotion as an antidote to excessive top-down repression.

The biggest mistake would be to think that democracy promotion is somehow the opposite of militarism, whereas in reality the two have always developed very much in symbiosis: as we see in the Libya intervention today, but this is far from new. Thus, in eastern Europe, the US Project on Transitional Democracies, which in 2003 grew out of the earlier Committee to Expand NATO,[12] was really driven by the arms industry, its leader Bruce P. Jackson being a former vice-president of Lockheed Martin. Effectively, it is a condition of acceding to NATO

---

[11] *CBS News*, "Musharraf: In the Line of Fire – Pakistan's President Tells Steve Kroft U.S. Threatened His Country", Sept. 24 2006 on http://www.cbsnews.com/stories/2006/09/21/60minutes/main2030165.shtml

[12] c.f. http://rightweb.irc-online.org/profile/1566

that each new member buy its membership by undertaking massive new arms expenditure.[13] NATO's 'Istanbul initiative' of 2004[14] in turn aimed to bring NATO operations directly into the Middle East through hook-ups with local states. This initially worried local elites, lest there be an agenda of promoting *internal* civil society (as the systemic turn in governance might envisage), but it soon became clear that there would be no such challenge to repressive polities. At most, 'democracy' was a tool in the anti-Russian facet of Bush policy,[15] but didn't threaten *friendly* elites.

The most likely instrument of democracy promotion would be aid, and this appears on the surface the perfect instrument for developing indirect, 'soft' power as an antidote to hierarchical, repressive control. But in reality, aid too has been very much captured by militarism.

In an ideal world of self-regulating capitalism, tame civil society would engineer itself: aspiring NGOs would compete for funding, and those conducive to the dominant agendas win while the rest atrophied. Now, the strength of the Reagan period was that this nonsense was only for propaganda and was not really believed: the 'polyarchy' approach was one of heavy interventionism through the United States Agency for International Development (USAID) (Hearn, 2001). But later, during the Clinton administration – as earlier research surprisingly revealed (Biel, 2003) – USAID was itself permitted to atrophy, jobs being cut and offices closed (Lyons, 2000). This must have been the heyday of faith in a laissez-faire complex order, one where capitalism – not just its economics but its institutions – self-engineer. But the lesson is that true emergence under capitalism is very limited, and this is why, in the subsequent correction under Bush, the rebuilding of USAID occurred not at all under the auspices of a 'soft' power agenda, but rather as part of the 'war on terror'. We get a flavour of this from the words of then USAID head Andrew S. Natsios to a British parliamentary meeting in 2005: "As Administrator of USAID, I am struggling with the damage done to my Agency during the 1990s, an era that was dubbed, not unfairly, 'a vacation from history'. I believe that the principal reason for the decline of official development assistance and the institutional

---

[13] *Guardian*, November 22 2002
[14] see http://www.nato.int/issues/ici/index.html
[15] as when, in May 2006, the US organised a conference with Ukraine, Georgia, Romania, Bulgaria, Estonia, Latvia, Lithuania and Poland, for the purpose of criticising Russia for being undemocratic

damage to USAID in the 1990s was the absence of a clearly understood foreign threat to Western interests which foreign aid could remedy. I am dealing with the legacy of the 1990s at the dawn of a new century, a time of global terror and a renewed emphasis on development" (Natsios, 2006). So the 'war on terror' and 'development' are bedfellows: this establishes the paradigm for the whole epoch. We can understand this same problematic in a different way by considering – as the complementary opposite to the aid 'carrot' – an increasing emphasis on the stick, namely sanctions. Interestingly, a congressional report was commissioned in 1999 to investigate whether sanctions were too damaging … not to the countries who suffered them, but to the *USA*, because of the loss of trade! It revealed how systematic their use has become, signalling "more than 190 provisions of U.S. law that potentially restrict some aspect of foreign commerce for foreign policy reasons"; (Farmer, 1999) but it also concluded that the fears were unfounded: sanctions are not harming US economic interests because they are mainly imposed on weak countries who would not be much use as trading partners anyhow!

The net result of all this is that any attempted corrective to excessive 'hard' power would draw upon a fairly limited set of colonial references, which are themselves deeply intertwined with hard power.

There is also the further limitation that the objective of controlling the system is to extract physical energy from it. It is true that a sophisticated experiment in governance would in a way conserve *managerial* energy because top-down rule is less efficient, which is the whole point of the new industrial management and its attempted extension into the field of manipulated civil society. But with physical energy drying up, wherever there is a conflict of interest between on the one hand a relatively simple institutional framework which is efficient for resource-extraction, and on the other, sophisticated governance experiments, the latter is likely to be sacrificed. Anti-Bush liberals attempted to paper over this contradiction, but only at the expense of descending into self-parody. Thus Nigeria became a key reference point for the liberal critique of excessive focus on the war on terror (Lubeck et al, 2007). If the situation there gets too chaotic, predictable extraction of oil will be impossible, and the liberal argument rationalises this by referring to a so-called 'paradox of plenty' whereby oil wealth is more a curse than a blessing because it favours corruption. (Lubeck et al, 2007) Such an argument – that in countries rich in natural resources the state is condemned to 'fail' – could provide an effective justification for a new wave of imperialism, but, importantly, its reference point lies in the past: anti-corruption is merely a modern form of the White Man's Burden whereby unselfish colonialists devote themselves to relieving the local population of the 'curse' of their resources! The early pilgrims who colonised North America were pleased to discover about "God in wisedom having enriched the Savage Countries, that those riches might be attractive for Christian suters, which there may sowe spirituals and reape temporals."(Pearce, 1965) The 'paradox of plenty' updates this, the new colonialists 'sowing' democracy (i.e. manipulated pluralism), and gathering oil as a reward.

Along the lines of Bunker's model, (Bunker, 1985) we might critique this argument from the Left perspective, while accepting part of its premises: there is indeed a depletion of institutional order in the periphery, which mirrors thermodynamic exploitation. But we cannot entirely accept the premises because the argument is too deterministic. Again, we return to Marx' fundamental teaching that the rate of exploitation is governed not by any mechanical law or correlation, but by struggle: (Marx, 1969 c) what Marx initially pointed out in relation to wages or the value of labour power is equally applicable to the fundamental processes addressed by the systems perspective, the extraction of exergy and export of social entropy. As with peak oil and everything else, the nice formulas are disrupted by politics, i.e. by reality. Grassroots struggle (class, women's and indigenous) conducts a dialogue with national struggle, and in principle, a successful movement to assert sovereignty over natural resources can reciprocally reduce the country's own social entropy, for example by investing in social programmes (but you would still need the internal class, women's and indigenous struggles to ensure it remained true to this orientation). Thus, extraction would not lead to a deficit of *contestatory* institutional order, and might indeed actually stimulate it (as in Latin America). On the other hand, there is certainly a deficit of *tame* institutional order, and this is precisely what undermines the possibility of imperialist governance. Social engineering imposed with the purpose of creating a stable and predictable institutional framework for exploitation is a contradiction in terms because the primary focus on extraction is going to limit investment in the order you are trying to build.

This brings us to what is perhaps the deeper agenda behind the liberal argument. The point of a liberal-interventionist crusade under the banner of anti-corruption is not just to build enough (simple) order to facilitate exploitation, but to pre-empt the creative use of chaos to experiment a *new* order, a contagion which might easily spread from

Latin America to Africa. To stifle this, all sorts of updated rationales serve to keep the Roosevelt Corollary on the boil. State failure has already been redefined in terms of a failed *enabling* state (the state doesn't just have to pay its obligations and remain 'civilised' as in 1904, it must actively pimp its country to the forces of globalisation); the liberal discourse now seeks to complement this by re-defining the tame version of democracy required to run such a state.

Among the tools of this 'Roosevelt Mark 2', particularly important is the current anti-poverty agenda. It is not difficult to invent a link between interventionism and the struggle against corruption, and interestingly we find an attempt to calculate an *economic* cost of state failure. Thus, in arguing that "the high cost of failing states ... *has implications for whether sovereignty might be rethought* [our emphasis]", a calculation is made to show that the cost of such failures is conveniently roughly equivalent to the sum which OECD countries would have to spend in order to meet their 0.7% GDP aid target (Collier and Hoeffler, 2007). What this effectively means is that if Africans could be forced to implement 'good governance', the North could save the expense of aiding them, and pocket the 0.7% GDP (in a fundamentally extractive system, it is a waste of effort to put anything back in)![16] We could develop this argument in interesting directions: if you invade the South to implement regime change, you could offset your military budget against the aid budget, and intervention would effectively have zero cost – a beautiful piece of creative accounting, and if on top of this the country in question was so unfortunate as to suffer the 'paradox of plenty', you could do it an even greater favour by relieving it of the 'burden' of its natural resources! Not surprising that sovereignty needs to be 'rethought'. It is indeed easy to see why, once the dominant discourse discovered institutional theory (as part of the post-Washington consensus), it embraced it like the Philosopher's Stone: without any cost, order would be created while the rate of exploitation could continue as before, or even increase.

Of course, like all attempts to manufacture order out of nothing, this is a purely imaginary escape from the entropy problem. From a material angle, the real cost is the accentuated entropy resulting from the liquidation of whatever resources one manages to grab. But we have to suspect that there is a kind of 'depletion' in the institutional sphere too: this definition of 'democracy' would have been so depleted as to

---

[16] 0.7% is the target set by the UN, though the Northern states as a whole don't actually meet it.

lose all content. This particularly occurs through its severance from sovereignty.

An assumption that sovereignty is the problem had insidiously been introduced from the NGO community (as in the argument from Médecins sans Frontières which we discussed earlier[17]) that sovereignty signifies a shield behind which states can with impunity massacre and torture their own citizens, corruptly embezzle aid and hinder humanitarian relief work. If it is repeated often enough (and enshrined in funded research) it will be believed. This makes it easy to attack the *good* aspect of sovereignty, i.e. that which serves to restrain the imperialist open-access regime. We will return to this link between sovereignty and regimes at various points in this chapter.

The notion of colonialist regime-change leading to 'good governance' – that you merely need to destroy nationalistic forms of sovereignty and replace it by a zero-cost social order funded by the removal of 'corruption' – is pure nonsense. In the hands of the right-wing it is frank propaganda; in the case of the liberals, if they really believe it, they are fooling themselves. If we take the case of Haiti as an example of colonial-style regime change, it is clear that the new 'order' is simply a destruction of an old sovereignty (however dysfunctional) and its replacement by something equally crude and simplified, which siphons entitlements to the wealthy; spatially, for example, it reflects the interests of wealthy neighbourhoods as against the ghetto; the whole effort of 'order'-creation being defined in opposition to the poor (Heyne, 2006). In effect, the anomie is contained, in the sense of 'bagging the mess', within poor areas, which become the object of sporadic violent incursions: this could be a microcosm of the whole political economy of contemporary capitalism. When in 2004 the UN Security Council baptised the Haiti occupation force a UN-mandated 'multinational force' and the occupation regime as 'sovereign', this stood exposed as a highly depleted institutional vocabulary, the only one acceptable to the ruling discourse.

A New International Power Balance Premised on Scarcity?

Because of these atavistic colonial points of reference, of the inability of capitalism really to innovate in the face of rapid change, its grasp of

---

[17] Le Monde diplomatique, *Le Libéralisme contre les Libertés*. Manières de Voir, Paris n.d.

order is very shaky. There are therefore possibilities for contestatory spheres to be carved out. We have seen how important is the notion of sovereignty in these struggles. If contestatory spheres *can't* be carved out, imperialism will rule the areas outside its direct control through a mixture of chaos-governance and simplified repressive forays. The stakes are therefore immense. Bearing in mind that the system is ultimately dependent on energy, the question then arises whether a changed distribution of thermodynamic power, in a context of peak oil and a general narrowing of the ecological parameters, can affect the power balance. The capitalist adaptive system must somehow take account of these new realities.

Let us focus this argument by relating it to two closely linked distributional issues. Firstly, the trend has been for the industrial world to become less and less energy-sufficient within itself, its own resources having been depleted relatively much more than those of developing countries. This looks strange because normally, isn't the core supposed to deplete the periphery, not itself? But the answer is that the South's movement for a New International Economic Order in the 1970s was a profound challenge to Eurocentrism and, precisely in order to carry on dominating the periphery, the hereditary rulers *bought themselves time* by exploiting their own resources to undercut the bargaining power of the South; this however merely shifted the problem to the future. Secondly, there has been a decline in the direct ownership of oil by transnationals. An influential report, hostile to Southern resource nationalism, laments the fact that multinationals now own, or have access to, less than 10 per cent of world oil resources (McNulty, 2007). A US Congressional report further reflects upon a very simple and true realisation: what counts is not the *absolute* peaking or non-peaking of oil, but the political context: the political reality is that the US faces a potential shortage because oil production has slipped out of the hands of OECD (USGAO, 2007). In fact, research remarkably contrasts the 1971–2000 period when OECD countries produced 40% of the world's primary energy, to the projection for 2000–2030 when it will have fallen to only 10%. (Jaffe, 2007)

Statistics further reveal how the decline of US oil production has begun to coincide with a rise in price. Figures released by the US Government Accountability Office, Report to Congressional Requesters, show how US oil production peaked around 1970 and has declined steadily since the late '80s (USGAO, 2007). Initially, this did not matter because the North's success in smashing the Third World producers' movement kept prices low, so energy could cheaply be imported.

The point of qualitative change came just before the turn of the millennium (a period which, as we have shown, seems to mark a tipping-point in many respects), when declining US production crossed paths with a sharp acceleration in price (USGAO, 2007). As we have argued, any system depends on importing energy in order to keep entropy at bay; and, as we have further argued, in a human system the immediate purveyor of information is politics, rather than objective scarcity.

We would then have to ask whether such major changes in the distribution of thermodynamic power would allow for (although not inevitably cause, since this too is an issue of politics) a possible new relationship between creative emergence and a redefinition of sovereignty in the South.

Let us consider the immediate background. In imperialism's ideal imagined world, local sovereignty places no barrier to its free access to the world's resources (it is only a secondary issue whether, as in classic imperialism, each power has its own reserved sphere of predictability or else, as in multilateral imperialism, they all share open access), and this Grail was seemingly attained in the 80s when the defeat of the Third World movement was rapidly followed by that of the Soviet bloc. But in reality it was not quite so simple. The system still needed the local state in a repressive sense, and this was gradually theorised in the form of the enabling state. This in fact 'enabled' imperialism to play a double game: while the humanitarian anti-sovereignty argument is sometimes useful to excuse intervention – in which case imperialism and NGOs may line up together – in other cases environmental NGOs may campaign *against* things dear to imperialism, such as biofuels or soybean plantations, and then it is convenient for international capital to shield itself behind the sovereignty of Southern governments, for example that of Brazil, as they override these protests.

But since, according to the data just considered, it seems that the balance of thermodynamic power may be moving to the periphery, the hypothesis suggests itself that under these circumstances the tame enabling state could be transformed into something more challenging for the global rulers. In practice, this is by no means as easy as it seems: there is much scope for co-opting would-be Southern nationalism, as we can again see in the case of Brazil, whose ruling elites obsessively pursue the illusory goal of using the global energy equation in order to build the country's national power (in an IR sense); the assumption is that this can be achieved by turning it into the world's biofuel workshop. Its National Economic and Social Development Bank (BNDES) aims for Brazil to control 50% of the global ethanol market, which would mean planting 80 million hectares of biofuel crops in order to increase production from its current level of 17 billion litres a year to 110 billion litres (Zibechi, 2007). Given the negative effects on biodiversity and food security, were this to succeed the diagnosis could only be "the operation was a success but the patient died." A wasted Brazil would emptily 'rule' a wasted world.

But historical development is not unilinear, and this is not the only way the equation could play out. There are other forms of international power redistribution which might favour unpredictable grassroots emergence. The peak oil situation, while narrowing conventional options (like the pursuit of the conventional trappings of IR power), actually widens the horizons for humanity by opening up the power of community. At one end of the spectrum, as in Cuba, one can manage fine without oil, if capability (the 'new' energy) rises to compensate for falling inputs of physical energy, and in this case even the changed distribution of the 'old' energy (fossil fuels) is irrelevant. But there is also a hybrid solution where a radical nationalism in an oil-producer country, like Bolivia, allies with grassroots movements to extract a better deal from the corporate interests. Described by a local analyst as "nationalization in the 21st century – based on higher tax payments"(Reuters, 2006), this solution may make possible a new balance of political power beneficial to the grassroots. The key difference from the NIEO movement of the '70s is that a new movement of the South cannot be top-down, if there is to be any hope of defending the gains. On the basis of the changed international balance, there is therefore a change in internal balance.

Even then, there are tricky questions we need to ask about the validity of *any* resource-based redistribution. Sovereignty conjures up a Baconian perspective of dominance, as in the 'Death of Nature' thesis. From common law we derive a principle that on the basis of something fundamentally unjust, no right can arise ('ex turpi causa non oritur actio'; or, 'ex injuria jus non oritur'). If a high-throughput system is a crime against nature, can the popular movement to appropriate more of the value arising through that act give rise to any right?

In the abstract, we might answer 'no', but what we must remember is that a rise in commodity prices is progressive, not only in terms of the transfer of *political* power, but because it is objectively conservationist. In contrast to the Malthusian perspective, price is determined not directly by scarcity, but by politics. In fact resource pricing is in any case political: (Nore, 1980) the North always deliberately manipulated pricing in order to rob producers, and all that the popular sovereignty movement is doing is to redress a situation where prices have been engineered to be artificially low. It is precisely because Southern capitalism is strategically blocked by the general contradictions of the capitalist mode of production overall that there are openings for the mass movement to negotiate with the state new definitions of sovereignty, ones which liberate sovereignty from the trappings of national interest. Pro-imperialist commentators condemn Venezuela on the grounds that revenues which 'should' have been invested to hasten the extraction of oil, have instead been 'diverted' into something which is anathema to the ruling order: increasing the people's welfare!(Jaffe, 2007) To such a crime, Venezuela must plead guilty: we need only contrast it with Thatcher's Britain where an oil bonanza was squandered at breakneck speed; or, the last gasp of the Thatcherite approach, the similar approach being advocated for the Canadian tarsands (Gindin, 2006). Venezuela's 'diversion' not only transforms the revenue into something tangible and lasting (in the shape of capacity) or into social measures which may themselves have a positive ecological impact (as in the distribution of low-energy light bulbs in the barrios[18]), but also preserves a portion of the precious resource to be carefully husbanded by a future society; if this is reflected in prices going up faster than absolute scarcity would theoretically allow, the result would be to reduce greenhouse gas at a world level, as well as providing an important incentive for communities to begin their energy descent right now, instead of doing so later in a catastrophic and reactive way. This is all progressive, and all a direct result of the social struggle.

The key lesson from the above analysis is something which both systems theory and real life should have taught us: there are different possible outcomes to crisis, and we can vision the best of these, struggle for it, and carve out spaces where the future can be built in a realistic, step-by-step way.

An Inter-dependent Exploitative System Held Together by the Core

So far in this chapter we have considered the problems faced by the core in controlling enough *particular* spaces, and it is indeed at this concrete level that the battle is ultimately conducted. Nevertheless,

---

[18] *International Herald Tribune*, February 2 2007

its power is manifested at the more general level too, that of the system as a whole. Hypothetically, it might increase its hold at this, more general level, to compensate for its weaknesses locally, for example by inhibiting the linking up of contestatory spaces. The definition of power which we highlight at this level is measured in control over the higher system's functioning, as distinct from the kind of power needed to invade individual countries, for example.

The historic core's advantage is that the rules of the global capitalist economy have developed in such a way that role of that core is so central to the system's very operation that it cannot be dispensed with. Even the export and processing of the core's entropy is, in a twisted sense, the lifeblood of the global system and no aspiring Southern capitalist interest, however contestatory it might imagine itself, can escape this reality for long. This systemic centrality might even, we may wonder, compensate the core for the partial redistribution of thermodynamic power in favour of the South.

There is of course an argument that this centrality, too, is diminishing, but in fact this assertion is nothing very new. Debates raged for years about the USA losing its leadership status, and in the period leading up to the 2008 crisis these were still going strong. While some argued that world economic activity was partially decoupled from the US (for example slowing US growth in 2007 had little impact on a global economy apparently adequately sustained by growth in India and China), on the opposite side it could be shown that US consumer spending, which played a critical role in the 1980s in resolving the earlier structural crisis, (Biel, 2000) still accounted in 2007 for 20% of the global economy, having risen uninterruptedly since 1991 (Gross, 2007). In fact the two propositions – decadence or centrality – do not stand in an either-or relation, they are different sides of the same coin. However much the entropy which the core, and specifically the USA, radiates through the IPE might be a product of weakness not of strength, it is still the medium of exchange which governs the functioning of the system. For those who could read the signs, even within the establishment, the finance crisis itself did not come as a surprise, and was in fact already well described long before it happened, as in Paul Krugman's characterisation of the US economy as Americans "selling each other houses, paid for with money borrowed from the Chinese"(Krugman, 2005), or in right-wing economist Niall Ferguson's catastrophist statements about an entire global order resting on US mortgage rates, the problem being the linkage between America's massive external deficit and its internal one (Ferguson, 2005). The deficit is indeed an expression of the entropy, and when things came to a head this merely signalled that the US, as entropy-factory par excellence, was more central than ever, and that the periphery had better prepare to pick up the tab. An astronomical analogy might be a system revolving around a black hole, but equally, we should not underestimate the interdependence between the centre and what orbits around it. Yeats' image, "Turning and turning in the widening gyre/ The falcon cannot hear the falconer", does not necessarily imply a weakening *centralised* system but rather the disruption of one regulated by an attractor generated through core-periphery interaction. Dos Santos' original formulation of dependency is valuable in picturing this: in this gravitational scheme, the parts (core and periphery) have a certain reciprocity. The point is to maintain the stability of these different sets of roles; or, if the roles slip, they should at least fall into a new alignment which should still embed relationships characteristic of capitalism. What was wrong with the Bush-era 'failed states' argument, the argument that "the fundamental character of regimes [i.e. political systems] matters more today than the international distribution of power", (Rice, 2005) was to underestimate the fact that a deficit of order at the international-system level would be every bit as serious as at the local one. If capitalism aspires to create a new AR, it would have to address this deficit.

One discourse would imagine a systemic solution to this problem in the shape of a new definition of 'alignment'.[19] Whereas in the Cold War alignment meant something top-down and hierarchical, one could reframe it in terms of systemic roles: a state which 'knows its place' in the system will conform to (align itself with) its role. There is some truth in this because, however non-Eurocentric they claim to be, peripheral elites cannot allow the collapse of a world-system which underwrites their own status; a system whose ground-rules include the recycling of core entropy. Certainly, Southern elites showed no readiness to grasp opportunities presented by the 2008 finance crisis to humiliate the historic core. Nevertheless, this argument falls apart at several levels. If even quite subservient Southern states need to be threatened with 'bombing back to the stone age', this does not say much for the spontaneous self-organisation of a dominated order. Nor would the mass movement be prepared to tolerate 'alignment' with such prescribed roles.

---

[19] as an example of this analysis, see Lahneman 2003

Throughout our discussion, we have pinpointed the problem of a system where the energy expended in controlling it outstrips that which it supplies. At the level of the international system, how might we quantify this?

The most obvious barometer would be the cost of militarism itself. Now, an official Congressional Research Service report of September 2006 estimated the cost of US 'war on terror' military operations at $437 billion in financial year 2006, with a further $549 billion projected for financial year 2007 – giving a total of roughly $1,000 billion over a two-year period (Balesco, 2006). This sounds a lot, but perhaps surprisingly, represents only about 1% of GDP, as against 9% at the time of Vietnam.[20] Of course, the economic calculation distorts the thermodynamic reality: we have remarked on the energy constraints affecting each different form of military intervention (rapid deployment, bases etc.): artificially, militarism is made to seem more cost-effective than it really is because energy is underpriced, but this benefit is merely temporary. We should also take into account the opportunity cost of losing control over the falcon's *mind*, which is crucial: it is mental servitude which should transmit the gravitational 'forces' in an effective neo-colonial mode, and this declines whenever armed force predominates. Nevertheless, we might from the above get the impression that imperialism is not in too bad a shape if it can control the system by force at a cost of 1% GDP. But there is something more profound underlying all this, which we need to grasp.

In an important sense, the crucial 'region' from the core's point of view has always been itself. The first question is in fact not whether it can afford to police the wider system, but whether it can – even with the aid of massive external dissipation – conquer the weakness which gnaws it from within. In this sense the quest to restore international order must, paradoxically, be introspective. But it is precisely the huge amount of energy poured into shoring up the core itself which leaches away from its ability to manage the periphery effectively. We see this in the pathetically small proportion of GDP available for development 'aid': since aid is essentially manipulative, the core would have an interest in spending more, if only it could afford it.

The core is of course not homogeneous but rather itself a subsystem of the larger IR system, and in this sense the problem of maintaining

---

[20] *Christian Science Monitor*, January 16 2007

global order can to a significant extent be narrowed down to one of maintaining the subsystem which manages the IR among the core states; much of the management energy which might otherwise go into the wider system is diverted to this task. But capitalism has one big advantage here: more emergence (i.e. less centralism) can be tolerated at the level of intra-core IR because (unlike with the periphery, where emergence is too dangerous) it is a relation among equals, i.e. among fellow-exploiters. Since emergent order is the most efficient, this should be beneficial.

In game theory, if one successfully escapes a Prisoners' Dilemma (PD) situation, as was the case with the qualitative reduction of inter-imperialist strife after World War II, the new equilibrium should be self-maintaining, since there is no incentive to depart from it. But this theory only holds good if the thermodynamic conditions exist to continue funding the payoffs. Whenever we look at a positive sum in game theory, we should be suspicious about the entropy. In this case, the positive-sum outcome to the PD does not arise from the act of co-operation itself (as Ricardian trade theory would allege), but from the heightened degree of resource-depletion possible under conditions of multilateral imperialism, compared to competitive imperialism. Obviously, then, intra-core stability is linked in a feedback relationship with the amount of energy obtained from the periphery and from nature. And under the new conditions which we have just discussed – shrinking ecological parameters, changes in energy distribution globally and its interlocking with mass struggles – the continuity of these payoffs is increasingly insecure. It is this nagging doubt which saps confidence in the global order, and more specifically in the intra-power subsystem which lies at its heart.

Of course the payoffs distributed within the core remain considerable. For example, Germany strongly expands its role in Africa, in particular in Angola, whose 'reconstruction' after decades of Western-manipulated civil war gives rise to lucrative contracts.[21] But since these payoffs ultimately depend on military dominance, whoever wishes to access them must submit to a strong collective discipline, from which in fact no-one is permitted to withdraw. The Federation has always possessed this duality, being both a tool of collective dominance *by* the Western states, and an instrument of dominance *over* them; it was

---

[21] German-Foreign-Policy 2006, July 6th, on http://www.german-foreign-policy.com/en/fulltext/56013

never explicable purely as a voluntary regime. Thus US Under-Secretary of State for Political Affairs Nicolas Burns, who at the first Euro-Atlantic Partnership Council Security Forum in 2005 vigorously campaigned for a role committing NATO to intervene practically anywhere, (Burns, 2005) was also the person who, when the Austrian government discovered about the CIA-led secret army in their country, had responded on behalf of President Clinton by vigorously upholding the programme, saying that the only mistake was that "successive Washington administrations simply decided not to talk to the Austrian government about it"(Ganser, 2005) (this was long after the Cold War which supposedly provided the stay-behinds' rationale, so we have to conclude that their ghost is still alive and kicking). As with the hidden dimensions in string theory, this undercover history may explain important features of the whole system which are not apparent when considering only the surface relationships. It has been observed that redefinition of the NATO role is central to recent debates, (Bhadrakumar, 2006) and the explanation of this, I would argue, is that to maintain the *internal* coherence of the Federation of Western States, its power must continually be projected externally. Militarism here serves, by analogy with paintballing sessions in contemporary management practices (but more lethally), as a ritualistic, conviction-strengthening collective bonding exercise.

War is thus a symbolic enactment, and the Alliance a 'pact', in a sense conjuring many resonances of collective suicide and of exterminism. Increasingly, and particularly after a key NATO summit in Riga in 2006, the whole future of NATO was embodied in the war in Afghanistan, the stabilisation of which became the alliance's "key priority".[22] Whenever withdrawal from Iraq was discussed, it was associated with intensification of war in Afghanistan, the two being somehow reciprocal, so that the total level of warfare should remain constant. Obama's successive 'surges' merely pursue this logic. Although the rational purpose of 'surging' is to secure a cosmetic 'victory' as a prelude to disengagement, the whole point is that militarism is *embedded* in a way where one 'rational' argument for it will seamlessly be succeeded by another: the Libyan intervention has somehow surfaced just when staying in Afghanistan begins to look seriously improbable. The great achievement of the PD image in game theory is to show that the actors are imprisoned, not so much by physical bars, but by logic. Two sources

---

[22] http://www.nato.int/docu/pr/2006/p06-150e.htm

of militarism have become locked in a feedback relation, on the one hand the centralist reflex as a response to the impossibility of ruling through complexity-appropriate systemic means; on the other, the spreading of chaos as a projection of the export of entropy.

Towards a Regulation Premised on Addressing Intra-core Entropy?

If entropy *within* the core could be reduced, this would marginally lessen the energy it must extract from the rest of the system, thus taking some of the heat off the wider international governance problem. Indeed, since most historical successes in regulation have been inspired by patching up intra-core relations, this could also help to inspire a regime of accumulation. The conventional way would be to follow the precedent of Keynes. There is also an unconventional alternative, but let's first see why the conventional approach will not work. It would consists of turning the symptoms of crisis itself into the raw material of an AR, thus treating the problem as the solution by converting stagnancy into growth.

It is not in fact difficult to pinpoint the symptoms of social imbalance in the core which might hypothetically be redressed as part of an AR solution. In the US, for example, wealth was being increasingly channelled into a very small segment at the top. Inland Revenue data reveals a remarkable change in the quarter century between 1979 and 2004: at the end of this period the total income of the top 1% of US households significantly exceeded that of the bottom 50%, whereas in 1979 their total income had been only one-third that of the bottom 50% (Johnston, 2007 a). In 2005 it even got much worse, with the top 1% receiving their largest share of national income since 1928; effectively the whole of the increase in national income went to the rich, while that of the poorest 90% actually fell (Johnston, 2007 b). Data from the 2005 census reveals that nearly 16 million people live on an individual income of less than $5,000 a year or a family income of less than $10,000. It is this group, classified as extreme poor, which had been growing in number more rapidly since 2000 (by 26%) than the poor in general.[23] An extremely marginalised segment seems to act as a sink for that entropy which it would be too destabilising to receive within the official economy. Productivity had been increasing in the US

---

[23] *The Independent*, 27 February 2007

since 1995, but, as important research by Dew-Becker and Gordon shows, the value was again siphoned to the very top of society: this means not only to the top 1%, but even more remarkably, the further up one climbs by establishing fragments of a percentile *within* the top 1%, the bigger the percentage of income increase. Most astonishingly, "the top one-tenth of one percent of the income distribution earned as much of the real 1997–2001 gain in wage and salary income, excluding non-labor income, *as the bottom 50 percent*."(Dew-Becker and Gordon, 2005) Krugman, who specialises as the establishment figure who first challenges cosy discourses, again intervened to debunk the notion that value accrues to those with the skills and knowledge to seize the opportunities provided by globalisation (Krugman, 2006). Instead, everything flows to those who already have the entitlements; and even more importantly, to finance capital (speculation, insurance, real estate) and away from the real economy.

Of course the core system has developed in symbiosis with its own decay, in the sense that people are so far more anxious to avoid dropping into the 'sink' than they are to overthrow the system which creates it, and will accept practically any exploitation to get a job. A certain mechanism therefore ensures that the more acute the decay, the more stable the ruling order. The myth is premised on social mobility, and up to a certain point, as we might perhaps expect whenever belief systems are faced by hostile information, the more unrealistic the myth the more fervently people cling to it: remarkably, whereas according to a New York Times survey in 2005 80% of Americans believed it possible to start out poor, work hard and become rich (an *increase* from 60% in 1983), a separate study in 2006 showed that only 1% of Americans *do* actually have a chance of doing so!(Bull, 2006) But at some point the contradiction between illusion and reality can be expected to explode, the key factor being again receipt of information.

This creates extreme vulnerability for the core ruling order, so if someone had a magic bullet to make the contradiction less acute, this could at least seem to provide an input into a new AR. To take an example, Stephen Roach (chief economist of Morgan Stanley) addresses the distribution effect of globalisation, attributing the improvement of productivity to the opening up of many sectors, in particular previously immobile 'services', to international competition (Roach, 2007). Analysing Roach's statistics from our own standpoint, it is striking how they show a brief improvement in labour compensation as against corporate profits beginning at our familiar tipping-point of 1998–9, followed in late 2001 (a point which happens to coincide with the 'war on terror') by a sharp movement in the opposite direction, with corporate profits shooting up and labour drastically declining. From a Marxist standpoint, it should be no surprise that the two are inversely related. But the official interpretation clings to the trickle-down assumption that capital-labour relations are not necessarily a zero-sum game, and that the extra wealth generated by globalisation could permit a positive-sum outcome. The problem then becomes the fact that, unless the gains from the supposedly greater efficiency (flowing from the increased competition opened up by open economies) can be more fairly distributed, loyalty to globalisation will break down, followed by a feedback loop where calls for protectionism further undermine it.

But this is of course just another facet of the same capitalist myth which is trumpeted to developing countries, that the benefits of globalisation can magically resolve all problems of poverty, if only some mysterious blockage could be removed. What this conveniently forgets is firstly that the essence of capitalist accumulation is anyway to channel wealth to the wealthy, and secondly that globalisation's 'gains' are outweighed by their cost – social as well as ecological.

In Europe, hints of a new accumulation regime premised on a refurbished Keynesianism have surfaced occasionally. Even before the 2008 crisis, the *Financial Times* was describing a session of the EU's council of finance ministers sounding 'like a trade union meeting', amid warnings to bosses to share with workers more of the profits from improved productivity, and remarks about the need for more demand.[24] But in Keynesianism's postwar heyday, core capitalists had been able to risk giving a bit more to workers while maintaining their relative class power, because of the huge value they could obtain both from a still-dynamic neo-colonialism in the periphery and from practically unlimited plundering of the ecosystem. These conditions no longer prevail. The American version of the conventional solution would be welfarism, and here some debates appear more innovatory. For example, a proposal by the New America Foundation (NAF) focuses on an indicator particularly apposite to the systemic approach: risk. Risk is on the increase, leading to a vulnerability which effectively restricts capacity (Hacker, 2007). The benefits of predictability have so far been usurped by capital in the form of stable access to resources and

---

[24] *Financial Times*, February 27 2007

expanded reproduction, but could a small proportion of this be shared more equitably?

The recommendation is for the introduction of Universal Risk Assurance, thus effectively redistributing risk more equitably (Hacker, 2007).

We might think that the ruling class could give up a portion of pre-dictability more easily than a portion of profit, so the argument is seductive: whereas the apportionment of *value* is a zero-sum relation-ship, with risk (or its opposite, security) this is less evident. But of course, this comes up against the fact that, in the real world of contem-porary capitalism security is increasingly 'gated', the ordered enclaves standing in a dissipative relationship to those regions excluded from the benefits. Risk can moreover only be conjured away by an accentu-ated depletion of negative entropy, i.e. resources. Thus, risk-reduction is not really a free resource, but has to be funded from somewhere.

We should emphasise that, in the spirit of Marx' *Wages, Price and Profit*, and of his general arguments against Malthusianism and against the 'iron law of wages', it is perfectly legitimate for the working class to improve their conditions (including both wage levels, welfare and by extension, reduction of risk) *at the expense of capitalist profits*. But this is not where the mainstream argument is coming from: NAF fellow James Pinkerton (former aide to Reagan and Bush snr.) makes this clear when he says that reforms would have be accompanied by a deci-sion by energy consumer countries to form their own version of NATO (Pinkerton, 2006). Presumably this would enable them to push down resource prices and deplete more freely (at least during the short period when there *are* still resources). The link between welfarism and social imperialism could not be more obvious, the only basis for its 'funding' being a redistribution of the profits from exploiting nature and the periphery. But unlike in 1945, the leeway to implement this simply doesn't exist.

Thus, the conventional approach to generating a new AR, through some sort of neo-Keynesianism, seems unlikely to happen; although it was being debated in the late 2000s in some circles, before and after the 2008 finance crisis, it has unsurprisingly not been pursued. But would there be better options available through an unconventional approach, and if so what form might this take?

Our starting point is to recognise that a return to Keynesian-style dirigisme would, from a systems perspective, go in exactly the wrong direction. The forward looking solution would be for capitalism to latch onto the human survival reflex, which, since human initiative is a genuinely free resource, escapes the need to fuel itself from impossible levels of socio-ecological depletion. In the remainder of this chapter, we will consider the scope for such an option, and its limitations ... as well as the possibilities for a counter co-optation whereby experiments which seem to be part of capitalism could work as plugins to a new social order.

The Human Response to Scarcity and Restriction

Before considering how it could be co-opted, let's first attempt to define this thing we are calling the human survival response: what pointers can help us comprehend it? In many ways, the central issue will be to rediscover co-operation.

Co-operation should not be confused with collectivism. An important lesson from our discussion of human rights is that they are attributes of the individual, rather than of a collectivity. But it is perfectly possible to uphold individually-attributed rights and values without following the reductionist 'individualist' *method* which reduces everything to the selfish and short-sighted actions of the atomised actor.

The pseudo-individualist method finds typical expression in the pretence of economic liberalism to liberate the individual, through an act which in fact subjugates her/him totally. The shibboleth to which the individual is sacrificed is made to appear as an abstraction, the emergent order of a market resulting from aggregate individual acts of selfishness. But because the 'free' market is itself a myth, the thing to which the individual is *really* subjugated is the repressive apparatus, whose task it is to enforce the market-fundamentalist diktat. In this sense, the generalised repressiveness of the 'war on terror' was, in its repudiation of human rights and subordination of the individual to raison d'état, a logical concomitant of neo-liberalism; and however much capitalism's hypothetical 'readjustment' might seek to de-emphasise overt repression, this will achieve little while its basis remains the same.

Since the self-organising market is premised on individual selfishness, it is not surprising that capitalism expends huge effort on refuting co-operation. A major terrain of this ideological agenda is biology: if a biological model can be created which borrows its categories from capitalist thinking (the unbridled pursuit of individual greed), then the argument could be turned the other way round and capitalism made to appear natural! The 'blind watchmaker' image popularised by Richard Dawkins correctly upholds the open-ended character of emergent order and criticises teleology, and this is the correct aspect of what both Darwin and Dawkins were saying. But Darwin was inspired by Malthus, and his work, at least in popular interpretation, assumed an absolutised notion of struggle which was to be taken literally rather than meta-phorically; (Gale, 1972) similarly, Dawkins' 'selfish gene' can be seen as a projection of the false individualism of the liberal model. Conflict is absolutised, and the reduction of the unit of analysis to the lowest level (at the expense of the wider ensemble) is similarly absolutised. Economics is reduced to the competitive pseudo-individual, while in biology the holistic being (at whatever level, including the real individual) disappears through reduction to the gene.

We can approach this from another angle by considering how entropy relates to information. What conveys meaning is not a particular bit of information, but the ensemble and the context. Thus, experiment suggests, we could decipher even an unknown language – including a naturally-ocurring coding system like the genome – by comparing the entropy of individual words (which would be low when clustering gives evidence of their significance) with their entropy in a scrambled version of the same text (which would effectively be mere noise, thus high in entropy) (Grossman, 2009, p.10). In Dennis Noble's reading of evolutionary theory, far from genes being 'selfish', what selects them is their ability to co-operate in creating the larger phenotype ... within which each gene may in fact have many different functions according to context (Noble, 2006). It still needs to be explained how evolution can select for co-operation, but this step too can be made: although models from game theory most obviously concern *rational* actors, they can be extended to emergent co-operative properties in biological systems; and as Martin Nowak shows, theoretical models of evolution – even those which at first sight appear solely competitive like the Prisoners' Dilemma – can easily encompass selection in favour of co-operative behaviour (Nowak, 2006). Co-operation is therefore a fundamental principle rooted in biology itself, and is then further explored through specifically human development. It is at least a plausible hypothesis that the size of the brain developed in association with the process of forming social networks; (Dunbar, 1998) nor is it merely a question of the brain's size, because certain types of cell may play a role in social network formation (Coghlan, 2006).

Co-operation would moreover take certain specific *forms*. This fact is derived from something fundamental to complexity: while there are infinite theoretical combinations of the building-blocks, only a bounded number of forms are viable in practice. This argument, which we can draw from general systems theory and biology, becomes quite interesting in a specifically human context. While the main form of our development has become cultural rather than biological, it could be argued that similar principles continue to operate: certain co-operative structures keep reasserting themselves, such as regimes.

However much our argument may be heavily critical of capitalism, we must also, taking the standpoint of human history (our history) as a whole, *assume* it, take it on board: as expressed in Tippett's song, "I would know my shadow and my light ...",[25] all the exploitation and atrocities are part of a dark side which we must acknowledge and understand. Thus capitalism – i.e. the pursuit of unbridled selfish accumulation – was always one logically possible line of human development ... which would tend to subvert the very thing which both makes us human and embeds us within the natural operation of the world, co-operation, and replace this with unbridled pseudo-individualism. Traditional systems seem to have acquired checks and balances against the emergence of just such a tendency, (Biel, 2000) and when these failed in Europe, the latter then imposed its mode of production – and a fundamentally Eurocentric path-dependency – on the rest of the world. But the co-operative reality continues to bubble beneath the surface. Thus cultural practices embed the co-operative option within social norms, continuing, even under nascent capitalism, to play out the battle whereby a co-operatively oriented protagonist continues to combat the destructive forces of personal dominance (Johnson et al, 2008). This resource continues to be available to be activated when the time is ripe, and it is precisely the source upon which the human survival reflex will draw.

In a Hobbesian world-view, where humanity is fundamentally conflictual unless constrained by top-down order, it would follow that the collapse of central rule (by the state, by the historic core), would result in an unstructured 'Mad Max'-style war of all against all (bellum omnium contra omnes). There was an aspect in Bush's millenarianism which might welcome such an outcome, probably fancying himself an apocalyptic horseman patrolling the wasted landscape.

---

[25] Tippett, Michael, *A Child of Our Time*

In the saner form of establishment futurology, this is the 'barbarism' scenario which should be avoided, (Raskin et al, 2002), not least because it is not a valid form of the capitalist mode of production. Our position is the opposite of the Hobbesian one because we would see humanity as fundamentally co-operative. Recent research strikingly reveals how crowds, far from 'stampeding' in an irrational manner, tend to increase their co-operative and rational behaviour in situations of stress or danger (Bond, 2009). Many disasters call forth tales of heroism and altruism, leading Rebecca Solnit to propose a counter-attack against the Hobbesian premise (Winn, 2009). But the ruling order has invested immensely in rubbishing co-operation. When Wendy Barnaby began researching a book on 'water wars' and was surprised to discover that the co-operative response to water scarcity overwhelmingly prevails over the conflictual, her publishers immediately withdrew their interest! (Barnaby, 2009) The dominant stereotype thus reinforces itself; this is what we have to break through. If, as Nowak further argues, "Cancer is a breakdown of cooperation", (quoted in Zimmer, 2007) we could transpose this argument to give an interesting perspective on exterminism, as a malignant bifurcation of the system's development.

Even though co-operation may be natural, we must fully appreciate the difficulty of getting back on the right track once we have deviated from it. Nevertheless the difference in world-view is fundamental. Facing crisis, our supposition is that we have at least the possibility of returning to our main line of development.

Having explained *why* we believe the crisis will trigger a self-organising survival reflex, we can now consider how capitalism may be able to parasitise upon this. We know that it has already evolved the ability to parasitise upon reciprocity and tacit knowledge, as in the case of industrial clustering, where non-capitalist features are encouraged to introduce themselves within the capitalist economy. We further know that the system can draw into its orbit institutional forms from outside mainstream capitalism, a factor highlighted in Chayanov's work and the feminist position on the household, and extended (as advocated for example by De Soto) to the entire informal economy. The next stage in this progression could logically be to move onto an attempt to co-opt the surivival mode triggered by today's socio-ecological crisis. This is the story we will now begin to tell. But we must never forget the fundamental contradiction which constrains such co-optation attempts: the more capitalism tries to conserve energy by accessing the free resource which is human self-organisation, the more energy it must expend in corralling this within acceptable forms. If the latter outstrips the former, it will come to a dead end.

Struggling to Contain the Forces of Informality and Human Adaptation

The system's drive to access energy encompasses not just physical energy but human resources. The latter are (as in the 'exergy' approach to defining physical energy) far from equilibrium, but in this case in an informational sense: there is much information and developmental initiative within the human lifeworld which stands sharply differentiated from the ambient noisy hum of chaotic capitalism.

Our main argument is that capitalism has evolved to establish some parasitic relationship with this sphere and its 'faculties'. My shorthand term, the 'Polanyi factor' draws on the contribution of both Polanyi brothers, Michael and Karl. They were not saying exactly the same thing, and it is precisely this dynamic contradiction to which the term draws attention: Karl Polanyi said that society's natural mode of organisation is incompatible with the self-regulating market (Polanyi K., 1944) whereas Michael Polanyi emphasised the importance of knowledge and particularly its embedded form, which is hard to 'codify' (Polanyi M., 1962). While the former argument is too threatening for capitalism to digest fully, Michael Polanyi's argument, despite a certain creative tension with other aspects of capitalism, can indeed be assimilated by it; it forms, for example, an important reference-point for mainstream work on industrial clustering, whose success is recognised to be conditional on tacit knowledge embedded in local networks and institutional cultures. Capitalism thus parasitises upon something *with which it is fundamentally incompatible*, but from which it can nevertheless draw value, a contradiction intrinsic to the neo-liberal era which on the one hand opened up many ways of exploiting emergence, and on the other pushed to extremes the thing which contradicts it, market fundamentalism. The richness of information in the lifeworld is only very imperfectly corralled by the simplifying categories (civil society, micro-credit) which capitalism imposes. Nevertheless, the system has not exhausted the possibilities of its co-optation of these resources. There is a strong argument that interaction across the boundary with the 'other' is what really regulates the system, since the 'pure' core relations of production would be ripped apart without the capacity to dissipate. The indictment of Bush-style militarism (from the standpoint of a would-be capitalist adaptive system) is precisely that it cuts this short.

As we will see, the new discourses of co-optation have a 'soft' and 'civilised' aspect, but we should always be aware of the savage dimension of exploitation which underlies them.

The functional role of the unacknowledged outsider is not an invention of capitalism: traditional systems too knew dualism between an in-group and out-group. As I argued elsewhere, (Biel, 2000) such divisions can be traced to gender and caste, and to their many ascribed characteristics; or, in systems terminology, *roles*. Roles are fundamental to all systemic interaction, and there is always a certain sense of co-dependence and co-evolution among them. The ambiguity is that the excluded *seem* not to have a role (precisely because the system excludes them), but they nevertheless have an unrecognised one, in the context of an undercover reality which underpins the surface of the political economy. In all stratified societies, the excluded were also the exploited, whose activities sustain the very ruling group which refuses to admit, or even recognise, them. The notion of 'tribute', which Samir Amin rightly emphasises, (Amin, 1980) signifies a transfer between spheres which are not isolated, but interact. The rise of capitalism critiqued these divisions in their *old* form (on the grounds of their being hereditary and immutable, and thus curtailing a 'career open to talents'), but re-introduced similar dualities in a new form, and at a global level. The excluded provide not just economic benefit, but *identity* to the in-group: as in Hegel's statement "What something is, … it is wholly in its externality,"(Hegel, 1969) the identity of the 'pure' sphere, of the core, is itself determined by the thing it excludes.

In today's circumstances, powerful objective forces sweep across the formal-informal divide. These might immediately be rationalised in a comforting sense as regulation mechanisms for capitalism, but are in a deeper sense uncontrollable by it. In particular, we can highlight two 'flows': of people (migrants), and of finance (in a form which bypasses the official economic flows of trade etc.). The two are closely linked in the sense that migrant remittances are themselves an important category of economic flows.

The regulatory function is seen in the fact that migration compensates skill shortages or changing demographics, so on the surface it looks like a demand-supply relationship which textbook economics would comfortingly think it understood. But we have to ask what is the material basis of these seemingly neutral economic processes. Most obviously, what incentivises people to migrate is super-exploitation and depletion of social order in their own countries, so in this sense, if there is indeed *exchange*, it is an exchange better understood through the language of dissipation than of economics. Migration permits the core to exploit subject peoples not only in situ, but within its own boundaries. Investment capital from the core insists on total deregulation, whereas the movement of peoples is increasingly restricted, not indeed in order to *prevent* labour movement but rather to force it into a clandestinity where it can be more savagely exploited. Nevertheless, it would be mistaken to see the relationship only in terms of cheap muscle-power: it is precisely because this parallel world falls outside the core's purview that it harbours creative and chaotic edges which the core aspires to convert into value. Core capitalism has in fact lost most of its own dynamism, but a measure of its primarily *parasitic* line of development – a term so correctly introduced by imperialism theory, although imperfectly explored by it – is that its main adaptation is now to assimilate the creativity of others.

The crisis, by depleting security (in the sense of those forms of predictability useful to working people, such as job security or food security) increases the scope for exploitation, which is highly convenient for capitalism … but only up to a point: the whole process threatens to tip over and become one of several chaotic features which now overwhelm it. Current responses merely keep the lid on the problem. In fact the conventional economic presentation of migration through supply-demand factors conceals something more intractable to control: since migration has always taken place and is in fact something inherently human, its contemporary upsurge may in the deepest sense be viewed as part of the human survival reflex. Again, this is not simply a 'blind' structural reaction because agency keeps rearing its head: in response to the failure of mainstream 'development', precisely that failure which forces people to migrate, collective remittances provide a way of re-visioning development from below.

Perhaps a qualitative point now approaches: the informal sector has grown at least to rival the official capitalist economy, the ILO estimating it to occupy half the world's workforce.[26] 200 million

---

[26] International Labour Office (ILO) press release on : http://www.ilo.org/public/english/bureau/inf/pr/2006/2.htm accessed February 2007

migrant workers are estimated to have sent home $300 billion in a single year, 2006.[27] Importantly, this was about three times the volume of official North-South development aid at that time[28] – thereby adding to the uncontrolled capital flows which bypass the official world. Superficially it may seem that the more informality there is, the more the opportunities for exploitation, and indeed the tools for doing so have improved over the course of the neo-liberal AR, for example the use of micro-credit to subject the excluded through debt-servitude. But the whole issue of tipping-points is to identify where things slip out of the control of the dominant attractor. When the struggle 'invades' (perhaps in the sense that the Argentinian *piqueteros* invade) too much terrain, the entropy of one order (capitalism) becomes the creative emergence of the other.

Worried about the uncontrollability of this situation, the rulers respond with an insubstantial parody of systems theory, slandering the creative processes of autonomy and emergence by assimilating them to the bad side of chaos. Thus pro-capitalist expert Raymond W. Baker (who desperately wants the system to clean up its act if it is to survive) estimates parallel cash flows (transactions outside the realms of official payments and trade) at around $1,000 billion per annum, about half of this flowing from developing and 'transition' countries (Baker, 2005). He presents this whole category of transactions as 'dirty money' resulting from corruption. Pretending that these flows neutralise the 'benefits' of globalisation and thus perpetuate poverty, the core would have a progressive duty to police them! While at one level this argument is an obvious smokescreen for aggressive intervention in the area of informal transfers, limiting their autonomy and making the process more easily exploitable, we must also take on board that this discourse reflects something deep about capitalism's response to crisis: *the tendency for everything which is annoyingly complex to be assimilated to chaos ...* and therefore repressed. We have encountered many examples of this.

While up to a point polarisation increases the scope of exploitation, at a certain level it may pass into its opposite, increasing the region of unpredictability. The ruling order cannot afford to leave the regions outside its control entirely to their own devices. Partly, in a hands-off attitude, it encourages the bad chaotic features like drugs and

---

[27] *New York Times*, April 22 2007
[28] The OECD Development Assistance Committee provided USD 103.9 billion in aid in 2006, down by 5.1% from 2005, in constant 2005 dollars. See http://www.oecd.org/document/17/0,2340,en_2649_33721_38341265_1_1_1_1,00.html

gang culture, in order to squeeze out creativity. Partly, it intervenes under the guise of policing these things, using 'exceptional' methods which are themselves chaotic and violent, as in the 'war on drugs'. By a combination of such methods, it undermines creative social experimentation outside its own direct sphere. But the danger from capitalism's standpoint is that if 'dirty war' overtakes the system as a whole – which is effectively a strong tendency – capacity to exploit informality will be eroded; this would be fatal. Distinctions between the tame periphery and the chaotic one would then have to be re-established. But if the notion of distinguishing the 'assimilated 'native' from the irreducable savage is as old as colonialism, today it has an added twist: the recalcitrant parallel sphere, far from being a region of tradition resistant to modernity, is contemporary history's special by-product. This means that the cutting edge of struggle will increasingly be manifested at the formal-informal boundary.

Against this background, what capitalism urgently needs is a creative response, drawing upon the 'soft' and less savage tradition of the core's exploitative relationship with its periphery, and developing this onto new terrain.

During the rising phase of the neo-liberal AR in the '80s, when the driver of ecological and social catastrophe was much less immediate, the Polanyi factor focused on things like the new industrial management and constrained political pluralism. The human faculties then existed in a latent way, but *not yet triggered in crisis mode*. Once the crisis really did begin (superficially a crisis of accumulation regimes, but more deeply one of the whole social fabric and its relations with the ecology), capitalism might adapt in different ways. In Chapters 4 and 5 we spoke of a highly decadent adaptation, which consists of parasitising upon the symptoms of capitalism's own (and the environment's) decay, and this approach will continue for sure, since it is heavily ingrained into feedback loops. But it could hypothetically be balanced by a different form of parasitism, in this case upon the currents of human renewal. The Obama presidency, though not an inevitable product of capitalist development, nevertheless appeared at its origins to signify an exploration in this sense: a quest for dynamism at the margins. While unlikely to lead to a fully-fledged accumulation regime, this might at least enable the system for a time to seem to be innovating.

As we have said, the core not only extracts energy from its periphery, but establishes a certain regulatory 'mechanics' in the relationship with it. The currently dominant capitalist attractors, which tend to circumscribe marginal creativity within a particular exploitative form, are challenged by others which look towards a post-capitalist mode of production. While the capitalist attractor rules for the moment, it does so only shakily, not least because it cannot take society forward to a valid new embodiment *even of capitalism itself*. The alternative, human line of development might therefore under the right circumstances grab into its orbit certain of the hybrid forms which for the moment appear manipulated by capitalism: an example could be industrial ecology, which tries to restructure manufacturing/residential 'flows' around ecological principles of closed cycles (using waste heat to heat buildings etc.). Since an adaptation of humanity cannot occur on a blank slate, it is bound to work initially with 'found objects'. Under conditions of imperialism, can capitalism 'grow over' into socialism? Drawing upon Lenin's argument that imperialism "drags the capitalists, against their will and consciousness, into some sort of new social order..." (Lenin, 1939), and however counter-intuitive this may seem, the answer must, at least in certain respects, be 'yes'. I am simply arguing for a non-modernist interpretation of what Lenin says: the thing transmitted to the future is not the superiority of central planning, but rather the use of emergence, clustering, capacity, tacit knowledge etc. The whole point is that under capitalism these experiments are so restricted (precisely because they cannot be allowed to develop in a way threatening to the existing mode of production) as to become too blocked to be of any use. The rise of an alternative attractor – socialism – can free them from this blockage. Whatever creativity capitalism may possess in scenting new opportunities for parasitism is limited by a fact of which we must always remind ourselves: imperialism is not something external to capitalism, it *is* what capitalism has become, it is itself an attractor which grips the mode of production within a highly decadent and non-creative framework (imprisoning it also moreover in its past). The paradox is that it presides over a complex system, but is nevertheless disgusted with the complexity it sees, only a microscopic fragment of which it can really comprehend.

The Historic Battle over Commons Regimes

Our hypothesis is that regimes are part of a set of viable institutional responses which concretely embody the co-operative response.

As we have argued, the fundamental incompatibility of a co-operative economy with capitalism does not deny the possibility of capitalism latching onto some elements of it as part of its adaptation, and there exists in practice a certain co-dependency between the human and capitalist responses to crisis in real situations. The focus of such interaction tends to be intermediate-range emergent institutional structures, which are of value to both. In this section we will refer to regimes in the strict sense as non-compulsory, lower- or intermediate-level structures involving some resource management (which could be physical resources, or intangibles such as knowledge). This strict usage differs from the ruling discourse, notably its doctrine of 'regime change', where the term is used to refer loosely to a political system. Nevertheless, there is some interesting interaction between the two usages, which we will explore.

From the capitalist side, intermediate-range structure was tradition-ally neglected both by its classic liberal and modernist forms, although for opposite reasons in the two cases. Classic liberalism sought emer-gent self-organisation, but only at a whole-systems level (i.e. the mar-ket, which by definition was a national or global one, since its mission was to sweep away particularisms), whereas modernism sought design, typically at a statist level. Through the supposed debate between these one-sided alternatives, the problem was defined in a phoney way, and socialism, despite its roots in co-operative resource management, tended to be sucked into this false debate on the modernist side. Then capitalism shifted its ground to encourage (provided it could control them) structures like clusters where the level of tacit knowledge is high, leaving official socialism out on a limb, often defending an outdated centralism. In this chapter we have referred to a desirable quality called predictability, but we must now nuance the argument. Predictability is indeed a valued good insofar as capitalism requires regions which sup-ply it with a reliable stream of value, but, while this holds true in a general sense, at the concrete intermediate level it may no longer hold, which is when it becomes interesting: so long as the overall goal of accumulation is served, global capitalism can respect the local auton-omy of the cluster, whose value arises exactly from the level of *unpre-dictability* generated through the innovatory capacity of its tacit knowledge. The whole creativity in emergence lies precisely in the fact that you don't know where it is leading.

While clusters do have a certain regime character (because of the common fund of tacit knowledge they manage), capitalism has always hated and feared regimes in a more general sense, as a repository of some irreducible popular resource-sovereignty which it must destroy. This has not changed in the recent phase, on the contrary, a counter-attack against regimes is very much on the agenda.

The imperialist 'regime change' notion does not openly address regimes in the strict sense. Implicitly, though, there is a deceptive manipulation at work. Typically, the discourse makes the surface claim that it is attacking centralised dictatorships, whereas the hidden agenda is to dispossess commons. Hostility to Cuba has been a constant of US policy over half a century, and most immediately what imperialism hates in this case is a strong centralised provision of public goods. Frustrated that it can't overthrow Cuba, the US sublimates its anger by transferring the fantasy to other regions. Thus, leading anti-Castro Cuban exile Alberto Fernández served as the State Department's Director of the Office of Iraq Affairs (before moving on to work on what was then the next regime change target, Iran, in 2006 (Rangwala, 2006)). As former Treasury Secretary Paul O'Neill revealed, plans to invade Iraq were central to the Bush agenda 'from day one',[29] so it must have symbolised something important, and since the Iraq occupation was not based on the realities of Iraq itself, the Coalition Provisional Authority (CPA) being staffed by people often lacking not only knowledge of local affairs but even any specialism in the sectors in which they worked, (Rajiv, 2007) this suggests that the project was mainly destructive. Most obviously, the thing targeted for destruction was sovereignty, in its conventional statist sense. We know that the proportion of oil controlled by the Majors had drastically shrunk, (Juhasz, 2007) and the post-occupation oil law of February 2007 duly established an open-access system of freedom to plunder.

On this basis, we might read regime change purely as an intervention from the top, aiming to destroy a top-down system which either delivers too much to the people, or limits imperialism's right to plunder. In this case, it would not address regimes in a strict sense of popular resource-governance.

But this is just where the deception lies, because in fact what is happening is very often an attack against commons disguised as one against centralism. The Cuban system has evolved increasingly towards a form

---

[29] "Bush Sought 'Way' To Invade Iraq? O'Neill Tells '60 Minutes' Iraq Was 'Topic A' 8 Months Before 9-11", *CBS broadcast* Jan 11 2004 on http://www.cbsnews.com/stories/2004/01/09/60minutes/main592330.shtml

of self-reliance which both nurtures the ecology, and uses it as a paradigm for experimenting with emergent forms of social organisation.
This challenges dominant paradigms in a much more radical way than
conventional public goods. Even in Iraq this issue is somehow visible.
Thus, the CPA's Patent, Industrial Design, Undisclosed Information,
Integrated Circuits and Plant Variety Law of 2004, (CPA Order No. 81,
26 April 2004) threatened the traditional methods of saving seed for
next year's harvest, by prohibiting this with respect to all new seed reg-
istered under the law (Focus on the Global South and GRAIN, 2005)
– particularly poignant given that the original development of one of
today's main staples, wheat, was probably the achievement of people
farming the land of today's Iraq. In this sense, regime change doesn't
just have the loose meaning of destroying top-down nationalisms, but
also that of attacking regimes in the stricter sense of popular institutional resource management. What fundamentally gives legitimacy to
national liberation is not so much the aspiration for an independent
anthem or flag, but self-determination in the sense of popular autonomy. And it remains true in today's context, that a meaningful state-
level defence of sovereignty must have some basis in decentralised
regimes, otherwise it would be too weak to stand up to imperialism.

Whenever we encounter the 'soft' facet of capitalism's discourse on
communities, we must never allow ourselves to forget this underlying
hostility to real autonomy.

Capitalism may indeed, in its most recent phase, evolve to gloss over
its this fundamental hostility, and instead encourage co-optable forms
of community management, which may have some features of commons regimes. This evolution has been visible for some time in subsidiarity doctrines, but really comes into its own in response to the
triggering of the human survival reflex.

Let us first revisit a key theoretical argument in establishment
debates, Garret Hardin's 1968 article on the Tragedy of the Commons
(Hardin, 1968). Using the purely theoretical example of herders on a
grassland, Hardin employed game theory to present a situation where
the individual tendency to interest maximisation will lead unavoidably
to a bad result, depletion[30] (Hardin's conclusions could be read as
an argument for ecological dictatorship, but when neo-liberalism

---

[30] this is a classic PD because even if participants are aware of the danger, they cannot avoid it

took power, it pretended to see only the opposite scenario – privatisation). We could say that this simply provides a new rationale for the
distrust of commons exhibited by ruling classes throughout history,
and apparently, Hardin provides an argument for merely getting rid of
commons, with no basis for co-optation. In order to understand where
the co-optation comes in, we have to look more closely at the logic of
the model. The general thrust of the anti-commons argument hinges
on the assumption that co-operative or altruistic behaviour is impossible, and we can refute this with the line of reasoning developed earlier
in this chapter. We can further refute it at an empirical level: for
instance, the example of herders is particularly ill-chosen, since anthropology reveals so clearly the cultural mechanisms which limit herd-
size to a level which the pasture can sustain (Rigby, 1985). But the
establishment is also capable of a more subtle approach to commons, as
indeed to informality in general and all the issues addressed in the
Polanyi factor: while continuing to outlaw forms of co-operation
threatening to capitalism, such as worker occupations, acceptable
forms which perform a useful service for the ruling order could be
allowed. From this follows the position which would recognise the
validity of commons, but safely confine them within a particular area
of the institutional map.

In institutional theory, certain goods are best administered as private goods, public goods or toll (club) goods. This leave commons to
occupy only the left-over segment of the institutional matrix, i.e., that
where 'excludability' is difficult (you can't easily prevent other people
accessing them) and 'subtractability' high (one person's usage diminishes that of the community, with an implied subtext of environmental
depletion because the goods can't easily be regenerated). In this spirit,
commons have been extensively theorised, notably in the work of
Elinor Ostrom (Ostrom, 2005). Her recent award of the Nobel Prize
marks yet another case of capitalism trying to revitalise itself from its
heterodox fringes.

I would argue that, to confine commons obediently in this way is in
fact a form of enclosure. Of course there is a progressive aspect to the
argument because it resists the market fundamentalist claim to rule the
whole institutional map: in Ostrom's model it is not just commons, but
also *the market* which is confined to its own appropriate sphere. There
is an interesting correspondence here with the work of ecologist
Herman Daly, who gives one of most vibrant defences of the market
(effectively systemic, because drawing on a similar logic to that of

Hayek), only to argue for it to be contained within the sphere of what it does best (Daly and Cobb, 1989).

But there is a danger in this approach which is not immediately apparent, until we take account of the 'complex social formations' argument: even though pure capitalist market relations only prevail within part of the political economy, *they still dominate the whole.* Those regions which are 'outside' the pure relations have their autonomy respected only insofar as the dominant order can 'milk' their emergent properties. Under these conditions, the apparent equality of the market sphere's relations with the non-market sphere will be no different from the 'separate but equal' of South African apartheid. Capitalism could then safely permit a tame definition of commons to develop within a restricted range of situations, without this in any way altering its more fundamental hostility to them.

For this reason, in our defence of commons we should be wary of arguing in a way which accepts the categories of the ruling institutional vocabulary. For example, one line of argument would challenge the dominant definition on the issue of excludability, and this opens up some interesting issues. Thus, as Bollier rightly points out, what Hardin really attacked is not a commons at all, but an open access system; (Bollier, 2001) in a true commons, the constituency which has access to it is delimited in some way. There may be a physical fence as in an allotment site, where we can demonstrate that the 'common weal' is sustainably administered through common endeavour and the free rider problem in practice is managed,[31] or, in the infosphere it may be a virtual boundary, where a particular community of interest has access to the password which permits them to modify a wiki. These examples are very effective in proving that commons can work, but of course this line of argument could have the unfortunate side-effect of providing further ammunition for a 'limiting' approach.

The stronger line of argument is, I believe, to say that, just because it is *possible* to exclude people, this does not mean that it is desirable to do so. We should therefore not rule out commons in any region of the institutional map. From this standpoint, they would no longer simply be confined to the left-over regions which the other approaches don't want.

---

[31] This is confirmed in my own unpublished research in Spa Hill allotments, South Norwood, London.

Capitalism's changing attitude to the institutional map can only be understood (and challenged) in the context of its response to a situation where entropy spreads and the ruling order requires, if it is to keep some handle on reality, to break down complexity into bite-sized regions of predictability.

Part of this adaptation goes in exactly the opposite direction to any spreading of commons. In this sense, the system parasitises upon a kind of 'scarcity of security'. Although it might appear in theory that security in the sense of stability and predictability of livelihoods, should be a commons or public good (because, in a given place, a city for example, one person's security would not diminish another's and might indeed augment it), in the reality of today's system security is increasingly treated as a scarce resource and 'gated' within enclaves. The parasitism arises when a security *industry* responds to the demand to protect these enclaves and then becomes locked in a feedback loop with the collapse of predictability, upon which it feeds.

And at a whole system level, as part of this 'scarce security' form of adaptation, imperialism has curiously evolved in such a way as to function *internally* as a kind of regime. Already, a superficially depoliticised form of regime theory would allow for this, (Young, 1983) one where no distinction is made between, on the one hand Hayek's avowedly right-wing notion of spontaneous order, and on the other, the radical, co-operative tradition. On this basis, the ruling order has organised to monopolise the benefits of regimes for itself: the international sphere provides an interesting focus of establishment regime theory, (Hasenclever et al, 1997) and this is not surprising given that, since the Hobbesian argument does not hold in the international sphere (because there is no sovereign), order must arise, if at all, on an acephalic premise. The core elite is a totally closed-off *community* (c.f. our arguments in Chapter 6 and the references to Schwarzenberger and Robert Cooper) wherein institutional goods to some extent function as a commons among the exploiters.

So much for the 'gated' form of adaptation. But if that were to be the sole approach, we would come to the point where, if the map beyond the enclaves becomes totally chaotic, this would be a poor basis for prolonging the mode of production. This provides the basis for an alternative adaptation, whereby the system would allow some regime-formation to 'leak' out of its own restricted sphere, into the wider society. If in this way certain regions could be stabilised in a non-threatening sense, this could limit a chaotic dérive of the system as a whole. The whole point of such a development would be to maintain some social structure as a basis for continued exploitation.

In Chayanov's theory, (Chayanov, 1966) the exploitable capacity revealed by non-capitalist modes of self-organisation is already not merely economic but institutional in a sense, but it is limited merely to a family level. It would be a big exploitative advance if this could unfold at a local community level, for example. This is particularly important because capitalism *must* intervene that level, both because it dare not leave the terrain free for radicalism, and because community initiative springing from the survival reflex is potentially a free resource which it cannot afford to neglect. This raises the possibility of an arm-wrestling match between communities and capitalism, and the question is whether capitalism is sufficiently confident to feel it can win. Here, Tony Blair was actually a better representative of the main line of capitalist development than Bush, because he sensed that there is still mileage in pushing the co-optation of the human survival reflex in the direction of community 'empowerment'. The main advantage to capitalism is in this case to stabilise society on a low-input basis. If this permits the wider exploitative system to flourish, it would not be necessary to have a *direct* exploitation of the communities themselves. Such an approach runs counter to the normal pattern of core-periphery relationships, where a 'tribute' is extracted by the core. To extract a tribute might be the preferred option, but in the current crisis it might be sufficiently beneficial to capitalism to encourage the emergence of ecological sub-units where the emphasis would be less on what can be extracted from them, and more on the fact that they are self-contained, their main characteristic being that they close loops, and create regions or agents where there is little input or output.

It goes without saying that this is more likely to be permitted within the imperialist countries themselves, and indeed the whole point of Blairism was to reserve 'civilised' methods for the 'civilised' regions. Nevertheless, elements of this approach could hypothetically spread to the South as well.

This would go beyond the issues addressed in things like industrial clusters, and target instead the social economy. Although society could not really be repaired under capitalism, it could be 'taped' in a palliative sense, without cost to the monetary economy. The basis for this is the realisation that, unlike in Luxemburg's model where the sphere of non-commodity transactions is merely destroyed by capitalist development, a social economy actually keeps regenerating itself as a response to keep society alive amid all the devastation. Hazel Henderson described the economy as a cake, where two 'recognised' layers at the top – private capital (the icing), and a cherry-coloured layer of public goods – sit on top of various layers of informality, all underpinned by nature.[32] Henderson's point was to advocate the *acknowledgement* of these layers, but what she missed was that that they might be 'embraced' on capitalism's own, exploitative terms. We can see the results in the discourse on 'sustainable communities', a notion now enshrined in an Act of Parliament (UK Government, 2007). But this emergence needs to be controlled. The Blair era's extreme culture of surveillance and aggressive social inclusion are thus the inseparable partner of 'sustainable communities'. The Transition Town movement which has grown since the mid-2000s in Britain and Ireland, is an excellent case of sustainable communities, as defined from below.[33] What Transition Towns and 'cold' imperialism have in common is that they totally reject the business-as-usual scenario, to which mainstream capitalism still clings. But in other respects it is the exact opposite of 'cold' imperialism because the level of information is very high. Although the Transition Town approach is in itself progressive, it does raise the possibility of something co-optable by capitalism, a model where segments within society maintain their socio-economic order without 'bothering' the mainstream system. In the British context of the Tory government which succeeded Blairism, David Cameron's professed admiration for the work of E.F. Schumacher expresses exactly this option: the exploitation which the mainstream system derives from the small local 'cells' is an indirect form of tribute, measured in the cuts of the expenditure for provisions which would otherwise have to be made by the state. Capitalism could then happily continue depleting at a whole-system level, without the tiresome distractions which would result from communities descending into anomie. It is important to be aware of the scope for co-optation implied in this scenario.

An interesting case, with ramifications in both the US and British contexts, is recent official backing for local food. There is a strong link with mainstream panic about social entropy (feedback loops of deprivation linked where poor nutrition leads to poor attention span, leading to alienation from the school system, and leading back to deprivation).

---

[32] see for example Henderson's presentation on http://www.fhs-forschung.at/ fileadmin/documents/zfz/HENDERSON_HAZEL_Konferenz_Zukunft _Lebensqualitaet_4_bis_6_Mai_2008.pdf

[33] *Guardian* Saturday April 7, 2007 on http://www.guardian.co.uk/oil/story/ 0,,2051911,00.html

In this way, the ruling order strives to regulate at least a small part of its self-depletion: while maintaining the mainstream food system intact, with all the abuses we discussed in Chapter 4, it counterbalances this slightly by its opposite, small-scale local production, an ingredient effectively 'borrowed' by capitalism from the human survival response to crisis, even while the mode of production's actual systemic rules – i.e. accumulation – push in the opposite direction. Translating this into the field of urban agriculture, this takes the form of carving out *spaces*, in this case cultivable spaces, where anomie is resisted in a non-threatening way.

Food as an Example for the Low-Input Economy

Food is both the area of greatest incompatibility in principle between capitalism and the natural system, and also paradoxically one of the most notable areas where the ruling order now adapts its discourses in an attempt to co-opt community empowerment.

In a purely fictional solution to the accumulation regime problem, capitalism might offset the worst excesses of factory farming by pushing sustainable principles a bit more. However, this is not really viable, because the two systems are incompatible: diminishing returns in conventional food production tend to be met by *increasing* still further the inputs (of chemicals, or of the wrong sort of knowledge, as in GM) which cause the problem, rather than reducing them. This is inbuilt into the rules. Mainstream agriculture will therefore continue as before with its unsustainable practices, which remain embedded in loops (capital accumulation loops, of course, not those of natural renewal). But while mainstream unsustainability remains inviolate, the system might, in parallel, accommodate elements of an alternative at a community level, notably in urban agriculture, in a manner wholly separate from mainstream agribusiness.

This is a terrain for struggle, where capitalism seeks to co-opt the human survival reflex, but where the latter has scope to draw hybrid forms into its own orbit. The reason why small-scale, low-input, knowledge-based agriculture has so much potential is the high level of human ingenuity which it encompasses, and this is of course also the reason why capitalism can benefit from co-opting it. In this sense, food production is one among many areas of economic activity which make use of the free resource of capacity. But it is also the foundation for all the others, for one simple reason: capacity is a free resource only as long as the people who exercise it can be 'fuelled' by nutritious food; if they are under-nourished or eat junk food, capacity will decline. So food is the condition for everything else.

The point of low-input agriculture is 'less is more': you allow nature to do the work as far as possible (for example, by worms circulating nutrients in the soil). This sounds like non-intervention, albeit the opposite of capitalism's laissez-faire (which advocates surrender not to natural circuits, but to the *un*natural ones of capital accumulation). But of course, the *transition* itself is not non-interventionist because it requires a lot of activism to struggle against the bad practices (for example, anti-GM activism); furthermore, the sustainable system has an aspect of intervention because we will intensively be modifying nature, the point is simply that this happens *with* its natural way of working, not against it. So there will be a massive input of knowledge. In fact it is the rise of knowledge which exactly parallels the reduction in inputs not just of fossil fuels and artificial substances, but of water and, importantly, of labour.

There is a natural mode of organisation which at one level we can relate to tradition. As in our earlier discussion of Peter Winch's argument, traditional societies were good at recognising the aspects of nature which they couldn't tame. They retained awareness of risk and vulnerability. On this basis, one would naturally *resist* the vulnerability by cultivating an element of predictability, which is simply how systems necessarily operate: they stabilise themselves because no system can have an identity if it is in constant flux. The embodiment of the quest for stability is in this case food security. But the whole essence of today's mainstream food system is the pursuit of *false* notions of security. Rather than embracing awareness of risk, and converting this understanding into resilience, it practices denial.

Security, stability and predictability within any system will in any case be disrupted periodically, because this is how change occurs in the real world. The pathway to resilience is to guard against risk in a non-entropic way, i.e. by maintaining diversity. Diversity of both biological resources and knowledge/initiative develop hand-in-hand, the diffusion of knowledge guaranteeing the preservation of genetic diversity.

We can begin to rediscover this approach by dialoguing in a dynamic way with tradition. Thus, the traditional farmer gets a buzz out of experimenting, which is probably an innate human trait, and the basis for this is to keep alive a diversity of different strains of genetic material: when faced with an unexpected challenge, they can then in a sense 'breed their way out of trouble'. Zeremariam Fre's research among pastoralists in East Africa shows how, when faced with a threat of cattle-rustling, they managed to breed, in a very short period of time, a type of cow which is faithful to its owner but extremely savage towards strangers, so if by chance someone manages to rustle it, it will simply walk back to its original owner at the first opportunity! (Fre, 1989) This encapsulates the traditional grassroots approach. The discipline of 'applied archaeology' translates ancient practices into a form where it can empower contemporary communities, as for example in the case of Inca terracing systems which were/are excellent at retaining moisture, stimulating microbiological activity and the recycling of nutrients; (Kendall, 2005) the feedback between past and present lies in the fact that only by experimenting the ancient techniques in practice can applied archaeology really begin to understand them.

But it is not only a dialogue with the past: because like commons regimes, these sustainable approaches form part of the 'set' of viable human responses which will keep reasserting themselves. For example, it is not surprising that small farms provide a good basis for re-awakening the intrinsic human resource of diffuse experimentation and 'redundancy' (dispersed and multiple foci of decision-making). This principle is in no way merely 'buried' within tradition, but keeps re-emerging in a (neglected) recent history. During World War II, the US used to produce 40% of its food in gardens, whereas by the 1980s this had shrunk to only 3% (Astyk, 2007). But the most important contribution is not quantitative, but qualitative. Surprisingly, small farms and gardens turn out to be more efficient than plantation agriculture. Complexity encourages an emergent order (mini-ecosystem within intercropped farming, natural balance between plant-feeding and predatory insects etc.) inaccessible to any approach which imposes simplicity (monocropping). Peter Rosset further demonstrates that the total output of multicropping systems is higher than the single-crop 'yield' of moncropping (Rosset, 1999). Actually, the existence of an "inverse relationship between farm size and output" is becoming noticed even within the mainstream, but the mainstream approach twists this in a way which fits in with the categories of conventional thinking: a notion that small farmers cannot hedge themselves against risk by accessing futures markets (Barret, 1993). If we turn this argument the other way round, it becomes quite interesting: the futures market encourages unsustainable agriculture! This should not surprise us, given that this is precisely what enables capitalism to accentuate its entropy while insulating itself from feedback.

On this basis we can easily understand why you don't need a direct link with tradition to reactivate the deep-seated human response to risk. At a material level, as the crisis catches people in a pincers between the erosion of disposable income and the fundamental entropy of the food system (expressed in soil exhaustion, fuel shortage, climate change etc. etc.), home-produced food begins to be seen as a lifeline (Morris, 2008 b). But there is also the psychological dimension, the need to feel 'grounded'. Evidence in the USA, suggests that, as international conflict got worse, people responded by cultivating food. (Phillips, 2003) They don't need to be told to do this by a top-down 'dig for victory' discourse.

It must continually be emphasised that the basis for apparent compromises between capitalist adaptation and grassroots survival is for capitalism to derive a parasitic value from the free resource of human capacity in order to give it leeway to push an outrageously dissipative conduct at the level of the system as a whole. The new scramble for Africa is not just a scramble for oil, but to grab regions, either for a colonial definition of food 'security', or for biofuels (which typically employ GM crops). (GRAIN, 2007) This is what has to be resisted. Cuba's remarkable success in creating a low-input economy has given it the moral entitlement to play a leading international role in attacking the ethanol scam, which Fidel Castro rightly described as genocidal (Castro, F., 2007). At a global level, therefore, there are antagonistic battle-lines in a decisive battle between two incompatible visions of the future of the world. Unless this battle is fought and won, small-scale *parallel* solutions will only be palliative.

Is there any point, then, in playing the game of community empowerment at a local level? The answer is that we have to, because we need to make the initial steps towards a new mode of production right now. The new agricultural revolution will not be easy because converting a portion of land to a thoroughly low-input system requires a period of time, during which its productivity may drop. It is precisely in such concrete ways we have to conceptualise transition, so that it becomes real. This is the real significance of urban agriculture, because if we can bring onstream an urban agriculture *with sufficiently high productivity to make a serious contribution to feeding the people* (this is the crucial condition), then we could afford to withdraw part of rural agriculture from the current, unsustainable system and still retain the total net food production while this part is being converted to organic, low-input methods. The work of Will Allen in Milwaukee is a remarkable example of an urban agriculture project whose fundamental orientation is entirely social, but which functions very well while capitalism is still in place by linking with the industrial ecology approach, because large amounts of waste can be composted. The aquaponic greenhouse system is heated by the composting process, which also supplies liquid nutrients; fish swim in channels bordered by salad crops. Phoning his farm while on a speaking tour, even Allen was surprised to learn that the system had spontaneously developed a state of equilibrium, with salads purifying the water in a manner analogous to river plants.[34] Because this approach outputs capacity (in the sense of combating the alienation of youth and improving nutrition) it actually manufactures negative entropy in the only way possible – and in a way which capitalism itself can never attain. Indisputably, such elements could form building blocks of a new mode of production.

The scope for co-optation is something of which radicals should be aware, but this is all the more reason for them to be involved in community regime-building experiments around such issues as local food. Because of the fear for freedom and the weight of pessimism, we can only rebuild confidence *in the concrete*, which is absolutely in accordance with the tradition of the Left. This is the argument for intervening from a radical perspective in these areas.

The Left's Role in the Struggle for a New Mode of Production

In relation to the commons debate, Ostrom is of course right to uphold an institutional diversity within which commons would be only one institutional form. But the crucial point is the difference between today's situation of class struggle, and the implicit future direction of human social development. In the latter case, one would no longer require defensive notions of exclusion, we would not require national sovereignty or 'closed' commons (defined as the opposite of an open-access regime). In this case the multiplicity of institutional forms (of which commons are only one) could arrange itself in a non-exploitative way, and there would be no problem having a 'map' which confines commons to one particular segment. But at the moment, capitalism

---

[34] Author's notes on Will Allen's presentation.

sets the overall agenda at a whole system-level, and this would need to be broken through before we arrive at the future scenario.

It is interesting here to consider the historical case of the Diggers of 1649, a radical movement during the English Civil War which asserted the right to farm land. The Diggers' self-identification as the dispossessed can in one way be seen as a response to the literal enclosures marking the transition to capitalism, whereby they were thrown off the land in their villages. But in a deeper sense, the dispossessed are all those excluded during the entire social history when people have been divided into in- and out-groups. By positing the earth as *a common treasury for all* the Diggers rejected the whole notion of exclusion, in favour of a non-exclusive definition of commons where any attempt to restrict it, physically or conceptually, would be an act of enclosure. This radical approach is relevant today in challenging manipulative divisions which seek to confine the commons into regions where it is 'proper' and safe.

This in no way denies the need to establish *concrete* experiments in commons when possible, *however limited or confined*, and it is precisely in this context that the defence (as in Bollier's contribution) of concrete grassroots experimentation is strongly progressive: the whole point is to *link* those regions where the experiment actually exists in practice. This would have the effect of spreading the commons as an institutional solution, to a point where it could constitute a building block for the emergent post-capitalist mode of production.

Then they would form component parts of a wider self-organising system, reaching right up to the global level. As Barkun points out, (Barkun, 1968) the analogy between the pre-stratified systems revealed by anthropology and the international system is that neither has a head, and this is promising for the future. The barrier is, for the time being, that the great powers have organised themselves as a kind of 'commons' of the exploiters, to usurp the fruits of international order, treat institutional goods (and of course also material ones) as a closed-access regime, shared by themselves but closed to outsiders (cosmetic arrangements like G20 notwithstanding).

An epic struggle thus unfolds within the sphere of commons, within which the Digger perspective remains strongly relevant. We need to pursue a concept of socialism which restores the dialogue – via the negation of the negation – with pre-stratified acephalic (headless) societies, (Sigrist, 1981) and this is the 'root and branch' aspect of the radical approach. But on the other hand, since we cannot wipe the slate clean and immediately rebuild the whole of society from scratch, it is essential to maintain some mode of production during the transition phase. Initially, this new system must be assembled by selecting and emphasising some existing components, under the auspices of a wholly different logic, and our hypothesis is that low-input and closed-loop structures will be brought together with commons in achieving this. Certain institutions can be 'pulled' away from capitalism, but only if there is a strong autonomous grassroots movement to liberate them from the hold of aggressive Blair-style 'inclusion'. Jürgen Habermas highlighted a contradiction between the systems of the official world, and the lifeworld, (Lloyd-Jones, 2004) and actually, even when the ruling order is functioning at its optimum, the lifeworld is not inchoate: it *always* has its own systems, its faculty of self-organisation – regimes and networks – which the official world can at best parody, control and draw tribute from.

A link with Gramsci's ideas here suggests itself: (Gramsci, 1971) society is influenced by a hegemonic attractor, but at a qualitative point that attractor might weaken. Cybernetics offers a particular take on the social science concept of 'anomie': disintegration into components, a lack of conventions and shared perceptions.[35] While this signifies an absence of structure (which looks like disorder), the other side of anomie is that, as social entropy increases, people become less subject to a hierarchy of control, and increasingly alienated from dominant norms (Spencer, 2006). This could well tip over into subversive social movements. From capitalism's standpoint, it could be claimed that failure to find an AR would leave society without structure, but from a human perspective, the lack of AR would be a good thing because it would weaken the attractor which now holds diffuse institutional initiatives in thrall.

As the capitalist attractor fails – which will occur unevenly, this is the important point – localised and plural regimes will arise to fill the gaps, with recognisable institutional commonalities and 'networkability' developing between them. Since the official world 'borrows' emergence from the lifeworld, it should not come as a shock if the latter, like a river which has to keep flowing somehow, overthrows the stultified discourses which presently channel it, and modifies its initial rules to seek

---

[35] *Principia Cybernetica*, (n.d.). Dictionary of Cybernetics and Systems on http://pespmc1.vub.ac.be/ASC/SOCIAL_ENTRO.html accessed February 2006

counter-systemic channels. It seems strange that the current order which produces very narrow benefits, makes heavier energy demands than one which would distribute them more widely; but this is precisely the essence of the difference between truncated capitalist forms of co-operation and the general human form whose external profile is reduced through the amount of internal energy (i.e. capacity) it creates.

What is the weak point of the ruling order? We might argue that it lies somewhere in the relationship between co-optation and repression. Repression, like the wonder herbicides promoted by capitalist agribusiness, should be selective and targeted. But this is not easy in practise, either for weeds or for recalcitrant civil society. The gut response, when complexity degenerates from capitalism's viewpoint into mere noise, is to shut it down altogether. For the *Financial Times*, for example, "where states are not doing their jobs properly, civil society activity can do more harm than good. It can become an alternative to traditional politics, increasingly absorbing citizens' energies and satisfying their basic needs while undermining political stability (by heightening dissatisfaction and societal cleavages) and providing rich soil for oppositional and revolutionary movements to grow."[36] This would lead straight to the cold/dark imperialism scenario, populated by energetically autonomous robots which munch their biomass without asking whether it emanates from good or bad NGOs. The saner elements in the capitalist mainstream would wish to avoid this, because blanket repression makes co-optation impossible, so they must remain faithful to the vision of the targeted civil society weedkiller. But where this leads in practise may simply be the same destination by a different route.

The symbol of 'bad' civil society conveniently presents itself in the shape of Lebanon's Hizbullah, an organisation which to some extent 'evolved' to exploit the niches within a failed polyarchy. Under the cover of a certain 'mutual parasitism' between Islamic fundamentalism and imperialism (each providing the other with the enemy which is its raison d'être), the ruling order can use its anti-Hizbullah tactics as a dress rehearsal for suppressing dissident social movements in strategic targets like Brazil or the Philippines. The reasoning is presumably that, once Hizbullah has been clinically eliminated, the good citizens will dutifully set about founding Transition Town Beirut. But of course,

---

[36] *Financial Times*, September 1 2006

what really happened in Lebanon was not clinical strikes to take out Hizbullah, but indiscriminate killing of everyone, which takes us back to the terrain of Guernica or Oradour-sur-Glane, and has absolutely nothing to do with the governance of complexity. In practice, there is always a strong tendency for indiscriminate repression to fall into a positive feedback relationship with the collapse of systemic power. The tipping-point arrives when the ruling order gives up on trying to adapt to the landscape of complexity, and begins angrily to swat at it, and this point may already have been passed.

If we look closely, any dissident civil society movement is vulnerable to the definition-creep of terrorism. For instance, nothing could appear on the surface less challenging than the notion of decentralisation: whereas centralised systems were the old way of controlling the people, decentralised ones are the new, systemically more efficient way, and concretely, decentralisation performs a good task in breaking down the peripheral state into bite-sized portions which are more easily ruled while appearing autonomous. But the reality inevitably draws imperialism into conflict situations where the repressive reflex rears its head. When in El Salvador, decentralisation became an excuse to privatise water (which could be regarded either as a commons or public good in the terminology of our discussion above), people protesting this found themselves accused under a new anti-terror law (CISPES 2007). The 'terrorism' label effectively revokes the human rights of anyone who resists global accumulation circuits.

Here of course, we are not arguing against decentralisation per se, but against its manipulated form: the objective is a more genuine decentralisation which reasserts community control through participatory regimes. It is important to emphasise that, while the struggle over resources has existed since the beginnings of capitalism/colonialism, it takes a special form today: the 21st century challenge is to see whether humanity can adapt to a new world with a radically different energy profile, and in this context the act of withdrawing resources from the accumulation circuits acquires a new significance. Low-input spaces are not just important in the negative sense of territory which they withdraw from the terrain of depletion, but also positively, as building blocks for a different mode of production.

As we have argued, the success of capitalism lies paradoxically in its ability to exploit what is *not* capitalist: the terrain ruled by pure capitalist relations has always been much smaller than that from which it draws value (or into which it dissipates). While recent developments bring some good news for capitalism, in the shape of new possibilities for parasitising on the survival reflex, this is outweighed by the spectre of radical movements over which it has no control. In place of the failed ideal type of 'governance' which would promote 'good' civil society, imperialism is then reduced to cultivating the negative features of chaos (diffuse militarism etc.) as a last-ditch tactic to squeeze out the creative ones. There are real tendencies towards a situation where the ruling order rules only in pockets, leaving huge areas where its writ runs (if at all) only in a mindlessly repressive way.

If that is true, how *can* it be said to rule? Partly, because it still rules the official world (however isolated from the real lifeworld); partly, because, even among the most marginalised (perhaps especially amongst them if one follows Freire's argument), it squeezes out notions of an alternative. In the objectively much less serious crisis of the 1970s there was more sense of a socialist alternative. The reason for the change is partly the complexity facing us. We must on the one hand avoid *denying* it, becaused complexity is real and can't be oversimplified away; on the other, we must prevent it leading to confusion and disorientation. What we should hold onto is the aspect of complexity which means rich diversity of information in distinction to noise (noise disorients because, with entropy being high, there is no recognisability in the information which comes at you from every direction). In fact the complexity is a good thing because it harbours so much raw material for a new mode of production, most of this information being unintelligible to capitalism. But the temporary loss of confidence occurs because we can no longer, as in the '70s, entertain notions of a relatively simplistic and non-emergent socialism, introduced merely by dispacing capitalism from the centre or the top; in contrast, the prospect of building a mode of production out of complexity appears daunting. This is nevertheless what must be attempted.

At a level of theory, we have emphasised throughout this book that the relevance of the basic ideas of Marxism is only confirmed, indeed intensified, by the current crisis. But we still need to translate this into practical politics.

The strategic importance of networking will be evident if we think back to the theme around 'spaces'. Capitalism has for the moment the advantage of claiming to offer *some* mode of production, and it seems an immense risk to give this up in exchange for the promise of something which doesn't yet exist. Nevertheless, objectively it struggles desperately to maintain the semblance of a mode of production from the spaces it still controls. There is therefore scope for beginning the experimentation for an alternative, through some process of *assemblage*: linking contestatory spaces, which might mean networking between localised experiments of the *same* type, such as commons, or else assembling a plurality of *different* organisational forms, typically with some element of self-reliance and closing of loops.

We can't criticise the new mode of production for failing to exist right now as an ideal type, because it can only be emergent: the ensemble would necessarily be greater than the sum of its parts. But at least some of its initial constituent elements already exist, and it is perfectly normal in a situation of complexity that once the mode of production begins to coalesce, feedback processes will rapidly strengthen those components conducive to the ensemble.

Even so, to have confidence that this is possible is asking much. A major task of the Left is therefore to build the confidence that a whole new mode of production is both necessary and possible, to maintain a strategic vision of the complex ensemble, but at the same time avoid misleading people with any notion that it can be drawn from blueprints. The *Communist Manifesto* is clear about not moulding the movement through any sectarian principles, (Marx and Engels, 1969) so it comes down to having faith in the process itself. It is further important to recognise, drawing upon Lenin's work on the role of the Peoples of the East within the context of imperialism, that the creative force lies on the *margins* of the Eurocentric world system.

While the emphasis is on the open-endedness of a future which will be very much what the social movement makes of it, there is at the same time a set of likely institutional solutions: this is the point of the discussion around co-operation and commons. Since the Left's historical roots go back to the struggle against enclosure and the co-operative movement, it is rooted in the defence of the natural human mode of organisation, and against encroachment. Marx' understanding of the future society was very definitely non-centralised, and we can link this with Marxism's insistence on the need to smash the bureaucratic-military apparatus rather than simply seizing possession of it. Thus, the highly centralised and top-down nature of some aspects of power under capitalism – existing alongside its diffuse and chaotic aspect – do not mean that it can be overthrown from the top. Although, following Lenin, there is indeed a sense where capitalism *itself* pushes towards socialism, this is not a smooth growing-over, instead, it is a dialectical moment of contradiction. The collapse of modernism and of the degenerate Soviet form of *pseudo*-opposition to capitalism should also be conducive to a resurgence of Marxism.

For all the above reasons, there is a heritage in the Left which fully conforms with what is required for a systemic and emergent approach to the organisation of social relations. It is important to make this argument, because adaptation of the Left to new realities is not a departure from its heritage, but a rediscovery of it. Having said this, there is indeed a radically changing reality which must be adapted to.

Our hypothesis that capitalism has 'run out' of dynamism in no way implies that revolution was impossible before the system had exhausted its potential: such an assertion would be determinist and completely at odds with the systems perspective. *Any* crisis has revolutionary potential. It is a fundamental of Marxism that struggle is justified, and in fact it would have been better to overthrow the system earlier, because the ecological damage would have been less. In the 1870s or 1930s or 1970s the contestatory movement was more clearly 'left-wing' because the Marxists were the precursors who had seen through the system early, and the adaptation by humanity as a whole had not yet been triggered. In today's situation, a complex mass movement has caught onto the fact that this is a serious crisis, but in a way which doesn't clearly target the mode of production. The context for the Left is therefore somewhat different, but in a sense more important than ever. The task of the ruling order is to split apart the Left from the lifeworld and prevent the two joining up. As long as we are aware of this danger, it can be avoided, but we need to be aware of it.

Implications of Cybernetic Theory for Combating Capitalism's
Hegemonic Pull over the Network Debate

As we have shown, capitalism, while in principle incompatible with the natural human mode of organisation, has evolved some abilities to co-opt it. The great coup of the 1980s was to persuade people that capitalism was better at mastering the human mode of organisation than socialism was. Fundamentally, this was totally phoney because of the issues around reductionism and pseudo-individualism which we discussed earlier, but at a practical level of socio-economic organisation it was more plausible because you had a networked capitalism with a high level of spontaneous emergent self-organisation through subcontracting chains etc., confronting a system which was supposedly socialist but was actually, in its Soviet form, 'rationalised' in a top-down way which squeezed out emergence almost entirely. Both at a local and at a global level, networking (in its capitalism-dominated form) was shown to work quite well.

This triumphalism is unravelling today, both in practice and in terms of its ideological hold. Although at a productive level, emergent forms like global value chains still function, at a social and institutional level there is little substance: vaunted experiments like the public-private partnership fail to create any order, emergent or otherwise, while the civil society aspect of emergent governance was always hollow; the highly militaristic and repressive turn signals the extent to which complexity simply can't be mastered. But although relatively weaker, capitalism's hold within the networking debate is not exhausted.

The strategic enemy has always been the Left, but capitalism has learned from its big mistake during the Cold War when, by *explicitly* targeting the Left, it pushed anyone with a grievance against the ruling order in that direction. The more recent tactic has been, by presenting the future in terms of pluralism, decentralisation and market-based self-organisation, to brand the Left as irrelevant because it has not adapted to new realities, turns its back on emergent order and networking, and instead persists in its outdated, simplifying institutional approach. Simultaneously, by claiming that the West's enemy is no longer a centralised Soviet-style monolith but rather some evil diffused within networks, the attempt is to justify the increasingly chaotic forms of imperialism itself, its increasing cultivation of self-modifying and non-centralised repressive agents. As we saw, this approach began by targeting the Zapatistas and then switched to Al Qaeda, and with the more recent readjustments, it is possible that a further re-formulation is on the cards.[37] But if the identity of the next main enemy is up for grabs, it will probably be framed in such a way as to keep quiet about the real enemy, i.e. the Left.

In fact, one feature inherited from the Zapatista phase is to maintain a cosy 'inimical' relationship with a certain facet of the anti-globalisation movement, one which is partly critical of capitalism but nevertheless amenable to co-optation. The main basis for this alliance seems to be a common commitment to making the old Left appear out of date.

---

[37] see for example, "Eight years on, Al-Qaida has withered, say experts", *Guardian*, September 11 2009

At one level the anti-globalisation movement may be seen as a case of capitalism creating its own grave-diggers, in the sense that that movement responds to a special phase of capitalism which has broken down national barriers, and indeed there is a strong progressive legacy reflecting the Zapatistas' role when anti-globalisation was first beginning in the '90s. This radical and progressive core is something we should continue to affirm. But precisely because of the risk that this will draw international civil society away from the ruling order's hegemonic control, imperialism needs to maintain a foot in the opposition camp. At one level, just because anti-globalisation addresses issues which are a special creation of highly globalised capital, its reformist wing could introduce ideas like the 'Tobin tax' on speculative capital which might well be taken on board by mainstream elements striving for a new accumulation regime. But there are also ambiguities in the movement's more radical side. The most obvious institutional form of global networking is the World Social Forum (WSF) of civil society organisations, and insofar as its raison d'être is to oppose globalisation one might expect the establishment to hate it. On the other hand, as Taimur Rahman points out, its Charter of Principles is framed in such a way that it not only excludes but implicitly anathematises communists and the organised left (Rahman, 2006). A certain post-modern discourse reinforces this by arguing that politics has fundamentally been transformed, through the healthy breakup of the old certainties characteristic of the cold war and the introduction of new means of communication and new definitions of identity (Toal and Shelley, 2002). Such arguments serve to conceal the fact that the old simplified and repressive realities of imperialism are not only still there, but in fact increasing, even (perhaps, especially) under the guise of an underlying ambiguity in its relations with international civil society.

Therefore, the cause which the old social movements (labour, the Left) have long represented is more relevant than ever. Any notion that we should allow the old forms of organisation – anti-imperialist movements, labour struggles, left-wing parties, national liberation – to wither away and be replaced by networks, would play into the hands of the ruling order. To say this is not an excuse for the old movements to keep to a narrow and sectarian character: they have for example never been very good at taking on board the autonomy of Black struggles, this problem goes right back to colonial times. Nor does it deny the relevance of the old Left being *complemented* by new movements which respond to different facets of today's complexity. The notion of 'new social movements' thus has validity, insofar as it signals the increasingly autonomous articulation of demands by indigenous peoples, women, informal sector workers, people who directly suffer environmental damage etc. etc. These movements are not in principle in contradiction to the old ones (workers' organisations, left-wing parties etc.), and the latter will be useless if they do not take on board feminism, indigenous rights, sexual orientation and of course recognise that ecology is the basis of everything; if they persistently refuse to do so, they would deservedly wither. But it is essential to preserve the labour, class, and liberation orientation, because this is just what the ruling order fears. The undying relevance of the 'old' Left is still as always to point out the truth about imperialism, and more specifically the fact that imperialism will inevitably either seek to control or repress whichever new movements it can't co-opt; the new movements would in turn be doomed if they failed to realise this.

The interesting challenge is to understand the implications of network theory not just for the external action of the Left (for example, in its relations with civil society), but for its internal workings. It would be weird to have an organisation working with emergence in the wider social fabric while avoiding this internally. Has the Left overemphasised centralism at the expense of self-organisation? It is very important to pose this question, and although it's beyond our scope to propose an answer, it is certainly worth setting out some parameters for the debate. The movement must indeed operate in a new way, because of the issues around linking spaces and the assemblage of components underlying a new mode of production, which can only be emergent. It is indeed necessary to think and act systemically. The Left must relate to a systems-oriented futurology … but must above all do so critically.

We could for example critically consider Jeff Vail's theory of power, which shares with cold imperialism the adaptation to a very new, and restrictive, socio-ecological environment, but in this case from a seemingly more radical perspective (Vail, 2004). Here, the model for the new social organisation is the rhizome. "Each node in a rhizome stands autonomous from the larger structure, but the nodes work together in a larger network that extends benefits to the node without creating dependence."(Vail, 2004) Now, the 'rhizome' image derives from the work of Deleuze and Guattari, who, as we remarked earlier, make the point that rhizomes include "the best and the worst: potato and couchgrass"; (Deleuze and Guattari, 1987) in Chapter 5 we focused on the worst, i.e. chaotic military/repressive forms of self-organisation. So could we apply this also to the 'best', i.e. resistance? Decentralised organisations are difficult to crush. But the problem with Vail's argument is that it is intrinsically social-Darwinist, the innovation being merely to take this reasoning beyond the point reached by the normal capitalist apologist (who lauds the spontaneous order of the free market as an expression of an inherently competitive nature), and into the terrain of the complex and low-energy situations *encountered during the decay of that order*. Like all social-Darwinism, it neglects agency. Also, if it were true that the decay of capitalism moved the whole situation onto *wholly* different terrain, then the struggles which took place on the old terrain, like labour movements, would be outdated – how convenient for the ruling order!

Nevertheless, we can accept that the complexity of the current era is indeed qualitatively new. Provided that our point of departure is still the anti-imperialism which gave the old radical movements their justification, institutional forms may in the future go in unexpected directions. For example, with the ruling order forced to move into more repressive mode, this has implications for the actors which have been left floating in the networked space, *even those which capitalism itself seems to have created*. There is something objectively fundamental about networks: as Capra shows, modern physics has confirmed traditional perspective, according to which the definition of reality is not particles but connections (Capra, 1982). This gives us a basis for interpreting the phenomenon rightly noted by Brafman and Beckstrom: the correspondence between traditional non-hierarchical institutional structures – such as those of the Apache Native Americans – and ones which have arisen in the infosphere through P2P: "when attacked, a decentralised organization tends to become even more open and decentralised."(Brafman and Beckstrom, 2006)

There is a link between open organisations and open source; and in IT, we very much find the point of reference to be the gift economy rather than the market. The point is that the market is not truly a principle for network organisation. The reason that the movement for renewal must be anti-capitalist is precisely that (as Karl Polanyi noted) the market is not a natural way of organising. The lesson of Marx' theory of commodity fetishism is that capitalism makes people relate to one another through commodities, and not directly as human beings. There is a tradition among the grassroots which has always questioned this, a point which comes across strikingly in Taussig's excellent analysis of Latin American peasant movements, (Taussig, 1980) and it is precisely upon this tradition that we should build. It runs from pre-capitalist commons regimes through to the *anti*-capitalist tradition of worker co-operatives. So there is something very radical in the new developments in the infosphere. But the other side of this is that the rise of the information economy, far from reducing exploitation in the 'old' sense (of the working class, migrants and marginalised), has greatly facilitated its *increase*. It would be easy for IT specialists to forget about this, but the 'old' Left never will.

Principles of the Emergent Mode of Production, and Found Objects, which May Be Incorporated

The Left's traditional vocation – bringing together the objective social movements for change, and giving them confidence to create a new mode of production – is updated in a qualitatively new way because of complexity and the thermodynamic perspective.

There are two converging ways to make the case for low-input self-organisation: in an informational sense, decentralised and non-hierarchical organisations are better because they have the benefit of redundancy and diffuse initiative; in an ecological sense, they tap the free resource of capacity and correspondingly reduce energy demands on the external environment. The interconnection is interesting: no-till agriculture minimises labour and disperses knowledge, in contrast to deep ploughing systems which have historically tended to convert leisure time into a source of surplus, and at the same time increased hierarchy. Today, in assembling the elements of a new mode of production, the goal is to maximise emergence and at the same time minimises inputs of scarce resources, such as water.

From the early imperialist period, we can derive one of the most far-sighted expressions of a link between physical energy and institutional systems in the work of Weber: "... the modern economic order ... is now bound to the technical and economic conditions of machine production which to-day determine the lives of all the individuals who are born into this mechanism, not only those directly concerned with economic acquisition, with irresistible force. Perhaps it will so determine them until the last ton of fossilized coal is burnt." (Weber, 1905) Although he doesn't develop the implications, there is some sense that the peculiar mode of bureaucratic top-down governance is somehow a logical expression of this high energy system. What Weber's failed to see that the two could be dissociated to some extent, and then, in a sense, substituted. Thus, in the 1980 AR, capitalism found it could tap into emergent structures like clusters and value chains in order to counterbalance the wastefulness of bureaucracy. This was driven by *exploitative* efficiency, but we could say that there was an implicit link with resource scarcity, in the sense that the 1980 AR was after all a resolution to the '70s crisis with its acute sense of limits and debates on the possible exhaustion of fossil fuels: we might argue that institutional efficiencies brought a saving which enabled the system temporarily to *repress* its consciousness of limits, and continue with a very high level of depletion.

Nevertheless, Weber is right that there has to be a double revolution in both thermodynamic and institutional organisation. Göran Wall was similarly right to indicate that common principles could be applied to both tasks (Wall, 1993). But what Wall fails to see is that the two sides will never come together under capitalism. The weak link is the fact that (something which can be confirmed by anyone having experienced the reality of 'Japanese' management) the supposed empowerment of human initiative under the new management systems is largely just an excuse to exploit workers more intensively by making them responsible for quality; and the same could be said of all aspects of the current community empowerment discourse. And because capitalism cannot deeply tap into capacity, its ecological profile must remain high to compensate, thus casting doubt on the claim of thermodynamic efficiency too. But it remains true that *the search for a low-energy mode of production is not only physical, but also institutional.* It is the historic task of the radical movement to take up this challenge where capitalism has failed.

This task, cannot, moreover, be left until capitalism has been (however we understand this) overthrown. On the one hand, some kind of productive system (most obviously of food, but of other necessary goods as well) must remain in place to bridge the transitional period; on the other – and this is the favourable factor – because the human survival reflex has been triggered while capitalism is still in place, there are already some positive elements to draw upon. While capitalism *at a whole-system level* opposes the creative low-input solution, a number of lower-level initiatives can indeed occur under the guise of capitalism, whose radical significance lies precisely in their hinting at a future direction which that system is incapable of realising. In waste management, for example, the idea of using biogas from processed waste is certainly workable and can make a real contribution, (Smith and Hughes, 2007) while in a more general sense, industrial ecology must begin to look in the direction of holistic and systemic approaches (Brunner and Ma, 2008). There is absolutely no question that this kind of systemic approach will form a component in a new mode of production: it involves specialist knowledge, but this is not at all contradictory to a democratisation of knowledge running through the mode of production as a whole. This is the basis for what we could call an 'institutional recycling'. After all, a whole range of new ways of running the economy is required, and thousands of institutional contributions will have to be assembled, and adapted, very quickly.

This takes us again to the issue of 'found objects': the new system will be built not just by processing physical waste, but in a sense also the institutional waste, the detritus of the old order. If the new one cannot be built from the top (which would go diametrically counter to the key element in the 'new social order' towards which the final stage of capitalism is 'dragged'), it is equally important to emphasise that it cannot be rebuilt from a blank slate. Any available low-energy structures may be 'plugged into' the project. In the Dada tradition, they may be seen as 'found objects', but at the same time we must realise that nothing is incorporated unchanged: recycling is a process of transformation ... or, to use the image so powerfully employed by Marx throughout Capital, Volume 1, metamorphosis.[38] The way this works is that in the act of smashing the repressive top-down institutions, those at the lower reaches are liberated from the capitalist logic which currently imprisons them. In a conventional capitalist view of environmental economics, individual decisions of firms or consumers are purely short-sighted and neglect environmental and social externalities, with the result that ecological commitments have to be pushed from the top of the system. But the reality may be the opposite: the system is rotten at the top, not just because of the corporations and hedge funds, but because any pretensions of the state to reflect longer-term interests (society, the environment) tend to be overwhelmed by its allegiance to imperialism. The myth of the environmental Kuznets curve (the greening of post-industrial capitalism) is sustained only by transplanting industrial

---

[38] The importance of this term is emphasised in Alexander Kluge's remarkable filmic exporation of Marx's Capital, 'Nachrichten aus der ideologischen Antike – Marx/Eisenstein/Das Kapital'

production to China, where its local manifestations now overlap with the global crisis. And in a broader sense, all the reactionary features which imperialism theory correctly highlighted – militarism, bureaucracy, speculation – are precisely the ones which dominate the system from the top and push *against* sustainability. Paradoxically, it is in the lower reaches of capitalism where the market still exists in pockets that the information from scarcity may make itself felt through 'price signals', in a way which encourages conservation or re-use.

The heritage of several centuries of capitalism is that we have forgotten how to organise differently, and will need to re-learn this. Of course, the natural co-operative reflex will help because it minimises institutional entropy; but there is still a massive amount of concrete experience to be acquired. So, alongside an extremely radical break with what went before, there is also the 'quieter' aspect of the revolution, the assemblage of any existing elements which may be helpful. This may at times appear reformist, but it is reformism guided by the radical strategic vision.

The New Epoch of History

Ever since Spengler and Toynbee we have had ideas of the rise and decline of civilisations, and even a notion that society would 'adapt' to its era of decline by assuming a merely decadent form. But the crucial difference is that, whereas these early debates assumed one civilisation could fall and another rise, if the issue is coupled to energy the ecosystem could not tolerate the rise of a replacement hierarchical social system, either in parallel or in succession to the current Atlantocentric capitalism. Even Capra, who should understand the ecological parameters much better than Spengler, tends to fall back on the tired old platitudes of rise and decline (Capra, 1982). In contrast, we should affirm the specificity and concreteness of the transition: the drivers of change and the social movements which constitute its agents will be specifically anti-capitalist ones. Despite the deprivation associated with crisis, the adaptation will, because it *must* access human capacity and overcome alienation, actually 'feel' better than what went before. Of course, this would necessarily be a 'decline of the West' because capitalism is indissociably linked with imperialism which in turn cannot be separated from its embodiment in IR terms, as predicted by Hobson, i.e. NATO/G7; but it would necessarily be an *anti-capitalist* 'decline of the West'. For example, China is objectively rising relative to the historic core, but the ecological conditions for it to develop in a conventional way to overtake or replace that core are missing. If China were to 'rise' this could only be in the context of a transition to a mode of production where labour and sustainability come together. There might be scope for some coming-together between grassroots movements and government both in reducing pollution, (Watts, 2007) and in improving labour standards;[39] but if it were to be successful, this movement would need to overcome resistance from the whole weight of forces hitched to global capital. The result would be the 'rise' not so much of China but of a wholly new mode of production.

This implies renaissance not just at an economic, but at an institutional level. The decadence of the current order leaves a void. In response, it would not be unreasonable to speak of a new civilisation, provided that this is defined in contrast, not to some notion of 'barbarism' from the past (as in the modernisation discourse), but rather to the terroristic tendency always latent within imperialism, of which fascism was one manifestation and today's politics another. In upholding civilisation against fascism-terrorism, we are therefore not turning the clock back to a mythical golden age of civilised capitalism, or even to a mythical pre-capitalist golden age, but rather universalising the hitherto-limited definition of *rights* in a way capitalism never could, and never tried to, achieve. And what fills the void is not a new force at the centre or at the top, but rather one diffused through the system, whose diversity necessarily challenges the normative outlines of past definitions of civilisation with their aggressive policing of deviance.

In this sense the force for civilisation is a social reality where ecological stewardship and 'old' labour struggles come together. In the Cochabamba Water Revolt in Bolivia from 2000, popular movements opposed the World Bank's policies forcing the country to privatise water in the interest of 'private' interests which are first and foremost multinational, in this case the giant US Bechtel corporation, which immediately forced prices up. Significant popular victories were achieved.[40] Underlying this is perhaps a different way of relating to the

---

[39] "The Global Battle Over New Rights for Chinese Workers", *Global Labour Strategies*, April 3rd 2007 on http://laborstrategies.blogs.com/global_labor_strategies/2007/04/in_a_historical.html#more

[40] The first victory was achieved, at the price of violent struggles, when the government was forced to back down. Bechtel then sued Bolivia for $50 million damages before the secretive International Centre for Settlement of Investment Disputes

natural world, one closer to indigenous perceptions. In the Bolivian case, the movement led by Morales in some sense reflects a fightback of indigenous peoples against a racist and Eurocentric order.

Conversely, where governments are too subservient or repressive to engage in any useful dialogue with society, they are beginning to be challenged by waves of struggle from below. What is extremely interesting in this respect is a renewed role of the 'old' social movements, i.e. the struggle for labour. In the Middle East, the Palestinians are no longer alone in waging struggle against the ruling dispensation, there are massive waves of labour struggle beginning to unfold. Suddenly (in what seems to have been a watershed around 2006–7 when the entropy of the system began to bite) the region became a hotbed of struggle. In Egypt, railway workers, textile workers, garbage collectors and many other categories launched a wave of militance;[41] over 200 such actions occurred in 2006 alone, particularly noteworthy being the strike in Al-Mahala Al-Kubra by 27,000 textile workers. Workers have totally rejected the official, top-down (manipulated) labour unions, and insisted on doing things their own way ... and the ruling order was forced to back down.[42] Attempts to counter this by increasing repression (in the name of anti-terrorism – of course) are a sign of desperation. Migrant construction workers in the Gulf likewise win industrial actions (DeParle, 2007) There is clearly a strong element of the 'new' social issues (migrant workers) coming in to reinforce the 'old' tradition of the labour movement. And they are already moving onto the terrain of resource management, as when Iraqi oil workers strike to resist the US-imposed legislation on the 'privatisation' of oil. This remarkable change at a level of class struggle certainly underpins the more recent political movements in the Middle East which have developed since December 2010. By one-sidedly emphasising the 'new' elements like social networking (however interesting), mainstream media accounts have tended to cover up the more profound currents, precisely those addressed by the 'old left', i.e. class and national liberation struggle.

Even in a day-to-day context where the circuits of capitalism are still more or less turning over, it would be narrow and economistic to think

---

(ICSID) in Washington. A second victory was achieved as a result of an international campaign, and Bechtel eventually had to settle for a token payment of 30 cents.

[41] see for example http://arabist.net/arabawy/2007/04/06/sit-ins-strikes-in-nile-delta-giza-cairo/

[42] *Al-Ahram Weekly*, 12–18 April 2007 on http://weekly.ahram.org.eg/2007/840/eg5.htm

that labour struggles are only limiting the *degree* of exploitation. They always raise the issue of rights, and this in turn suggests a new conception of civilisation, which must be upheld against the ruling order's unprecedented attacks. More specifically, working class struggles target the issue of security, an area where capitalism is highly vulnerable.

Security is related to stability, and the end product will be to enter into the stable phase of a new mode of production, creating predictability of access to things like employment and healthcare. Of course, this can only come about through a period of chaos: chaos which is the responsibility of the current ruling order, and of its environmental effects. While embracing the creative possibilities of this chaos, the popular struggles never cease raising issues of the new phase of stability which is their goal. For example, they expose the social-Darwinist logic whereby if a company goes bust, this is a gain for efficiency. The capitalist crisis is manifested in shutdowns, but working people have to respond in way which makes sense in livelihood terms. They don't simply welcome the entropy of capitalism if this means the loss of their job, but the important point is *how* they respond: institutional solutions like workplace occupation and worker co-operatives enable livelihoods to be maintained in the interstices of a capitalist order which is for the moment still in place, while preparing institutional experience for a new mode of production. In fact, knowledge must be rapidly accumulated. Across Latin America a regional conference of cooperative-run businesses in 2005 brought together delegates under the slogan Occupy, Resist, and Produce (Trigona, 2006). Such experience could be shared internationally – in the same way as, for example, the grassroots agriculture movement shares seed – through global information networks, which possess the virtue of 'redundancy': not the bad sense of redundancy meaning workers getting the sack, but the good sense of many different solutions to a problem, the institutional equivalent to biodiversity in the ecosystem. There is often a direct relationship to physical resources. Tower Colliery in Wales, with a historic claim to be the first place where the red flag was flown by the workers' movement under capitalism (in 1830), lived through the experience of the top-down transfer to public ownership in 1945 (where relations within the productive process remained intact), through the bitter attacks of Thatcher and eventual closure, only to be reopened as a co-operative. The change is subtle: hierarchical systems privilege certain spaces of social interaction, where the habitus of the operative is concerned only with detail; under co-operative relations, interactive modes expand their sphere to encompass the whole process, while those propitious to hierarchy shrink (Arthur et al, 2004). This is the kind of experience which shows us how, concretely, to rebuild co-operative relations. Obviously, the resource in this case (coal) is unsustainable and the colliery eventually had to close, but the lasting legacy is precisely the free resource which we can eventually substitute for fossil fuels: capacity, and the institutional forms which embody it.

In refutation of the capitalist notion of 'efficiency' (which cheerfully sacrifices livelihoods), such experiments are efficient in the institutional sense (diversity and diffuse initiative as a guarantor of resilience), and potentially also (because they serve to liberate this free resource), thermodynamically too. They can thus survive within a still-existing capitalism, and later emerge as the crucial building block of a new order, where the intra-capitalist experiments like industrial ecology and social/environmental enterprise will probably play a more subordinate role. The 'other' is thus something which begins to mature in the interstices of capitalism.

The notion of 'spaces' of struggle (occupied workplaces, community-organised unconventional spaces for food-growing, as in Argentina) would emphasise an irreducible area of contention within the heart of a system which on the surface appears uniformly capitalist (Artur et al, 2004). While we must be wary of any reading of the end of the Cold War which welcomes the collapse of the old 'certainties' (i.e. Communism), it is sensible to expect that new content will be introduced into socialism, and that this will, as Venezuelan minister Hector Navarro argued, draw on the premise that people require not just material needs but, precisely, 'spaces', into which to project their creativity (Fuentes, 2007).

In the context of the 'old-new' fusion, international solidarity may be instrumental in helping the 'spaces' to coalesce into something wider. In January 2007, Palestinians staged a nonviolent demonstration at Huwara Checkpoint in southern Nablus dressed in a loose version of the traditional outfits of Native Americans.[43] A Canadian draft military manual of 2005 lists Native American groups alongside Islamists as targets of counter-terrorism operations (Curry, 2007). Third-generation descendants of Japanese Americans wrongly detained during World War II have spoken out in solidarity with Muslims (Bernstein, 2007).

---

[43] http://www.kibush.co.il/show_file.asp?num=17824

The development, *and linking*, of contestatory spaces thus objectively forms the opposite, the negation of the attempt by imperialism, which we described at the beginning of this chapter, to assemble a definition of order from the scraps of information it still comprehends in the shrinking spaces under its direct control.

Struggle goes in 'waves', and an interesting hypothesis would be to view the wave as a coalescence of 'spaces', the beginning of the situation where they can begin to bring about qualitative change. At the time of writing, the rapidly-developing feedback from entropy is stimulating the development of increasing numbers of 'spaces' which are yet to coalesce to become a wave, but this is exactly what we may expect to happen soon. The working population thus reconstitutes itself as a subject, and as an active force. A key aspect of this will be, as we have argued in this chapter, the way that the natural co-operative tendency becomes institutionally embodied in regimes. As Massimo De Angelis puts it, "'Our outside' is the realm of the production of commons"; (De Angelis, 2006) and he is surely right in principle to say that the 'detritus' of capital accumulation (an area where "the problematic of social reproduction is uniquely in the hands of the dispossessed") is also the region of 'conatus' (a term taken from Spinoza, signifying the drive to preservation) which clashes with that of capital (De Angelis, 2006).

A human survival reflex has been triggered by the crisis, but this is of course not merely an instinctive ('knee-jerk) reflex, but rather something conscious and normative. The crucial point is the information about the future which social movements possess: what is being created is an institutional experience of autonomy and self reliance and for the rebuilding of community and this is precisely the basis for 'cells' which can survive a decaying capitalism, and begin, by coalescing, to reconstitute the new order. In its search for an institutional vocabulary, the social movement can thus draw upon several elements such as (modern) commons regimes and acephalic traditions or 'panarchism': (Stienhauer, 2006) not anarchy but a mode of organisation appropriate to a social order which is not chaotic, but highly complex, and within which rule is diffused. In this sense, the different traditional and modern forms (e.g. workers' co-operatives) can be synthesised using dialectics to explore the logical relations between them. The overarching organising principle is the indigenous perception that, whereas everyone has a share in the world, they can't go 'take' their share (Steinhauer, 2006).

In a complex order, the uncertainty principle should be a vehicle of creativity. But this is what has been perverted under capitalism, because disorder is exported into the livelihoods of the masses – both in the social form of insecurity of employment and exposure to conflict, and in the ecological form of direct exposure to environmental hazard. It is crucial that the most 'advanced' form of capitalism, i.e. its networked form, has increased this perversion, spreading, as Boltanski and Chiapello point out, its own peculiar *inquiétude* (Boltanski and Chiapello, 1999).

On this basis, we can suddenly understand that the terrorist phase of imperialism (evident since the end of the 1990s), which in some respects seems to contradict the more diffuse and indirect rule appropriate to its networked phase, is actually implicit within it. There is a kind of 'strategy of tension' diffused within the industrial networks themselves, and this in turn creates the climate of thinking whereby militarist 'security' – i.e. actual terrorism – seeks to justify itself. As the 'strategy of tension' is increasingly globalised, much of contemporary politics is focused around fear. This both feeds into the 'fear of freedom' discussed by Fromm, and at the same time potentially negates it: as Brazilian activist Moema Miranda points out, the current climate includes "fear of crime, of the neighbour, of the immigrant, of the competition for my job, of war and instability. Fear of loneliness, of grow[ing] old and losing the pension. We have to make combating fear a central part of our new thinking about politics (Miranda, 2007)." If insecurity has become so intrinsic and endemic to the mode of production, and specifically to the neoliberal/terrorist AR from which it is unable to disembed itself, then the realisation may dawn that liberation from the mode of production is also the pathway to liberation from fear. This would suddenly invalidate capitalism's 'fear of freedom' trump card.

Then, in the process of transition, the oppressive form of uncertainty can be processed into its opposite, and anomie as a depletion of order become anomie as collapse of hegemonic discourses. Central to this outcome will be a re-definition of security, rebuilt from the ground up as a common-pool resource where it is no longer conceived as private, fenced-off, zero-sum. Having clawed its identity away from the militaristic discourses, this redefinition of security would become a principle for the rebuilding of society, embracing the unpredictability of emergent order as a cause for hope, rather than of fear, and as the only pathway to the eventual stability of a new mode of production.

REFERENCES

Abbott, C. et al, 2006, *Sustainable security for the 21st century – global responses to global threats*, Oxford (Oxford Research Group)

Agamben G., 2005, *State of Exception*, Chicago (University of Chicago Press)

Ahearn, L.A., 2001, "Language and Agency", *Annual Review of Anthropology*, vol. 30 pp 109–37

Ahmed, N.M., 2002, *The War on Freedom*, Joshua Tree, CA (Media Messenger Books)

Amin, S., 1970, *L'Accumulation à l'échelle mondiale: Critique du sous-développement*, Paris (Anthropos)

——, 1973, *Le Développement Inégal: Essai Sur les Formes Sociales du Capitalisme périphérique*, Paris (Les Editions de Minuit)

——, 1977, *La Loi de la Valeur et le Matérialisme historique*, Paris (Les Editions de Minuit)

——, 1980, *Class and Nation – Historically and in the Current Crisis*, London (Heinemann)

——, 1981, *L'Avenir du Maoisme*, Paris (Les Editions de Minuit)

——, and Frank A.G., 1981, "Let's not wait for 1984!" in Frank, *Reflections on the Economic Crisis*, New York (Monthly Review Press)

Anon, 1992, "The Current Crisis, a Crisis for Over-Production of Capital", *Social Relations* (Milan), March

Anslow, Mark, 2007, "Biofuels – facts and fiction", *The Ecologist,* February 19 on http://www.theecologist.org/archive_detail.asp?content_id=755

Anyang' Nyong'o, P., 1987, (ed) *Popular Struggles for Democracy in Africa*, London (Zed Books/UNU)

Astyk, S., 2007, "How Much Did the Green Revolution Matter? or Can We Feed the World Without Industrial Agriculture?", *Energy Bulletin,* 29 Jan 2007 on http://www.energybulletin.net/25315.html

Aufderheide, P., 2007, "Is Wikipedia the New Town Hall?" *In These Times*, March 12, on: http://www.inthesetimes.com/article/3067/is_wikipedia_the_new_town_hall/

Babbage, C., 1832, *On the Economy of Machinery and Manufactures*, London (Charles Knight).

Bahr, H., 1980, "The Class Structure of Machinery: Notes on the Value Form" in Slater P. (ed) *Outlines of a Critique of Technology*, London (Ink Links)

Bailey, K.D., 1996, "Advances in Social Entropy Theory", *Slovak Sociological Review*, Vol. 1 Fall.

Baillie, J., E.M.C. Hilton-Taylor and S.N. Stuart (eds.) 2004, *A Global Species Assessment*, Cambridge (World Conservation Union – IUCN)

Baker, Raymond W., 2005, interviewed on Australian radio station ABC, December 12, on http://www.abc.net.au/pm/content/2005/s1529454.htm

Bakhtiari, A., 2006, Peak Oil – Four Phases of Transition – interview with Byron W. King, on http://www.thepeakist.com/peak-oil-four-phases-of-transition/#more-212

Baran P.A., 1973, *The Political Economy of Growth*, London (Penguin)

Baranger, M., n.d., *Chaos, Complexity, and Entropy* discussion paper, Center for Theoretical Physics, Laboratory for Nuclear Science and Department of Physics, Massachusetts Institute of Technology, on http://www.necsi.org/projects/baranger/cce.pdf

Barkun, Michael, 1968, *Law Without Sanctions: Order in Primitive Societies and the World Community*, New Haven (Yale University Press)

Barma, N., 2003, *The Prospects and Pitfalls of Information Technology-Driven Development Strategies and Assistance*, Conference paper: The American Political Science Association, Philadelphia

Barnaby, W., 2009, "Do nations go to war over water?", *Nature*, 458, 282–283 (19 March).

Barret, C.B., 1993, *On Price Risk and the Inverse Farm Size-Productivity Relationship*, University of Wisconsin-Madison, Department of Agricultural Economics Staff Paper Series no.369, on http://www.aae.wisc.edu/pubs/sps/pdf/stpap369.pdf

Bauwens, M., 2007, *P2P and Human Evolution: Peer to peer as the premise of a new mode of civilization*, on http://www.networkcultures.org/weblog/archives/P2P_essay.pdf accessed April 2007. This is an ongoing essay under constant development: a slightly revised version can be accessed on http://integralvisioning.org/article.php?story=p2ptheory1

Beck, U., 1992, *Risk Society: Towards a New Modernity*, London (Sage)

Beckett, A., 2004, "Friends in High Places," *Guardian*, November 6

Belasco, A., 2006, *CRS Report for Congress, The Cost of Iraq, Afghanistan, and Other Global War on Terror Operations Since 9/11*, Washington DC (CRS), Sept., Order Code RL33110.

Bellinger, Gene et al, n.d., *Data, Information, Knowledge, and Wisdom* on http://www.systems-thinking.org/dikw/dikw.htm

Belshaw, D., 1980, "Taking Indigenous Technology Seriously, the Case of Inter-Cropping Techniques in East Africa" in Brokensha D. et al (eds) *Indigenous Knowledge Systems and Development*, Lanham MD (University Press of America)

Bender, B., 2007, "Pentagon study says oil reliance strains military, urges development of alternative fuels", *Boston Globe*, May 1.

Bergsten, C.F., 2004, *Speech to the Deputies of the G-20*, Leipzig, March 4, on http://www.iie.com/publications/papers/bergsten0304-2.htm

Bernstein, N., 2007, "Relatives of Interned Japanese-Americans Side with Muslims", *New York Times*, April 3

Bettelheim, C., 1965, "Les Cadres généraux de la Planification chinoise" in Bettelheim C. et al, *La Construction du Socialisme en Chine*, Paris (Maspéro).

Bhadrakumar, M.K., 2006, "A journey into the new American century" *The Hindu*, January 11

Biel, R., 2000, *The New Imperialism*, London (Zed Books)

——, 2003, "Le Capitalisme a besoin des femmes" in Bisilliat J. (ed) *Regards de Femmes sur la Globalisation - Approches critiques*, Paris (Karthala)

——, 2003 a, "The Political Economy of Migration", in Schmid E. et al (eds) *Listen to the Refugee's Story*, London (Corner House)

——, 2003 b, "Imperialism and International Governance - the Case of US Foreign Policy Towards Africa", *Review of African Political Economy*, No.95

——, 2004, "Por formas radicais de decisão popular: Elas podem ajudar na luta contra a violência total da guerra ao terror", *Reportagem* (Brasil) N.63 Dezembro

——, 2006, "The interplay between social and environmental degradation in the development of the international political economy" *Journal of World-Systems Research*, xii, July

——, 2010, "Critical Perspectives on Issue of Global Poverty" in Boran A. (ed.) *Poverty - Malaise of Development*, Chester (Chester University Press)

Blair, Tony, 2006, speech to the Foreign Policy centre, March 21, on http://www.pm.gov.uk/output/Page 9224.asp

Bollier, D., 2001, *Public Assets, Private Profits - Reclaiming the American Commons in an Age of Market Enclosure*, Washington DC (New America Foundation)

Boltanski, L. and Chiapello, E., 1999, *Le nouvel Esprit du Capitalisme*, Paris (Gallimard)

Bond, M., 2009, "Critical Mass", *New Scientist*, July 18

Bowcott, O., 2007, "Spy left out in the cold: how MI6 buried heroic exploits of agent 'Griffin'", *Guardian*, September 22

Bowring, Philip, 2006, "A World Awash in Dangerous Liquidity" *Asia Sentinel* October 27 on http://www.asiasentinel.com/index.php?option=com_content&task=view&id=236&Itemid=32

Brafman, O. and R.A. Beckstrom, 2006, *The Starfish and the Spider – the Unstoppable Power of Leaderless Organizations* New York (Penguin)

Braverman, H., 1974, *Labour and Monopoly Capital,* New York (Monthly Review)

Brecht, B., *The Threepenny Opera*

Brenner, T. and D. Fornahl, 2003, "Introduction: Towards a Political Perspective and Unifying Concept" in Fornahl and Brenner (eds.) *Cooperation, Networks, and Institutions in Regional Innovations Systems,* Cheltenham (Edward Elgar), pp. 1–11

Brunner, P.H. and H.W. Ma, 2008, "Substance Flow Analysis – An Indispensable Tool for Goal-Oriented Waste Management", *Journal of Industrial Ecology,* 13, 1

Bryce, R., 2008, *Gusher of Lies – the dangerous delusions of 'energy independence'* (Public Affairs Books)

Bull, A., 2006, "America's rags-to-riches dream an illusion: study", *Reuters News Service* Apr 26, on http://www.libertypost.org/cgi-bin/readart.cgi?ArtNum=138980

Bunker, S.G.,1985, *Underdeveloping the Amazon – Extraction, Unequal Exchange and the Failure of the Modern State,* Chicago (University of Chicago Press)

Burkett, P. and J. Bellamy Foster, 2006, "Metabolism, energy and entropy in Marx' critique of political economy: beyond the Podolinski myth", *Theory and Society,* vol. 35

Burnham, G. et al, 2006, "Mortality after the 2003 invasion of Iraq: a cross-sectional cluster sample survey", *The Lancet,* www.thelancet.com. Published online October 11

Burns, N., 2005, on http://www.nato.int/docu/speech/2005/s050525o.htm

Busby, C. and S. Morgan, 2006, *Evidence from the measurements of the Atomic Weapons Establishment, Aldermaston, Berkshire, UK.* Aberystwyth (Green Audit) Occasional Paper 2006/1 on http://www.llrc.org/aldermastrept.pdf.

Butz, D. and D. Leslie, 2001, "Risky subjects – changing geographies of employment in the automobile industry", *Area* (Royal Geographical Society), 33, 2.

Byakola, T., 2007, "Massive protests in Uganda over agrofuel projects" in GRAIN, *The New Scramble for Africa* on http://www.grain.org/seedling_files/seed-07-07-6-en.pdf

Caldwell, M., n.d., *The Energy of Imperialism, and the Imperialism of Energy,* London (School of Oriental and African Studies) [ca 1970], duplicated,

——, 1977, *The Wealth of Some Nations,* London (Zed Books)

Campbell, A., 1945, *It's Your Empire,* London (Left Book Club)

Capra, F., 1982, *The Turning Point: Science, Society, and the Rising Culture,* New York (Simon and Schuster). See text on http://www.wplus.net/pp/Julia/Capra/CONTENTS.htm

Carlson, C., 2007, "Washington's New Imperial Strategy In Venezuela" Venezuelanalysis. com May 13, on http://www.venezuelanalysis.com/articles.php?artno=2035

Carr, N., 2006, "Avatars consume as much electricity as Brazilians", December 5, on http://www.roughtype.com/archives/2006/12/avatars_consume.php

Castro, F., 2007, *More than three billion people in the world condemned to premature death from hunger and thirst*, Granma March 29 on http://www.granma.cu/ INGLES/2007/marzo/juev29/14reflex.html

Catalinotto, J., 2006, *Civil War: a new strategy of the United States to dominate Iraq* Lecture at the International Seminar on the Assassination of Iraqi Academics and Health Professionals, Madrid, April 22, on http://iraktribunal.de/internat/madrid _april2006/catalinotto.htm

Cattori, S., 2007, *The Strategy of Tension – NATO's Hidden Terrorism – Interview with Daniele Ganser*, January, on http://www.voltairenet.org/article144748.html

Cavanaugh, G.J., 1976, review article, *American Historical Review*, Vol. 81, No. 1, February

Césaire, A., 1972, *Discourse on Colonialism*, London (Monthly Review Press)

Chandler, D., 2004, *Constructing Global Civil Society*, Basingstoke (Palgrave Macmillan)

Chandrasekaran, R., 2007, "The Project", *Guardian*, Feb. 20.

——, 2007, "Defense Skirts State in Reviving Iraqi Industry" *Washington Post*, May 14

Chayanov, A.V., 1966, *On the Theory of Peasant Economy*, Manchester (Manchester UP)

Chipaux, F., 2007, "Les Afghans dénoncent les victimes civiles des bombardements américains", *Le Monde*, May 11

Chossudovsky, M., "Osamagate", Centre for Research on Globalisation (CRG), Montréal on http://www.globalresearch.ca/articles/CHO110A.html

——, 2003, "Rwanda: Installing a US Protectorate in Central Africa – The US was behind the Rwandan Genocide", *Global Research*, May 8, on http://www .globalresearch.ca/index.php?context=va&aid=373

Churchill, W., 2005, *Lessons Not Learned and the War on Free Speech*, on http://www .dissidentvoice.org/Feb05/Churchill0203.htm

Cispes (Committee in Solidarity with the Peoples of El Salvador), 2007, "Protestors & Movement Leaders Charged with Terrorism after Police Action in Suchitoto, El Salvador", July 5 on http://www.cispes.org/index.php?option=com_content&task =view&id=235&Itemid=27

Clairmonte, F. and J. Cavanagh, 1981, *The World in their Web – The Dynamics of Textile Multinationals*, London (Zed Books)

Clark, N., 2006, "You cannot be serious – The Belarus saga exposes the hollowness of the west's support for human rights and democracy", *Guardian*, March 27.

Coalition for the International Criminal Court, *Overview of the United States' opposition to the International Criminal Court* on http://www.iccnow.org/documents/CICCFS_US_Opposition_to_ICC_11Dec06_final.pdf

Coghlan, A., 2006, "Whales boast the brain cells that 'make us human'", *New Scientist*, November 27

Cole, H.S.D. et al, 1973, *Thinking About the Future – A Critique of the Limits to Growth*, University of Sussex, Science Policy Research Unit

Cole, S. and I. Miles, 1984, *Worlds Apart – Technology and North-South Relations in the Global Economy*, Brighton (Wheatsheaf for UNITAR)

Collier P. and A. Hoeffler, 2007, "The Costs of State Failure and the Limits to Sovereignty", *Research Summary 2007*, Oxford (Centre for the Study of African Economies)

Collins, M., 2007, "Ensembles and probabilities: a new era in the prediction of climate change", *Philosophical Transactions of the Royal Society A*, vol. 365, June, pp. 1957–70

Cooper, R., 2002, "Why we still need empires", *The Observer*, April 7

Council on Foreign Relations, 2005, *Building a North American Community – Report of an Independent Task Force*, New York (Council on Foreign Relations), on http://www.cfr.org/content/publications/attachments/NorthAmerica_TF_final.pdf

Cracker, J., 1983, "Sociobiology: The Capitalist Synthesis", *Radical Science Journal*, No.13, pp. 55–72

Cross, J.C., 1998, "Co-optation, Competition, and Resistance: State and Street Vendors in Mexico City", *Latin American Perspectives*, Vol. 25, No. 2, March, pp. 41–61

Crouchy, M.D. Galai D. and R. Mark, 2006, *The Essentials of Risk Management*, New York (McGraw Hill)

Curry, B., 2007, "Forces' terror manual lists natives with Hezbollah", *Globe and Mail*, Toronto March 31

Curtis, M., 1998, *The Great Deception – Anglo-American Power and World Order*, London (Pluto)

Daalder, I.H., and R. Kagan, 2007, "America and the Use of Force: Sources of Legitimacy", Brookings Institution (the Stanley Foundation's Bridging the Foreign Policy Divide project), June on http://www.brookings.edu/views/articles/daalder/2007june_kagan.htm

Daly, H.E. and J.B. Cobb, Jr, 1989, *For the Common Good – Redirecting the Economy toward Community, the Environment and a Sustainable Future* London (Green Print)

Darwin, C., 1959, *The Voyage of the Beagle*, London (Everyman)

Davis, M., 2007, "Sinister symmetry – Both Iraq's car bombers and the White House see the Shia resurgence and Iran as the main enemies" *Guardian*, April 21

De Angelis, M., 2006, "Enclosures, commons and the 'outside'", in Bond P., Chitonge H. and Hofmann A., *Accumulation of Capital and Southern Africa*, University of Kwazulu Natal, School of Development Studies

de Rosnay, Joël, 1979, *The Macroscope*, New York (Harper & Row); electronic text on http://pespmc1.vub.ac.be/MACRBOOK.html

de Soto, H., 2000, *The Mystery of Capital: Why Capitalism Triumphs in the West and Fails Everywhere Else*, New York (Basic Books)

——, 2001, "The Mystery of Capital" in *Finance and Development*, Volume 38, Number 1, March

Dean, C., 2007, "Experts Discuss Engineering Feats, Like Space Mirrors, to Slow Climate Change", *New York Times*, November 10

Dearman, Peter, 2007, "Please Lord, not the bees – Everything you didn't want to know about Colony Collapse Disorder", GNN, Wed, May 2 on http://www.gnn.tv/articles/3063/Please_Lord_not_the_bees

Defra, 2005, (Department for Environment, Food and Rural Affairs, UK Government): *Joint announcement by the agricultural departments of the United Kingdom, Organic Statistics United Kingdom*, June

Deleuze, G. and F. Guattari, 1987, *A Thousand Plateaus: Capitalism and Schizophrenia* (University of Minnesota Press)

Delpeuch, B., 1985, "L'Espoir déçu de la Révolution verte" in Alaux J.P. and Norel P. (eds) *Faim au Sud, Crise au Nord*, Paris (L'Harmattan)

Delwiche, P., 2006, *Du Potager de Survie au Jardin solidaire*, Namur (Nature et Progrès)

DeParle, J., 2007, "Emirates making peace with army of restive migrant workers", *International Herald Tribune*, August 5

Dew-Becker, I. and R.J. Gordon, 2005, *Where did the Productivity Growth Go? Inflation Dynamics and the Distribution of Income*, paper presented at the 81st Brookings Panel on Economic Activity, Washington DC, September 8–9, on http://www.brookings.edu/es/commentary/journals/bpea_macro/forum/200509bpea_gordon.pdf

Dincer, I., 2002, "The role of exergy in energy policy making", *Energy Policy*, 30 (2), pp. 137–149

Dinmore, G., 2006, "US marines probe tensions among Iran's minorities", *Financial Times*, February 23.

Donnelly, T. et al, 2000, *Rebuilding America's Defenses – Strategy, Forces and Resources For a New Century*, Washington DC (Project for the New American Century)

Dos Santos, T., 1970, "The Structure of Dependency", *American Economic Review*, LX, No. 2, May

Drozdiak, W., 1999, "NATO General Predicts Victory in Two Months" *Washington Post*, May 24

Du Bois, W.E.B., 1965 [1946], *The World and Africa, An Inquiry into the Part Which Africa has Played in World History*, New York (International Publishers)

Du Bois, W.E.B., 1970 [1900], "Address to the Nations of the World" in *W.E.B. Du Bois Speaks*, New York (Pathfinder).

Duke, L., 1998, "US faces surprise, dilemma in Africa", *Washington Post*, Tuesday, July 14

Dukes, J.S., 2003, "Burning Buried Sunshine: Human Consumption Of Ancient Solar Energy", *Climatic Change*, 61 pp. 31–44

Dunbar, R.I.M., 1998, "The social brain hypothesis", *Evolutionary Anthropology*, 6, pp.178–190

Dupré, Georges (ed.). 1991, *Savoirs paysans et Dévoloppement*, Paris (Karthala-ORSTOM)

Durand-Lasserve A. and M. Mattingly, 2005, "Sticking with tradition – How effective are new customary land delivery systems?" *ID21 Insights* no. 48 on http://www.id21 .org/insights/insights48/insights-iss48-art03.html

Edwards, David and D. Cromwell, 2005, *Guardians of Power – The Myth of the Liberal Media*, London (Pluto)

Ehrenreich, Barbara, 2007, "Pathologies of Hope", *Harper's*, February

Eliot, T.S., 1943, "Little Gidding" from *Four Quartets*

Elizondo, Rolando, 2001, *Theoretical and Methodological Elements for a Research on the Transference of Environmental Responsibilities within Subcontracting of Hazardous Processes in Mexican Domestic Industrial Firms*, paper, University College London

Encylopedia of Human Thermodynamics, http://www.eoht.info/page/Far-from-equilibrium

Engels, Frederick, 1969, *Anti-Dühring*, Moscow (Progress Publishers)

Ernst, Dieter and Kim, Linsu, 2002, "Global Production Networks, Knowledge Diffusion, and Local Capability Formation", *Research Policy*, 31, pp. 1417–1429

Escobar, Pepe, 2006, "Hezbollah south of the border", *Asia Times*, August 3

Euston Manifesto, statement of March 29 2006, on http://eustonmanifesto.org/joomla/ index.php?option=com_content&task=view&id=12&Itemid=38

Eve, Raymond A., 1997, "Afterword" in Eve, R.A., S. Horsfall, and M.E. Lee (eds.), *Chaos, Complexity, and Sociology*, London (Sage)

Fanon, F., 1968, *Wretched of the Earth*, New York (Grove Press)

Farmer, Richard D., 1999, *Statement of Richard D. Farmer (Principal Analyst Natural Resources and Commerce Division Congressional Budget Office) on the Domestic Costs of Sanctions on Foreign Commerce before the Subcommittee on Trade Committee on Ways and Means*, U.S. House of Representatives, May 27, on http://www.cbo.gov/showdoc.cfm?index=1293&sequence=0

Felker, Greg B., 2003, "Southeast Asian industrialisation and the changing global production system", *Third World Quarterly*, Vol. 34, no. 2, pp.255–282

Ferguson, N., 2005, "Sinking Globalization", *Foreign Affairs*, March/April

Fevre, Ralph, 1985, "Racism and Cheap Labour in UK Wool Textiles" in Newby H. et al (eds.) *Restructuring Capital – Recession and Reorganisation in Industrial Society*, Basingstoke (Macmillan)

Focus on the Global South and GRAIN, "World Food Day: Iraqi farmers aren't celebrating", 15 October 2004, revised Feb. 2005, on http://www.grain.org/nfg/?id=253

Forero, Juan, 2007, "Colombia May Seek Chiquita Extraditions – Eight Executives Targeted in Paramilitary Payment Scandal", *Washington Post*, March 21

Foucault, M., 1975, *Discipline and Punish: the Birth of the Prison*, New York (Random House)

——, 2003, *Society Must be Defended – Lectures at the Collège de France 1975–76*, London (Allen Lane)

Frank, A.G., 1978, *World Accumulation 1492–1789*, Basingstoke (Macmillan)

——, 1998, *ReOrient: Global Economy in the Asian Age*, Berkeley (Univ. of California Press)

Frazer, J.G., 1998, *The Golden Bough: a Study in Magic and Religion*, Oxford (Oxford University Press)

Fre, Zeremariam, 1990, *Pastoral Development in Eritrea and Eastern Sudan – Implications for Livestock* Extension Programmes, PhD thesis, Reading University

Freire, P., 1972, *Pedagogy of the Oppressed*, Harmondsworth (Penguin)

Fröbel, F., J. Heinrichs J. and O. Kreye, 1980, *The New International Division of Labour – Structural Unemployment in Industrial Countries and Industrialisation in Developing Countries*, Cambridge (Cambridge UP)

Fromm, Erich, 1942, *The Fear of Freedom*, London (Routledge and Kegan Paul)

Fuentes, Federico, 2007, "Pioneering the new socialism of the 21st century", *GreenLeft* online 25 January on http://www.greenleft.org.au/2007/696/36142

Fusaro, Peter C. and Gary M. Vasey, 2005a, "Today's Energy and Environmental Hedge Funds", *Commodities Now*, September

——, 2005b, *Energy hedge funds: it's all about risk/reward*, third quarter 2005 on www.energyhedgefunds.com

Gale, B.G., 1972, "Darwin and the Concept of a Struggle for Existence: A Study in the Extrascientific Origins of Scientific Ideas", *Isis*, Vol. 63, No. 3 (September), pp. 321–344

Gale, Fred P., 1998, "Theorizing Power in Ecological Economics", *Ecological Economics*, 27, pp. 131–138

Galland, David, 2007, "African Madness…Coming Soon to a Gas Pump Near You", *Resource Investor*, May 4 on http://www.resourceinvestor.com/pebble.asp?relid =31470

Ganser, Daniele, 2005, "Terrorism in Western Europe: An Approach to NATO's Secret Stay-Behind Armies", *Whitehead Journal of Diplomacy and International Relations*, Winter/Spring on http://www.php.isn.ethz.ch/services/publist/docu-ments/Terrorism_Western_Europe.pdf

Gelbspan, Ross, 2005, "Hurricane Katrina's real name", *Boston Globe*, August 31

George Mason University, *History News Network, Washington Update*, Vol. 12, #25; June 1 2006 on http://hnn.us/roundup/entries/26015.html

Georgescu-Roegen, Nicholas, 1975, "Energy and Economic Myths", *Southern Economic Journal*, 41, no. 3, January; on http://www.geocities.com/combusem/GEORGESC .HTM

Gereffi, Gary, 2001, "Shifting Governance Structures in Global Commodity Chains, with Special Reference to the Internet", *American Behavioral Scientist*, Vol. 44 No. 10, pp. 1616–1637

German-Foreign-Policy 2006, July 6th, on http://www.german-foreign-policy.com/en/ fulltext/56013

Gindin, Jonah, 2006, "To Sow the Oil, or Give it Away? Canada and Venezuela are pursuing very different oil policies. In the war of the wells, whose investment will bring the biggest return?" *Z Magazine* Dec 4 on http://www.zmag.org/content/ print_article.cfm?itemID=11562&sectionID=1

Ginzberg E. et al, 1986, *Technology and Employment*, Boulder Col. (Westview)

Glaeser, B. and K. Phillips-Howard, 1987, "Low-energy Farming Systems in Nigeria" in Glaeser (ed.) *The Green Revolution Revisited – Critique and Alternatives*, London (Allen and Unwin)

Glendinning, Lee, 2007, "RAF pilots asked to consider suicide flight", *Guardian*, April 3

Global Labour Strategies, 2007, "The Global Battle Over New Rights for Chinese Workers", April 3 on http://laborstrategies.blogs.com/global_labor_strategies/2007/ 04/in_a_historical.html#more

Good K. And S. Hughes, 2002, "Globalisation and Diversification: Two Cases in Southern Africa", *African Affairs*, 101, pp. 39–59

Goonatilake, Susantha, 1982, *Crippled Minds – An Exploration into Colonial Culture*, New Delhi (Vikas)

Gorz, A., 1992, "L'écologie politique entre expertocratie et autolimitation", *Actuel Marx*, No. 12

Gowans, Stephen, 2007, "What's Really Going On in Zimbabwe: Mugabe Gets the Milosevic Treatment", *Counterpunch*, March 23, on: http://www.counterpunch.org/gowans03232007.html

GRAIN, 2007, *The New Scramble for Africa* on http://www.grain.org/seedling_files/seed-07-07-6-en.pdf

Gramsci, A., 1971 [1927–33], *Selections from Prison Notebooks*, London (Lawrence and Wishart)

Grange, David L., 2007, "Developing Irregular Warfare Leaders for the 21st Century", *National Strategy Forum Review*, Vol. 16, issue 3, Summer, on http://www.nationalstrategy.com/Asymmetry.Summer07NSFR.pdf

Gresh, Alain, 1988, "Une fondation au-dessus de tout soupçon", in *Le Monde diplomatique: Le Libéralisme contre les Libertés*, Paris.

Griffin, R., n.d. *The Meaning of 'Sacrifice' in the First World War* on http://www.ideologiesofwar.com/papers/griffin_sacrifice.html

Gross, Daniel, 2007, Does It Even Matter if the U.S. Has a Cold?, *New York Times*, May 6

Grossman, L., 2009, "Hidden patterns reveal a book's true meaning", *New Scientist*, August 15

Guerrera, Francesco and James Politi, 2007, "Moody's slams private equity" *Financial Times*, July 8

Guha, R., 1983, *Elementary Aspects of Peasant Insurgency in Colonial India*, Delhi (OUP)

Guyatt, N., 2000, *Another American century? : the United States and the world after 2000*, New York (Zed Books)

Hacker, Jacob S., 2007, "Universal Risk Insurance" in New America Foundation, *Ten Big Ideas for a New America*, Washington DC on http://www.newamerica.net/publications/policy/ten_big_ideas_for_a_new_america

Hamilton, C., 2007, "Building on Kyoto", *New Left Review*, May-June

Hansen, James, 2007, "Huge sea level rises are coming – unless we act now", *New Scientist*, July 25 on http://environment.newscientist.com/article.ns?id=mg19526141.600&feedId=climate-change_rss20

Hardin, Garret, 1968, "The Tragedy of the Commons", *Science*, vol. 162

Harris, Jerry, 2005, "Emerging Third World Powers: China, India and Brazil", *Race and Class*, 46, 3

Hartsock, Nancy, 1983, *Money, Sex and Power – Toward a Feminist Historical Materialism* (Northeast University Press)

Hasenclever A., P Mayer and V Rittberger, 1997, *Theories of International Regimes*, Cambridge (Cambridge University Press)

Hawken P., A Lovins. and L.H. Lovins, 1999, *Natural Capitalism: Creating the Next Industrial Revolution*, Boston (Little Brown), downloadable on http://www.natcap .org/sitepages/pid20.php

Hayek, Friedrich A., 1964, "The Theory of Complex Phenomena", in Bunge M (editor), *The Critical Approach to Science and Philosophy*, London (Collier-Macmillan)

——, 1973, *Law, Legislation and Liberty*, Vol. I, London (Routledge)

——, 1978, *New Studies in Philosophy, Politics, Economics and the History of Ideas*, London, (Routledge and Kegan Paul)

Hearn, Julie, 2001, "The 'Uses and Abuses' of Civil Society in Africa", *Review of African Political Economy*, No. 87, March

Hedges, Chris and Laila al-Arian, 2007, "The carnage, the blown-up bodies I saw … Why? What was this for?", *Guardian*, July 13

Hegel, G.F., 1969, *The Science of Logic*, trans. A.V. Miller, London (George Allen and Unwin)

Heinberg, Richard, 2006, "Fifty Million Farmers", *Energy Bulletin*, 17 Nov on http://energybulletin.net/22584.htm

Helm, Dieter, 2007, *British Energy Policy – After the White paper and the September package*, presentation to the Prime Minister's Strategy Unit, November 5th, on www .dieterhelm.co.uk/presentations/PMSU_Nov_07.ppt

——, Robin Smale and Jonathan Phillips, 2007, "Too Good To Be True? The UK's Climate Change Record", *Guardian*, December 12

Henderson, David, 1999, *The MAI Affair – A Story and its Lessons*, London (Royal Institute of International Affairs)

Herman, Edward, 2007, "Iraq: The Genocide Option", *ZNet*, January 24

Hersh, Seymour M., 2007, "The Redirection: Is the Administration's new policy benefitting our enemies in the war on terrorism?", *New Yorker*, March 5

Heylighen, Francis and Paul Cilliers, and Carlos Gershenson, 2006, "Complexity and Philosophy", in *Complexity, Science, and Society*, Oxford (Radcliffe)

Heyne, Christian, 2006, "Haiti – Two views of a world", *Z Magazine*, March 21

Hirsch, Robert et al, 2005, *Peaking of world oil production: impacts, mitigation, and risk management*, United States Government [Department of Energy]

Hobson, John A., 1902, *Imperialism – A Study*, New York (James Pott & Co.)

Hodgson G.M. and T. Knudsen, 2006, "Why we need a generalized Darwinism, and why a generalized Darwinism is not enough", *Journal of Economic Behaviour and Organization*, Vol. 61, No. 1, September, pp. 1–19

Holland, Greg J. and Peter J. Webster, 2007, "Heightened tropical cyclone activity in the North Atlantic: natural variability or climate trend?", *Philosophical Transactions of the Royal Society A*

Holzer, Jessica, 2006, "The Joys Of Going Nuclear?", *Forbes,* May 25

Howden, Daniel, 2007, "The fight for the world's food", *The Independent,* June 23

Humphrey, John and Hubert Schmitz, 2002, "How Does Insertion in Global Value Chains Act Upgrading in Industrial Clusters?", *Regional Studies,* 36, 9, pp. 1017–1024

Hymer, S.H., 1990, "The Large Multinational 'Corporation': an Analysis of Some Motives for the International Integration of Business" in Casson M. (ed.) *Multinational Corporations,* Aldershot (Edward Elgar)

Isaksen, Arne, 2001, "Building Regional Innovation Systems: Is Endogenous Industrial Development Possible in the Global Economy?", *Canadian Journal of Regional Science,* XXIV, 1, pp. 101–120

Jackson, John H., 1998, *The World Trade Organisation – Constitution and Jurisprudence,* London (Royal Institute of International Affairs)

Jaffe, Amy Myers, 2007, *The Changing Role of National Oil Companies in International Energy Markets – Introduction and Summary Conclusions,* James A. Baker III Institute for Public Policy, Rice University, March on: http://www.rice.edu/energy/publications/docs/NOCs/Presentations/Hou-Jaffe-KeyFindings.pdf

James A. Baker Institute of Public Policy, Rice University, 2005 *Energy and Nanotechnology – Strategy for the Future,* on http://www.rice.edu/energy/publications/docs/NanoReport.pdf

James, CLR., 1982, The *Black Jacobins: Toussaint L'Ouverture and the San Domingo Revolution,* London (Allison & Busby)

Jenkinson, Jacqueline, 2007, "Black Sailors on Red Clydeside: Rioting, Reactionary Trade Unionism and Conflicting Notions of 'Britishness' Following the First World War", *Twentieth Century British History,* October.

Jensen, Derrick, n.d., *Endgame, Vol. I, The Problem of Civilization,* http://www.endgamethebook.org/index.html

Jervis, Robert and Jack Snyder (eds.), 1991, *Dominoes and Bandwagons – Strategic Beliefs and Great Power Competition in the Eurasian Rimland,* New York (Oxford University Press)

Jessop, Bob, 2001, 'Regulationist and Autopoieticist Reflections on Polanyi's Account of Market Economies and the Market, *New Political Economy,* 6 (2), pp. 213–232

Johnson B, 2009, "The meat's off: flesh-eating robots turn vegetarian", *Guardian,* July 21

Johnson, J.A., J. Carroll, J. Gottschall, and D. Kruger, 2008, "Hierarchy in the library: Egalitarian dynamics in Victorian novels", *Evolutionary Psychology,* Vol. 6 No. 4

Johnson, Nathanael, 2006, "Swine of the times: The making of the modern pig" *Harper's*, May

Johnston, David Cay, 2007 a, "'04 Income in U.S. Was Below 2000 Level" *New York Times*, November 27

Johnston, David Cay, 2007 b, "Income Gap Is Widening, Data Shows" *New York Times*, March 29

Jones, Mark, 2001, *Stand-off between Opec and Russia?* 20 November on http://wsarch .ucr.edu/wsnmail/2001/msg01791.html

Juhasz, Antonia, 2007, "Whose Oil Is It, Anyway?" *New York Times*, March 13

Jung, Sung-ki, 2005, "USFK Lost Depleted Uranium: Activist" *Korea Times*, Dec. 23, on http://search.hankooki.com/times/times_view.php?term=depleted+uranium++ &path=hankooki3/times/lpage/200512/kt2005122317370310230.htm&media=kt

Kagan, Robert, 2005, "A Higher Realism", *Washington Post*, January 23

Kanter, James, 2007, "Despite warnings, oil usage expected to increase", *International Herald Tribune*, July 9

Kaplan, Robert D., 2007, "On Forgetting the Obvious", *The American Interest*, Vol II, no. 6, July/August, on http://www.the-american-interest.com/ai2/index.cfm

Kaplinski, Raphael, 1995, "Technique and System: the Spread of Japanese Management Techniques to Developing Countries", *World Development*, 23, 1, pp. 57–71

Kauffman S.A. and S. Johnsen, 1991, "Coevolution to the Edge of Chaos: Coupled Fitness Landscapes, Poised States and Coevolutionary Avalanches", *Journal of Theoretical Biology*, No. 149, pp. 467–505

Kautsky, K., 1914, "Ultra-Imperialism" *Die Neue Zeit*, September 1914 on http://www .marxists.org/archive/kautsky/1914/09/ultra-imp.htm

Keck, M.E. and K. Sikkink, 1998, *Activists Beyond Borders – Advocacy Networks in International Politics*, Ithaca (Cornell UP)

Keeble, D. and F. Wilkinson, 1998, "Collective Learning and Knowledge Development in the Evolution of Regional Clusters of High Technology SMEs in Europe", *Regional Studies*, 33, 4, pp. 295–303

Kegley, C.W. and E.R. Wittkopf, 1979, *American Foreign Policy, Patterns and Process*, New York (St Martin's Press)

Kendall, Ann, 2005, "Applied archaeology: revitalizing indigenous agricultural technology within an Andean community", *Public Archaeology*, volume 4

Kim Young-Ho, 1987, "Towards an Articulation of Dependency and Development Paradigms: Development of Semi-Development in the Korean Economy" in Kim Kyong-Dong (ed) *Dependency Issues in Korean Development*, Seoul (Seoul National University Press)

Kindiki, M., 2007, *The Role of International Regimes in the Governance of Global Value Chains: A Study of Apparel 'Exportism' in Kenya*, University College London

Kings College London, International Centre for Prison Studies, *Prison Brief for the United States of America* on www.kcl.ac.uk/depsta/rel/icps/worldbrief/north_america_records.php?code=190

Klein, Naomi, 2007, "Baghdad Burns, Calgary Booms" *The Nation*, June 18

Knight, Rebecca, 2007, "Home loans are more expensive for minorities" *Financial Times*, March 16

Kojima, K., 1977, *Japan and a New World Economic Order*, Boulder Col. (Westview)

Kolko, G. 2007, "Israel's Last Chance", AntiWar.com, March 17, on http://www.antiwar.com/orig/kolko.php?articleid=10689

Kopinak, Kathryn, 1995, "Transitions in the Maquilization of Mexican Industry", *Labour, Capital and Society*, 28, 1

Koponen, Juhani, 1991 "Agricultural Systems in late Pre-Colonial Tanzania" in Morner M. and Svensson T. (eds) *The Transformation of Rural Society in the Third World*, London (Routledge).

Krugman, Paul, 1994, "The Myth of Asia's Miracle", *Foreign Affairs*, November-December

——, 2005, "Safe as Houses", *New York Times*, August 12

——, 2006, "Graduates Versus Oligarchs", *New York Times*, February 27

Lahneman, W., 2003, *The War on Terrorism and International Stability: A New Precarious Balance?*, American Political Science Association conference paper, August

Lam, D. K-K. and I. Lee, 1992, "Guerrilla Capitalism and the Limits of Statist Theory" in Clark C. and Chan S., *The Evolving Pacific Basin in the Global Political Economy*, Boulder (Lynne Rienner)

Lampe, David, 1968, *The Last Ditch: Britain's Resistance Plans against the Nazis*, London (Cassell)

Lancaster, Brad, 1996, "The man who farms water", *Permaculture Drylands Journal*, April on http://ag.arizona.edu/oals/ALN/aln46/lancaster.html

Landim, Leilah, 1993, "Brazilian Crossroads" in Wignaraja P. (ed.) *New Social Movements in the South – Empowering the People*, London (Zed Books)

Langley, Chris, 2005, *Soldiers in the Laboratory: Military involvement in science and technology— and some alternatives*, Folkestone (Scientists for Global Responsibility)

Lappé, Frances Moore and Rachel Schurman, 1989, *Taking Population Seriously*, London (Earthscan)

Lawrence, Felicity, 2007, "Pioneering Welsh town begins the transition to a life without oil", *Guardian*, April 7

Lazarus, David, 2001, "CalPERS, Carlyle profit from Afghan war", *San Francisco Chronicle*, December 2

Le Houérou, Henry, 1989, *The Grazing Land Ecosystems of the African Sahel*, Berlin (Springer-Verlag)

Lecler, Yveline, 2002, "The Cluster Role in the Development of the Thai Car Industry", *International Journal of Urban and Regional Research*, 26, 4, pp. 799–814

Leffler, M.P., 1994, "National Security and United States Foreign Policy" in Leffler and Painter D. (eds.) *Origins of the Cold War*, London (Routledge)

Leggett, J., 2006, "What they don't want you to know about the coming oil crisis", *The Independent*, January 20

Lenin, V.I., 1961 [1915], "On the question of dialectics" *Lenin Collected Works*, Vol. 38, London (Lawrence and Wishart)

——, 1939, *Imperialism, the Highest Stage of Capitalism*, New York (International Publishers)

Lerner, Gerda, 1987, *The Creation of Patriarchy*, Oxford (Oxford UP)

Lévi-Strauss, Claude, 1958, *Anthropologie structurale*, Paris (Plon)

Lewchuk, W. and P. Stewart, 2001, "Empowerment as a Trojan Horse – New Systems of Work Organisation in the North American Automobile Industry" *Economic and Industrial Democracy*, 22, 4

Lidal, B., 2005, "Lockdown America Revisited – A Conversation with Christian Parenti on Prisons, Policing, and the War on Terror", *Z Magazine*, December, on http://www.zmag.org/content/showarticle.cfm?SectionID=43&ItemID=9292

Lima, Ivan B.T. et al, 2007, "Methane Emissions from Large Dams as Renewable Energy Resources: A Developing Nation Perspective", *Mitigation and Adaptation Strategies for Global Change*, April

Linear, M., 1985, *Zapping the Third World – the Disaster of Development Aid*, London (Pluto)

List, Friedrich, 1983 [1837], *The Natural System of Political Economy*, London (Frank Cass)

Liu, Henry C.K., 2007, posting to A-List discussion group March 16, on http://lists .econ.utah.edu/pipermail/a-list/2007-March.txt.gz

Lloyd-Jones, D., 2004, *Technical Cosmopolitanism: Systems, Critical Theory and International Relations*, Leeds University School of Politics and International Studies, Working Paper No. 6, February

Lobell, David B. and Christopher B. Field, 2007, "Global scale climate–crop yield relationships and the impacts of recent warming" *Environmental Research Letters* 2

Lovelock J. and L. Margulis, 1974, "Atmospheric Homeostasis by and for the Biosphere", *Tellus*, XXVI

Lowther, William and Colin Freeman, 2007, "US funds terror groups to sow chaos in Iran", *Sunday Telegraph*, February 25

Lubeck, Paul M., Michael J. Watts and Ronnie Lipschutz, 2007, *Convergent Interests: U.S. Energy Security and the "Securing" of Nigerian Democracy*, Washington DC (Centre for International Policy) February on http://www.ciponline.org/NIGERIA _FINAL.pdf

Lugar, Richard G., 2006, (Chairman, Committee on Foreign Relations United States Senate), *The Backlash against Democracy Assistance*, Washington DC (National Endowment for Democracy), on http://www.ned.org/publications/publications .html

Luminet, J.-P., 1992, *Black Holes*, Cambridge (Cambridge University Press)

Luttwak, Edward N., 2007, "Dead End – Counterinsurgency warfare as military malpractice", *Harper's*, February

Luxemburg, R., 1913, *Die Akkumulation des Kapitals – eine Beitrag zur Ökonomischen Erklarung des Imperialismus*, Berlin (Paul Singer)

——, 1972, *The Accumulation of Capital – an Anti-Critique*, New York (Monthly Review Press)

Lydersen, K. 2007, "Pollution Fight Pits Illinois vs. BP, Indiana" *Washington Post*, August 23

Lyons, Terence, 2000, "US Diplomacy" in: Centre for Strategic and International Studies, Washington DC, *A Review of US Africa Policy – Draft discussion document for presentation at the Woodrow Wilson Centre Conference, 'The Future of US Africa Policy'*, December

Macarov, D., 2003, *What the Market Does to People – Privatisation, Globalization and Poverty*, Atlanta (Clarity Press)

Mackay, Neil, 2007, "How Britain created Ulster's murder gangs" *Sunday Herald*, January 28.

Mackinder, H.J., 1904, "The Geographical Pivot of History", *The Geographical Journal*, Vol. 23, no. 4

Mackintosh, James and Martin Arnold, 2007, "French probe buy-out collusion" *Financial Times*, June 7

Mackovich, Bill, 2007, "Mining black gold, and profits, from northern sands", *People's Weekly World Newspaper*, August 23 on http://www.pww.org/article/articleview/ 11600/1/387/

Magdoff, Fred, 2006, "The Explosion of Debt and Speculation", *Monthly Review*, November

Malaina, Alvaro, n.d., *Edgar Morin et Jesus Ibañez : la sociologie et les théories de la complexité*, duplicated

Malerba F. and Orsenigo L., 2000, "Knowledge, Innovative Activities and Industrial Evolution" *Industrial and Corporate Change*, 9, 2

Mamdani, Mahmood, 2007, "The Politics of Naming: Genocide, Civil War, Insurgency", *London Review of Books* Vol. 29 No. 5, 8 March

Manwaring, Max G., 2007, *Latin America's new security reality: irregular asymmetric conflict and Hugo Chavez*, Carlisle, PA (Strategic Studies Institute, U.S. Army) August on www.StrategicStudiesInstitute.army.mil

Mao Zedong, 1969, "The Situation and our Policy after Victory in the War of Resistance against Japan", Mao Tse-tung [Mao Zedong] *Selected Works Vol. 4*, Peking [Beijing] (Foreign Languages Press)

Mao Zedong, 1985, Interview with Anna Lousie Strong, Jan 17 1964, in Strong, Tracy B. and Helene Keyssar, "Anna Louise Strong: Three Interviews with Chairman Mao Zedong", *The China Quarterly*, No. 103, pp. 489–509; Sept

Marglin F. and Marglin A., (eds) 1990, *Dominating Knowledge – Development, Culture and Resistance*, Oxford (Clarendon Press)

Marks, Kathy, 2007, "Australia's epic drought: The situation is grim" *The Independent*, April 20

Marx, K., 1954, *Capital Vol. I*, Moscow (Foreign Languages Publishing House)

——, 1965, Letter to Engels in Manchester, 8th October 1858, Marx, Karl and Frederick Engels, *Selected Correspondence, second edition*, Moscow (Progress Publishers)

——, 1969 a [1848]. "Manifesto of the Communist Party", *Marx and Engels, Selected Works. Vol I*, Moscow (Progress Publishers)

——, 1969 b [1849] "Wage Labour and Capital", Marx and Engels, *Selected Works Vol. I*, Moscow (Progress Publishers)

——, 1969 c [1865]. "Wages, Price and Profit", Marx and Engels, *Selected Works Vol. II*, Moscow (Progress Publishers)

——, 1969 d The Civil War in France [1871], Marx and Engels, *Selected Works Vol. II*, Moscow (Progress Publishers)

——, 1969 e, *Theories of Surplus Value, Volume 2*, London (Lawrence and Wishart)

——, 1970, "Marginal Notes to the Programme of the German Workers' Party", Marx and Engels *Selected Works Vol. III*, Moscow (Progress Publishers)

——, 1971, *Capital Volume II*, Moscow (Progress Publishers)

Masood, Salman, 2007, "Throngs Attend Speech by Pakistan's Suspended Justice" *New York Times*, May 7

Massarat, Mohsen, 1987, "The Energy Crisis", in Nore, Petter and Terisa Turner, (eds.), *Oil and the Class Struggle*, London (Zed Books)

Mazzocchi, Fulvio, 2008, "Complexity in biology. Exceeding the limits of reductionism and determinism using complexity theory" in *EMBO reports* 9, 1, 10–14, on http://www.nature.com/embor/journal/v9/n1/full/7401147.html

McDonald, Joe, 2007, "China Forming Fund to Invest Reserves", *Washington Post*, March 9

McKibben, Bill, 2008, *Deep Economy: The Wealth of Communities and the Durable Future*, (Holt)

McNulty, Sheila, 2007, "Nationalism and state ownership seen as main threats to oil supply", *Financial Times*, May 10

Meadows, D.L. et al, 1972, *The Limits to Growth*, London (Earth Island)

Meikle, S., Ramasut T. and J. Walker,1999, *Sustainable Urban Livelihoods – Concepts and Implications for Policy*, London (Development Planning Unit)

Meister, R., 1994, *Beyond Satisfaction: Desire, Consumption and the Future of Socialism*, London SOAS September (duplicated)

Merchant, Carolyn, 1990, *The Death of Nature*, New York (Harper)

Merk, J., 2004, "Regulating the Global Athletic Footwear Industry – the Collective Worker in the Production Chain" in van der Pijl K. et al (eds.) *Global Regulation – Managing Crises after the Imperial Turn*, Basingstoke (Palgrave Macmillan)

Miller, T. Christian, 2007, "Private contractors outnumber U.S. troops in Iraq", *Los Angeles Times*, July 4

Miranda, Moema, 2007, "Rebuild politics as a place for alternatives and common goods" in Wainwright H. et al (eds.) *Networked politics – Rethinking political organisation in an age of movements and networks*, Amsterdam (Transnational Institute)

Molden, David and Charlotte de Fraiture, 2004, *Investing in Water for Food, Ecosystems and Livelihoods*, discussion paper, Stockholm (Comprehensive Assessment of Water Management in Agriculture)

Monbiot, George, 2005, "Worse than Fossil Fuel", *Guardian*, December 6

——, 2006, "We need omega-3 oils for our brains to function properly – but where will they come from?", *Guardian*, June 20

——, 2006, "The emerging disaster at Dounreay is a powerful argument for open government", *Guardian*, September 12

——, 2007 "An audit of the government's planned carbon cuts shows they will achieve only half of what it claims", *Guardian*, March 5

Morgenson, Gretchen, 2007, "Crisis Looms in Mortgages", *New York Times*, March 11

Morris, Steven, 2008 a, "Council used terror law to spy on fishermen", *Guardian*, May 14

——, 2008 b, "Veg seed sales soar as credit crunch bites", *Guardian*, April 22

Morrison, Kevin, 2007, "US's ethanol future depends on foreign fertiliser supplies", *Financial Times*, March 27

Mouawad, Jad, 2007, "Oil Innovations Pump New Life Into Old Wells", New York Times, March 5

Murswiek, Dietrich, 2003, *The American Strategy of Preemptive War and International Law*, Albert-Ludwigs-Universität Freiburg, Institute of Public Law, March

Nabudere, D., 1977, *The Political Economy of Imperialism*, London (Zed Books)

National Peasant Front Ezequeil Zamora (Venezuela) 2006, *We will defeat the paramilitaries with the people organized*, June on http://a-manila.org/newswire/display/391/index.php

Natsios, Andrew S., 2006, "Five Debates on International Development: The US Perspective", *Development Policy Review*, 24, 2

Newman, Peter J. and Victor A. Burk, 2005, *Presenting the full picture – oil and gas: reserves measurement and reporting in the 21st century*, Deloitte Touche Tohmatsu, briefing paper

Nicholas Petreley, *Open source closes backdoors*, LinuxWorld.com 11/10/00 on http://www.itworld.com/AppDev/1303/lw-11-penguin_2/

Noble, Dennis, 2006, *The Music of Life – Biology beyond genes*, Oxford (Oxford University Press)

Nore, Petter and Terisa Turner, (eds.), 1980, *Oil and the Class Struggle*, London (Zed Books)

Norris, Floyd, 2007, "Bulging Profits in U.S. Often Originate Overseas", *New York Times*, August 4

North, Gary, 2006, "There Are Two Ways To Gain Cooperation", LeeRockwell.com March 9 on http://slate.msn.com/id/2112608/

Norton-Taylor, Richard, 2007, "At the sharp end of war", *Guardian*, February 15

Nowak, M., 2006, "Five Rules for the Evolution of Cooperation", *Science*, December 8

Nwoke, Chibuzo,1987, *Raw Materials and Global Pricing*, London (Zed Books)

O Tuathail, Gearoid, 1996, *Critical Geopolitics – The Politics of Writing Global Space*, London (Routledge)

OECD, Accueil : Science et innovation: "Brazil, China and India Share Knowledge Strategies, Wilton Park (UK), 17 April 2001" on http://www.oecd.org/document/9/0,2340,fr_2649_37417_2373065_1_1_1_37417,00.html

Offe, Claus, 1996, *Modernity and the State: East, West*, Cambridge Mass. (MIT Press)

Okamuro, H., 2001, "Risk sharing in the supplier relationship: new evidence from the Japanese automotive industry", *Journal of Economic Behavior and Organization*, Vol. 45, pp. 361–381

Oliver, N. and B. Wilkinson, 1988, *The Japanization of British Industry*, Oxford (Blackwell)

Organisation for Economic Co-operation and Development (OECD), 2007, "Development aid from OECD countries fell 5.1% in 2006" (press release), April 3 on http://www.oecd.org/document/17/0,2340,en_2649_33721_38341265_1 _1_1_1,00.html

Ostrom, Elinor, 2005, *Understanding Institutional Diversity*, Princeton (Princeton University Press)

Palpacuer, Florence and Aurelio Parisotto, 1998, *Global production and local jobs: new perspectives on enterprise networks, employment and local development policy*, discussion paper, International Institute for Labour Studies, Geneva

Panitchpakdi, Supachai, 2004, *American Leadership and the World Trade Organization: What is the Alternative?*, National Press Club — Washington D.C., February 26, on http://www.wto.org/english/news_e/spsp_e/spsp22_e.htm

Pearce, Fred, 2005, "Forests paying the price for biofuels", *New Scientist*, November 22

Peoples' Global Action against 'Free' Trade and the World Trade Organisation, Chiapas, 29 November 1997, on www.hartford-hwp.com/archives/25a/024.html

Perl, Raphael F., 1998, *Terrorism: US Response to Bombings in Kenya and Tanzania – A New Policy Direction*, Congressional Research Service Report 98–733F, September

Peschard-Sverdrup, Armand B., n.d. *North American Future 2025 Project*, Washington DC (Centre for Strategic and International Studies) on http://www.canadians.org/ water/documents/NA_Future_2025.pdf

Petermann, Anne, 2005, "International Status of GE Trees": UN FAO Report quoted in *The International Status of Genetically Modified Trees*, Global Justice Ecology Project, on http://www.worldagroforestrycentre.org/downloads/International%20Status %20of%20GE%20Trees.pdf

Phillips, Kathleen, 2003, "In war times, growing gardens may yield relaxing, useful benefits", *AgNews* (Texas A&M University System Agriculture Program), April 4 on http://agnews.tamu.edu/dailynews/stories/HORT/Apr0403a.htm

Pigou, Arthur C., 1932, *The Economics of Welfare*, London (Macmillan) Fourth edition

Pearce, Roy Harvey, 1953, *The Savages of America: A Study of the Indian and the Idea of Civilization*, Baltimore (John Hopkins Press)

Pimentel, David, and Tad W. Patzek, 2005, "Ethanol Production Using Corn, Switchgrass, and Wood; Biodiesel Production Using Soybean and Sunflower", *Natural Resources Research*, Vol. 14, No. 1, March

Pinkerton, James, 2006, "The world should prepare for a Nato-style oil alliance", *Financial Times*, April 20

Piombo, Jessica R., 2007, "Terrorism and U.S. Counter-Terrorism Programs in Africa: An Overview" in *Strategic Insights*, (US Navy) Volume VI, Issue 1 (January) on http://www.ccc.nps.navy.mil/si/2007/Jan/piomboJan07.asp#references

Podobnik, B., 2002, "Global Energy Inequalities: Exploring the Long-Term Implications", *Journal of World-Systems Research*, VIII, 2

Polanyi, K., 1944, *The Great Transformation*, New York (Rinehart & Company)

Polanyi, M., 1962, *The Tacit Dimension*, New York (Doubleday)

Ponna, Wignaraja and Akmal Hussain (eds), 1989, *The Challenge in South Asia: Development, Democracy and Regional Cooperation*, New Delhi (Sage Publications, India)

Portes, Alejandro and J. Walton, 1981, *Labor, Class and the International System*, New York (Academic Press)

Principia Cybernetica, (n.d.), *Dictionary of Cybernetics and Systems* on http://pespmc1. vub.ac.be/ASC/SOCIAL_ENTRO.html accessed February 2006.

Psoinos, A. and S. Smithson, 2002, "Employee empowerment in manufacturing – a study of organisations in the UK", *New Technology, Work and Employment*, 17, 2

Pyka, Andreas, 1999, *Innovation Networks in Economics: from the Incentive-based to the Knowledge-based Approaches*, working paper, INRA-SERD, Grenoble, France

Queuille, P., 1969, *L'Amérique latine – la Doctrine Monroe et le Panaméricanisme*, Paris (Payot)

Rahman, Taimur, 2006, *World Social Forum Karachi : A left critique*, March 17, circulated by e-mail

Rangwala, G., 2006, *Planning for regime change – again*, Labour Left Briefing -June on http://middleeastreference.org.uk/llb060520.html

Raskin, P. et al, 2002, *Great Transition: The Promise and Lure of the Times Ahead*, (revised ed. 2008) on http://www.eoearth.org/article/Great_Transition:_The _Promise_and_Lure_of_the_Times_Ahead_%28e-book%29

Ravallion, M., 2003, *The Debate on Globalization, Poverty and Inequality: Why Measurement Matters,*. Washington DC: World Bank Policy Research Working Paper 3038

Reason, P., and, B.C. Goodwin, 1999, "Toward a Science of Qualities in Organizations: Lessons from complexity theory and postmodern biology", *Concepts and Transformations*, 4, 3, pp. 281–317

Reiff, David, 2003, "Were Sanctions Right?", *New York Times*, July 27

Reuters, 2006, "Energy Firms Bow to Demands Set by Bolivia", October 30

——, 2007, "U.S. military cemetery running out of space", September 20, on http://uk.reuters.com/article/latestCrisis/idUKN2039677420070920

Revkin, Andrew C., 2007, "The Climate Divide – Reports From Four Fronts in the War on Warming", *New York Times*, April 3

Ricardo. D., 1951, *On the Principles of Political Economy and Taxation* – The Works and Correspondence of David Ricardo ed. Sraffa, Vol. I, Cambridge (Cambridge University Press)

Rice, Condoleezza, 2005, "The Promise of Democratic Peace", *Washington Post*, December 11

Richards, Paul, 1985, *Indigenous Agricultural Revolution – Ecology and Food Production in West Africa*, London (Hutchinson)

Rigby, P., 1985, *Persistent Pastoralists*, London (Zed Books)

Roach, Stephen, 2007, (chief economist, Morgan Stanley) From *Globalization to Localization*, January 07, on http://www.morganstanley.com/views/perspectives/index.html#anchor4201

Robb, John, 2006, "Security – power to the people", *Fast Company Magazine*, issue 103, March, on http://www.fastcompany.com/magazine/103/essay-security.html

——, blog, http://globalguerrillas.typepad.com/globalguerrillas/2007/04/nigerias_open_s.html

Roberts, A., 2006, *A History of the English Speaking Peoples Since 1900*, London (Weidenfeld and Nicholson)

Roberts, Les, 2007, "Iraq's death toll is far worse than our leaders admit – The US and Britain have triggered an episode more deadly than the Rwandan genocide" *The Independent*, February 14

Robinson, William L., 1996, *Promoting Polyarchy – Globalisation, US Intervention and Hegemony*, Cambridge (Cambridge University Press)

Rode, R. and D.A. Deese, 2004, *Governance and Hegemonic Regime Stabilzation in the Doha Round*, Conference Paper, ISA Convention, Montréal, March

Rodney, W., 1972, *How Europe Underdeveloped Africa*, London (Bogle-l'Ouverture)

Roederer, Juan G., 2003, "On the Concept of Information and its Role in Nature", *Entropy*, 5

Roig-Franzia, Manuel, 2007, "A Culinary and Cultural Staple in Crisis: Mexico Grapples With Soaring Prices for Corn – and Tortillas", *Washington Post*, January 27

Ronfeldt, David F., J. Arquilla, G.E. Fuller and M. Fuller, 1998, *The Zapatista Social Netwar in Mexico*, Washington D.C. (RAND)

Ronneburger, Jan-Uwe, 2007, "Ethanol: Washington's biological weapon against Chavez", *Deutsche Presse-Agentur* March 9, on http://canadiandimension.com/articles/2007/03/09/967/

Roosevelt, Theodore, 1904, *Annual Message to Congress*, December 6

Rosenberg, Tina, 2007, "Reverse Foreign Aid", *New York Times*, March 25

Rosset, P., 2000, "Cuba: A Successful Case Study of Sustainable Agriculture" in Magdoff, Fred, John Bellamy Foster and Frederick H. Butte (eds.): *Hungry for Profit: The Agribusiness Threat to Farmers, Food and the Environment*, New York (Monthly Review Press)

Rosset, Peter, "Small Is Bountiful", *The Ecologist*, v.29, i. 8, December 9 on http://www .mindfully.org/Farm/Small-Farm-Benefits-Rosset.htm

Rostow, W.W., 1960, *The Process of Economic Growth*, Oxford (Clarendon) 2nd edition

Rousseau, Jean-Jacques, 1964, "Extrait du Projet de Paix perpétuelle de Monsieur l'Abbé de Saint Pierre" [1759] in Rousseau, *Oeuvres complètes, Tome III* Paris (Gallimard)

Roy, Arundhati, 2007, *On India's Growing Violence: 'It's Outright War and Both Sides are Choosing Their Weapons'*, March 25, on http://www.commondreams.org/ archive/2007/03/25/77/print/

Rubinstein, W.D., 1986, *Wealth and Inequality in Britain*, London (Faber and Faber)

Rucker, Patrick, 2007, "Wall Street often shelved damaging subprime reports" *Reuters*, July 27.

Rumsfeld, Donald, 2002, "Transforming the Military", *Foreign Affairs*, May-June

Ryn, Claes G., 2003, "The Ideology of American Empire", *Orbis*, Summer

Rynn, Jonathan, 2003, *A Systems-based, Production-centered Theory of Political Economy*, conference paper, American Political Science Association, August

Salas, María Angélica, 1991, "The Categories of Space and Time and the Production of Potatoes in the Mantaro Valley, Peru" in Dupré, Georges (ed.) *Savoirs paysans et Développement*, Paris (Karthala-ORSTOM)

Sauvy, A., 1952, "Trois mondes, une planète", *L'Observateur*, 14 août, n°118; full text in http://www.homme-moderne.org/societe/demo/sauvy/3mondes.html

Savage, Charlie, 2006, "Bush challenges hundreds of laws: President cites powers of his office", *Boston Globe*, April 30

Scahill, Jeremy, 2006, "Cleansing Serbs in Kosovo", *The Nation*, June 19

——, 2007, Bush's Shadow Army, *The Nation*, March 15

Schmitter, P.C., 1990, "Sectors in Modern Capitalism – Modes of Governance" in Brunetta R. and Dell'aringa C. (eds.) *Labour Relations and Economic Performance*, Basingstoke (Macmillan)

Schumpeter, Joseph A., 1992, *Capitalism, Socialism and Democracy*, London (Routledge)

Schwarzenberger G., 1964, *Power Politics- A Study of World Society*, London (Stevens) 3rd. ed.

Scott, Dale P., 2006, "Homeland Security Contracts for Vast New Detention Camps", *Pacific News Service*, February 8, on http://news.pacificnews.org/news/view_article .html?article_id=eed74d9d44c30493706fe03f4c9b3a77

'Securing of Nigerian Democracy', *International Policy Report*, Washington DC (Center for International Policy) 2007

Sen, Amartya, 1982, *Poverty and Famines: An Essay on Entitlements and Deprivation*, Oxford (Clarendon Press)

Sheehan, N. (ed.) 1971, *The Pentagon Papers as Published by the New York Times*, New York (Bantam Books)

Shiva, Vandana, 1988, *Staying Alive - Women, Ecology and Development*, London (Zed Books)

Sibley, David, 1995, *Geographies of Exclusion - Society and Difference in the West*, London (Routledge)

Sigrist, C., 1981, "Akephale politische Systeme und nationale Befreiung" in Grevemeyer J.H. ed. *Traditionale Gesellschafter und europäischer Kolonialismus*, Frankfurt am Main (Syndikat).

Silverstein, Ken, 2006, "The minister of civil war", *Harper's*, August

Singel, R., 2006, "One Million Ways to Die", *Wired News*, September 11 on http://www.wired.com/news/technology/1,71743-0.html

Sit, Victor and Liu Weidong, 2000, "Restructuring and Spatial Change of China's Auto Industry under Institutional Reform and Globalization", *Annals of the Association of American Geographers*, 90, 4, pp. 653–673

Slack, Martin, 2007, "Veterans wait with minds scarred by war", *Yorkshire Post*, March 12

Slaughter, J., 2006, "Robots in the Fields", *People's Tribune*, Chicago, July on http://www.peoplestribune.org/PT.2006.07/PT.2006.07.18.html

Smith, Jeremy and Jon Hughes, 2007, "Growing crops to solve the planet's energy needs doesn't work - Recycling the energy in our waste just might have a significant part to play", *The Ecologist*, March

Smith, Kevin, 2007, "The Carbon Neutral Myth - Offset Indulgences for your Climate Sins", Transnational Institute on http://www.tni.org/detail_pub.phtml?&know _id=56

Smith, W. Leon, 2007, "Battle of Baghdad Cover-Up Four Years Later", *Lone Star Iconoclast*, April 2, on http://www.lonestaricon.com/absolutenm/anmviewer.asp?a =1294&z=123

Social and Spatial Inequalities Research Group, University of Sheffield, *WorldMapper*, on http://www.sasi.group.shef.ac.uk/worldmapper/index.html accessed March 2007.

Solomon, John, 2007, "In Intelligence World, A Mute Watchdog – Panel Reported No Violations for Five Years", *Washington Post*, July 15

Sowell, T., 1960, "Marx' 'Increasing Misery' Doctrine", *American Economic Review*, Vol. 50, No. 1

Spencer, N., (n.d.), *Network Propositions* on: http://www.normanspencer.co.nz/PsNetwork/00500.html accessed February 2006

Spengler, Oswald, 1928, [1922]. *The Decline of the West, Vol. II: Perspectives of World-History*, London (George Allen and Unwin)

Sprout, Harold and Margaret Sprout, 1965, *The Ecological Perspective on Human Affairs*, Princeton (Princeton University Press)

Steinhauer, Stewart, 2006, Panarchists To The Rescue – Out Of The Pan And Into The Fire, *The Dominion* (Canada), Issue 33, February on http://www.dominionpaper.ca/opinion/2006/02/02/panarchist.html

Stone, Judith F., 1998, "Insurgent Identities: Class, Community and Protest in Paris from 1848 to the Commune (book review)", *Labour History*, February

Strategic Research Institute, 2007, *Programme for 2007 Oil Sands Investor Symposium*, New York, June, on http://www.srinstitute.com/conf_page.cfm?instance_id=30&web_id=948&pid=555 accessed March 2007

Sudbury, Julia (ed.) 2005, *Global Lockdown: Race, Gender, And The Prison-Industrial Complex*, London (Routledge)

Sumiya, Toshio, 1989, "The Structure and Operation of Monopoly Capitalism in Japan" in Morris-Suzuki T. and Seiyama T. *Japanese Capitalism Since 1945*, Armonk NY (M.E. Sharpe)

Suskind, R., 2006, *The One Percent Doctrine – deep inside America's pursuit of its enemies since 9/11*, London (Simon and Schuster)

Sutton, Antony C., 1984, *America's secret establishment: An Introduction to the Order of Skull and Bones*, reprinted 2002

Tacsir, Andrés, 2005, *Modular Production in the Automobile Industry and the Brazilian Economy as a World Laboratory*, paper, School of Public Policy, University College London

Taussig, Michael T., 1980, *The Devil and Commodity Fetishism in South America*, Chapel Hill (University of North Carolina Press)

Taylor, Mark C., 2001, *The Moment of Complexity: Emerging Network Culture*, Chicago (University of Chicago Press)

Teather, D., 2007, "London closes gap on New York as share of hedge funds doubles", *Guardian*, April 17

Tett, Gillian, 2007 a, "Pension funds left vulnerable after unlikely bet on CDOs", *Financial Times*, July 6

——, 2007 b, "The effect of collateralised debt should not be underplayed", *Financial Times*, May 18.

Thompson, Edward, 1980, "Notes on Exterminism, the Last Stage of Civilization", *New Left Review* I/121, May-June on http://www.newleftreview.org/?page =article&view=1468

Thompson, George, 1941, *Aeschylus and Athens*, London (Lawrence & Wishart)

Thorner, D., 1971, "Peasant Economy as a Category in Economic History" in Shanin T. ed., *Peasants and Peasant Societies*, London (Penguin)

Thornton, Philip, 2006, "IMF: risk of global crash is increasing", *The Independent*, September 13

Tippett, Michael, 1939, *A Child of Our Time* (oratorio)

Toal, G. and F. Shelley, 2002, "Political Geography: From the 'Long 1989' to the End of the Post-Cold War Peace", in Gale G. and J. Willmott (eds) *Geography in America*, Columbus Ohio (Merrill)

Toolis, Kevin, 2004, "Rise of the terrorist professors", *New Statesman*, June 14

Townsend, Peter, 1979, *Poverty in the United Kingdom – A Survey of Household Resources and Standards of Living*, Harmondsworth (Penguin)

Toye, John, 1993, *Dilemmas of Development: Reflections on the Counter- Revolution in Development Theory and Policy*, Oxford (Basil Blackwell)

Tran-Thanh, K., 2003, *Needle in a Haystack: Searching for Civil Society in the Socialist Republic of Vietnam*, University College London Development Planning Unit, Working Paper No. 127, on: http://www.ucl.ac.uk/dpu/publications/working %20papers%20pdf/WP%20127.pdf

Trewavas, A., 2001, "Urban Myths of Organic Farming", *Nature*, Vol. 41

Trigona, Marie, 2006, *Recuperated Enterprises in Argentina: Reversing the Logic of Capitalism*, International Relations Center (IRC), Americas Program, Citizen Action in the Americas, Paper No. 19, March on http://americas.irc-online.org/am/3158

UK Government, 2000, *Eliminating World Poverty: Making Globalisation Work for the Poor*, White Paper on International Development Presented to Parliament by the Secretary of State for International Development December, Cmd 5006 on http://www.dfid.gov.uk/pubs/files/whitepaper2000.pdf

——, 2005, Department for Environment, Food and Rural Affairs (Defra), *Joint announcement by the agricultural departments of the United Kingdom, Organic Statistics United Kingdom*, June

——, 2007, *Sustainable Communities Act*, on http://www.opsi.gov.uk/ACTS/acts2007/ pdf/ukpga_20070023_en.pdf

United Nations, 2000, Interim Administration Mission in Kosovo (UNMIK), "Kosovo Protection Corps", on http://www.unmikonline.org/1styear/kpcorps.htm

——, 2004 a, *A more secure world: Our shared responsibility*: Report of the High-level Panel on Threats, Challenges and Change, on http://www.un.org/secureworld/report3.pdf

——, 2004 b, *Robots are taking an increasing number of jobs, new UN report says*, press communique 20 October on http://www.un.org/apps/news/story.asp?NewsID =12287&Cr=robot&Cr1=

United Nations Economic Commission for Europe, 2005, Press Release ECE/ STAT/05/P03 Geneva, October 11 on http://www.unece.org/press/pr2005/05stat _p03e.pdf

United Nations Food and Agriculture Organisation (FAO), 2006, *Food Outlook – Global Market Analysis, no 2*. Dec., on http://www.fao.org/docrep/009/j8126e/ j8126e01.htm

United Nations General Assembly, 2000 *United Nations Millennium Declaration*, A/ RES/55/2, September, on http://www.un.org/millennium/declaration/ares552e.pdf

United Nations Industrial Development Organisation (Unido), 2004, *Inserting Local Industries into Global Value Chains and Global Production Networks: Opportunities and Challenges for Upgrading*, Vienna (UNIDO)

United Nations University, 2005, World Institute for Development Economics Research (WIDER), *Wider Angle*, 2

United States, 1962, Department of Defense, Joint Chiefs of Staff, Memoramdum to the Secretary of Defense "Justification for US Military Intervention in Cuba", March 13, downloadable from National Security Archive, George Washington University, on http://www.gwu.edu/~nsarchiv/news/20010430/northwoods.pdf

United States Department of Defense, 2005 a, *Base Structure Report* (A Summary of DoD's Real Property Inventory), Washington DC (Office of the Deputy Under-Secretary of Defense), on http://www.globalpolicy.org/empire/intervention/2005/ basestructurereport.pdf

——, 2005 b, *Capstone Concept for Joint Operations*, version 2.0, Washington DC on http://www.dtic.mil/futurejointwarfare/concepts/approved_ccjov2.pdf

United States Government, 2000, *Written Testimony of Ralf Mutschke Assistant Director, Criminal Intelligence Directorate, International Criminal Police Organization – Interpol General Secretariat* before a hearing of the Committee on the Judiciary, Subcommittee on Crime, December 13, "The Threat Posed by the Convergence of Organized Crime, Drugs Trafficking and Terrorism" on http://www.globalsecurity .org/security/library/congress/2000_h/001213-mutschke.htm

——, 2004, National Intelligence Council, *Mapping the Global Future*, Washington DC (Government Printing Office) December. Summary on http://www.cia.gov/nic/ NIC_globaltrend2020_s1.html

——, 2007, *State of the Union Policy Initiatives, Twenty in Ten – Strengthening America's Energy Security* on http://www.whitehouse.gov/stateoftheunion/2007/ initiatives/energy.html

United States Government Accountability Office, 2007, *Report to Congressional Requesters Crude Oil – Uncertainty about Future Oil Supply Makes It Important to Develop a Strategy for Addressing a Peak and Decline in Oil Production*, Washington DC (GAO) February on: http://www.gao.gov/new.items/d07283.pdf

United States Government, Defense Advanced Research Projects Agency, 2009, *Strategic Plan* on http://hbr.harvardbusiness.org/hbr-main/resources/pdfs/darpa-strat-plan-2009.pdf

United States Government, Energy Information Agency, n.d., *Energy Use – Aluminum Industry Analysis Brief* on http://www.eia.doe.gov/emeu/mecs/iab/aluminum/page2.html

University of Winsconsin, 1993, Department of Agricultural Economics, Staff Paper Series no.369, on http://www.aae.wisc.edu/pubs/sps/pdf/stpap369.pdf

Vail, Jeff, 2004, *A Theory of Power*, New York etc. (iUniverse)

Valle, Sabrina, 2007, "Losing Forests to Fuel Cars: Ethanol Sugarcane Threatens Brazil's Wooded Savanna", *Washington Post*, July 31

Vasey, Gary M., 2005, *Energy Prices, Hedge Funds and the Coming Energy Crisis*, UtiliPoint International, Issue Alert, September 26, on http://energyhedgefunds.com/ehfc/modules/articles-4/content/IA_REPRINT_September_26_2005.pdf

Vidal, John, 2005, "Monster of the Moment", *Guardian*, July 1

——, et al, 2006, "Could scrapping Trident save the planet?", *Guardian*, November 4

Vidal, John, 2008 "The Green Scare", *Guardian*, April 3

Voltaire, 1968, *Candide ou L'optimisme*, Genève (Droz)

von Tunzelmann, N., 2003, "Historical coevolution of governance and technology in the industrial revolutions", *Structural Change and Economic Dynamics*, 14, pp. 365–384

Wall, Göran, 1993, *Exergy, Ecology and Democracy – Concepts of a Vital Society or a Proposal for an Exergy Tax*, conference paper, International Conference on Energy Systems and Ecology, Krakow July, on http://exergy.se/goran/eed/

Walls, Michael, 2007, *Commons Theory: A framework for analysis of constitutional-level collective action*, discussion paper, University College London

Waltz, Kenneth, 1979, *Theory of International Politics*, Reading Mass. (Addison Wesley)

Watts, Jonathan, 2007, "China blames growing social unrest on anger over pollution" *Guardian*, July 6

Weber, Max, 2002 [1905], *The Protestant Ethic and the Spirit of Capitalism*, Harmondsworth (Penguin)

Wilde, Oscar, 1891, *The Picture of Dorian Gray*, London (Ward, Lock, and Company)

Willan, Philip, 2003, "Moro's ghost haunts political life", *Guardian*, May 9

Williams, Eric. D., Robert U Ayres, and Miriam Heller, 2002, "The 1.7 Kilogram Microchip: Energy and Material Use in the Production of Semiconductor Devices", *Environmental Science and Technology*, Vol. 36, no. 24

Williams, H., 2007, How green is my tank?, *The Ecologist*, March

Wilpert, Gregory, 2007, "Chavez Dismisses International Disapproval of Venezuela's Media Policy – Hundreds of Thousands March in Support of Chavez", Venezuelanalysis.com Jun 05, on http://www.trinicenter.com/articles/2007/050607 .html

Winn, Steven, 2009, "A Paradise Built in Hell – The Extraordinary Communities That Arise in Disaster by Rebecca Solnit (book review)", *San Francisco Chronicle*, August 23

Wokusch, H., *The Powell Doctrine: Baghdad/Jenin/My Lai* on http://www.disinfo.com/ archive/pages/article/id2584/pg1/index.html

Wolf, Naomi, 2007, "Fascist America, in 10 easy steps", *Guardian*, April 24

Wolfe, M.S., n.d., *Recognising and realising the potential of organic agriculture*, Elm Farm Research Centre, Hamstead Marshall, Newbury, Berks; duplicated

World Resources Institute, 2003, *EarthTrends Data Tables, Energy Consumption by Economic Sector*, Washington DC, http://earthtrends.wri.org/pdf_library/data _tables/ene5_2003.pdf, on www.youtube.com/watch?v=na3ZWOIus78

Worldwatch Institute, 2005, *Unnatural Disaster – the lessons of Katrina*, September 1, on http://www.worldwatch.org/press/news/2005/09/02

Yeats, 1963, The Second Coming, from Michael Robartes and the Dancer, *Collected Poems of W.B. Yeats*, London (Macmillan)

Young, Oran, 1983, 'Regime dynamics: the rise and fall of international regimes', in Krasner, Stephen D. (ed.) *International Regimes*, Ithaca, NY (Cornell University Press)

Young, R.M., 1990, 'Darwinism and the Division of Labour', *Science as Culture*, no. 9, pp. 110–24, on http://human-nature.com/rmyoung/papers/pap109.html

Zagare, Frank C., 1984, *Game Theory: Concepts and Applications*, Beverly Hills (Sage)

Zarembka, P. (ed.), 2006, *The Hidden History of 9-11-2001*, Research in Political Economy Vol. 23, Amsterdam (Elsevier)

Zelem, Marie Christine, 1991 "L'Evolution des Techniques fromagères dans le Cantal, France du XVIII au XIX Siecle" in Dupré G. (ed) *Savoirs paysans et Développement*, Paris (Karthala/Orstom)

Zibechi, Raul, 2007, "Horror in the Brazilian California – The Dark Side of Agrofuels", *Counterpunch*, August 9, on http://www.counterpunch.org/zibechi08092007.html

Zimmer, C., 2007, "In Games, an Insight Into the Rules of Evolution", *New York Times*, July 31

Zwick, Martin, n.d., *Incompleteness, Negation, Hazard: on the Precariousness of Systems*, Discussion paper, Portland State University, Portland, Oregon

INDEX OF NAMES

INDEX OF SUBJECTS

208, 216–220, 222, 224, 227–230, 232,
236–238, 240–243, 245, 249, 250, 252,
255–258, 260, 270, 274–277, 279, 280,
282–284, 286–289, 291, 292, 294, 295,
298, 305, 306, 313, 316, 318, 320, 321,
323, 326, 328, 332, 335, 336
Hard/soft 150
Precautionary principle (see also
Massive hazard) 147, 173
Predatory 85, 108, 154, 164, 320
Predictability 2, 12, 14, 19, 55, 98,
105, 136, 151, 169, 175, 176, 177,
179, 225, 229, 241, 255, 258, 259,
270, 273–276, 279, 288, 298, 299,
306, 307, 310, 315, 319, 340, 343
Primitive 87, 88, 110, 181
Prisons 108, 203, 336
Prisoner's dilemma (PD) 61, 62, 65, 294,
295, 312
Privatisation (see also Enclosure) 12, 59,
171, 202, 203, 313, 339
Public goods 171, 313
Product cycle 89, 101
Profit 133, 177

Racial division/racism 51, 87, 215, 272
raison détat 216, 300
RAND Corporation 115, 116, 250
Realism (in International Relations
theory) 241, 242, 246, 253, 256
Reciprocity 6, 28, 31, 86, 87, 102, 103,
114, 214, 292, 303
Reductionism 51, 55, 58, 59, 119, 121,
143, 329
Redundancy 114, 147, 265, 320, 334,
340
Regime change 195, 208, 285, 286,
310–312
Regimes (see also Accumulation
regime) 5, 6, 14, 16, 23, 31, 47, 57, 61,
62, 68, 120, 141, 170–172, 177, 178,
255, 259, 266, 280, 286, 292, 302,
308–312, 315, 320, 324, 326, 334, 342
Regulation 20, 28, 33, 43, 56–59, 74, 80,
82, 111, 112, 117, 144, 155, 157, 158,
227, 276, 296, 305, 306
Relative and absolute 36, 128
Remittances 305, 306
Renditions 204, 206, 223
Repression 2, 9, 11, 16, 19, 20, 22, 23,
28, 52, 57, 77–79, 108, 116, 127, 148,
177, 179, 181, 184, 186, 189, 210,
214, 216, 224, 225, 228, 230, 250,
271, 281, 300, 325, 326, 339

Repressive definition 98
Resilience 43, 319, 341
Resources (natural) 4, 13, 14, 22, 23, 29,
32, 33, 39–42, 47, 60, 62, 63, 66–68,
70, 71, 73, 74, 84, 88, 96, 124, 134, 136,
138, 146, 147, 151, 157–159, 163, 165,
167, 168, 170, 171, 194, 195, 205, 218,
232, 236, 239, 258, 273, 274, 276, 278,
281, 283–285, 287, 288, 298, 299, 304,
310, 319, 326, 334, 340
Rhizomes (as metaphor for
non-hierarchical emergent forms;
see also Networks) 181, 182, 184, 332
Risk 9, 16, 26, 61, 72, 84, 90, 94, 96, 101,
105–107, 144, 147, 151, 152, 154–162,
168, 169, 177, 178, 182, 190, 200, 203,
204, 226, 245, 248, 298, 299, 319–321,
327, 331
Robots/robotics 83, 84, 201, 271, 325
Roosevelt Corollary 111, 221, 253,
257, 285

Sanctions 11, 150, 196, 283
Scarcity 15, 26, 66, 124, 136, 137, 148,
162, 165, 166, 236, 268, 270, 286,
288–290, 300, 303, 315, 335, 337
Seattle conference (1999) 116, 240,
260, 261
Second Law 21, 57, 165
Security 2, 10–12, 14, 15, 32, 59, 68, 98,
100, 105, 106, 114, 115, 139, 140, 145,
151, 152, 155, 156, 158, 160, 162, 163,
167–173, 177, 179, 183, 185, 186, 188,
197, 203, 204, 206, 207, 213, 218, 220,
228, 230, 244, 245, 265, 269, 278, 279,
286, 289, 295, 299, 306, 315, 319, 321,
340, 343
Self-determination 219, 312
Self-exploitation 7, 85, 88
Self-organisation 3, 5, 7, 8, 31, 48, 52,
73, 82, 85, 90, 91, 95, 99, 207, 268, 304,
310, 316, 324, 329, 330, 332–334
self-organising/self-regulating 6, 7, 14,
16, 31, 59, 74, 76, 84, 90, 99, 109, 213,
218, 221, 237, 241, 282, 300, 304, 232
September 11th attacks (9/11) 79, 172,
175, 182, 187, 194, 216
Shocks (see also Extreme events) 1, 21,
25, 35, 43, 131, 141, 146, 147, 172
Sink 6, 36, 40, 50, 57, 60, 87, 105, 128,
139, 145, 150, 157, 159, 160, 166, 181,
183, 187, 212, 225, 296, 297
Social 3–5, 7, 10, 13, 15, 16, 19–37, 39,
41, 42, 44, 46–60, 63, 67, 70, 73–78,

CPSIA information can be obtained
at www.ICGtesting.com
Printed in the USA
LVOW04s1001020516

486262LV00014B/44/P